Family-Centered
Early Intervention
with Infants and Toddlers

This book is printed on recycled paper.

Family-Centered Early Intervention with Infants and Toddlers
Innovative Cross-Disciplinary Approaches

edited by

Wesley Brown, Ph.D.
Professor and Director
Center for Early Childhood Learning and Development
East Tennessee State University
Johnson City, Tennessee

S. Kenneth Thurman, Ph.D.
Professor of Special Education
Temple University
Philadelphia, Pennsylvania

and

Lynda F. Pearl, Ph.D.
Assistant Professor and Associate Director
Center for Early Childhood Learning and Development
East Tennessee State University
Johnson City, Tennessee

·P A U L·H·
BROOKES
PUBLISHING CO.

Baltimore • London • Toronto • Sydney

Paul H. Brookes Publishing Co.
P.O. Box 10624
Baltimore, Maryland 21285-0624

Typeset by The Composing Room of Michigan, Inc., Grand Rapids, Michigan.
Manufactured in the United States of America by
The Maple Press Company, York, Pennsylvania.

Library of Congress Cataloging-in-Publication Data

Family-centered early intervention with infants and toddlers: innovative
cross-disciplinary approaches / edited by Wesley Brown, S. Kenneth
Thurman, and Lynda F. Pearl.
    p.   cm.
    Includes bibliographical references and index.
    ISBN 1-55766-124-3
    1. Handicapped children—Government policy—United States. 2.
Handicapped children—Services for—United States. 3. Handicapped
children—United States—Development. 4. Handicapped children—
Education (Preschool)—United States. I. Brown, Wesley, 1947–
. II. Thurman, S. Kenneth. III. Pearl, Lynda F., 1948–   .
HV888.5.F34   1993
362.4′048′083—dc20   93-16068
                                                        CIP

British Library Cataloguing-in-Publication data are available from the
British Library.

Contents

Contributors

Theresa Bologna, Ed.D.
Assistant Professor and
Director of Early Childhood
  Programs
Fordham University Graduate
  School of Education
New York, New York 10023

Carole Brown, Ed.D.
Assistant Professor and Director
Early Intervention Program
Department of Teacher Preparation
  and Special Education
2201 G Street N.W., Suite 524
Washington, DC 20052

Wesley Brown, Ph.D.
Professor and Director
Center for Early Childhood
  Learning and Development
East Tennessee State University
Box 70434
Johnson City, Tennessee 37614-0434

Mary Beth Bruder, Ph.D.
Associate Professor
Department of Pediatrics
UCONN School of Medicine
Farmington, Connecticut 06062

James L. Hamilton, Ph.D.
Chief, Early Childhood Branch
Office of Special Education
  Programs
400 Maryland Avenue S.W.
Switzer 4611
Washington, DC 20202

Katherine McCormick, Ph.D.
Assistant Professor
Department of Counseling and
  Clinical Programs
Columbus College
Columbus, Georgia 31907

Mary McLean, Ph.D.
Center for Teaching and Learning
Box 7189
University Station
University of North Dakota
Grand Forks, North Dakota 58202

Lynda F. Pearl, Ph.D.
Assistant Professor and Associate
  Director
Center for Early Childhood
  Learning and Development
East Tennessee State University
Box 70434
Johnson City, Tennessee 37614-0002

Sarah Rule, Ph.D.
Associate Professor, Special
  Education
and
Director, Outreach Division
University-Affiliated Center for
  Persons with Disabilities
Utah State University
Logan, Utah 84322-6805

Nancy D. Safer, Ed.D.
Director, Division of Education
  Services
Office of Special Education Programs
400 Maryland Avenue S.W.
Switzer 4630
Washington, DC 20202

Susan R. Sandall, Ph.D.
Individual and Family Studies
University of Delaware
111 Alison Annex
Newark, Delaware 19716

Robert Sheehan, Ph.D.
Professor of Educational Research
  and
Director, Center for Applied
  Research in Education
College of Education
Cleveland State University
1860 East 22nd Street
Cleveland, Ohio 44115

David Smith, Ph.D.
301 Bixler Hall
Ashland University
401 College Avenue
Ashland, Ohio 44805

Scott Snyder, Ph.D.
Department of Counseling, Human
    Services, and Foundations
Room 119, School of Education
University of Alabama at
    Birmingham
University Station
Birmingham, Alabama 35294

S. Kenneth Thurman, Ph.D.
Professor of Special Education
Temple University
Ritter Annex, 291
Philadelphia, Pennsylvania 19122

Foreword

In this era of fast-paced communication through journals, newsletters, videotapes, and electronic media, why another book? From conception to delivery, most books have a gestational period of 2 years or more. Is a book an anachronism, or does it remain an important resource? This carefully selected collection of chapters on early intervention, edited by Drs. Brown, Thurman, and Pearl, clearly demonstrates the continuing importance of the book as a repository of accumulated wisdom.

There is a growing activist movement surrounding children with special needs in the United States and throughout the world. Federal and state mandates have acknowledged several important facts: children with developmental concerns require individualized attention, interventions should begin as early as possible, family needs and preferences are preeminent, and prevention is more effective and less costly than amelioration. By strongly encouraging states to develop a comprehensive, coordinated system of early intervention services that are responsive to the needs of children and families, Part H of IDEA pushed this country to garner new resources and knowledge. States will continue to adapt to this change for many years to come, but much progress has been made in a very short time. Unless the details of this progress are chronicled and analyzed, and the lessons that they teach disseminated, the movement will falter. We do not have time to learn everything through individual experience, but rather must rely on experts such as those who share their first-hand knowledge with us in this volume. To this end, the editors have sifted through a mass of data to glean only the most relevant and accurate information in the field.

Family-Centered Early Intervention with Infants and Toddlers: Innovative Cross-Disciplinary Approaches provides insight into the evolution of recommended practices in early intervention. No one can yet claim to have achieved the ideal system of services, but over the past several decades we have learned much about the special needs of children with, or at risk for, developmental problems, and most recently, about the needs of their families. We know that there are sensitive, if not critical, periods in early human development, and that infants and toddlers cannot wait for eventual improvements in their learning environments. Fortunately, as is evident in this volume, early interventionists, educators, service providers, legislators, administrators, families, and students now have specific guidelines and techniques for addressing those needs within a family-centered context.

From the national infrastructure level to hands-on specifics, the authors of this volume provide critical discussion on the challenges of providing early intervention services within a family-centered framework. The book begins with a legislative review of the key elements of eligibility, assessment, and evaluation. The authors then turn to the details of early intervention: service coordination, curricula, special intervention settings, tracking, training, and quality assurance. Together, the chapters in this volume provide a comprehensive presentation for the readers.

This work is a welcome addition to our still modest library in the field of early intervention. The authors have utilized their many years of experience in government, academia, and front-line service delivery settings in forging a comprehensive and coherent presentation. The resulting product is relevant to a wide interdisciplinary audience of teachers, students, and practitioners of early intervention.

James A. Blackman, Ph.D.
Professor of Pediatrics
University of Virginia

Preface

BACKGROUND

Books, like families and so many other things, never seem to end up faithful to our original intentions. This volume has been no exception. Pleasantly, we believe that over the course of its evolution, it has been greatly enhanced in terms of its range and quality of content. What began as a two-author text focused on transition from neonatal intensive care to the home community has culminated in a multi-contributor volume dealing with a much broader range of topics surrounding early intervention for infants and toddlers with disabilities, with special attention to the developing concept of family-centered services. Our contributors were carefully selected for their experience and qualifications. They have greatly enhanced the final product by providing essential information in a much better form than the editors would have been able to provide alone.

Family means a great deal to all of the contributors. During this book's developmental period, the editors' families have gained four children—two through adoption, two by marriage—and have also seen the transition of one young adult through the later part of college and into the world of work. This period of development has been momentous not only for early intervention, but for our own families as well.

The book is designed for early interventionists, present and future, including members of many different disciplines and role groups. We hope that it will contribute to the preparation of professionals from all of these role groups and that it can serve as a reference for practitioners.

Developments in early intervention for infants and toddlers with disabilities and their families have proceeded so rapidly since the passage of PL 99-457 in 1986 that we could not be more pleased. Many states have experienced delays in implementation, and some seem to have encountered overwhelming difficulties meeting the intent or specific requirements of the legislation. At the same time, however, we have never before experienced such a rapid growth of services for an individual specialized population.

Our concluding chapter indicates that early intervention, as a field, has advanced to a period of adolescence from its prior childhood. Family-centered practices once seemed to be more rhetoric than reality. Now they are beginning to be reflected in philosophical and programmatic shifts in the implementation of early intervention. Real partnerships with families are being established, and services are truly becoming more comprehensive and transdisciplinary.

CHAPTER INTRODUCTIONS

In Chapter 1 Nancy Safer and Jim Hamilton have lent us their unique perspectives as federal officials critically close to the purpose and intent of Part H.

While this chapter represents their views in their private capacities, it provides a clear macro view of implementation. This enables the reader to follow their distinct understanding of the context for early intervention with infants and toddlers and their families.

In Chapter 2, Wesley Brown and Carole Brown explore the sometimes troublesome variables surrounding eligibility for early intervention services. With each individual child and family, eligibility issues are encountered and must be examined in light of a wide range of considerations related to prevention, risk, resilience, and intervention. This chapter carefully explores the current procedures and practices surrounding eligibility.

In Chapter 3, Mary McLean and Katherine McCormick provide a thorough, excellent examination of evaluation and assessment in early intervention. With careful consideration of family and child variables, their materials illuminate evolving, regulated recommended practices for dealing with these processes. The authors provide clear guidelines for implementation and examine a number of important variables in screening and instrumentation.

Direct attention to families' needs, resources, and perspectives is provided in Chapter 4, in which editor Lynda Pearl explores family-centered care as an early intervention philosophy. The importance of understanding the child with developmental delays as also having many other roles (i.e., granddaughter, little sister) is discussed. Important concepts of systems theory are discussed in the context of early intervention, along with information specifically on fathers, siblings, and family support activities.

In Chapter 5, collaboration and service coordination receive attentive consideration from Mary Beth Bruder and Theresa Bologna. From the opening example of 18-month-old Polly, they provide various viewpoints on interagency processes at the state and local levels and promote essential features of collaboration in early intervention.

Chapter 6 focuses on curriculum and its role in the design and delivery of early intervention. Susan Sandall fully explores the individualized family service plan and provides a clear framework for the activities and experiences included in early intervention while examining a wide range of instructional methods, curricular adaptations, and exemplary curricula.

In Chapter 7, editor Kenneth Thurman examines intervention in the neonatal intensive care unit. The reader is introduced to the treatment of critically ill infants, as well as the physical, social, and working environments that the infants and their families experience. The personnel in the NICU and the most common medical conditions treated there are presented, along with developmental and behavioral interventions commonly utilized.

Chapter 8 contains Lynda Pearl's examination of developmental follow-up of high-risk infants. Research on various groups of infants is carefully reviewed, and the components of developmental follow-up and transition are presented, with particular attention to family-centered practices. The chapter concludes with several specific program models.

In Chapter 9, personnel and professional disciplines for early intervention receive the attention of Wesley Brown and Sarah Rule. The roles and services of each group of early intervention providers are examined, and personnel standards and state regulations for their practice are discussed. Also included are the roles of parents and paraprofessionals and the current status of early intervention specializations within the disciplines. The chapter seeks to clarify the common and unique roles of each discipline.

In Chapter 10, Scott Snyder and Rob Sheehan provide a comprehensive primer on evaluation in early intervention, examining its purposes and demonstrating several types of decisions that its results affect. A corresponding program-evaluation method is provided for decision area with a case example.

As a concluding chapter, Kenneth Thurman provides his perspectives on the continuing challenges in early intervention. He discusses many of the topics previously presented, and some areas that did not receive the direct attention of the contributors. His discussions of family-centeredness, natural settings, and advocacy are thought provoking, and thus provide an excellent conclusion for the volume.

Finally, a glossary contributed by David Smith defines many of the key terms that appear in this volume.

We believe that the reader in search of information on family-centered early intervention for infant and toddlers will find the contents of this book timely and thorough. We acknowledge that no volume can fully explore the rapid developments in early intervention, but we are confident that this volume, supported by continuing related literature, will assist families in receiving more sophisticated and responsive early intervention services.

ACKNOWLEDGMENTS

We would like to first acknowledge our families and the families of our contributors. In every case, their tolerance and support has enabled our professional perspectives to develop and be documented. We also greatly appreciate the special impact of our contributors on this volume. We acknowledge our employing institutions, which enable our professional participation in early intervention.

We appreciate all of the people at Paul H. Brookes Publishing for their help in making this book a reality. They have had a wonderfully responsive team spirit and continuous positive outlook that has greatly assisted us in the development of this volume. We also greatly value Jim Blackman's interest and perspectives related to our work and his definitive contributions to early intervention.

None of the past developments in our field have been more important than the movement from child-focused to family-centered services. The full evolution of family-centered practices will entail continuing challenges, as will true partnerships of parents with professionals. With recent progress, the course is clear and the promise is stronger than ever. We welcome and acknowledge your contributions to the future progress of early intervention.

Family-Centered
Early Intervention
with Infants and Toddlers

Legislative Context for Early Intervention Services

Nancy D. Safer
and James L. Hamilton

The 1960s, 1970s, and 1980s have seen a rapid proliferation of research, programs, and policies on early intervention for young children with disabilities. Shonkoff and Meisels (1990) have recently described the historical underpinnings of early intervention services and argued that PL 99-457, the Education of the Handicapped Act Amendments of 1986 (changed by PL 101-476 to the Individuals with Disabilities Education Act, or IDEA), is the most important legislation ever enacted for young children with disabilities. Others (e.g., Gallagher, Trohanis, & Clifford, 1989; Smith, 1988) have described the early childhood provisions of IDEA as watershed legislation that is clearly as important and far-reaching for young children with disabilities and their families as PL 94-142 (the Education for All Handicapped Children Act of 1975) was for school-age children and their families.

As a statement of public policy, IDEA, and in particular the provisions that established the Part H Infants and Toddlers with Disabilities program and amended the Preschool Grants Program, represented

This chapter was prepared by the authors in their private capacity. The views expressed are those of the authors, and no official support by the U.S. Department of Education is intended or should be inferred.

the zeitgeist, the general intellectual and moral spirit of that time, concerning young children with disabilities. Examination of the various provisions of the legislation reveals the prevailing values of American society, ideas about best practices in service provision, and a contemporary vision of the ideal service system for young children with disabilities and their families. This chapter is about that legislation: how it came about, how it was shaped by the beliefs and values of the time, its key provisions, and some issues and challenges that accompany its implementation.

The enactment of PL 99-457 was the culmination of a movement that began with the pioneering efforts of program developers and researchers who demonstrated that providing early intervention services for young children often yielded important and lasting benefits for both the children and their parents. While much of the evidence supporting early intervention was gathered from studies of programs for economically disadvantaged children, research that assessed the effects and costs of intervention for young children with disabilities was also promising (for integrative reviews of these studies, see Casto & Mastropieri, 1986; Farran, 1990; Guralnick & Bennett, 1987; White & Casto, 1985). In addition to efficacy studies, there was an inherent logic, as well as a moral/humanitarian rationale (see Turnbull & Turnbull, 1985), for providing services immediately when a disability is detected, which for many children is at birth or shortly thereafter.

A number of efficacy studies illustrating the benefits of providing early intervention for children with disabilities were completed prior to 1975, and thus predated the passage of PL 94-142. Despite that available evidence, Congress, while requiring services for school-age children with disabilities under PL 94-142, included preschool-age children only on a permissive basis, providing modest incentives for states to serve these children. No support was provided for serving infants and toddlers with disabilities, although states could use some of the federal funds for this purpose. Congress did, however, continue to appropriate funds for the establishment of model programs, research, and other activities through programs such as the Handicapped Children's Early Education Program (HCEEP), which was first established in 1968 under PL 90-538 (the Handicapped Children's Early Education Assistance Act) to demonstrate and evaluate the feasibility of providing early intervention to young children with disabilities. Later, in 1983, under PL 98-199 (the Education of the Handicapped Act Amendments of 1983), Congress established the State Planning Grant program under the HCEEP, providing small grants to states for planning, developing, and implementing services for children with disabilities from birth through 5 years old. By the 1985–

1986 school year, however, only 24 states had mandated special education and related services for all children with disabilities beginning at 3 years of age or younger, and only six states had mandated services beginning at birth. Thus, while progress had been made to establish universal services for young children with disabilities through federal incentives, discretionary projects, and state planning grants, the majority of states still did not provide early intervention or preschool programs for all young children with disabilities.

By 1985–1986, parents, professionals, and other advocates were exerting substantial pressure on Congress to enact comprehensive early intervention legislation both for children with disabilities from birth through 2 years old and those 3 through 5 years old (Garwood, 1987). Armed with results from efficacy studies, with arguments made on humanitarian and moral grounds, with the examples of model programs and of states that had already mandated services, and with information demonstrating uneven and inequitable availability of services both within and across states, these advocates presented a convincing case for establishing a national comprehensive policy for serving young children with disabilities. In response, on October 8, 1986, after several days of hearings and testimony from over 50 witnesses, Congress enacted PL 99-457.

PL 99-457 established the Part H program for infants and toddlers with disabilities and their families and amended several other sections of the Education of the Handicapped Act, including Section 619 of Part B. The amendments to Section 619 changed the name of the Preschool Incentive Program to the Preschool Grants Program and required that states, in order to continue receiving federal funds and avoid certain sanctions, provide a free, appropriate public education (FAPE) for all children with disabilities 3 through 5 years old by the 1991–1992 school year. As noted above, when PL 99-457 was enacted in 1986, fewer than half of the states required a FAPE for all children with disabilities of age 3 or younger. By September, 1991 all states had mandates in place, and all but one was providing a FAPE to all children with disabilities 3 through 5 years old (one state's mandate would not take effect until the 1992–1993 school year). Thus, PL 99-457 was crucial legislation both for children with disabilities birth through 2 years old and those 3 through 5 years old.

UNIQUE FEATURES OF PL 99-457

PL 99-457 is considered landmark legislation because of the promise it made to provide services for all young children with disabilities and their families. There were other features of PL 99-457 that also made it unique. This section will describe those features and concepts as a framework for considering the issues and challenges in early intervention.

The first surprising aspect of PL 99-457 was the fact that it was enacted at all. It was federal entitlement legislation passed at a time when the prevailing philosophy of government was moving away from the expansion of the federal role in the delivery of human services and from the belief that social problems could be solved through federal actions. How was the passage of PL 99-457 possible? It is clear that the growing base of information illustrating the benefits and cost-effectiveness of early intervention was a key factor (Silverstein, 1989). At the same time, the development of policy options that meshed the prevailing values concerning governance and the family was also a key factor. Each of these factors is examined further below.

The Influence of Research

By the mid-1980s, a body of research existed that not only suggested significant outcomes from early intervention and preschool services for young children with disabilities, but that began to frame these outcomes in cost–benefit terms (U.S. Department of Education,1984, 1985). This provided advocates with the information base needed to argue for extending the free, appropriate public education required under Part B of IDEA to 3- through 5-year-old children with disabilities. The fact that nearly half the states already served all preschool children with disabilities, and additional states served some, when combined with the accumulating cost–benefit information, provided impetus and a rationale for extending this program, despite a general wariness about establishing new federal entitlements.

New Beliefs about Governance and the Role of the Family

Because children of ages 3 through 5 could be included under Part B and many states were already serving them under the provisions of that program, amending Part B to require services for all 3- through 5-year-old children with disabilities was a logical approach. The same base of research and efficacy information, however, also suggested the benefits of serving children below the age of 3 (a step that only six states had undertaken on a statewide basis). Congress certainly could have extended Part B to birth, but, instead, a new program for infants and toddlers with disabilities and their families was created—Part H, a program that differed from the Part B program in some very fundamental ways. Some of those differences may have stemmed from discrepancies between the needs of children birth through 2 and those of children age 3 through 5. But it is also likely that these differences arose partly from the changing beliefs about governance and the role of the family. Whereas the federal programs enacted in the 1960s and 1970s could be seen as growing out of a belief that many of the nation's social problems could be solved by federal programs and policies, the 1980s saw a growing disillusionment with such an approach. As reflected in the Omnibus Budget and Reconciliation Act of 1981, people increasingly believed that many problems, particularly health and social problems, could be more efficiently and effectively solved at the state or the community level, if governments at these levels were given the flexibility to do so. This flexibility is a central theme of Part H, and deliberately so, for the drafters believed that Washington did not have all the answers (Silverstein, 1989). Under Part H, the state designates whatever agency is most appropriate to serve as the lead agency, determines what population of infants and toddlers will be served (within certain broad parameters), and designs the service delivery system, drawing upon public or private providers. Although the legislation prescribes 14 key components of the statewide system (described below), it gives wide latitude to develop a system unique to and serving the needs of the particular state. Thus, although it is federal legislation, the Part H program still reflects the belief that states (and communities) have the responsibility, and should be given the flexibility, to meet human service needs.

The decade of the 1980s was also a time when increasing attention was paid to the family and to family values. Under legislation such as Part B of IDEA, parents were given a significant role, reflecting the concept of parents as protectors and advocates for their children's rights, or as partners with the schools in developing an individualized education program (IEP) that the school would then deliver. By the early 1980s, many individuals were articulating a new view of the family. This view recognized the family as the constant in the child's life, as most knowledgeable about particular aspects of the child, and as the provider of the stimulation and emotional support needed by children to grow and thrive (Shelton, Jeppson, & Johnson 1987). This new respect for the family was reflected in language such as "family-centered" or "family-focused" care, and was a key tenet of the drafters of Part H of IDEA (Silverstein, 1989). Thus, Part H reflects not only a respect for families and what they know, but also an assumption that the family plays the key role in the development of the young child, and that the responsibility of the service system is to support that role. The needs of the family are as much a focus of Part H as are the needs of the child, and the family is given the authority to determine which services it will accept and which it will not.

Coordination of Services and Accountability

The focus on families is related to another key feature of Part H, that of coordinating the service system to make it responsive to the needs of families and children. A series of studies by the Rand Corporation during the mid-1970s (Brewer & Kakalik, 1979), drew attention to fragmented, sometimes redundant education, health, and social service programs at the community level. Such a piecemeal set of programs was often intimidating or difficult for families to understand or access because of differences in legislation, mandates, or eligibility. The services provided were often driven by the structure and procedures of different agencies, rather than the needs of clients and their families. The conclusion of such studies was that mechanisms were needed to meld disparate services and programs into a service system, as well as to help families access the system on behalf of their children. This perspective undoubtedly affected Part H, as well as other legislation of the time such as the Maternal and Child Health Block Grant Program. In Part H it resulted in a requirement for service coordination through clear and detailed interagency agreements and, most importantly, through the appointment of a service coordinator for each child and family. This individual is responsible for ensuring the coordination of all services (including medical and non developmental services) and the delivery of the services listed in the individualized family service plan (IFSP). This concept places the family and child at the center of the service delivery system and ensures that family needs, rather than agency procedures, drive the system.

In addition to its negative effects on families, service fragmentation was also perceived as limiting the services provided under existing programs. It appeared that there was much redundancy in the services that could be provided under the various programs, and, therefore, that resources could be stretched much further if properly coordinated. Thus, the drafters of the Part H legislation conceived of Part H funds as the "glue money" that would allow the existing service providers to work cohesively to provide the services needed by infants and toddlers with disabilities and their families (Silverstein, 1989).

Thus far we have seen how the Part H legislation was consistent with changing beliefs about governance and suspicion of prescriptive programs from Washington, with the changing perception of the family's role, and with concern about fragmented services. Another value or belief articulated during the 1980s was that of accountability, which has been a consistent component of flexibility and restructuring initiatives. This is also a clear focus of Part H (Silverstein, 1989); the lead agency is given flexibility in designing the statewide system, but also responsibility for ensuring that all services are provided, for assigning financial responsibility, and for ensuring that existing resources for providing particular services do not fade away. Thus, in Part H, some of the mechanisms for ensuring a coordinated service system for families also perform an accountability function in ensuring that services are provided and paid for.

For any major piece of federal legislation to be enacted, it must meet an agreed-upon need in a way that is consistent with the prevailing beliefs and values of the nation. In the mid-1980s, the available research information made an overwhelming case for enacting programs entitling young children with disabilities to services. At the same time, shifts in beliefs and values concerning the role of the federal government and families ensured that the new legislation would reflect and emphasize ideas different from those that had given rise to previous legislation. The next section will show how these concepts are reflected in the key components of the statewide system envisioned in Part H.

KEY PROVISIONS OF THE PART H PROGRAM

The Part H Program for Infants and Toddlers is a formula grant program that provides financial assistance to states to help them develop a comprehensive, coordinated, multidisciplinary, interagency program of early intervention for infants and toddlers and their families. As originally conceived, this system was intended to be constructed largely through the coordination of services and resources already available in a given state. Congress provided for a phase-in period during which various state agencies were to enter into interagency agreements that would provide or pay for certain of the required services. To receive Part H funds for the first year of the phase-in period, the governor of the state was required to designate a lead agency and members of an interagency coordinating council (ICC) who would advise and assist the lead agency in planning a statewide system. Education was designated the lead agency in approximately one-third of the states, Health in one-third, and Human Services or other state agencies in the remaining third. During the third year of the phase-in period, the law required that states adopt a policy showing their commitment to implementing a statewide system of services for infants and toddlers with disabilities and their families. Congress also specified 14 components of the statewide system. Briefly, they are:

1. A state definition of the term "developmental delay"
2. A timetable to ensure services
3. A multidisciplinary evaluation of each eligible child
4. An individualized family service plan (IFSP), including service coordination, for each eligible child and family
5. A comprehensive child find system
6. A public awareness system
7. A central directory of services and other resources
8. A comprehensive system of personnel development
9. Designation of a single line of responsibility in the lead agency
10. A policy on contracting with local service providers
11. Procedures for timely reimbursement of funds
12. Procedural safeguards
13. Policies for personnel standards
14. A system for compiling data

To be eligible for Part H funds in the 4th year of the phase-in period, each state was required to have policies and procedures in place for each of these components, conduct multidisciplinary assessments, develop IFSPs, and make service coordination available. To receive 5th-year Part H funds, the original legislation required states to ensure that all eligible children (as defined by each state) were receiving services. (In 1991, through PL 102-119, Congress amended the Part H program to permit states experiencing hardships in meeting the Part H requirements to remain in the program for up to 2 additional years. Termed "extended participation" and "differential funding," this amendment reduces funding to these states while giving them up to two additional years to meet the 4th- or 5th-year requirements of the program. By fiscal year 1993, all states must be serving all eligible children in order to continue receiving Part H funds.)

Children eligible under Part H are those from birth through 2 years of age in need of early intervention services because they are experiencing developmental delays in one or more developmental domains (physical, cognitive, communicative, social or emotional, or adaptive development) as measured by appropriate diagnostic instruments and procedures, or because they have a diagnosed physical or mental condition that has a high probability of resulting in developmental delay. In addition, states may elect to serve infants and toddlers who are at risk for delay if early intervention services are not provided. The definition of the term "developmental delay" is determined by each individual state.

A significant feature of the Part H program is its emphasis on the family. The strengths and needs of both children and families must be determined, and early intervention services must be documented in an IFSP. Early intervention services must include service coordination and may include audiology, family training/counseling/home visits, certain health services, medical services for diagnostic purposes, nursing services, nutrition services, occupational therapy, physical therapy, psychological services, social work services, special instruction, speech-language pathology, vision services, assistive technology devices and services, and transportation. Families, however, may decide to accept or reject any particular service.

Part H funds are allocated in proportion to each state's general population of children birth through 2 years of age. States may use Part H funds to plan, develop, and implement a statewide system of services; Part H funds cannot be used for services that are provided or paid for through other sources (i.e., Part H funds are payor-of-last-resort funds). The major sources of funds for services include Medicaid, Maternal and Child Health Block Grants, the Chapter 1 Handicapped Program, state appropriations, the federal Developmental Disabilities Program, federal Social Services Block Grants, third party insurance, and Part H funds, when necessary. Importantly, Part H legislation also allows states to establish a sliding fee scale if state law permits; however, families may not be denied services because of their inability to pay.

ISSUES AND CHALLENGES IN IMPLEMENTING THE PART H PROGRAM

Although the Part H program has been hailed as exemplary legislation for the special-needs population that it targets, there are challenges that, if not met, may limit its outcomes. Some of these challenges stem from the unique concepts of the legislation, some from outside factors such as the economic difficulties of individual states. Certain problems can also be anticipated from experiences with other programs. Before discussing these issues, it is important to review the goals of Congress in enacting the legislation. These were:

to provide financial assistance to states (1) to develop and implement a *statewide*, comprehensive, coordinated, multidisciplinary, *interagency program* of early intervention services for infants and toddlers with disabilities and their families, (2) to *facilitate the coordination of payment* for early intervention services from federal, state, local, and private sources (including public and private insurance coverage), and (3) to enhance its capacity to *provide quality early intervention services* and expand and improve existing early intervention services being provided to infants and toddlers with disabilities and their families. [emphasis added] (Section 471, PL 99-457)

This suggests that the success of the program will be measured by the implementation of a statewide, interagency program of early intervention for all infants and toddlers with disabilities in all states, the financing of this system through the coordination of resources and payment, and, ultimately, the delivery of high-quality services.

The issues and challenges confronting policymakers, state officials, professionals, and parents can be related to these three goals of the Part H program. Before discussing these, it is important to note that different states are at different points in the implementation of the Part H program, that the issues and challenges described are not common to every state, and that the issues and challenges are not meant to be exhaustive, nor are they discussed in order of importance.

Statewide Service Coordination

IDEA mandates the development and implementation of a statewide, coordinated, interagency program of early intervention services available to all children and families. Accomplishment of this goal at the state level is dependent on several factors, including the history and infrastructure of the state, the availability of service personnel, and the interaction of these factors with the scope and outcomes of the planning process.

State Infrastructure   When PL 99-457 was enacted in 1986, states varied enormously in the extent to which their underlying foundations and existing systems were amenable to incorporating the requirements of the Part H program. Certainly there were states that had one or more of the following: 1) working relationships or formal interagency agreements between state agencies such as Health and Education; 2) a system of local service providers that could form the basis of a statewide system of services; 3) an extensive network of personnel-training resources that was available for both preservice and inservice training of early intervention personnel; and 4) legislative, professional, and lay groups that had been planning or supporting the establishment of programs for young children with disabilities. Other states could not claim to have as adequate an infrastructure; systems that could readily accommodate the challenge of planning and implementing a Part H system of services were simply not in place. For most states, the immediate challenge was to transform existing fragmented services into a coordinated, comprehensive system of services operating throughout the state (Gallagher, Harbin, Thomas, Clifford, & Wenger, 1988). To the extent that certain structures were already in place or were established during the phase-in period of the program, states were more likely to effect a successful transformation.

An especially important part of a state's infrastructure was the agency designated by the governor as the lead agency for the Part H program. Ideally, the agency designated as lead agency was already involved in systems planning, was administratively responsible for a service delivery system for young children, and had working relationships with other state agencies that could contribute funds or services to the statewide system. Furthermore, the lead agency would ideally be involved in personnel-development activities (training, certification, licensing), have data systems that could be modified for the Part H program, and have influence with key policymakers in the state for purposes of creating or amending legislation and securing funds and other resources to make the program work. The choice of lead agency in a given state's infrastructure has proven to be a critical factor in the Part H program; during the phase-in period, several states have changed lead agencies to provide for a better match between the Part H requirements and the existing infrastructure of the state.

Personnel Needs   Securing well-qualified personnel to serve infants and toddlers and their families has been a major concern since the passage of PL 99-457 (Campbell, Bellamy, & Bishop, 1988). In an early survey of state officials involved with the Part H program, Meisels, Harbin, Modigliani, and Olsen (1988) reported that the lack of qualified personnel was a serious problem facing states in providing services to children and families. Over two-thirds of the states reported a lack of sufficient training programs. Over four-fifths of the states reported shortages of early intervention personnel, and nearly all reported a shortage of therapists. Although the Meisels study was carried out early in the phase-in of the Part H program, there is no evidence that the situation has improved enough to meet emerging needs. To gain some understanding of barriers to developing or expanding university training programs, Gallagher and Staples (1989), surveyed 249 deans of schools of education regarding programs for preparing early childhood special educators. One hundred and sixty-two deans reported that they had no program at all at the undergraduate, master's, or doctoral level. Furthermore, only 40% of the deans indicated a willingness to initiate or expand a program, and then, only if certain incentives were offered (e.g., funding, job-demand data, establishment of state certification for trainees).

In addition to these personnel shortages, research by Bailey, Palsha, and Huntington (1990) has documented that there is a paucity of curriculum content related to infants or families in typical undergraduate and graduate special education programs. Similar findings were obtained in a study of other disciplines that prepare professionals to serve infants and families (Bailey, Simeonsson, Yoder, & Huntington, 1990).

The nature of the services and the service system required under the Part H program is changing training programs from child-centered and discipline-specific to child- and family-centered and interdisciplinary. This change in training focus is producing a substantial demand for inservice training of practicing professionals and paraprofessionals and a restructuring of preservice training programs to accommodate new skills, new roles, and expanded personnel responsibilities. New skills needed by most professionals include those in working with families, conducting family assessments, developing IFSPs, understanding and working with professionals from other disciplines, and performing service-coordination functions. Thus, four major challenges in personnel training are: 1) restructuring preservice training programs to include new competencies, 2) providing inservice training to upgrade the skills of practicing professionals, 3) recruiting new personnel or retraining personnel to work with infants and toddlers and their families to meet personnel shortages, and 4) developing a permanent personnel-training system that will address current and future personnel-training needs.

Interactions with the Planning Process   Professionals and parents involved in planning a statewide system of services are confronted with an enormously complex task. First, as described earlier, states were given great flexibility in some key aspects of the program, such as defining eligibility. This resulted in a number of issues that had to be addressed in planning the system: How should "developmental delay" be defined in our state? Should our state include children at risk for developmental delay in the Part H program and, if so, which at-risk children? What kinds of services are these children likely to need? Where will those services be provided? Does our state have enough personnel to serve all eligible children? What are potential funding sources for each of the required Part H services (e.g., service coordination) and for each of the services that these children may need? What are the resource implications of the general supervision and monitoring of service programs within the state? If we expand our eligibility criteria, should our public-awareness system be expanded as well?

A second reason for the complexity is that many of the elements that the system comprises interact with other elements, such that changing one often has major implications for one or more of the others. For example, in determining which children and families will be eligible for the Part H program, what kinds of services they are likely to receive, and the nature of the service delivery approaches that would be used, state planners have had to generate numerous estimates of the corresponding financial requirements.

Further complicating the planning process have been uncertainties about the size and stability of funding sources. Will federal and state appropriations remain stable or increase? (This problem is described in greater depth in the next section.) Will we be successful in amending our state Medicaid plan? If we establish a sliding fee scale system, will we generate enough money to offset its administrative costs and provide program income? Are any of our major funding sources likely to be reduced or eliminated?

As state planners considered each of the elements of their statewide system and their interactive effects, many states changed their original plan to a more modest effort. For example, early in the phase-in period, 18 states planned to include children at risk for developmental delay as eligible for Part H services (Gallagher et al., 1988). As of February 1992, only nine states still planned to include at-risk children, and most of these states were narrowly defining the risk categories that will be included.

Whether or not this first goal for the Part H program, the establishment of a coordinated statewide system, will be achieved is related to the second goal, which is discussed below.

Coordination of Payment for Early Intervention Services from All Sources

For most states, the most challenging aspect of the Part H program has been identifying and coordinating financial and other resources to support the administrative and programmatic requirements of building and operating a statewide system of services. Several studies conducted by the Carolina Policy Studies Program revealed, for example, that states have been especially slow in establishing interagency agreements that assigned financial responsibility for services among state agencies (see Harbin, Gallagher, & Lillie, 1989; Harbin, Gallagher, Lillie, & Eckland, 1990). Evidence of this can be seen in PL 102-119, the Individuals with Disabilities Education Act Amendments of 1991, which require that each state designate an individual or entity to be responsible for assigning financial responsibility among appropriate state agencies. This amendment was made in response to lead agencies' difficulty in leveraging funds for Part H purposes from other state agencies. Other evidence of the importance of financial issues in the implementation of the Part H program is the recent amendment to the Part H legislation described above, which allows states to apply for extended participation because of hardships in meeting 4th- or 5th-year requirements; in fiscal year 1990, 11 states applied for extended participation, with financial hardships in meeting 4th-year requirements typically mentioned as the major reason for exercising this option.

Funds provided through the Part H program were intended to be "glue money" (to coordinate and leverage funds and other resources from other sources within a state) and to serve a payor-of-last-resort purpose (Silverstein, 1989). Actual payment for services was to be made from federal, state, local, and private sources. As Clifford (1991) has documented, states have explored the use of a wide variety of funding sources, including Medicaid, federal and state health funds, Chapter 1 Handicapped Program funds, state education funds, private insurance, parent fees, and local funds, to name a few of the potential sources. One of the major dilemmas facing the states, however, is that most of the sources have inherent restrictions on the use of funds or are targeted to a narrower purpose (e.g., health services) or a broader population (e.g., persons from birth through 21 years old) than that targeted by the Part H program. For example, Medicaid funds can be accessed only for those Part H–eligible children who meet the program's family income requirement; reimbursement for services is restricted to those services included in the state Medicaid plan; and the state matching requirement often discourages the widespread use of Medicaid or the amendment of the state Medicaid plan to cover a broader range of services. Accessing other funding sources (e.g., federal Developmental Disabilities funds that can be used for persons from birth through 21 years old), often requires diverting funds from other groups with special needs (e.g., older children and adolescents). What many state planners have learned is that, while other funding sources can be accessed for the Part H program, this effort often falls short of meeting the total financial requirements of implementing their statewide system of services. There is a growing recognition that Part H funds and state-appropriated funds are often the most useful funds, as they can be used to pay for any Part H–eligible child and any early intervention service required under the program. The federal appropriation for the Part H program has increased by approximately 50% in both Fiscal Year 1991 and in Fiscal Year 1992, and some states have provided significant state appropriations for early intervention, further supporting the observation that additional funds have been needed for both gluing purposes and filling funding gaps.

Given the current economic difficulties of many states, finding sufficient funding and other resources for the Part H program is likely to be a continuing challenge to the viability of the program. A number of alternative funding schemes and recommendations have been proposed (e.g., Clifford, 1991; Clifford, Kates, Black, Eckland, & Bernier, 1991), however, and there is a growing understanding among key policymakers that the absence of an adequate and stable financial foundation will threaten the Part H program.

An initial measure of the progress made toward the first two goals will be available in 1993, when the extended-participation option ends. At that time, we will know the extent to which states have developed a statewide system of services and identified and coordinated resources to pay for those services. Then states can focus on refining their system to ensure the high-quality services envisioned by Congress.

States Will Provide High-Quality Services to Children and Families

PL 99-457 does not describe how states should meet the goal of providing high-quality services, nor does it define what "high-quality services" are. The law does contain several provisions that the authors believe are closely related to quality, or are at least meant to enable the delivery of high-quality services. For the most part, however, determining whether high-quality services are being provided will depend on each observer's values, philosophy, and knowledge of the scientific basis of different practices. Importantly, professionals involved in conducting research, evaluation, personnel training, model development, and dissemination will, over time, contribute to improved practices and will report on the quality of services being provided. In this section, we offer six dimensions of quality. Under each dimension, we pose several questions that may serve as an initial framework for considering the quality of services.

1. Timeliness Are eligible children and families identified and referred as quickly as possible? Is the multidisciplinary assessment and the development of the IFSP completed and implemented without delay? Is the IFSP revised as needed in response to growth and change in the child and family? Are early intervention services provided to children and families in a timely way?

2. Effectiveness Are the early intervention services provided to children and families effective, and do these services improve the quality of their lives? Do they lead to important and beneficial outcomes, allowing each child to realize his or her full potential? Are the service approaches being used the most efficacious ones available, yet least disruptive of family routines and relationships?

3. Individualization Are the services for children and families truly individualized? Are the services and service approaches responsive to, and accommodating of, each child and family's needs and circumstances? Are the services provided in a sensitive and competent manner, recognizing the uniqueness of each child and family? Are the services tailored to cultural, linguistic, and other child and family characteristics that must be addressed with special sensitivity?

4. Transitions Is there a continuum of services available over time to each child and family? Do professionals help the child and family successfully negotiate changes in service providers, settings, and locations? Do transition strategies assist the child and family by providing for counseling and support, by helping the child develop necessary new skills, by assisting with logistical changes, and by preparing the new service provider and service setting to successfully accommodate the child and family?

5. Child- and Family-Centered Are services provided in a nonstigmatizing way that avoids labeling of the child and the family? Are services provided, to the greatest extent possible, in the child's and family's natural environments? Do services enable the family to participate in the same range of activities possible for other families? Is the service system sufficiently flexible that a family's needs and preferences determine how, where, and when services are provided? Does the service system allow parents to easily decline particular services, respecting their knowledge of the needs of the child and family? Is the family satisfied with the services?

6. Coordination of Services Are multiple services, service providers, and service agencies truly coordinated? Do multiple services individually and collectively produce the desired outcomes? Are multiple services integrated into a nonfragmented system of assistance that supports the development and well-being of the child and family?

Unlike the first two goals, there will be no particular point in time when we will be able to gauge the extent to which the goal of high-quality services is being met, for our definition of high-quality services will evolve. At the same time, there is little point in meeting the first two goals if we do not also concern ourselves with the quality of services provided. Thus, the third goal will become the enduring goal that pushes us to expand our vision as to what is possible for young children with disabilities and their families, and then to work to make that vision a reality for all children and families.

CONCLUDING COMMENTS

PL 99-457 is landmark legislation, both in terms of the promise that it held for young children with disabilities and their families, and in the values and beliefs it reflected. The concepts it embodied have generated both excitement about the promise and implementation challenges for states. This is not surprising, as experience has shown that, with any major new social program, the initial focus is necessarily on defining and putting into place the procedures and services related to the basic components, and only later on refining and improving those procedures and services. Furthermore, experience has shown that the refining-and-improving stage never really ends, as our efforts are continually fueled by new knowledge or expanded target populations. What is important is that both our initial and later activities are driven by the best possible knowledge base.

REFERENCES

Bailey, D.B., Palsha, S.A., & Huntington, G.S. (1990). Preservice preparation of special educators to work with infants and their families: Current status and training needs. *Journal of Early Intervention, 14*(1), 43–54.

Bailey, D.B., Simeonsson, R.J., Yoder, D.E., & Huntington, G.S. (1990). Infant personnel preparation across eight disciplines: An integrative analysis. *Exceptional Children, 57*(1), 26–35. .

Brewer, G.D., & Kakalik, J.S. (1979). *Handicapped children: Strategies for improving services.* New York: McGraw-Hill.

Campbell, P.H., Bellamy, G.T., & Bishop, K.K. (1988). Statewide intervention systems: an overview of the new federal program for infants and toddlers with handicaps. *Journal of Special Education, 22,* 25–40.

Casto, G., & Mastropieri, M.A. (1986). The efficacy of early intervention programs for handicapped children: A meta-analysis. *Exceptional Children, 52,* 417–424.

Clifford, R. (1991). *State financing of services under P.L. 99-457, Part H.* Chapel Hill: Carolina Policy Studies Program, Frank Porter Graham Child Development Center, University of North Carolina.

Clifford, R. Kates, D.A., Black, T. Eckland, J., & Bernier, K. (1991). *Reconcepualization of financing under P.L. 99-457, Part H.* Chapel Hill: Carolina Policy Studies Program, Frank Porter Graham Child Development Center, University of North Carolina.

Education for All Handicapped Children Act of 1975, PL 94-142. (August 23, 1977). Title 20, U.S.C. 1401 et seq: *U.S. Statutes at Large, 89,* 773–796.

Education of the Handicapped Act Amendment of 1983, PL 98-199. (1983). Title 20, U.S.C. 101 et seq: *U.S. Statutes at Large, 97,* 1357–1375

Education of the Handicapped Act Amendments of 1986, PL 99-457. (October 8, 1986). Title 20, U.S.C. 1400 et seq: *U.S. Statutes at Large, 100,* 1145–1177.

Farran, D.C. (1990). Effects of intervention with disadvantaged and disabled children: A decade review. In S.J. Meisels & J.P. Shonkoff (Eds.), *Handbook of early childhood intervention* (pp. 501-539). Cambridge: Cambridge University Press.

Gallagher, J.J., Harbin, G., Thomas, D., Clifford, R., & Wenger, M. (1988). *Major policy issues in implementing Part H-P.L. 99-457 (infants and toddlers).* Chapel Hill: Carolina Policy Studies Program, Frank Porter Graham Child Development Center, University of North Carolina.

Gallagher, J.J., & Staples, A. (1989). *Available and potential resources for personnel preparation in special education: Dean's survey.* Chapel Hill: Carolina Policy Studies Program, Frank Porter Graham Child Development Center, University of North Carolina.

Gallagher, J.J., Trohanis, P.L., & Clifford, R.M. (Eds.). (1989). *Policy implementation and PL 99-457: Planning for young children with special needs.* Baltimore: Paul H. Brookes Publishing Co.

Garwood, S.G. (1987). Political, economic, and practical issues affecting the development of universal early intervention for handicapped infants. *Topics in Early Childhood Special Education, 8*(1), 1–11.

Guralnick, M.J., & Bennett, F.C. (Eds.). (1987). *The effectiveness of early intervention for at-risk and handicapped children.* Orlando, FL: Academic Press.

Handicapped Children's Early Education Act, PL 90-538. (September 30, 1968). Title 20, U.S.C. 621 et seq: *U.S. Statutes at Large, 82,* 901–902.

Harbin, G., Gallagher, J.J., & Lillie, T. (1989). *States' progress related to fourteen components of P.L. 99-457, Part H.* Chapel Hill: Carolina Policy Studies Program, Frank Porter Graham Child Development Center, University of North Carolina.

Harbin, G., Gallagher, J.J., Lillie, T., & Eckland, J. (1990). *Status of states' progress in implementing Part H of P.L. 99-457: Report #2.* Chapel Hill: Carolina Policy Studies Program, Frank Porter Graham Child Development Center, University of North Carolina.

Meisels, S., Harbin, G., Modigliani, K., & Olsen, K. (1988). Formulating optimal state early childhood intervention policies. *Exceptional Children, 55,* 159–165.

Shelton, T.L., Jeppson, E.S., & Johnson, B.H. (1987). *Family-centered care for children with special health care needs.* Washington, DC: Association for the Care of Children's Health.

Shonkoff, J.P., & Meisels, S.J. (1990). Early childhood intervention: The evolution of a concept. In S.J. Meisels & J.P. Shonkoff (Eds.), *Handbook of early childhood intervention* (pp. 3-31). Cambridge: Cambridge University Press.

Silverstein, R. (1989). A window of opportunity: P.L. 99-457. In *The intent and spirit of P.L. 99-457: A sourcebook* (pp. A1-A7). Washington, DC: National Center for Clinical Infant Programs.

Smith, B. (1988). Early intervention public policy: Past, present, and future. In J.B. Jordan, J.J. Gallagher, P.L. Hutinger, & M.B. Karnes (Eds.), *Early childhood special education: Birth to three* (pp. 213–228). Reston, VA: Council for Exceptional Children.

Turnbull, A.P., & Turnbull, H.R. (1985). Stepping back from early intervention: An ethical perspective. *Journal of the Division for Early Childhood, 10,* 106–117.

U.S. Department of Education. (1984). *Sixth annual report to Congress on the implementation of Public Law 94-142: The Education for all Handicapped Children Act.* Washington, DC: Author.

U.S. Department of Education. (1985). *Seventh annual report to Congress on the implementation of Public Law 94-142: The Education for all Handicapped Children Act.* Washington, DC: Author.

White, K.R., & Casto, G. (1985). An integrative review of early intervention efficacy studies with at-risk children: Implications for the handicapped. *Analysis and Intervention in Developmental Disabilities, 5,* 7–31.

Defining Eligibility
for Early Intervention

Wesley Brown
and Carole Brown

> The determination of disability in childhood rests on certain as-
> sumptions about the fundamental nature of disability and the nature
> of childhood. We have made considerable inroads in our under-
> standing about how children develop by incorporating a "develop-
> mental model" into the disability determination process. We still
> have conceptual work to be done related to disability and function.
> (Brown & Seklemian, in press)

This chapter carefully examines a variety of concepts related to the
definitions of developmental delays and of infants and toddlers with
disabilities. The requirements of PL 99-457, as amended by PL 102-119,
are also analyzed, and a variety of state definitions are noted. Biological and environmental risk factors are also discussed; and concepts of
risk are introduced, with a focus on established and cumulative risk
factors. Chapter 3, "Assessment and Evaluation in Early Intervention," supports and extends the discussion on eligibility begun here.

WHO ARE INFANTS AND TODDLERS WITH DISABILITIES?

Infants and toddlers are a difficult group among whom to determine
the existence and magnitude of disability. First, infant tests have not

been found to be highly predictive of later functioning (McCall, 1979). Second, the potential influence of environmental conditions and early intervention on the long-term effects of illness and other disabling conditions varies for each individual. Deciding which infants and toddlers are eligible to receive early intervention services is an essential component of a state's system of early intervention services.

Regulations for the early intervention (Part H) program provide specifically for three subgroups, or categories of eligibility, in the definition of infants and toddlers with disabilities. States have been given considerable flexibility in establishing criteria for eligibility in these subgroups. The first group includes children with *established conditions*. These children have a diagnosed physical or mental condition or group of conditions that establishes their eligibility because of the high probability of the occurrence of developmental delay. However, there are differences of professional opinion on which conditions should be included in this group. The second group includes children who are *developmentally delayed* in one or more developmental domains. States are required to define the term *developmental delay* and to establish procedures to determine when such a condition is present. Many states have defined the term as a certain percentage of difference between performance level and chronological age, or a certain number of standard deviations below chronological age, and various additional criteria are also used by some states (Harbin & Maxwell, 1991). Finally, a state can determine, at its own option, whether to serve children who are *at risk* for becoming substantially developmentally delayed if early intervention services are not provided. This optional at-risk subgroup allows states the discretion of determining which children, if any, to serve, while still remaining in compliance with the federal requirements for the program for infants and toddlers with disabilities. Various state criteria for eligibility for each of these subgroups are presented later in this chapter.

Perspectives on Prevention and Promotion

One of the major purposes of early intervention is the prevention of developmental delays in children. Since the 1960s, the health, medical, and psychiatric communities have delineated levels of prevention by using the terms *primary, secondary,* and *tertiary prevention.* This terminology has been used to increase our awareness that even with effective treatment of existing conditions, there is often a failure to provide sufficient attention to preventable causes or factors influencing the development of the condition. Primary prevention seeks to prevent the conditions or developmental delay from ever developing or becoming established. Such primary preventive approaches require systemic and societal changes in the way children are nurtured during their development, as well as the elimination of specific conditions that lead to later disability. For example, by increasing the availability of prenatal care to a group of women without health insurance, we can decrease the rate of premature births among this group and, as an outcome of this intervention, we can expect to see fewer children born with disabling conditions.

Secondary prevention seeks, through timely, focused intervention, to lessen the magnitude of the disability or delay, reducing or preferably eliminating its future impact on both the individual and society. Secondary prevention is effective when the individual considered to be delayed is able to leave that status, or does not require interventions that otherwise would have been required. For example, children with frequently occurring otitis media (ear infections) will suffer transient hearing loss that may affect their ability to learn language. By treating the otitis media, we would expect to see improved hearing and, thus, few or no impairments in language skills.

Finally, tertiary prevention seeks to reduce the outcomes and effects of disability or delay through various forms of intervention. Here, the delay can not be avoided entirely, as in primary prevention, or eliminated through treatment, as in secondary prevention, but the effects can still be lessened and the development of the individual fostered. An example of tertiary intervention might involve a child who is born with a hearing impairment, for whom intervention is aimed at enhancing communication through hearing aids or an alternative communication system such as signing. These three levels of prevention are closely related to the legislative purposes of the program for infants and toddlers with disabilities. The reader is referred to Simeonsson (1991b) for an excellent discussion of this topic.

Dunst, Trivette, and Thompson (1990) have advocated the concept of *promotion*, as opposed to treatment or prevention, as a basis when developing interventions. Promotion models focus on positive growth through the enhancement of the individual capacities and functioning of children and families, rather than on avoidance, remediation, or reduction of developmental delay. Working on factors that facilitate the child and family is viewed here as a far better way to influence developmental outcomes for an infant or toddler with disabilities. An example of promotion might be an approach that fosters a resource of the family. For example, a child who is deaf and has parents who are also deaf would be encouraged to learn signing as his or her main mode of communication. A child with the same hearing level, but raised in a hearing family, might be promoted differently.

For example, the parents might be introduced to other parents in a similar situation, who could then serve as a primary resource to promote and empower the family.

Established Conditions

Children who have certain established physical or mental conditions automatically become eligible for early intervention services in participating states. While the federal law and regulations do not specify which conditions are to be included, examples are provided for guidance. It would not be realistic for states to exclude conditions with which developmental delays are often associated. Examples of conditions that "have a high probability of resulting in a developmental delay" include Down syndrome and other chromosomal abnormalities, sensory impairments (e.g., vision and hearing loss), inborn abnormalities in metabolism; microcephaly; severe attachment disorders, including failure to thrive; seizure disorders; and fetal alcohol syndrome.

Unfortunately, experts do not always agree about which conditions in early childhood have a high probability of resulting in developmental delay. An examination of the conditions that various states have determined should qualify children for this group shows a lack of agreement among states (Harbin & Maxwell, 1991). Clarifying language in the Part H regulations indicates that "high probability of resulting in developmental delay" is not intended to be viewed as a statistical term and that "established conditions" refers to those conditions with known etiologies and developmental consequences. Table 1 contains a list of categories of established conditions, with selected examples of individual diagnoses under many of the categories.

Having an established condition constitutes *presumptive eligibility,* and children with such conditions are eligible for early intervention services regardless of whether the delay is present at the time of identification. For example, some children with Down syndrome may not be developmentally delayed in the first few months of life, but there is universal agreement that these children should receive early intervention services to minimize the future delay. Therefore, the first step in determining eligibility for services for a child is to note whether or not the child's condition falls into a presumptive eligibility category. If so, additional assessments or evaluations are not necessary for eligibility determination.

Besides recognizing individual clinical conditions, such as Down syndrome, some states also recognize that certain combinations of

Table 1.   Selected examples of established conditions

Chromosomal Anomalies/Genetic Disorders

Trisomies, translocations, and deletions
   Cri-du-chat syndrome
   Down syndrome
   Trisomy 18
Sex-linked
   Fragile X syndrome
   Klinefelter syndrome
Other types of abnormalities
   Marfan syndrome

Neurological Disorders

Neuromotor/muscle disorders
   Cerebral palsy
   Muscular dystrophy
   Paralysis
   Wilson disease
Cerebrovascular disease
   Intracranial hemorrhage
Degenerative diseases
   Leukodystrophies
Neurocutaneous disorders
   Neurofibromatosis
   Tuberous sclerosis
Malignancies
   Intracranial tumors
   and other malignancies of the central nervous system
Head and spinal cord trauma
   Fracture of vertebral column
Seizure disorders
   Nonrefractory and intractible type
   Refractory and tractible type (controllable)

Congenital Malformations

Cardiovascular
   Patent ductus arteriosus
   Transposition of great arteries
Orofacial
   Cleft lip and/or cleft palate
Genitourinary
   Renal insufficiency
Musculoskeletal
   Arthrogryposis
   Cornelia de Lange syndrome
Pulmonary/respiratory
   Tracheostomy
Central nervous system
   Uncorrected hydrocephalus
   Microcephaly
   Spina bifida

(continued)

Table 1. (*continued*)

Inborn Errors of Metabolism

Mucopolysaccharidoses
  Hunter syndrome
  Hurler-Scheie syndrome
Abnormalities of amino acid metabolism
  Phenylketonuria (PKU)
Abnormalities of carbohydrate metabolism
  Galactosemia
  Glycogen storage disease
Abnormalities of lipid metabolism
  Tay-Sachs disease
Abnormalities of purine/pyridimine metabolism
  Lesch-Nyhan syndrome
Abnormalities of the parathyroid
  Hyperparathyroidism
  Untreated hypoparathyroidism
Abnormalities of the pituitary
  Hyperpituitary
  Hypopituitary
Abnormalities of adrenocortical function
  Hyperadrenocortical function
  Hypoadrenocortical function

Sensory Disorders

Eye
  Amblyopia
  Blindness
  Congenital cataract
  Retinopathy of prematurity (ROP)
Ear
  Hearing loss

Severe Atypical Developmental Disorders

Atypical pervasive developmental disorder
Autistic disorder
Reactive attachment disorder

Toxic Exposure

Prenatal
  Fetal alcohol syndrome (FAS)
  Maternal phenylketonuria (PKU)
  Maternal substance abuse
Postnatal
  Lead exposure
  Mercury exposure

Chronic Medical Illness

Complex health care needs
  Technology-dependent
Medical illness
  Bronchopulmonary dysplasia (BPD)
  Cancer
  Chronic hepatitis

(*continued*)

Table 1.   (*continued*)

Cystic fibrosis
Diabetes
Heart problems
Renal failure

Infectious Disease

Congenital infections
  Cytomegalovirus (CMV)
  Herpesvirus
  Human immunodeficiency virus (HIV)
  Rubella
  Toxoplasmosis
Acquired infections
  Bacterial meningitis
  Encephalitis
  Poliomyelitis.
  Viral meningitis

Adapted from NEC*TAS. (1989).

less severe factors, taken together, constitute a condition with a high probability of resulting in developmental delay. *Multiplicity of risk,* as this condition is termed, can, at a state's discretion, be considered an established condition. Such conditions could include, for example, a combination of low birth weight, neonatal sepsis, and maternal substance abuse. Other such risk factors will be discussed later in this chapter.

Developmental Delay

Developmental delay is a major building block in the definition of infants and toddlers with disabilities. This term was used for the first time in special education legislation in 1986, when PL 99-457 was passed. In the program for infants and toddlers with disabilities, states are required to develop procedures for determining the presence of a developmental delay in each of five developmental domains: physical development, cognitive development, communicative development, social or emotional development, and adaptive development. Procedures to determine the presence of delays include the use of tests, informed clinical opinion, and multidisciplinary team decisionmaking.

After referral, the process of determining eligibility usually begins with the use of a screening test or other norm- or criterion-referenced instrument or protocol. The child's delay may be described in terms of his or her level of functioning or other criteria. When standardized procedures for determining the presence of developmental delay are considered appropriate, levels of functioning may include: percentage of delay, standard deviation, number-of-months delay, developmental quotients, and the rate of developmental change over a prescribed period of time. Other criteria might include observational data that describes a pronounced discrepancy in a pattern of development, or a combination of functional, clinical, or other data.

Qualitative assessment methods can be based on the observation of discrepancies in development, without specifying a particular level of delay. Regulation section 303.22(c)(2) requires states to ensure that informed clinical opinion is used in determining a child's eligibility. These opinions become especially important when there are no standardized measures, or the standardized procedures are not appropriate for a given age or developmental area, as described in detail later in this chapter.

Each state must describe the quantitative and qualitative methods or techniques that are used in evaluation and assessment and indicate how informed clinical opinion is included in the process. How is the decisionmaking process handled? What is the nature of parental involvement? And how are decisions on eligibility made when consensus is not immediately reached? All of these points must be addressed in the states' procedures.

There is currently a great deal of variety from state to state in the procedures that have been proposed to define developmental delay and eligibility for services under Part H (Harbin & Maxwell, 1991). While states have flexibility in determining developmental delay, 16 rely solely on test-based criteria, and 22 states use a combination of test-based and non–test-based criteria. Four states, however, use professional judgment and/or documentation of atypical development (Harbin & Maxwell, 1991). Table 2 shows each state's current criteria for determining developmental delay.

As a matter of professional practice and policy, it is recommended that the determination of developmental delay always be based on more than test results. Tests, and even many criterion-referenced instruments, rely on the existence of well-normed standards for developmental domains. Unfortunately, we do not always have standards for each developmental domain, and often, the populations on which the norms are based do not match a child's condition (e.g., visual impairment). Parental concern that a disability or delay may be present is often one of the most reliable indicators of the existence of developmental delay. A recent doctoral study (Henderson, 1991) found that parental input greatly reduced the number of misclassifications of preschool children. Professional's classifications, using the Early Screening Inventory, were found to be accurate 84% of the time; parent's classifications, using the Parent Questionnaire,

Table 2. Developmental delay criteria from state definitions

Alabama	25% delay in one or more areas
Alaska	15% or 1.5 SD delay in one or more areas
Arizona	50% delay in one or more areas
Arkansas	2 SD in one area or 35% for birth to eighteen months
	2 SD in one area, 1.5 SD in two areas, or 25% delay for 18-36 months
California	determined by multidisciplinary team
Colorado	1.5 SD or equivalent in percentile (7%) or standard scores
Connecticut	2 SD
Delaware	1.5 SD in one area or 2 month delay for B - 12 months
	3-4 month delay for 13-24 months
	5-6 months delay for 25-36 months
	atypical development
Florida	Less than 2 months- atypical development
	2-12 months- 2 months delay in one area
	13-24 months- 3 months delay in one area
	24-36 months- 4 months delay in one area
Georgia	2 SD in one area; 1.5 SD in two areas
Hawaii	determined by multidisciplinary team
Idaho	30% below age or 6 month delay or 2 SD in one area
	1.5 SD in two areas
Illinois	2 SD or 25% delay in one area; 1.5 SD or 20% delay in two or more
	areas or in one area with additional risk factors
Indiana	1.5 SD in one area or 20% delay; 1 SD in two areas or 15% delay
Iowa	25% delay in one or more areas
Kansas	25% delay or 1.5 SD in one area; 20% delay or 1 SD in two areas
Kentucky	2 SD in one area; 1.5 SD in two areas or less than 75% developmental quotient
Louisiana	determined by multidisciplinary team
Maine	under 24 months- multidisciplinary team
	over 24 months- 2 SD or 25% delay in one area or 1.5 SD or 15% delay, or
	1 SD or 10% delay with additional risk factors
Maryland	25% delay in one area; atypical development/behavior
Massachusetts	age 6 months, 1.5 months delay; age 12 months, 3 months delay;
	age 18 months, 4 months delay; age 24 months, 6 months delay;
	age 30 months, 7 months delay
Michigan	determined by multidisciplinary team
Minnesota	cognitive, 1.5 SD; communication, 2 SD; other areas involve clinical opinion
	and/or 1 - 2 SD delays
Mississippi	1.5 SD or 25% delay
Missouri	50% delay in one area or atypical development
Montana	50% delay in one area or 25% delay in two areas
Nebraska	developmental delay, no criteria
Nevada	25% delay or clinical opinion during birth to 12 months
New Hampshire	determined by multidisciplinary team
New Jersey	33% delay in one area; 25% delay in two or more areas
New Mexico	25% delay in one area or score indicating significant delay
	birth to 12 months, clinical opinion only
New York	2 SD in one area
North Carolina	1.5 SD in one area or 20% delay; atypical development
North Dakota	50% delay in one area; 25% delay in two or more areas

(continued)

Table 2. (*continued*)

Ohio	"measurable delay" or not reaching developmental milestones
Oklahoma	50% delay in one area; 25% delay in two or more areas
Oregon	56-75% of chronological age in 3 or more areas
	40-55% of chronological age in 2 areas
	less than 40% of chronological age in 1 area
Pennsylvania	25% delay or 1.5 SD
Puerto Rico	informed clinical opinion
Rhode Island	25% or 2 SD in one area; 1.5 SD in two areas
South Carolina	2 SD or 30% in one area; 1.5 SD or 22% in two areas
South Dakota	25% or 6 month delay or 1.5 SD
Tennessee	25% delay in two areas; 40% in one area
Texas	age less than 2 months- atypical behavior or medical diagnosis
	age 2-12 months- 2 month delay
	age 13-24 months- 3 month delay
	age 25-36 months- 4 month delay
	atypical behavior
Utah	2 SD or below 2nd percentile in one area
	1.5 SD or below 7th percentile in two areas
	1 SD or below 16th percentile in three areas
Vermont	observable, measurable delay
Virginia	25% delay in one area
Washington	1.5 SD or 25% delay in one area
West Virginia	25% delay in one area; 6 month delay in two or more areas
Wisconsin	25% delay or 1.3 SD in one area; atypical development; or team decision
Wyoming	1.5 SD or 25% delay in one or more areas

Adapted from Shakelford (1992).
Criteria based on September 1992 state plans. Program regulations require all states to use informed clinical opinion, the use of which has various qualifications in individual state plans.
SD = standard deviation

were accurate 76% of the time. However, when the screening inventory and parent questionnaire were used in combination, the accuracy rate of classification was raised to 93% (Meisels, 1992).

At Risk

The term *at risk* refers to children who are in danger of having substantial developmental delays if early intervention services are not provided. These children may currently demonstrate no abnormality, but have biological or environmental factors associated with their medical history or home context that increase the risk of delay in the future. They may also show abnormalities in their developmental patterns that lead informed sources to predict that early intervention services are necessary to prevent substantial developmental delay. There are two major categories of risk for developmental delay. The first, *biological risk,* includes those children whose personal or family medical history includes biological conditions that imply a greater probability of delay. Commonly noted factors for infants include low birth weight, respiratory distress as a newborn, lack of oxygen, brain hemorrhage, and infection. Sameroff and Chandler (1975) labeled a somewhat similar category of risk as *reproductive casualty*, in which non optimal outcomes are viewed as being caused by genetic, prenatal, and perinatal factors. Except where there has been significant damage to the central nervous system, most researchers have noted that single biological factors have had only a limited impact on the child independent of caregiving factors. In other words, children in nurturing environments often appear to overcome the effects of single biological risk factors.

The second category, *environmental risk*, includes children whose histories of care involve risk factors that imply a greater probability of delay. This category, in which psychosocial and environmental factors contribute to non-optimal outcomes, was labeled as *caretaking casualty* by Sameroff and Chandler (1975). Research studies have shown that the risk is much greater when several risk factors are present and not compensated for by areas of strength or positive functioning. Findings have indicated that the actual number of risk factors present for an infant or toddler with disabilities is clearly more important than the presence of any specific factors. Table 3 is a list of environmental and biological risk factors developed by Benn (1991) after an extensive research review.

Benn examined research on 27 risk factors for developmental outcomes. While she found the studies methodologically unsophisticated, she also found evidence of short-term adverse effects for each factor and long-term negative effects for multiple factors. Benn's work supports the inclusion of certain conditions (i.e., child abuse, impaired attachment, parental substance abuse that results in toxic exposure to the infant, chronic illness, and infectious diseases) in the "established risk conditions" or "presumptive eligibility" category. Beyond this, she found that developmental outcome cannot be reliably predicted by individual factors. She recommends considering multiple risk factors in the context of balancing positive factors as significant mediating influences in the child's environment.

Regardless of the method of examination, environmental factors stand out in their impact, as contrasted with biological factors. Kochanek and Buka (1991) systematically screened infants in Rhode Island and found about 4% to be at risk. Of this risk group, only 20% were included due to child characteristics (biological), while 80% were included because of parental and environmental characteristics. Kochanek concluded that in his sample, 75%–80% of the at-risk infants could only be identified as such within a family-centered context. Research has demonstrated, for example, that maternal educational

Table 3. Sample eligibility for service provision based on multiple risk factors

A combination of any four risk factors selected from lists below denotes eligibility for service provision:

Biological

Very low birth weight (VLBW) (<1,500 g)
Failure to thrive (FTT)
Asphyxia
Chronic otitis media
Bronchopulmonary disease (BPD)
Apnea
Acute physical illness/accident
Maternal prenatal and postnatal habits (e.g., alcohol, tobacco, or marijuana use)
Observed infant neonatal behavior state abnormalities
Any severe perinatal complication (e.g., intraventricular hemorrhage (IVH), seizures, abnormal neurological examination, multiple births)
Severe prenatal complications
Small for gestational age
Parental medical history characteristics (e.g., parent has a history of perinatal loss due to SIDs, of family sensory impairment, of several birth complications [e.g., multiple pregnancies, previous birth of child with a disability].)

Environmental

Serious concern expressed by a parent, regular caregiver, or health provider regarding a child's development (e.g., emotional well-being, physical health status), parenting style, or parent–child interaction
Parental chronic or acute mental illness/developmental disability/retardation
Drug- or alcohol-dependent parent or caregiver
Disordered infant–parent attachment
Teenage mother (<age 20)
Homeless family
Acute family crisis
Chronically disturbed family interaction
Parental developmental history characteristics of loss, abuse
Caregiver with chronic physical illness
Parent–child separations (e.g., due to divorce, incarceration, hospitalization)
Lack of prenatal care beyond the 5th month
Physical, cultural, or social isolation
Lack of adequate social support
Family within 200% of federal guidelines for poverty
Parent with four or more preschool-age children
Presence of one or more of the following:
    Parent education less than 12th-grade
    Unemployed parent
    Single parent
Absence of regular health supervision or pediatric care
Parent with inadequate health care or no health insurance
Presence of one of social/cultural/ecological factors that may adversely affect the child (e.g., transient lifestyle, lack of stable residence, high-crime area)

Source: Benn (1991).

level is "a more accurate predictor of adolescent functioning than [was] the child's developmental status from birth to 12 months" (Kochanek, Kabacoff, & Lipsitt, 1987).

Low birth weight (LBW) is a common biological risk factor. Mc-Cormick (1989) found that 18.5% of her sample of very low birth weight (VLBW) infants had moderate or greater problems at age 8. However, when she examined the families for socioeconomic status (SES), there was a startling difference in the outcomes. In families in which there was low parental educational attainment, 54.5% of the VLBW infants were found to have developmental problems. When parents were better educated, only 8.7% had poor developmental outcomes, less than one sixth the incidence of difficulties for children of parents with limited education.

In other studies of obstetric complications (Littman & Parmelee, 1978), no correlation has been found among the 41 items of the Obstetric Complications Scale and the child's developmental quotient at 4, 9, 18, or 24 months. Recently, Craig, Evans, Meisels, and Plunkett (1991), tracked 30 LBW premature infants. Four of the 30 had significant language problems at age 3, but these problems were not found to be related to birth weight, gestational age, length of hospitalization, SES, respiratory status, family factors, or cognitive status of the child.

Many states, in the program for infants and toddlers with disabilities, indicate that they may, in the future, choose to serve children who are at risk. Other states offer early intervention services to some such children under other laws or programs. Therefore, if a child does not fit a particular state's Part H definition, the possibility of early intervention services should not be ruled out. Other programs may take a categorical approach, using biological and other factors as criteria for eligibility.

Procedures To Determine Eligibility

Informed clinical opinion is a required part of evaluation, assessment, and eligibility determination under Part H. Informed clinical opinion is recognized as being necessary because most tests are not normed for the purpose of determining if a disability is present, and certainly are not tailored to the individual eligibility requirements of various states' definitions or of federal standards. Furthermore, tests cannot capture a full developmental picture of an infant or toddler.

Informed clinical opinion is based on the knowledge and skill of the multidisciplinary team, including the child's parents. Thus, being "informed" implies that determination of a child's developmental status occurs in a socially valid way for that child and family (Biro, Daulton, & Szanton, 1991). The use of test-based thresholds for eligibility is insufficient without further interpretation, observations, and information gathered in interviews, informal assessment, and team decisionmaking. A coherent body of informed clinical opinion emerges from the documentation and synthesis of information from these varied sources (Biro et al., 1991).

The appropriate use of these procedures to achieve informed clinical opinion should lead to a greater compatibility between services for which the child is eligible and the specific needs of the child and family (Biro et al., 1991, p. 4). It has also been viewed as useful to determine the extent of the risk of future delay in a child's development. Simeonsson has suggested that a cumulative risk model in which the numbers of risk factors are simply tallied would lead to far greater numbers of children being identified as needing services (e.g., 25% of all children for three or more factors) than would a model that takes into account the effect that context and combination can have on the synergistic potential of risk factors (which would lead to the identification of 16% of children as needing services) (1991a, p. 53).

Simeonsson (1991a) has suggested an alternate model for making decisions about providing early intervention services. He makes the point that:

> Determination of eligibility should be considered as a continuing process rather than a static event. The fluctuations characterizing infant development in general, coupled with variations in biological and environmental factors, may result in a child's moving in and out of risk or eligibility status. (p. 55)

Prevention efforts might be more appropriately seen as a function of degree of concern. He concludes that a concerns-based approach "lends itself more readily to the use of clinical judgment as the basis for identification of children needing services" (p. 55). Using informed clinical opinion in a systematic manner that captures level of concern can more accurately target the children who are at risk for developmental delay if early intervention services are not provided.

RESILIENCE TO RISK

With the difficulty of predicting risk for single factors, researchers have sought to understand why a factor leads to poor outcomes with some children and not others. This has led to discussions about and research on resilience and protective factors that offset risk. Dunst (1992) recently reported that he has found patterns that appear to numerically demonstrate the counterbalancing of positive and negative factors. These developments have important implications for early intervention and clearly discourage looking at risk factors in isolation.

   While Dunst (1992) has identified the facilitating or protective factors in the child's environment, Werner (1990) has identified typical child-centered factors that contribute to the child's resilience, such as temperament, stress-handling capabilities, intelligence, self-esteem, and the quality of learning experiences and supportive relationships.

   In her work towards formulating a structural/behavioral model of development, F.D. Horowitz (1987) has proposed a three-dimensional model to illustrate the interaction of the individual, the environment, and potential developmental outcomes. In an adaptation of her work, Figure 1 is labeled for two hypothetical children. Child A's location represents high vulnerability as an individual in a nonfacilitative envi-

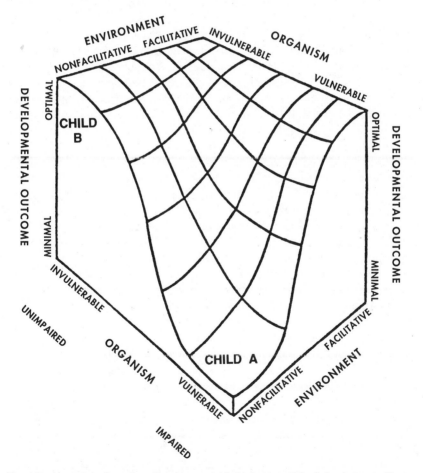

Figure 1. Horowitz's three-dimensional structural/behavioral model of development. (From Horowtiz, F. D. [1987]. *Exploring developmental theories: Toward a structural/behavioral model of development.* Hillsdale, NJ: Lawrence Erlbaum Associates; reprinted by permission.)

ronment whose potential developmental outcomes are viewed as being minimal. No protective factors support this child's development. Child B is also positioned in a nonfacilitative environment, but has protective factors or resilient capabilities that make the child invulnerable, with excellent potential developmental outcomes.

SPECIAL CONSIDERATIONS RELATED TO ELIGIBILITY

Attitudes toward individuals with disabilities among the public, and even among professionals, are often negative. The labeling of a child may create a social stigma for both the child and his or her family. Therefore, some parents and professionals may object to labeling a child with a disability. This will, however, vary with the values and attitudes of the community and family in which the child lives. There is evidence that the designation of a disability can sometimes be as debilitating as the disability itself. For example, some studies have demonstrated the phenomena of "learned helplessness," in which children, because of the attitudes of those around them, mistakenly come to believe that they are incapable of carrying out certain tasks.

Parents will fight for or against the designation of a disability, depending in part on what benefits might accrue to the child if he or she is considered eligible for a service. Many child advocates see a need to identify all children who may have special needs, so that those needs can be met. They want a very inclusive approach to eligibility in order to ensure that no child is missed. They believe that definitions should be broadly stated and flexible. In contrast, some public agencies are concerned about the costs of establishing a wide safety net and see the establishment of "eligibility criteria" as primarily a gate-keeping function meant to restrict the numbers of children who will be recognized as needing services, thereby containing costs, and perhaps preventing the provision of services that may not be needed.

ELIGIBILITY IN RELATED PROGRAMS

Traditional categorical approaches to determining eligibility for special education services, which consist of classifying children as having learning disabilities, mental retardation, serious emotional disturbance, and so forth, have long been considered inappropriate for young children. For example, because learning in young children is pre-academic, it is unusual that, based upon the current definition, a preschool-age child can be accurately diagnosed as having a learning disability. Young children are also more apt to have transient conditions that may not result in a long-term disabling condition. Placing a categorical label on a preschool child would appear to be inexact at best, and potentially harmful because of the possibility of social stigma. For these reasons, the term "developmental delay" is preferred by the professional community for the young child with disabilities (McLean, Smith, McCormick, Schakel, & McEvoy, 1991). PL 102-119, the 1991 amendments to IDEA, includes a new provision that gives states the option of creating a new category, termed *developmental delay,* for 3- to 5-year-olds. This section will examine how some major programs or classification systems have approached eligibility. This is important because early interventionists will have significant contact with each of these systems, either when children transfer out of Part H early intervention services at age 3 or when additional funding sources are utilized for children from birth to 3 years.

Head Start

In Head Start, traditional categorical definitions are used to determine if a child has a disability. Head Start primarily serves children of ages 3 through 5 who meet certain low-income eligibility requirements, but 10% of the participants in each program must be children with a diagnosed disability, and 10% do not have to meet strict income criteria. The definitions of disability in Head Start are similar to the special education categories for school-age children. Some differences currently being recommended are that the "seriously emotionally disturbed" category in special education be termed "emotional/ behavioral disorder" in Head Start and that the "Other" category under Head Start include attention deficit disorder (ADD) or attention deficit hyperactivity disorder (ADHD), might be classified under "other health-impaired" or "learning disability" under special education law. It could also possibly fit a state's "developmental delay" category for children ages 3 through 5). Head Start will also use any state definition of disability that is recognized in the jurisdiction in which the program is located. Finally, Head Start is considering restricting the use of the term "learning disability," particularly for children who are considered too young to be accurately identified as having a learning disability.

Medical Classifications

ICD   *The International Classification of Diseases—9th Revision Clinical Modification* (ICD-9-CM) is a system to classify the entire range of diseases and conditions related to disease. While the first ICD was developed to aid in reporting the causes of death, subsequent revisions have been used for other purposes, including medical research, and have evolved to serve a variety of uses for practitioners.

DSM-III-R *Diagnostic and Statistical Manual of Mental Disorders* (DSM-III-R) has been developed to be fully consistent with portions of the latest version of the ICD in providing additional diagnostic information about mental disorders. Mental disorders of childhood have posed challenges to classifiers and coders of information, and this coding system continues to evolve. Multiaxial evaluation for "mental disorders" involves evaluating each individual on five "axes," each providing a different class or category of information. The first two, clinical syndromes (Axis I) and developmental and personality disorders (Axis II) cover the entire range of mental disorders and have coding consistent with ICD-9-CM. The third axis is for recording relevant physical disorders and conditions of the individual from the other sections of ICD-9-CM. The final two axes, severity of psychosocial stressors (Axis IV) and global assessment of functioning (Axis V) are numerical rating scales that indicate the severity of stress contributing to the individual's condition and an overall judgement of their functioning. Special codes, known as V codes, are also provided to indicate prescribed areas for treatment that are not attributable to specific disorders. An example of a V code subject is a parent–child interaction pattern (V-61.20). Research leading to a new revision of this classification system, DSM-IV, is currently being completed.

Both classification systems are of particular interest to early intervention practitioners because they provide diagnostic descriptions of what might be considered established conditions under Part H. In addition, information gained through the ICD and other medical diagnostic systems may have an influence on insurance and other types of financing of early intervention services. As health services cost-containment efforts have increased, ICD codes have become more important, as they are used to file for insurance reimbursements. Since 1989, claims submitted by physicians on behalf of Medicare beneficiaries have had to include ICD-9-CM diagnostic codes. Currently, ICD-9-CM codes classifying a medical diagnosis are used in conjunction with Current Procedural Terminology (CPT) codes that specify procedures used to treat each diagnosis as part of the billing process for reimbursement from Medicare or other insurance providers.

Medicaid

Medicaid is a major federal program and provider of health services for children from families with low incomes. Because many of the "health services" under Medicaid can also be viewed as early intervention services, the Medicaid program is a potential provider of intervention services for half of the infants and toddlers with disabilities. This makes the eligibility process for receiving Medicaid benefits especially important to providers of early intervention services. It is important to note that Medicaid is a state-administered program, and that certain requirements, such as maximum income level, will vary according to the state in which the child resides. Under Medicaid, the first eligibility factor is the financial-means test. For children under age 6, every state is required to provide Medicaid to families with incomes up to 33% above the poverty level. Some states will also provide Medicaid to children under 1 year of age in families with incomes up to 85% above the poverty level.

If eligible for Medicaid, families with young children are eligible for the Early Periodic Screening Diagnosis and Treatment (EPSDT) program. While in the past states have had the option of specifying in their state Medicaid plan which specific services will be provided, recent legislation requires that treatment for conditions discovered through screening be covered, whether or not such services are covered under the State Medicaid plan. Essentially, this requirement means that if a condition that needs treatment is discovered in an EPSDT screen, then any services that are needed to ameliorate that condition should be covered as a benefit.

Medicaid has not established Federal diagnostic requirements for determining a need for a treatment; while a *Good Practices Handbook* was published by the Health Care Financing Administration, it is up to each state to determine minimal standards. Therefore, standards may vary, and it is important that professionals be sure that they are using best practice guidelines when making a determination of disability or a related condition. In most cases, state standards are adequate. However, when they are not up to date, it is a professional responsibility to insist on adequate standards and to document the need for services or ameliorative treatment.

The implications for state and local policy planners and practitioners of the new requirement for EPSDT to provide treatment are very significant. It will be important to establish procedures to ensure that the EPSDT screening process is utilized and coordinated with other efforts to identify conditions that require early intervention treatment services (Williams & Kates, 1990).

Social Security Administration

Benefits under Supplemental Security Income (SSI) provide financial assistance to low-income families of children with disabilities or chronic illness who meet a test of financial means. Additionally, in most states, children who are eligible for SSI are also eligible for free health care through Medicaid. Thus, qualifying for SSI represents a significant financial advantage for these families for the reasons already noted in the "Medicaid" section above.

Under the Social Security Administration's regulations, an "individualized functional assessment" has now become a Federal requirement for determining if a child has a disability in early childhood that would allow him or her to qualify for SSI benefits. These assessments are to "take into consideration all relevant factors and evidence in assessing a child's developmental milestones, functional domains, and certain behaviors, varying according to the age of the child" (Association of Maternal and Child Health Programs, 1991, p. 12) and multiple steps are taken in disability determination.

In its new regulations, Social Security has established two age categories for infants and toddlers from birth to age 3: "newborn and young infants" covers birth to age 1, and "older infants and toddlers" covers age 1 to age 3. Premature infants of 37 weeks or less and weighing less than 1,200 grams, and premature infants weighing at least 1,200 grams but less than 2,000 grams and who are at least 4 weeks small for gestational age, are considered eligible under the age of 1 year solely on the basis of low birth weight (Federal Register, November 11, 1991, p. 5,561). Professional determination of expected disability can be sufficient for an eligibility decision for the youngest group. Advocates would like the period for informed professional opinion to be extended because:

> there are many conditions that cannot be fully evaluated until the child is much older. For example, children under 3 are too young for the vision test . . . children under age 5 are too young for most hearing tests . . . and the ability to ambulate cannot be evaluated in children below walking age. (Manes & Ford, 1991, p. 7)

CONCLUDING COMMENTS

The process of defining and determining eligibility for early intervention, special education, or any special service for an individual with a disability cannot be understood without first understanding the cultural contexts of the child, family, and institutions that are involved in that decision. Family- and environment-centered factors must be considered along with biological and medical factors. The difficulties in predicting developmental outcomes from these factors remain highly problematic. Both environmental and biological factors must be taken into account when attempting to determine risk status and eligibility. At the same time, the unpredictability of individual risk factors has lead some researchers (Baumeister, Kupstas, & Klindworth, 1990; Simeonsson, 1991a) to characterize risk as being synergistic. From this perspective on risk, factors are considered transactional and dynamic, rather than static. The interrelationships of the factors are considered far more powerful than the direct effects of individual factors or groups of risk factors. This predicament presents great challenges to both front-line practitioners and distant policymakers regarding eligibility. The chapters that follow, on assessment, families, and collaboration and coordination, provide additional essential information to aid in the eligibility-determination process.

REFERENCES

American Medical Association. (1992). *Physicians' current procedural terminology 1992*. Chicago, IL: Author.
American Psychiatric Association. (1987). *Diagnostic and statistical manual of mental disorders* (3rd ed.—revised). Washington, DC: Author.
Association of Maternal and Child Health Programs. (1991). *MCH related federal programs: Legal handbook for program planners—Supplemental security income (SSI) for disabled children*. Washington, DC: The National Maternal and Child Health Clearinghouse.
Baumeister, A.A., Kupstas, F., & Klindworth, L.M. (1990). New morbidity: Implications for prevention of children's disabilities. *Exceptionality, 1*, 1–16.
Benn, R. (1991). *A state wide definition of eligibility under P.L. 99-457, Part H: A final research report*. Detroit, MI: Merrill-Palmer Institute.
Biro, P., Daulton, D., & Szanton, E. (1991). Informed clinical opinion. *NEC*TAS Notes, 4*, 1–4.
Brown, C.W., & Seklemian, P. (in press). The individual functional assessment process for young children with disabilities: Lessons from the Zebley decision. *Journal of Early Intervention*.
Craig, H.K., Evans, J.L., Meisels, S.J., & Plunkett, J.W. (1991). Linguistic production abilities of 3-year-old children born premature with low birth weight. *Journal of Early Intervention, 15*(4), 326–337.
Dunst, C.J. (1992). *Taking aim on intervention practices with children at-risk and their families*. Paper presented at the Ninth Annual Smokey Mountain Winter Institute.
Dunst, C., Trivette, C., & Thompson, R. (1990). Supporting and strengthening family functioning: Towards a congruence between principles and practice. *Prevention in Human Services, 9*(1), 19–43.
Federal Register. (1991, February 11). *Rules and Regulations, Department of Health and Human Services, Social Security Administration (20, Part 416)*.
Harbin, G.L., & Maxwell, K. (1991). *Progress toward developing a definition for developmentally delayed: Report #2*. Chapel Hill: The University of North Carolina, Carolina Policy Studies Program.
Henderson, L.W. (1991). Parental involvement in the developmental screen-

ing of young children: A multiple risk perspective (Doctoral dissertation, University of Michigan, Ann Arbor, 1991). *Dissertation Abstracts International, 52,* 3520A.

Horowitz, F.D. (1987). *Exploring developmental theories: toward a structural/ behavioral model of development.* Hillsdale, NJ: Lawrence Erlbaum Associates.

Kochanek, T.T., & Buka, S.L. (1991). Using biologic and ecologic factors to identify vulnerable infants and toddlers. *Infants and Young Children, 4(1)* 11–25.

Kochanek, T.T., Kabacoff, R.I., & Lipsitt, L.P. (1987). Early detection of handicapping conditions in infancy and early childhood: Toward a multivariate model. *Journal of Applied Developmental Psychology, 8,* 411-420.

Littman, B., & Parmelee, A.M. (1978). Medical correlates of infant development. *Pediatrics, 61,* 470–474.

Manes, J., & Ford, M. (1991). *Comments Re: SSI Rules for Determining Disability in Children.* 56 FR 5533, Mental Health Law Project and Association for Retarded Citizens—United States, July 3rd.

McCall, R.B. (1979). The development of intellectual functioning in infancy and the prediction of childhood IQ. In J.D. Osofsky (Ed.), *Handbook of infant development* (pp. 707–741). New York: John Wiley & Sons.

McCormick, M.C. (1989). Long-term follow-up of infants discharged from neonatal intensive care units. *Journal of the American Medical Association, 261(12)* 1767–1772.

McLean, M., Smith, B.J., McCormick, K., Schakel, J., & McEvoy, M. (1991). *Developmental delay: Establishing parameters for a preschool category of exceptionality* (Division for Early Childhood position paper). Reston, Va: Council for Exceptional Children.

Meisels, S.J. (1992). Early intervention: A matter of context. *Zero to Three, 12(3),* 1–6.

NEC*TAS. (1989). [Established conditions and the probility of developmental delay]. Unpublished raw data.

Sameroff, A.J., & Chandler, M.J. (1975). Perinatal risk and the continuum of caretaking causality. In F. Horowitz, M. Hetherington, S. Scarr-Salapatek, & G. Siegel (Eds.), *Review of child development research* (Vol. 4, pp. 187–244). Chicago: University of Chicago Press.

Shackelford, J. (1992). State/jurisdiction eligibility definition for Part H. *NEC*TAS Notes, 5,* 1–13.

Simeonsson, R.J. (1991a). Early intervention eligibility: A prevention perspective. *Infants and Young Children, 3(4),* 48–55.

Simeonsson, R.J. (1991b). Primary, secondary, and tertiary prevention in early intervention. *Journal of Early Intervention, 15,* 124–134.

Werner, E.E. (1990). Protective factors and individual resilience. In S.J. Meisels & J.P. Shonkoff (Eds.), *Handbook of early intervention* (pp. 97–116). New York: Cambridge University Press.

Williams, S., & Kates, D. (1990). *An interagency process for planning and implementing a financing system for early intervention and preschool services.* Chapel Hill, NC: National Early Childhood Technical Assistance System.

U.S. Department of Health and Human Services. (1900). *International classification of diseases* (9th Revision, Clinical Modification [ICD-9-CM]). (U.S. Department of Health and Human Services Publication No. [PHS] 91-1260.) Washington, DC: Author.

Assessment and Evaluation in Early Intervention

Mary McLean
and Katherine McCormick

The first section of this chapter covers the specific regulations and definitions included in PL 99-457, the original legislation that provided for early intervention services, and in PL 102-119 (now known as IDEA), the most recent legislation pertaining to the identification, evaluation, and assessment of infants and toddlers with disabilities and their families. PL 99-457 mandates that each state system include provisions for the performance of a timely, comprehensive, multi-disciplinary evaluation of each child birth through age 2 who has been referred for evaluation. In addition, these evaluation and assessment procedures should: 1) respect the unique developmental nature and characteristics of the infant or toddler and his or her family, 2) include the active participation of parents and other significant caregivers, 3) be sensitive to cultural and ethnic differences, and 4) utilize appropriate assessment procedures and instruments.

Evaluation Evaluation is defined as the procedures used by appropriately qualified personnel to determine a child's initial and continuing eligibility consistent with the legal definition of infants and toddlers with disabilities and includes determining the status of the child in each development area. Evaluation can be described as a systematic process of collecting and interpreting information on a child's health status, medical history, current level of functioning, and family in order to best enhance the child's development. Specifically, PL 99-457 defines evaluation as "a timely, comprehensive, multidisciplinary evaluation of the functioning of each handicapped infant and toddler in the state and the need of the families to appropriately assist in the development of the handicapped infant or toddler" (Section 300.322).

Assessment   Assessment is defined as the ongoing procedures used by appropriately qualified personnel throughout the period of a child's eligibility to identify the child's unique needs; the family's resources, priorities, and concerns regarding the development of the child; and the nature and extent of early intervention services that are needed by the child and family. The evaluation and assessment of each child must:

Be conducted by personnel trained to utilize appropriate methods and procedures.

Be based on informed clinical opinion.

Include a review of pertinent records related to the child's current health status and medical history.

Include an evaluation of the child's level of functioning in each of the following developmental areas: cognitive development; physical development, including vision and hearing; communication development; social or emotional development; and adaptive skills.

Include an assessment of the unique needs of the child in each of the developmental areas, including the identification of services appropriate to meet those needs.

Family Assessment   Family assessments under Part H must be designed to determine the resources, concerns, and priorities of the family related to enhancing the development of the child. Any assessment that is conducted must be voluntary on the part of the family. If an assessment of the family is carried out, the assessment must be conducted by personnel trained to utilize appropriate methods and procedures and must be based on information provided by the family through a personal interview. PL 102-119 further mandates that family assessments be family-centered and may,

> with the concurrence of the family include an assessment of the family's resources, priorities, and concerns and identification of family preferences, supports, and services necessary to enhance the parents' and siblings' capacity to meet the developmental needs of their infant or toddler with a disability. (Section 14)

To further support the desires of the family, a statement of family needs may be included in the written individualized family service plan (IFSP), but only with the family's consent. Furthermore, at the family's request, the family-assessment portion of an evaluation may be completely omitted. In addition, services may not be withheld from a child in a situation in which the family chooses not to participate in family assessment.

Timelines The evaluation and initial assessment of each child must be completed within 45 days. In exceptional circumstances that make this impossible, public agencies may document those circumstances and develop and implement an interim IFSP.

Nondiscriminatory Procedures Nondiscriminatory assessment, evaluation, and accompanying procedural safeguards are also necessary components of early intervention services. Each state lead agency is required to adopt nondiscriminatory evaluation and assessment procedures. PL 94-142 requires that tests and other evaluation materials:

Be provided and administered in the child's native language or other mode of communication.

Be validated for the specific purpose for which they are used.

Be administered by trained personnel in conformance with the instructions provided by the producer of the materials.

Include instruments tailored to assess specific areas of educational needs, and not merely those that are designed to provide a single general intelligence quotient.

Be selected and administered to best ensure that when a test is administered to a child with impaired sensory, manual, or speaking skills, the test results accurately reflect the child's aptitude or achievement level, or whatever other factors the test purports to measure, rather than simply reflecting the child's disability (except, of course, in cases in which the effects of the disability are the specific factors that are being measured).

No single procedure may be used as the sole criterion for determining an appropriate educational program for a child, and the evaluation must be made by a multidisciplinary team that includes at least one specialist with knowledge in the area of suspected disability.

SPECIAL CONSIDERATIONS IN
THE ASSESSMENT OF INFANTS AND TODDLERS

Instrumentation Variables

One of the first steps in evaluation is determining which instruments will be appropriate for the purpose of the intended outcome. One factor that must be considered when choosing an assessment instru-

ment, especially a standardized one, is the set of assumptions underlying the instrument's development and use. Robinson and Fieber
(1988) present three assumptions commonly acknowledged by the
users of norm-referenced standardized assessments. When using any
assessment, professionals assume that there is *adequate representation*
within the standardization group of infants and toddlers similar to
the child being assessed. We also assume *comparable opportunities for
acculturation* with the standardization group. Finally, we assume that
the instrument has demonstrated *adequate validity for prediction.*

If norm-referenced instruments are chosen, then it must be acknowledged that children with disabilities are typically excluded from
standardization groups. Furthermore, experiential deficits (e.g., dissimilar opportunities for acculturation) may have profound results,
especially for an infant or toddler with motor or sensory disabilities.
Early interventionists must be aware that violation of these assumptions compromises the outcomes rendered by many standardized assessments, especially in regard to the infant's position relative to the
norm. Therefore, particular caution must be exercised in the interpretation of outcomes, especially when we consider the poor predictive ability of early intellectual or performance tests.

Gibbs (1990) provides three explanations for the poor predictive
quality of assessments of young children. First, development may be
discontinuous from infancy to childhood. Second, what we attempt
to measure in infancy may be distinctly different from what we measure in childhood. This is especially critical in the cognitive domain.
Prediction is made more difficult when we compare the largely sensorimotor functioning of infants with the much more social, verbal,
and representational functioning of later development. Furthermore,
developmental domains are more strongly interrelated during infancy, making domain-specific testing difficult. A third possible explanation is the degree to which development may be influenced by social
and environmental factors from infancy to later ages. It can be argued
that the inability to predict from infancy to later childhood is a function of the malleability of this period. In summary, standardized assessments have very poor predictive ability when used with infants
and toddlers. They may, however, help us to determine the child's
current level of functioning.

Also of concern is the issue of reliability of outcome. Growth is
rapid and uneven during this period, affecting the stability of performance within and across domains, so that assessment outcomes may
be quite different from day to day or from week to week (Peterson,
1987).

Family Variables

Unlike it's predecessor, PL 94-142, which required parent involvement primarily in the areas of procedural safeguards and involvement in decisionmaking, PL 99-457 provides early intervention services to both the child and the family. The new law recognizes the
unique position of the family in the life of an infant or toddler and
mandates services designed to enhance the parents' ability to meet
the special needs of their infants or toddler. A child's development is
more controlled and influenced by his or her environment in infancy
than at any other time during development. Gibbs and Teti (1990)
suggest that the interdependence of infant development and family
functioning demands that the family be fully involved in infant assessment. Furthermore, families are accurate observers of their child's
behavior (Beckman, 1984; Vincent, Laten, Salisbury, Brown, & Baumgart, 1981). Their knowledge of the child's typical behavior is superior
to that of any member of the assessment team, and is a valuable
addition to the assessment process.

Child Variables

Bailey and Rouse (1989) cite four major areas of consideration in assessing infants and toddlers: 1) activity levels/distractibility, 2) variable states/attention span, 3) wariness of strangers or unfamiliar
adults, and 4) inconsistent performance in unfamiliar environments.
In addition, examiners must be cognizant of poorly developed verbal
expressive skills, separation factors, noncompliance, and lack of willingness to please the examiner (Peterson, 1987). These are attributes
common to all young children, however; examiners must also be
aware of the unique influence of specific disabling conditions on the
behavior of young infants and toddlers. For example, fatigue may be
exacerbated by the effort of the infants to move, visually track, or
auditorially localize. The effects of medication may further complicate
readiness or desire to participate in the social interaction or object
play required during most assessments. Furthermore, disabilities
may produce a differential developmental sequence for the acquisition of some skills. Robinson and Fieber (1988) suggest that limited
motor behaviors may inhibit object exploration, which is commonly
believed to precede concept development, but that concept development may still occur without the fine motor skills necessary for object
manipulation. In other words, some infants are able to compensate,
through other developmental pathways, for the missing information
typically gained through motor behaviors.

Researchers must be cautious in using the motor behaviors of some infants as indices of intelligence, and no domain should be viewed in a nonintegrated fashion. What must be considered are the limitations that a "missing pathway of information" places on a child's interpretations of his physical and social environment (Robinson & Fieber, 1988, p. 130).

In the evaluation of infants and toddlers with visual impairments, examiners must make the best possible use of residual vision with strategies such as the use of high-contrast visual stimuli, materials of increased size, close presentation, and allowance of ample time to explore materials (Fewell, 1983). In the evaluation of children with hearing impairments, examiners should present tasks in an organized manner in order to facilitate habituation and response expectations. Examiners should also be cognizant of the difficulty of providing appropriate hearing aids for infants and toddlers.

Examiner Variables

Competent assessment of young infants and toddlers with disabilities is not easily or quickly accomplished. The early interventionist must be knowledgeable about typical child development, must plan carefully within a team, and must be able to build and maintain rapport with young children. She or he must be able to adjust the tempo of the activities, presenting the task, removing materials easily and quickly, and immediately presenting the next task. He or she must be skilled enough to keep the child's attention, present materials, observe the child's response, and record the child's behavior simultaneously (Paget, 1983). While all of these skills are important, the ability to observe the child's interaction with materials and the environment is perhaps the most essential aspect of good assessment. The ability to work with professionals from other disciplines and use a hypothesis-building approach is also critical (Bailey & Rouse, 1989).

Perhaps the most important factor in the assessment of infant status is the use of professional judgment. The choice of instrument, use of materials and observation, and continual evaluation of the infant's interaction with the environment are dynamic processes based on a knowledge of child development and on clinical skill. Interventionists must not only be well aware of how to administer the chosen instrument, but must also be cognizant of the critical function of the individual items. For example, seeking a hidden object under a cup may be the overt demonstration of the acquisition or use of the concept of object permanence, but this act of seeking may be demonstrated in any one of many ways. The critical function is the act of seeking a hidden object; not picking up the cup. This is an important distinction when evaluating infants and toddlers with sensory or motor impairments. The interventionist must use his or her clinical skills to best ensure that the presence or absence of the critical function is being evaluated, rather than the disability. Furthermore, interventionists must be able to move beyond the documentation of the presence or absence of a specific skill or concept to an analysis of the use or quality of the skill or concept. More critical than the demonstration of a pincer grasp in picking up a sugar pellet is the use of the grasp in daily living.

GUIDELINES FOR ASSESSMENT

In 1989, a national task force on screening and assessment published a monograph that provided guidelines for screening and assessment procedures for young children (Meisels & Provence, 1989). A review of these guidelines is provided below, followed by a discussion of specific instruments and procedures that can be used in the screening, evaluation, and assessment of infants and toddlers.

   "Processes, procedures, and instruments intended for screening and assessment should only be used for their specified purposes" (p. 23). Professionals involved in the assessment of young children with special needs must clearly identify the purpose of various levels of assessment and must ensure that the instruments used are appropriate for the task at hand. Harbin (in press) identifies four distinct levels of assessment, each having a separate purpose: 1) public awareness, location, and pre-screening; 2) screening; 3) diagnostic assessment; and 4) assessment for intervention. Harbin suggests that disagreement among professionals about the purpose of different levels of assessment has led to fragmented and unsystematic assessment procedures that, in turn, lead to frustration and less-than-appropriate services for children and families.

   "Multiple sources of information should be included in screening and assessment processes" (p. 23). PL 99-457 specifies that each infant and toddler shall receive a multidisciplinary assessment of his or her unique needs. It is most important that, in the assessment process, information be obtained from a variety of sources. Sources of information that might be utilized by the assessment team include standardized assessment, observational recordings, parent report, health records, developmental checklists, and behavior checklists. A child's development is effected by multiple environmental and biological factors. No single source of information can be adequate.

   "Developmental screening should be viewed as only one path to more in-depth assessment. Failure to qualify for services based on a

single source of screening information should not become a barrier to further evaluation for intervention services if other risk factors (financial, environmental, medical) are present" (p. 24). No single procedure should be used to determine a child's eligibility for an in-depth evaluation. Studies of developmental screening measures have clearly indicated the occurrence of false negatives in the process. Therefore, even if a child passes a developmental screening, if the screening team identifies other factors that suggest developmental difficulty, further evaluation is warranted.

"Developmental screening should take place on a recurrent or periodic basis. It is inappropriate to screen young children only once during their early years of life; similarly, provisions should be made for reevaluation or reassessment after services have been initiated" (p. 24). During the period of development from birth through age 5, development can be affected by many factors. A screening process measures only a sample of the child's development at one moment in time. The provision of recurrent screenings is most important in order to adequately identify all of the children who may need early intervention services. Furthermore, continued reassessment is equally important so that children no longer in need of early intervention services can transfer out of early intervention.

"Screening and assessment procedures should be reliable and valid" (p. 25). The psychometric integrity of existing screening and assessment procedures for very young children is poor. Since the passage of PL 99-457 and the widespread development of early intervention services, there has been an increase in activity in this area. It will, however, take a considerable amount of research and development of new instruments to improve the situation. Professionals involved in screening and assessment during the interim must be careful to use existing instruments only for the specific purposes for which they were developed.

"Family members should be an integral part of the screening and assessment process" (p. 25). Family members should be fully informed of, and should consent to, all screening or assessment procedures prior to their implementation. Furthermore, professionals should actively solicit information from the family regarding their perceptions of the child's development and their desires for intervention goals.

"Screening and assessment should be viewed as services—as part of the intervention and not only as means of identification and measurement" (p. 23). The family should begin to develop a sense of trust in the intervention staff and process from the very first contact. Screening and assessment procedures not only serve as opportunities to gain information about the child's developmental and health status, but also provide an opportunity for facilitating the family's understanding of their child's development and of the early intervention process.

"**All tests, procedures and processes intended for screening or assessment must be culturally sensitive**" (p. 25). Professionals involved in the screening and assessment of young children must be able to differentiate the effects of developmental problems from the effects of cultural differences. Young children are heavily influenced by their caregiving environment. Differences in cultural and language environment may be reflected in the outcomes of developmental assessments that are based on norms obtained from the dominant culture.

"**Extensive and comprehensive training is needed for those who screen and assess very young children**" (p. 25). Professionals who provide screening and assessment services must not only be knowledgeable and skilled in the administration of assessment instruments for young children, they must also be able to develop trusting relationships with families and must have the clinical skills needed to interpret assessment results and explain those results to families.

ELIGIBILITY AND SCREENING

The definition of eligibility adopted in each state has significant implications for the evaluation and intervention system that develops in that state (see chap. 2, this volume). Clearly, fewer children will be identified and eligible for services if a more restrictive criteria (e.g., 50% delay in one or more areas) is adopted. If, however, a state is serving the "at-risk" population, and the state definition of "at-risk" requires identification of only one factor, rather than three, a larger number of children will be identified as being at risk.

The purpose of screening is to identify those children who may be in need of further assessment. Screening yields only a general evaluation of the child's functioning, since the purpose is to quickly and efficiently assess a larger number of children. Screeners answer the question: does a possible disability or problem exist? Because of their reliance on gross estimates of performance, screening measures do not provide adequate information for placement decisions. Screening efforts typically lead to one of three findings: 1) the child is in need of further evaluation, 2) the child is in need of repeated screening or follow-up, or 3) the child is not in need of further evaluation. Screening program personnel must be careful that a mechanism is in place to follow those children whose condition is in question so that, if necessary, appropriate intervention may be speedily delivered.

Factors Necessary for Successful Screening

Comprehensive screening programs will provide multiple points of contact so that infants and toddlers can be systematically evaluated in order to identify problems as they occur. Screening must result in follow-up evaluation and service, if necessary. If potential problems are identified through the screening process, follow-up is critical so that problems may be identified and intervention begun, or status determined to be within normal limits and possible parental anxiety alleviated. Parents and caregivers must be well-informed about the purpose of the screening so that their wealth of information may be accessed during the screening process. Parents can also provide much assistance in determining if performance is typical and representative.

Hanson and Lynch (1989) suggest the following criteria for exemplary screening programs:

Screeners should be *simple*. Assessment instruments should be short, quick, easy to administer and usable by a wide variety of professionals from diverse disciplines, including paraprofessionals. Procedures should also be systematic for continued ease of use and replication of efforts.

Screeners should be *accurate*. Instruments should demonstrate adequate validity and reliability for screening. The number of false positives (children identified as having a problem who are truly without problems) or false negatives (children with problems who are not identified) should not be excessive.

Screening programs should be *comprehensive*. Programs should be available to the entire community and should include educational, behavioral, health and environmental problems.

Screening programs should be *cost-effective*. Programs should be organized so that inappropriate referrals are minimal and referrals may be quickly identified and intervention begun.

Screening programs should foster *partnerships with parents*. Programs should acknowledge and respect parental knowledge and strive to empower parents. Parental need for information should be responded to quickly and as comprehensively as possible. [emphasis added] (Hanson & Lynch, 1989, p. 91)

Screening efforts should be well-coordinated within a catchment area, so that duplication of services can be avoided and infants and toddlers in need of services can be efficiently and effectively identified. Efforts should be coordinated with other education, health, and social service programs, such as Maternal and Child Health programs under Title V of the Social Security Act, Medicaid's Early Periodic Screening, Diagnosis and Treatment (EPSDT) program under Title XIX of the Social Security Act, and Developmental Disabilities and Head Start programs. The national EPSDT program was initiated in

1972 with two major goals: to strengthen case-finding efforts at both the national and local level, and to establish a linkage between service providers and infants and toddlers in need of services. It has been suggested that because of inadequate screening instruments, inadequate personnel and facilities, and inadequate referral strategies, the EPSDT program has not adequately met the needs of young children with disabilities (Wolery, 1989a).

Present Screening Efforts

Screening efforts are quite varied across the nation. Although PL 94-142 mandated that school districts identify all children with disabilities from birth through 21 years, efforts have been less than comprehensive. But with the passage of PL 99-457, efforts have been revived and expanded. Screening procedures are also quite diverse. Programs may seek to include all the children within a defined age range or may screen only those infants and toddlers who are referred to the system. The characteristics of screening programs will of necessity depend on variables in geography and use of resources. For example, rural programs may use a rotating-clinic approach, while urban areas may perhaps provide a more easily accessible program and more opportunities for contact between professionals and parents and children. Team membership is also variable. Screening teams may consist of nurses, pediatricians, social workers, occupational and physical therapists, psychologists, audiologists, and early interventionists. Teams may also include paraprofessionals or volunteers trained to assist the screening team.

Screening is also varied in comprehensiveness. Generally, in addition to developmental status, screening efforts also include measures of health, vision, and auditory functioning. Peterson (1987) suggests that a screening program include the following:

Pediatric examination
Recording of developmental history
Parental or caregiver interview to determine if special problems have been evidenced
Assessment of general developmental status using a screening instrument

Screening procedures and settings are dependent on desired comprehensiveness and the resources available. Some instruments have been designed so they may be responded to quickly by parents or caregivers at a pediatrician's office or well-baby clinic, or even through the mail. Examples of these instruments include: 1) Infant/ Child Monitoring Questionnaires (Bricker & Squires, 1989; Bricker,

Squires, Kaminski, & Mounts, 1988), 2) the Revised Denver Prescreening Developmental Questionnaire (Frankenburg, Fandal, & Thorton, 1987), and 3) the Revised Parent Developmental Questionnaire (Knobloch, Stevens, Malone, Ellison, & Risemberg, 1979). An example of the Infant Monitoring Questionnaire is provided in Figure 1.

Other screening procedures may be carried out in any location visited by caregivers, such as grocery stores, malls, or shopping plazas. Additional opportunities include neighborhood health fairs and mobile units that may be taken to churches, school gymnasiums, or recreation centers. For families who receive routine medical care, screening efforts may be easily provided by the physician, but reaching those families who have difficulty accessing health or social services may be more challenging. Issues such as public awareness of screening efforts, as well as practical problems of transportation, adequate staffing, and availability of appropriate settings, must be resolved in initial and continued planning efforts.

Available Screeners

The Battelle Developmental Inventory Screening Test (BDI), published by DLM, provides items across five developmental domains: personal–social, adaptive, motor, communicative, and cognitive. Although publishers suggest the screening can be administered in 20–30

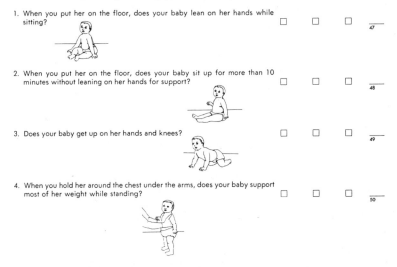

II. GROSS MOTOR   *(Please try the activity if you are not sure.)*

1. When you put her on the floor, does your baby lean on her hands while sitting?   □   □   □   ___
                                                                                                    47

2. When you put her on the floor, does your baby sit up for more than 10 minutes without leaning on her hands for support?   □   □   □   ___
                                                                                                                                        48

3. Does your baby get up on her hands and knees?   □   □   □   ___
                                                                           49

4. When you hold her around the chest under the arms, does your baby support most of her weight while standing?   □   □   □   ___
                                                                                                                          50

Figure 1.   An example from a parent-answered questionnaire. (From Bricker, D., Squires, J., & Mounts, L. [1990]. *Infant child monitoring questionnaires.* Eugene, OR: Center on Human Development, University of Oregon; reprinted by permission.)

minutes, results from a recent study (McLean, McCormick, Baird, & Mayfield, 1987) suggest a longer administration time is needed. Furthermore, the BDI Screener yielded a referral rate of 40% in this study.

The Denver Developmental Screening Test II (DDST II) (Frankenburg & Dodds, 1990) yields outcomes across four domains: gross motor, fine motor, personal–social, and language. The Denver II can be used with children between 2 weeks and 6 years of age and is widely used in medical settings, as well as in early intervention programs. The original DDST was found to underidentify children who need further evaluation. Frankenburg, Camp, and van Natta (1971) studied the validity of the DDST with a group of children under 30 months of age and found that 13% who did poorly on the Bayley Scales of Infant Development (BSID) were not identified by the DDST.

The Minnesota Infant Development Inventory (MIDI) (Ireton & Thwing, 1980) measures development in the gross motor, fine motor, language comprehension, and personal–social areas. It is used with infants from 1 to 15 months of age and is individually administered to the infant's mother.

EVALUATION

The purpose of evaluation is to determine which infants and toddlers have developmental disabilities that qualify for early intervention services. An evaluation that attempts only to determine eligibility, however, will fall short of its intended purpose. The nature of the child's disability and the child's current level of functioning should also be ascertained, so that appropriate services can be provided and further assessment, which will be the basis for the IFSP, will be facilitated.

The Evaluation Process

Harbin (in press) has suggested that professionals "would do well to think of themselves as detectives, uncovering clues in an attempt to solve a mystery" during the evaluation (p. 12). This team of "detectives" must come together and share their clues in order to completely understand the situation. An effective strategy for beginning this process is *pre-assessment planning* (Johnson, McGonigel, & Kaufman, 1989). As described in the procedures of Project Dakota, (Kjerland & Kovach, 1989) pre-assessment planning basically involves two steps. The service coordinator, who serves as facilitator for the evaluation process, obtains information from the family on questions that they have about their child and on their desires concerning the time, location, and extent of their participation in the evaluation process. Second, the facilitator reviews this information, along with any available records on the child, with the evaluation team. The team then decides which assessments should be used and plans the evaluation to fit the family's requests.

From the very beginning, evaluation activities should be designed to respond to the *family's agenda*. Johnson et al. (1989) define a family's agenda as their "priorities for how early intervention will be involved in family life" (p. 13). This agenda should shape the evaluation and assessment process, rather than vice versa. In concrete terms, this means that family questions about the child's condition and development will be central to the evaluation process. The family will be involved in the actual evaluation to the extent that they themselves desire. The family should be allowed a voice in determining the time and location of the evaluation, as well as the individuals to be present. Responding to the family's agenda has a significant effect on the manner in which evaluation and assessment are accomplished.

The specific evaluation process that is utilized is an especially important factor. McCune, Kalmanson, Fleck, Glazewski, and Sillari (1990) suggest that what is most significant about recent changes in infant assessment is the shift away from assessment of intelligence to assessment of a number of interrelated areas of development, which frequently involve professionals from a variety of disciplines. It is recognized that assessing differentiated areas of development is an artificial undertaking, due to the considerable interrelatedness of these areas (Stern, 1985). However, collecting information in this manner and then reintegrating the information through a team effort allows identification of strengths and needs in an individual child's development, yielding not only a determination of need for intervention, but also hypotheses about possible causes of developmental difficulties.

This process is facilitated through an integrated team approach to evaluation that is built on close collaboration among team members. An integrated team approach to evaluation, called *arena assessment*, not only facilitates collaboration among team members but also facilitates the sometimes difficult process of assessment of a very young child by a group of professionals from a variety of disciplines (Foley, 1990; Linder, 1990; Wolery & Dyk, 1984). In arena assessment, members of the team, led by the family, plan in advance what specific questions they will be attempting to answer, which assessment instruments will be used, and what time and location would best facilitate child performance. Typically, one team member will be designated as the *facilitator* for the evaluation. The facilitator and the parent will be the primary individuals to engage the child in activities during the evaluation. Other team members will also be present, and may be engaged in completing individual assessment instruments, but may interact only briefly with the infant, if at all.

McCune and her colleagues (McCune et al., 1990) suggest the use of the Bayley Scales of Infant Development (BSID) as a "core" assessment instrument in this process. They point out that the Bayley provides a quantitative measure for establishing the infant's current developmental status and therefore provides a framework for other information the team may wish to obtain. In addition, many other instruments include a number of the same items as the BSID, which allows the team to score more than one instrument at a time.

It is also important to emphasize that standardized assessment should not become a necessary or central part of evaluation; there are certainly situations in which it is best to forego the administration of such an assessment. For example, a 14-month-old child who was recently referred to the authors' intervention project had been diagnosed as having arthrogryposis; suffered from frequent infantile spasms; exhibited no communicative behavior, either receptive or expressive; and had impaired vision and hearing. No reach or grasp was present, and the child was unable to roll over or change his position. If administered the BSID, for example, this child would be able to pass few, if any, of the items. Scoring would not be possible using typical procedures, and the administration of the assessment and presentation of results to the family could only be discouraging. Clearly, this is a case in which a standardized assessment would serve no useful purpose.

While the situation described above is rare, it must also be remembered that standardized tests include few, if any, infants or children with disabilities in the standardization population. Furthermore, heavy sensory and motor components of items administered to infants further compromise scores for children with sensory or motor impairment. For these reasons, standardized assessments should never be the sole basis for determining eligibility for early intervention services. Furthermore, they should always be administered and interpreted with sensitivity and sound clinical judgment and should be utilized only in the context of a multidisciplinary assessment (McCune et al., 1990; Meisels, 1991).

The multidisciplinary evaluation serves another purpose in addition to that of determining eligibility. As stated above, the evaluation process should also seek to identify the nature and extent of the child's disability so that appropriate service delivery can be outlined (Harbin, in press). Information from the evaluation will not provide specific objectives to become part of the IFSP, but will lay the foundation for the more finely tuned assessment procedures that will follow.

The arena assessment format lends itself well to this purpose of evaluation, since all members of the team will be available to observe the infant's behavior in the assessment situation and to complete assessments specific to their area of expertise.

Evaluation Instruments

As indicated before, there currently are very few psychometrically sound, standardized assessments that can be used with children from birth through age 2. Table 1 lists selected standardized instruments commonly used with children under age 3. The paucity of instruments available for use with this population may serve to simplify the process of selecting specific assessments, but it also serves to increase the importance of professional training and experience. At this point in time, professional judgment is one of the most important aspects of evaluation.

Standardized instruments developed for children under age 3 include the BSID (Bayley, 1984), the Battelle Developmental Inventory (BDI) (Newborg, Stock, Wnek, Guidubaldi, & Svinicki, 1984) and the Griffiths Mental Development Scale (Griffiths, 1954). Of these instruments, the Bayley Scales are clearly the most widely used (Simeonsson, 1986).

Table 1. Standardized instruments

Assessment instrument	Domains/ components	Age	Publisher
Gesell Developmental Schedules (Knobloch, Stevens, & Malone, 1990)	Adaptive, gross motor, fine motor, personal–social	0–3 years	New York: Harper & Row
Batelle Developmental Inventory (Newborg, Stock, Wneck, Guibaldi, & Svincki, 1984)	Personal–social, adaptive, motor, communication, cognitive	0–8 years	Allen, TX: DLM Teaching Resources
Griffiths Mental Developmental Scale (Griffiths, 1954)	Locomotor, personal–social, hearing and speech, eye and hand performance, practical reasoning	0–2 years 2–8 years	High Wycombe, United Kingdom: The Test Agency
Bayley Scales of Infant Development (Bayley, 1969)	Mental scale, motor scale, infant behavior record	2–30 months	New York: Psychological Corporation

The Bayley Scales are currently undergoing restandardization by the Psychological Corporation (it is anticipated that the revised scales will be available for use in 1993). The Bayley Scales were designed for use with children from 2 through 30 months of age and include the Mental Scale, which yields a Mental Development Index (MDI), and the Motor Scale, which yields a Psychomotor Development Index (PDI). Both are based on a normal distribution with a mean of 100 and a standard deviation of 15. The Infant Behavior Record, which provides a record of the child's response to the environment in the testing situation, is completed following the evaluation and is not normed.

The Bayley items do not have to be administered in a predetermined order. This facilitates the evaluation process by allowing the examiner to choose items based on the child's interest at any given moment. The Bayley norms do not provide an MDI or PDI below 50; extrapolation tables must be used for this process (Naglieri, 1981). Scores that must be calculated through extrapolation should be clearly identified as estimates, since they are not obtained from the norming sample.

The Battelle Developmental Inventory (BDI) may be used with children from birth through age 8 years. The BDI covers five developmental domains: personal–social, adaptive, motor, communicative, and cognitive. Each domain and subdomain can yield a standard score and an age-equivalent score. The BDI was developed for use with children with disabilities, as well as with children who are normally developing. Adaptations in administration are provided for children with sensory, motor, and behavior problems. The BDI correlates well with the Bayley for children under 30 months (Sexton, McLean, Boyd, Thompson, & McCormick, 1988), but several disadvantages in using the BDI with this population have been identified. In a study of children with disabilities under 30 months of age, McLean, McCormick, Bruder, and Burdg (1987) found that the BDI took, on average, almost an hour longer to administer than the Bayley. The BDI was also more difficult to administer to infants and toddlers than the Bayley, due to the requirement that the items be presented in a specific order. Most problematic, however, was the need to extrapolate any deviation quotient (DQ) below the first percentile, which is a DQ of 65. In the study by McLean et al. (1987), the vast majority of DQs had to be extrapolated, and 13% of them yielded negative scores (one as high as −80).

The Griffiths Mental Development Scales (Griffiths, 1954) also include five independent measures: locomotor, personal–social, hearing and speech, eye–hand coordination, and performance. The

Griffiths were developed in England and are not currently marketed in the United States. Recent studies also indicate that scores on the Griffiths tend to be inflated (McLean, McCormick, & Baird, 1991).

The Gesell Developmental Schedules (Knobloch, Stevens, & Malone, 1980) are also used in some programs as if they yielded a standardized score (Kahn, 1988). These scales, originally devised by Arnold Gesell in the 1940's (Gesell & Armatruda, 1947), were designed as a clinical assessment tool to describe a child's current developmental status. The developmental quotient that is yielded by these scales is not a standardized score, and was not intended to be predictive or to be used as an IQ.

Areas of Evaluation

Cognitive Development Standardized cognitive assessments typically used include the Bayley Scales of Infant Development— Mental Scales; the Battelle Developmental Inventory—Cognitive Domain; and the Griffiths Mental Development Scales—Performance Scale. However, if it is decided to forego the use of standardized instruments with a particular infant, valuable cognitive information may still be obtained with the use of Piagetian instruments such as the scales developed by Uzgiris and Hunt (1975). When used in conjunction with the clinical manual developed by Dunst (1980), the Uzgiris and Hunt scales allow determination of an estimated developmental age (EDA) of an infant's functioning on seven scales—visual pursuit and object permanence, means ends abilities, operational causality, spatial relationships, schemes for relating to objects, verbal imitation, and gestural imitation. The EDA values have no predictive uses, but can help evaluators gauge current developmental functioning (Dunst, Holbert, & Wilson, 1990). It is not, however, the age-equivalent scores on these scales that will provide the most insight into the nature of the infant's developmental difficulties. Rather, to the informed professional, the identification of the cognitive stage of functioning will provide the most useful clinical information (Robinson & Fieber, 1988).

Communicative Development Assessments in the area of communication frequently used with infants and toddlers include the Sequenced Inventory of Communicative Development (SICD)—Revised (Hedrick, Prather, & Tobin, 1984) and the Receptive Expressive Emergent Language (REEL) Scale (Bzoch & League, 1971). Both the SICD and the REEL provide norm-based measures of receptive and expressive language in children under 3 years of age. The REEL relies heavily on parent report, but both instruments combine parent report with observation. Obtained developmental ages from both of these instruments are questionable (Graham, 1990). The Communication Domain of the Battelle Developmental Inventory will also yield age-equivalent information and a standard score in both receptive and expressive communication.

The communication disorders specialist who is a member of the evaluation team may use one of the instruments above to obtain a general picture of how the infant is functioning in the area of communication development. At the same time, and in further observations during the assessment for program planning, this professional will be observing the child's performance in specific areas of communication, including pragmatics, semantics, syntax, and phonology. For the child who is using words, a language sample should be collected for analysis (Miller, 1981). The communication disorders specialist or the occupational therapist may also conduct an oral peripheral examination to determine the presence of motor-control problems, structural problems, or atypical reflexes that may affect feeding and pre-speech development (Morris, 1984).

Motor Development   Development of fine and gross motor abilities is an area that will be changing rather rapidly in the infant or toddler. Early in life, motor skills are a better indicator of differences in developmental levels than are communication skills, which have a somewhat later start. As a result, most infant assessments will include a significant number of items that are based on motor responses. The Bayley, Battelle, and Griffiths assessments all include scales that specifically measure motor development.

Another widely used instrument, the Peabody Developmental Motor Scales (PDMS) (Folio & Fewell, 1983) can provide an age-equivalent sum, developmental quotient, percentile, or Z score for both gross and fine motor skills for children from birth to 83 months. The PDMS assesses reflexes, balance, nonlocomotor, locomotor, and receipt and propulsion in the gross motor area, and grasping, hand use, eye–hand coordination, and manual dexterity in the fine motor area.

It is important to point out that an evaluation that yields only a standard score or a developmental age in this area as an outcome will be less than complete. It is very important that information on the quality of movement also be obtained. A motor milestone may be scored as correct by the naive or untrained observer simply because the child can demonstrate the milestone. However, to the trained observer who is assessing quality of movement, it may be indicative of motor dysfunction that will require intervention so that abnormal patterns of movement will be minimized as the child develops. So that quality of movement may be assessed, motor evaluation should also include assessment of muscle tone, primitive reflexes, automatic reactions, posture, and volitional movements (McCune et al., 1990; Smith, 1989). The evaluation team must include someone who has been trained in neuromotor assessment, so that atypical motor patterns will be recognized.

Instruments that might be helpful in neuromotor assessment include the Milani-Comparetti Motor Development Screening Test (Milani-Comparetti & Gidoni, 1967) and the Movement Assessment of Infants (MAI) (Chandler, Andrews, & Swanson, 1980). The Milani-Comparetti Test covers postural control, active movement, primitive reflexes, and automatic reactions. This assessment has not been standardized. Scoring systems for use with the Milani-Comparetti have been developed by Ellison, Browning, Larson, and Denny (1983) and by Trembath (1977).

The MAI (Chandler et al., 1980) was developed for use with children who function below the 12-month level in motor areas. The MAI assesses tone, primitive reflexes, automatic reactions, and volitional movement, and yields an index of risk for infants at 4 and 8 months of age.

Infants and toddlers who have difficulties in the area of motor development are likely to also have difficulties in fine motor development. It is common in this area as well to utilize developmental milestones to assess fine motor development, as is done in the Bayley Scales, Battelle Developmental Inventory, Griffiths Scales, and Peabody Motor Development Scales. If, however, this is the only information obtained, the evaluation team will be lacking information on the quality of fine-motor movements. The Erhardt Developmental Prehension Assessment (EDPA) (Erhardt, 1989) is a neurodevelopmental assessment of prehension used with children from birth to 15 months. The EDPA is a criterion-referenced test that includes intervention strategies. The EDPA is divided into three clusters: involuntary arm–hand patterns, voluntary movements, and prewriting. Erhardt has also developed an instrument to measure visual–motor functioning, the Erhardt Developmental Visual Assessment (Erhardt, 1989).

Social and Emotional Development   The area of social and emotional development encompasses a wide range of constructs, including temperament, reactivity, readability, play, and interaction with adults and peers. The social aspects of child development represent one area in which it is particularly difficult to obtain reliable information in a brief period of time. Therefore, only global measures will be discussed here in relation to conducting the evaluation. Further investigation of social development is possible during the assessment process.

The Bayley includes a social scale, the Infant Behavior Record (IBR) (Bayley, 1984). The IBR is designed to be used clinically during the administration of the Bayley mental and motor scales. The IBR consists of 30 items, most of which are rated on a 5- or 9-point rating scale. Recently, Wolf and Lozoff (1985) have developed an empirical basis for interpreting the IBR that indicates which areas should be targeted for further assessment.

The Carolina Record of Individual Behavior (CRIB) (Simeonsson, 1979) was developed in response to the shortcomings of the IBR. The CRIB consists of two parts, which are completed after a period of interaction or observation of the child. The first part documents the behavioral state of the child during the observation. The second part involves rating three groups of behavior: section A behaviors are ordinal (e.g., motivation, endurance), section B behaviors are normally distributed (e.g., activity, reactivity, attention span, tone), and section C behaviors are rhythmic habit patterns (e.g., tongue thrusting, body rocking) (Huntington, 1989).

Multi-domain assessment instruments also include procedures for measuring social development. The Battelle Developmental Inventory (Newborg et al., 1984) includes a Social Domain, which is divided into adult interaction, affect, self-concept, peer interaction, coping, and social role subdomains. The Griffiths Scales (Griffiths, 1954) include a personal–social scale. Also, the Gesell Scales (Knobloch et al., 1980) include personal–social items.

Adaptive Skills   The Vineland Adaptive Behavior Scales, interview edition (Sparrow, Balla, & Cicchetti, 1984), can be used from birth to age 19 years. The Vineland includes the following domains: communication, daily living skills, socialization, and motor skills. The Vineland yields a standard score for each domain, plus a composite score. McLean, McCormick, Bruder, and Burdg (1987) found in a study of infants and toddlers with disabilities that a floor effect occurred while using the Vineland, in that a raw score of 0 for infants could be equivalent to a standard score of 70 or even 80.

The Early Coping Inventory (ECI) (Zeitlin, Williamson, & Szczepanski, 1988) consists of 48 items divided into three areas—sensorimotor organization, reactive behavior, and self-initiated behavior. The ECI can be used with children from 4 to 36 months. The ECI yields effectiveness scores from each of the three areas, which are used to complete an adaptive behavior index. In addition, a coping profile is generated that can be used to identify the focus of intervention efforts.

Finally, the Battelle Developmental Inventory (Newborg et al., 1984) also includes an adaptive domain that yields age-equivalent scores or standard scores in the following subdomains: attention, eating, dressing, personal responsibility, and toileting. Only two of these subdomains have items in the 0- to 5-month age range: the dressing subdomain begins at 12 months, personal responsibility begins at 18 months, and toileting begins at 24 months.

It can be seen that definitions of what constitutes adaptive behavior differ among instruments that purport to measure development in that area. Furthermore, adaptive behavior and social development overlap to some degree. PL 102-119 changed the wording in this area of assessment from "self-help" to "adaptive" development, no doubt in response to the realization that "self-help" or "self-care" skills, which commonly include feeding, dressing, and toileting independently, are only beginning to be developed in the 0- to 3-year age range. Adaptive behavior, which refers to an individuals' personal independence, is perhaps better represented in the infant/toddler population by the construct of coping that Zeitlin et al. (1988) define as a process of adapting to meet personal needs and to respond to environmental demands.

Play   Including play in the evaluation battery will be helpful with many infants and toddlers in adding to information about cognitive and communication development. It will also allow for observation of functional movement and of social behavior. In many cases, assessment of play behavior will occur at the beginning of the evaluation, allowing the child to explore and become adjusted to the situation before more directive activities are attempted. Play can be analyzed according to Piaget's (1962) work. The outcome of this analysis of representational behavior is important in the interpretation of the child's cognitive level and communicative development (Belsky & Most, 1981; McCune-Nicolich, 1983).

ASSESSMENT

When it is clear that a particular infant or toddler is eligible for services under the state criteria for eligibility, further assessment activities will be undertaken so that the IFSP, which will outline the aspects of the intervention, can be written. An advantage provided to infant/toddler programs by the law is the stipulation that services may begin for the child and family prior to the completion of the IFSP. Therefore, the young child and his or her family will not be deprived of intervention services while waiting for the completion of this next level of assessment activities.

The purpose of assessment at this level is to determine the content of the intervention plan for the child and family. The outcome will be goals and objectives for child and family, determination of related services to be provided, and also additional "baseline" measurement of the child's functioning, which will serve as a point of comparison for the measurement of progress.

The same "detective work" described by Harbin (in press) for the evaluation process will continue during the assessment activities that lead to the development of the IFSP. At this point, however, there will be a bit more time for observation of particular behaviors, and assessment will be leading to the prioritization of outcomes desired for the child and family. Family input in defining these goals should be strongly encouraged and facilitated throughout this process.

Family Involvement in Child Assessment

Parents know their child better than any other member of the assessment team. It has been demonstrated that parents can accurately evaluate their child's current level of skill (Beckman, 1984; Vincent et al., 1981). For this, and many other reasons, family members should be an integral part of the assessment process as providers of assessment information and as members of the team process that leads to the delineation of goals and objectives in the IFSP.

Two instruments developed by Lisbeth Vincent and her colleagues can be particularly helpful in gathering information from families and in assisting families to identify goals for the child. The Parent Inventory of Child Development in Nonschool Environments (Vincent et al., 1986) allows parents to rate their child's development by identifying behaviors the child currently exhibits in five areas: interactions, communication, self-help, adaptive behavior, and maladaptive behavior. From this rating, parents can then identify whether they want more information about a particular area and whether they wish a behavior to be targeted in the IFSP. The Daily Routine Recording Form (Vincent, Davis, Brown, Teicher, & Weynand, 1983) is used along with the parent inventory to identify aspects of the daily routine that make it especially difficult to care for the child, as well as areas that family members find pleasurable. Intervention can then help to ease the difficult times and build on the pleasant ones.

The family should be involved in all team discussions of assessment results. If an arena assessment format is used, information should be shared with the family at the post-session meeting, which may take place immediately after the assessment, or at a later time when the family can attend (Kjerland & Kovach, 1990; Linder, 1990). Including the family in all team discussions not only assures family input in the assessment process, but also helps the family to prepare for the identification of goals, objectives, and services that they desire for their child.

Curriculum-Referenced Instruments

Multi-domain curriculum-referenced instruments that might be used in assessment are listed in Table 2 and include the *Carolina Curriculum for Infants and Toddlers with Special Needs, Second Edition* (Johnson-Martin, Jens, Attermeier, & Hacker, 1991), *the Hawaii Early Learning Profile* (HELP) (Furuno et al., 1979), the *Early Intervention Developmental Profile—Revised Edition* (EIDP) (Rogers et al., 1981) and the *Assessment, Evaluation, and Programming System* (AEPS) (Bricker, 1993). As can be seen in the table, there is much similarity among these instruments in terms of the domains of development included. All of these instruments were designed to facilitate the process of identifying intervention targets and measuring child progress toward the attainment of objectives over time. These instruments were developed in relation to a curriculum; that is, the test items are behaviors that we might in fact wish to teach a child, rather than items designed with the sole intent of providing evaluative information. However, these

Table 2.   Curriculum-referenced instruments

Assessment instrument	Domains/ components	Age	Publisher
Carolina Curriculum for Infants and Toddlers with Special Needs (2nd ed.) (Johnson-Martin, Jens, Attermeier, & Hacker, 1991)	Cognitive, communication, social-skills adaptation, self-help, fine and gross motor	0–3 years	Baltimore: Paul H. Brookes Publishing Co.
Hawaii Early Learning Profile (Furuno, O'Reilly, Hosaka, Inatsuka, Allman, & Zeisloft, 1979)	Cognitive, language, gross and fine motor, social–emotional, self-help	0–3 years	Palo Alto, CA: VORT Corporation
Assessment, Evaluation, and Programming System for Infants and Children (Bricker, 1993)	Sensorimotor skills, physical development, gross and fine motor, social, self-care, communication	Birth–3 years	Baltimore: Paul H. Brookes Publishing Co.
Early Intervention Developmental Profile-Revised Edition (Rogers, Donovan, D'Eugenio, Brown, Lynch, Moersch, & Schafer, 1981)	Perceptual/fine motor, cognition, language, social–emotional, self-care, gross motor	0–5 years	Ann Arbor, MI: University of Michigan Press

instruments all have the potential to be used ineffectively if they become "cookbooks" for identifying intervention targets. If the interventionist simply identifies all of the behaviors that the infant or toddler already has in their repertoire and then targets the first failed item as an objective for intervention, the quality of the intervention plan will be reduced (Wolery, 1989b). The "detective work" is then reduced to filling out a checklist, the content of which may or may not be appropriate to the individual child and family.

Cognitive-Stage Information

If the determination of the child's level of cognitive development was not attempted during evaluation, it would be most helpful in planning the intervention program to obtain this information as part of the assessment process. The most widely used instrument for this purpose is the Infant Psychological Development Scale (IPDS) developed by Uzgiris and Hunt (1975) for research purposes. Work by Carl Dunst has since produced a manual that facilitates the use of the Uzgiris and Hunt Scales for clinical and educational purposes (Dunst, 1980).

The IPDS, used with the Dunst manual, will yield information on the child's level of functioning (stages I–VI) in the following areas of sensorimotor development:

Object permanence
Means ends abilities
Vocal imitation
Gestural imitation
Preoperational causality
Spatial relationships
Schemes in relation to objects

Figures 2 and 3 present profiles of two children's performance on an assessment of sensorimotor functioning. Jason (Figure 2) is 26 months old and has Down syndrome, but no hearing or vision impairment. The overall designation for Jason is Stage V. This information is helpful in determining intervention targets and strategies for intervention. Jason is currently producing several words (hi, daddy, ball, cookie, juice). However, these words are elicited by the presence of the objects or the context in which the word is typically used; Jason is not yet using spoken words symbolically. His play is also reflective of his Stage V behavior in that he is not yet pretending or using an object to stand for something else. A goal for Jason, then, may be to facilitate the development of the use of symbols in play and commu-

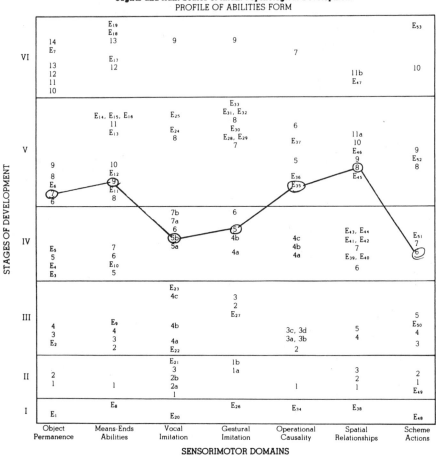

Uzgiris and Hunt Scales of Infant Psychological Development
PROFILE OF ABILITIES FORM

Figure 2. Profile showing Jason's performance on an assesment of sensorimotor functioning. (From Dunst, C.J. [1980]. *A clinical and educational manual for use with the Uzgris and Hunt Scales of Infant Psychological Development*. Austin, TX: PRO-ED; reprinted by permission.)

nication. Imitation, as well as simple verbal directions, could be used as a teaching strategy with Jason.

Brittany (Figure 3) is also 26 months old, was born with vision and hearing impairments, mild spastic diplegia, and cleft lip and palate. Brittany's level of functioning is very different from Jason's; we would say that her overall level of functioning is Stage III, although deficits in her gestural imitation and action schemes are more severe due to her impaired vision. Brittany's goals will focus on chaining two actions to reach a goal and on learning discriminated re-

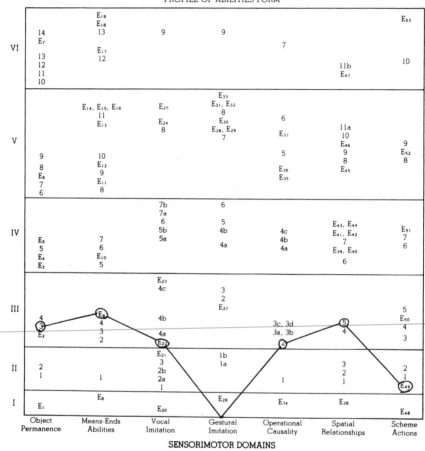

Uzgiris and Hunt Scales of Infant Psychological Development
PROFILE OF ABILITIES FORM

© Copyright 1980 ProEd, Inc.

Figure 3.   Profile showing Brittany's performance on an assesment of sensorimotor functioning. (From Dunst, C.J. [1980]. *A clinical and educational manual for use with the Uzgris and Hunt Scales of Infant Psychological Development.* Austin, TX: PRO-ED; reprinted by permission.)

sponses in relation to environmental objects and events. Modeling will not yet be useful in teaching Brittany, since she does not imitate, but physical prompting will be used. Imitation may, in fact, become an objective of intervention for Brittany.

Analysis of Communication

Information derived from the assessment of early cognitive development will be extremely helpful in analyzing the communication abilities of children who are functioning at the sensorimotor level of development. This information will identify the child as being symbolic (Stage VI) or presymbolic, and as being intentional (Stage IV) or pre-intentional.

Over the past 20 years, research in early communication development has focused increasingly on the precursors of symbolic behavior. Although most language-assessment instruments still begin after the point at which the child is producing words, the number of instruments that facilitate assessment of the communication behavior of the pre-verbal child is increasing. The following instruments can be helpful in assessing the preverbal child:

Assessing Prelinguistic and Early Linguistic Behaviors in Young Children (Olswang, Stoel-Gammons, Coggins, & Carpenter, 1987: University of Washington Press, Seattle)
The Early Language Milestone Scale (Coplan, 1987: Modern Educational Corporation, Tulsa, Oklahoma)
Environmental Prelanguage Battery (Horstmeier & MacDonald, 1979: The Psychological Corporation, New York).

If a delay in language development is discovered, it becomes most important to explore the possible causes for this delay. It will be important to assess differences between the child's level of development in the comprehension and production of language. Observation of a child's response to spoken language in conjunction with an analysis of a language sample can facilitate the process of identifying particular areas of weakness that the child may exhibit. A manual of strategies for assessing language production in young children developed by Miller (1981) can be very helpful in this process. Comprehension is more difficult to assess in the very young child. A variety of informal assessment procedures have been developed that can be used in conjunction with information gained from parents (Bates et al., 1986; Rosetti, 1990). However, as Rosetti (1990) indicates, assessment of language comprehension in children under 3 years of age "taxes the clinical judgment of even the most experienced examiner" (p. 166). The analysis of communication should include assessment of *semantic* development (meaning), assessment of the *form* of language (phonology, morphology, and syntax), and assessment of the child's *use* of communication (pragmatics).

Communication assessment information cannot be interpreted accurately, of course, unless information on the child's auditory ability is available. If there is any question about hearing, an audiological evaluation should be completed. Similarly, if there is any question about the oral–motor mechanism, an oral–peripheral examination must be completed.

Parent–Child Interaction

Assessment of parent–child interaction is one part of assessing the child's social interaction abilities and may also assist interventionists as they try to help the family facilitate the child's development. Barnard and Kelly (1990) identify four scales that evaluate parent–child interaction, all of which have published data supporting their reliability and validity and are appropriate for clinical use.

The National Early Childhood Technical Assistance System Teaching and Feeding Scales (Barnard, 1979) evaluate both maternal and infant characteristics in a familiar (feeding) situation and a novel (teaching) situation. Outcomes of the scale include information on parent sensitivity to child cues, response to child distress, social–emotional growth fostering, cognitive growth fostering, and, from the teaching scale, contingent responsiveness. Results include measures of the clarity in each area and responsiveness to parents.

The Parent Behavior Progression (PBP) (Bromwich, 1983) was designed to help interventionists working with infants with special needs evaluate parent–infant interactions. A scale with six levels is employed to determine current functioning of the parent relative to increasing parent ability to provide an environment that fosters developmental growth of the infant.

The Maternal Behavior Rating Scale (Mahoney, Finger, & Powell, 1985), like the PBP, rates only maternal behavior, with no measure of child behavior. It is a global rating scale applied to a 10-minute videotaped sample of home-based toy play and was developed to include maternal behaviors that research had found to be related to variability in cognitive, social, or language development in children. A shortened form that includes fewer items is also available (Mahoney, Powell, & Finger, 1986).

The Parent/Caregiver Involvement Scale (PCIS) (Farran, Kasari, Comfort, & Jay, 1986) measures parent behavior by tallying behaviors observed in a videotaped sample of parent–child play. Eleven different caregiver behaviors are rated according to amount, quality, and appropriateness. The outcome of the scale leads to suggestions for intervention and may also be used for program evaluation.

ASSESSMENT OF FAMILY CHARACTERISTICS AND PRIORITIES

Part H now provides for the assessment of family strengths, needs, concerns, priorities, and resources as part of the assessment process so that families can be supported in their efforts to facilitate their child's development. It is important to again consider the family agenda in this process so that assessment becomes truly family-centered (Shelton, Jeppson, & Johnson, 1987) rather than an assessment of the family itself. Johnson et al. (1989) remind us that "only family members can determine for themselves which aspects of their family life they feel are relevant to their ability to help their child grow and develop" (p. 37). Many of the instruments available in this area are actually self-assessment instruments (e.g., checklists, questionnaires) that can be completed by the family alone, or through an interview process with early intervention staff.

A strong word of caution has been sounded in relation to this process by Johnson et al. (1989):

> There are a host of psychosocial instruments that measure stress, depression, locus of control, and numerous other personality characteristics and life circumstances. Such measures are not recommended for the purpose of identifying strengths and needs as part of the IFSP process. The need to limit identification of family strengths and needs to those areas that a family decides are relevant to its family agenda places these standardized family assessment instruments out of context for the purposes of developing most IFSP's. (p. 38)

If an assessment of family characteristics is carried out, the assessment must: 1) be conducted by personnel trained to utilize appropriate methods and procedures, 2) be based on information provided by the family through a personal interview, and 3) incorporate the family's description of its strengths and needs related to enhancing the child's development. PL 102-119 also mandates that family assessments must be family-directed and may:

> with the concurrence of the family include an assessment of the family's resources, priorities, and concerns and identification of family preferences, supports, and services necessary to enhance the parents' and siblings' capacity to meet the developmental needs of their infant or toddler with a disability.

To further support the desires of the family, a statement of family needs may be included in the written IFSP, but only with the family's consent. Furthermore, at the family's request, the family assessment portion of an evaluation may be completely omitted. Services may not be withheld from a child in a situation in which the family chooses not to participate in family assessment. It is important to note that this part of the assessment may also take place at a later time, after the development of the IFSP, if the family so desires.

A variety of measures have been developed that can help a family identify its strengths, needs, and resources, including the following:

Family Functioning Style Scale (Deal, Trivette, & Dunst, 1988)
Family Need Survey (Bailey, 1988)

Family Needs Scale (Dunst, Cooper, Weeldreyer, Snyder, & Chase, 1988)

Family Strengths Scale (Olson, Larsen, & McCubbin, 1983)

Family Support Scale (Dunst, Jenkins, & Trivette, 1988)

Parent Needs Survey (Darling, 1988)

Personal Network Matrix (Trivette & Dunst, 1988)

It is important to remember that the assessment of family strengths, needs, and resources is a process, just as child assessment is a process. Most of the instruments for use in this area do not yield scaled scores, nor do they automatically identify what should be written in the IFSP. The sensitivity and skill of the service coordinator is of utmost importance in this process. The manner in which strengths, needs, and resources are identified will differ across families. Sometimes it will not occur at all (at family request), and sometimes it will take place later, only after a trusting relationship has been established with the intervention staff.

Central to family assessment is the premise that information must be used to plan a program to enable families to meet the needs of their infant or toddler with special needs. Information is not intended to identify emotional disturbance or disability or a need for marital or family counseling. In the use of family assessment, interventionists must be ever diligent to ensure cultural sensitivity and respect for the unique goals and attributes of the family. Interventionists must recognize that their own cultural, religious, or personal values may not be shared by the family, and that intervention goals may not be equally valued by parents and professionals. Therefore, professionals must be aware of their own subjective opinions and mindful of subtly imposing their own desires or values upon the families with whom they work.

PUTTING IT ALL TOGETHER

Toni Linder has developed a guide to assessment that she calls transdisciplinary play-based assessment (TPBA) (Linder, 1990). This guide provides not only excellent descriptions of normal development in the cognitive, social–emotional, communicative, and sensorimotor areas, but also procedures for conducting a transdisciplinary arena-type assessment of the young child that utilizes a play format and involves all team members and the family.

Linder's description of how to interpret assessment information and plan intervention is also very helpful as a model for the manner in which assessment results can be reviewed by the team in preparing to develop the IFSP. Under the TPBA model, a post-assessment meeting to review preliminary findings is held immediately or soon after the assessment. The family is in attendance at this meeting as team members share initial impressions and questions that may require additional assessment. As observations are shared, hypotheses are formed about the child's development. Disagreements may arise at this time, but this is part of a process that will lead to a better understanding of the child's development. Following the post-session meeting, team members may perform further assessment, summarize their findings, and develop preliminary recommendations. A program-planning meeting is then held to review the final assessment information and plan the IFSP. At this meeting, "parents assume a preeminent role" (Linder, 1990, p. 61) in identifying their priorities for the child and the amount and type of early intervention that they feel should become a part of their lives.

CONCLUDING COMMENTS

The assessment process as described by Linder exemplifies the spirit of Part H of IDEA, incorporates a family-centered approach, and outlines exemplary assessment practices as well. To be implemented as designed, this process requires knowledgeable and competent professionals who are able to utilize a range of formal and informal assessments from their discipline, are skilled and experienced in working with infants and toddlers, are able to work in a family-centered system, and are able to collaborate with a team of professionals from other disciplines. When implemented correctly, this process exemplifies best practice in assessment in early intervention.

REFERENCES

Bailey, D.B. (1988). Assessing family strengths and needs. In D.B. Bailey & R.J. Simeonsson (Eds.), *Family assessment in early intervention* (pp. 95–118). Columbus, OH: Charles E. Merrill.

Bailey, D.B., & Rouse, T. (1989). Procedural considerations in assessing infants and preschoolers with handicaps. In D.B. Bailey & M. Wolery (Eds.), *Assessing infants and preschoolers with handicaps* (pp. 47–63). Columbus, OH: Charles E. Merrill.

Barnard, K.E. (1979). *Instructor's learning resource manual.* Seattle: Univ. of Washington, NCAST Publications.

Barnard, K.E., & Kelly, J. (1990). Assessment of parent–child interaction. In J. Shonkoff & S. Meisels (Eds.), *Handbook of early intervention* (pp. 278–302). Cambridge: Cambridge University Press.

Bates, E., Beeghly, M., Bretherton, I., Harris, C., Marchiman, V., McNew, S., O'Connell, B., Reznick, S., Shore, C., Snyder, L., Thal, D., & Volterra, V. (1986). *Early Language Inventory.* LaJolla: University of California.

Bayley, N. (1984). *Bayley Scales of Infant Development.* New York: Psychological Corporation.

Beckman, P.J. (1984). Perceptions of young children with handicaps: A comparison of mothers and program staff. *Mental Retardation, 22*(4), 176–181.

Belsky, J., & Most, R.K. (1981). From exploration to play: A cross-sectional study of infant free play behavior. *Developmental Psychology, 17,* 630–639.

Bricker, D. (1987). *Infant Monitoring Questionnaire for At-Risk Infants 4 to 36 Months.* Eugene: University of Oregon Center on Human Development.

Bricker, D. (Ed.). (1993). AEPS test manual. In D. Bricker (Ed.), *Assessment, evaluation, and programming system (AEPS) for infants and children: Vol. 1 AEPS measurement for birth to three years* (pp. 65–214). Baltimore: Paul H. Brookes Publishing Co.

Bricker, D., & Squires, J. (1989). Low cost system using parents to monitor the development of at-risk infants. *Journal of Early Intervention, 13*(1), 50–60.

Bricker, D., Squires, J., Kaminski, R., & Mounts, L. (1988). The validity, reliability, and cost of a parent-completed questionnaire system to evaluate at-risk infants. *Journal of Pediatric Psychology, 13*(1), 5–68.

Bromwich, R. (1983). *Parent Behavior Progression—manual and 1983 supplement.* Northridge: California State University, Department of Educational Psychology, The Center for Research, Development and Services.

Bzoch, K.R., & League, R. (1971). *Assessing language skills in infancy.* Baltimore: University Park Press.

Chandler, L.S., Andrews, M.S., & Swanson, M.W. (1980). *Movement assessment of infants: A manual.* Rolling Bay, WA: Infant Movement Research.

Darling, R.B. (1988). Parent Needs Survey. In M. Seligmen & R. Benjamin Darling (Eds.), *Ordinary families, special children: A system approach to childhood disability.* New York: Guilford Press.

Deal, A., Trivette, C., & Dunst, C.J. (1988). Family functioning style scale. In C.J. Dunst, C.M. Trivette, & A.G. Deal (Eds.), *Enabling and empowering families: Principles and guidelines for practice* (pp. 177–184). Cambridge, MA: Brookline Books.

Dunst, C.J. (1980). *A clinical and educational manual for use with the Uzgiris and Hunt Scales of Infant Psychological Development.* Austin, TX: PRO-ED.

Dunst, C.J., Cooper, C.S., Weeldreyer, J.C., Snyder, K.D., & Chase, J.H. (1988). Family Needs Scale. In C.J. Dunst, C.M. Trivette, & A.G. Deal (Eds.), *Enabling and empowering families: Principles and guidelines for practice* (pp. 149–151). Cambridge, MA: Brookline Books.

Dunst, C.J., Holbert, K.A., & Wilson, L.L. (1990). Strategies for assessing infant sensorimotor interactive competencies. In E.D. Gibbs & D.M. Teti (Eds.), *Interdisciplinary assessment of infants: A guide for early intervention professionals* (pp. 91–112). Baltimore: Paul H. Brookes Publishing Co.

Dunst, C.J., Jenkins, V., & Trivette, C.M. (1988). Family Support Scale. In C.J. Dunst, C.M. Trivette, & A.G. Deal (Eds.), *Enabling and empowering families: Principles and guidelines for practice* (pp. 155–157). Cambridge, MA: Brookline Books.

Education for All Handicapped Children Act of 1975, PL 94-142. (August 23, 1977). Title 20, U.S.C. 1401 et seq: *U.S. Statutes at Large, 89,* 773–796.

Education of the Handicapped Act Amendments of 1986, PL 99-457. (October 8, 1986). Title 20, U.S.C. 1400 et seq: *U.S. Statutes at Large, 100,* 1145–1177.

Ellison, P., Browning, C., Larson, B., & Denny, J. (1983). Development of a scoring system for the Milani-Comparetti and Gidoni method of assessing neurologic abnormality in infancy. *Physical Therapy, 63*(9), 1414–1423.

Erhardt, R.P. (1989). *Developmental hand dysfunction: Theory, assessment, treatment.* Tucson, AZ: Therapy Skill Builders.

Erhardt, R.P. (1989). *Erhardt Developmental Visual Assessment.* Tucson, AZ: Therapy Skill Builders.

Farran, D.C., Kasari, C., Comfort, M., & Jay, S. (1986). *Parent/Caregiver Involvement Scale.* Greensboro: University of North Carolina–Greensboro, Department of Child Development–Family Relations.

Fewell, R. (1983). Assessment of visual functioning. In K. Paget & B. Bracken (Eds.), *The psychoeducational assessment of preschool children* (pp. 359–386). New York: Grune & Stratton.

Foley, G.M. (1990). Portrait of the arena evaluation: Assessment in the transdisciplinary approach. In E.D. Gibbs & D.M. Teti (Eds.), *Interdisciplinary assessment of infants: A guide for early intervention professionals* (pp. 271–286). Baltimore: Paul H. Brookes Publishing Co.

Folio, R., & Fewell, R. (1983). *Peabody Developmental Motor Scale and Activity Cards.* Allen, TX: Teaching Resources.

Frankenburg, W.K., Camp, B., & van Natta, P.A. (1971). Validity of the Denver Developmental Screening Test. *Child Development, 42,* 475–485.

Frankenburg, W., & Dodds, J. (1990). *Denver Developmental Screening Test II.* Denver: Denver Developmental Materials.

Frankenburg, W., Fandal, A., & Thorton, S. (1987). Revision of the Denver Prescreening Developmental Questionnaire. *Journal of Pediatrics, 110,* 653–657.

Furuno, S., O'Reilly, K.A., Hosaka, C.M., Inatsuka, T.T., Allman, T.L., & Zeisloft, B. (1979). *The Hawaii Early Learning Profile.* Palo Alto, CA: VORT Corp.

Gesell, A., & Armatruda, C.S. (1947). *Developmental diagnosis.* New York: Hoeber.

Gibbs, E.D. (1990). Assessment of infant mental ability: Conventional tests and issues of prediction. In E.D. Gibbs & D.M. Teti (Eds.), *Interdisciplinary assessment of infants: A guide for early intervention professionals* (pp. 77–90). Baltimore: Paul H. Brookes Publishing Co.

Gibbs, E.D., & Teti, D.M. (1990). Issues and future directions in infant and family assessment. In E.D. Gibbs & D.M. Teti (Eds.), *Interdisciplinary assessment of infants: A guide for early intervention professionals* (pp. 311–320). Baltimore: Paul H. Brookes Publishing Co.

Graham, M. (1990). *Evaluation, assessment and IFSP development for infants and toddlers.* Tallahassee, FL: Developmental Services.

Griffiths, R. (1954). *The abilities of babies.* High Wycombe, United Kingdom: The Test Agency.

Hanson, M., & Lynch, E. (1989). *Early intervention: Implementing child and family services for infants and toddlers who are at-risk or disabled.* Austin, TX: PRO-ED.

Harbin, G.L. (in press). Issues in the assessment of infants and toddlers with handicaps. In J. Siders & M. Huch (Eds.), *Ecological framework for team assessment: Young children with special needs.* Austin, TX: PRO-ED.

Hedrick, D., Prather, E., & Tobin, A. (1984). *Sequenced inventory of communication development revised.* Seattle: University of Washington Press.

Horstmeier, D., & MacDonald, J. (1979). *Environmental Pre-language Battery.* New York: The Psychological Corporation.

Huntington, G. (1989). Assessing behavioral characteristics. In D. Bailey & M. Wolery (Eds.), *Assessing infants and preschoolers with handicaps* (pp. 225–248). Columbus, OH: Charles E. Merrill.

Individuals with Disabilities Education Act Amendments of 1991, PL 102-119. (October 7, 1991). Title 20, U.S.C. 1400 et seq: *U.S. Statues at Large, 105,* 587–608.

Ireton, H., & Thwing, E. (1980). *Minnesota Infant Development Inventory.* Minneapolis: Behavior Science Systems.

Johnson, B., McGonigel, M., & Kaufman, R. (1989). *Guidelines and recommended practices for the individualized family service plan.* Washington, DC: National Early Childhood Technical Assistance System and Association for the Care of Children's Health.

Johnson-Martin, N., Jens, K.G., Attermeier, S.M., & Hacker, B.J. (1991). *The Carolina curriculum for infants and toddlers with special needs* (2nd ed.). Baltimore: Paul H. Brookes Publishing Co.

Kahn, J. (1988). Cognitive assessment of mentally retarded infants and preschoolers. In T.D. Wachs & R. Sheehan (Eds.), *Assessment of young developmentally disabled children* (pp. 164–182). New York: Plenum.

Kjerland, L., & Kovach, J. (1990). Family–staff collaboration for tailored infant assessment. In E.D. Gibbs & D.M. Teti (Eds.), *Interdisciplinary assessment of infants: A guide for early intervention professionals* (pp. 287–298). Baltimore: Paul H. Brookes Publishing Co.

Knobloch, H., Stevens, F., & Malone, A.F. (1980). *Manual of developmental diagnosis: The administration and interpretation of the revised Gesell and Armatruda Developmental and Neurologic Examination.* New York: Harper & Row.

Knobloch, H., Stevens, F., Malone, A., Ellison, P., & Risemberg, H. (1979). The validity of parental reporting of infant development. *Pediatrics, 63,* 873–878.

Linder, T.W. (1990). *Transdisciplinary play-based assessment: A functional approach to working with young children.* Baltimore: Paul H. Brookes Publishing Co.

Mahoney, G., Finger, I., & Powell, A. (1985). Relationship of maternal behavioral style to the development of organically impaired mentally retarded infants. *American Journal of Mental Deficiency, 90,* 296–302.

Mahoney, G., Powell, A., & Finger, I. (1986). The Maternal Behavior Rating Scale. *Topics in Early Childhood Special Education, 6,* 44–56.

McCune, L., Kalmanson, B., Fleck, M., Glazewski, B., & Sillari, J. (1990). An interdisciplinary model of infant assessment. In S.H. Meisels & J.P. Shonkoff (Eds.), *Handbook of early childhood intervention* (pp. 219–245). Cambridge: Cambridge University Press.

McCune-Nicolich, L. (1983). *A manual for analyzing free play.* New Brunswick, NJ: Department of Educational Psychology, Rutgers University.

McLean, M., McCormick, K., & Baird, S. (1991). Concurrent validity of the Griffith's Mental Development Scales with a population of children under 24 months. *Journal of Early Intervention, 15*(4), 338–344.

McLean, M., McCormick, K., Baird, S., & Mayfield, P. (1987). A study of the concurrent validity of the Battelle Developmental Inventory Screening Test. *Diagnostique, 13*(1), 10–20.

McLean, M., McCormick, K., Bruder, M.B., & Burdg, N. (1987). An investigation of the validity and reliability of the Battelle Developmental Inventory with a population of children younger than 30 months with identified handicapping conditions. *Journal of the Division for Early Childhood, 11*(3), 238–246.

Meisels, S. (1991). Dimensions of early identification. *Journal of Early Intervention, 15*(1), 26–35.

Meisels, S., & Provence, S. (1989). *Screening and assessment: Guidelines for identifying young disabled and developmentally vulnerable children and their families.* Washington, DC: National Center for Clinical Infant Programs.

Milani-Comparetti, A., & Gidoni, E. (1967). Routine developmental examination in normal and retarded children. *Developmental Medicine and Child Neurology, 9*, 631–638.

Miller, J. (1981). *Assessing language production in children.* Baltimore: University Park Press.

Morris, S.E. (1984). *Pre-speech assessment scale: A rating scale for the measurement of pre-speech behaviors from birth through two years.* Clifton, NJ: A.J. Preston.

Naglieri, J.A. (1981). Extrapolated developmental indices for the Bayley Scales of Infant Development. *American Journal of Mental Deficiency, 85*, 548–550.

Newborg, J., Stock, J.R., Wnek, L., Guidubaldi, N.J., & Svinicki, J. (1984). *The Battelle Developmental Inventory.* Allen, TX: Developmental Learning Materials.

Olson, D.H., Larsen, A.S., & McCubbin, H.I. (1983). Family Strengths. In D.H. Olson, H.L. Muxen, & M.A. Wilson (Eds.), *Families: What makes them work* (pp. 261–262). Beverly Hills, CA: Sage Publications.

Olswang, V., Stoel-Gammons, C., Coggins, T., & Carpenter, R. (1987). *Assessing linguistic behaviors.* Seattle, WA: University of Washington Press.

Paget, K. (1983). The individual examining situation: Basic considerations for preschool children. In K. Paget & B. Bracken (Eds.), *The psychoeducational assessment of preschool children* (pp. 51–62). New York: Grune & Stratton.

Piaget, J. (1962). *Play, dreams and imitation in childhood.* New York: Norton.

Peterson, N. (1987). *Early intervention for handicapped and at-risk children.* Denver: Love Publishing.

Robinson, C., & Fieber, N. (1988). Cognitive assessment of motorically impaired infants and preschoolers. In T. Wachs & R. Sheehan (Eds.), *Assessment of young developmentally disabled children* (pp. 127–162). New York: Plenum.

Rogers, S.J., Donovan, C.M., D'Eugenio, D.B., Brown, S., Lynch, E., Moersch, M.S., & Schafer, S. (1981). *Early Intervention Developmental Profile—Revised Edition.* Ann Arbor: The University of Michigan Press.

Rosetti, L. (1990). *Infant-toddler assessment: An interdisciplinary approach.* Baltimore: University Park Press.

Sexton, D., McLean, M., Boyd, R., Thompson, B., & McCormick, K. (1988). Criterion-related validity of a new standardized developmental measure. *Measurement and Evaluation in Counseling and Development, 21*, 16–21.

Shelton, T., Jeppson, E., & Johnson, B. (1987). *Family-centered care for children with special health care needs.* Washington, DC: Association for the Care of Children's Health.

Simeonsson, R. (1979). *The Carolina Record of Individual Behavior.* Chapel Hill: University of North Carolina, Chapel Hill.

Smith, P. (1989). Assessing motor skills. In D. Bailey & M. Wolery (Eds.), *Assessing infants and preschoolers with handicaps* (pp. 301–338). Columbus, OH: Charles E. Merrill.

Sparrow, S., Balla, D., & Cicchetti, D. (1984). *Vineland Adaptive Behavior Scales.* Circle Pines, MN: American Guidance Service.

Stern, D. (1985). *The interpersonal world of the human infant: A view from psychoanalysis and developmental psychology.* New York: Basic Books.

Trembath, J. (1977). *The Milani-Comparetti Motor Development Screening Test.* Omaha: University of Nebraska Medical Center, Meyer Children's Rehabilitation Institute.

Trivette, C.M., & Dunst, C.J. (1988). Personal Network Matrix: A system for assessing family needs and support. In C.J. Dunst, C.M. Trivette, & A.G. Deal (Eds.), *Enabling and empowering families: Principles and guidelines for practice* (pp. 165–174). Cambridge, MA: Brookline Books.

Uzgiris, I., & Hunt, J.M. (1975). *Assessment in Infancy: Ordinal Scales of Psychological Development.* Urbana: University of Illinois Press.

Vincent, L., Davis, J., Brown, P., Broome, K., Funkhouser, K., Miller, J., & Grunewald, L. (1986). *The Parent Inventory of Child Development in Nonschool Environments.* Madison: University of Wisconsin, Department of Rehabilitation Psychology and Special Education.

Vincent, L., Davis, J., Brown, P., Teicher, J., & Weynand, P. (1983). *Daily Routine Recording Form.* Madison: University of Wisconsin, Department of Rehabilitation Psychology and Special Education.

Vincent, L., Laten, S., Salisbury, C., Brown, P., & Baumgart, D. (1981). Family involvement in the educational processes of severely handicapped students: State of the art and directions for the future. In B. Wilcox & R. York (Eds.), *Quality education for the severely handicapped: The federal investment.* Washington, DC: U.S. Department of Education.

Wolery, M. (1989a). Child find and screening issues. In D.B. Bailey & M. Wolery (Eds.), *Assessing infants and preschoolers with handicaps* (pp. 119–143). Columbus, OH: Charles E. Merrill.

Wolery, M. (1989b). Using assessment information to plan instructional programs. In D.B. Bailey & M. Wolery (Eds.), *Assessing infants and preschoolers with handicaps* (pp. 478–495). Columbus, OH: Charles E. Merrill.

Wolery, M., & Dyk, L. (1984). Arena assessment: Description and preliminary social validity data. *Journal of The Association for the Severely Handicapped, 9,* 231–235.

Wolf, A.W., & Lozoff, B. (1985). A clinically interpretable method for analyzing the Bayley Infant Behavior Record. *Journal of Pediatric Psychology, 10,* 199–214.

Zeitlin, S., Williamson, G., & Szczepanski, M. (1988). *Early Coping Inventory.* Bensenville, IL: Scholastic Testing Service.

4

Providing Family-Centered Early Intervention

Lynda F. Pearl

"Early intervention by its nature is an intimate service that touches a family's life at a time of double vulnerability" (Healy, Keesee, & Smith, 1989, p. 3). Families involved in early intervention may be vulnerable in two ways: 1) they have recently become the parents of a young child, and 2) they have learned that their child may be developmentally delayed. Even in the best of circumstances, both of these situations require a great deal of adjustment. During a child's first years, all family members are developing relationships with the new member. Families are learning all of the ways that this new person fits into and changes the family structure. For most families, the infant/toddler period is one of significant readjustment of resources and priorities. In addition to dealing with many challenges faced by typical families, a family with an infant/toddler exhibiting significant delays in development, or the potential to develop delays later, is also dealing with all of their various feelings related to the special needs of the child.

Imagine the family of Brandon, the first child of the P. family:

> Brandon was born at 26 weeks gestational age after Ms. P. went into premature labor. He weighed 1 pound, 5 ounces at birth and, in the first week of his life, experienced many complications associated with prematurity, including severe respiratory distress syndrome requiring high levels of oxygen delivered by me-

81

chanical ventilation and bleeding in the brain area surrounding the ventricles. He had to be fed intravenously and required 24-hour monitoring in a neonatal intensive care unit. After the first week of life, Brandon required surgery to correct a heart condition and was flown to another hospital 150 miles away where he spent 3 weeks.

Brandon's family were brought to see him during his first day of life. He appeared very tiny and weak, with loose skin, and eyes that were fused closed. Ms. P. was shocked by his size and appearance and saddened that they were unable to hold or feed him. She was alarmed by the maze of tubes attached to her tiny son. Both parents were frightened that he would not live, and about the problems that he might have if he did. They were astounded by the cost of the technology that was keeping Brandon alive. They had many questions about why this had happened to them. Ms. P. expressed anger at the physician who had provided prenatal care, feeling that he should have been able to prevent her early labor. Also, she felt guilty because she had been told to avoid certain foods because of gestational diabetes, but had gone on a "binge" several days before she delivered Brandon.

Mr. P. was trying to be strong and calm to help his wife, but actually felt very anxious about the situation. His visits to the nursery made him feel helpless, but he worried constantly when he wasn't there. He was also receiving many telephone calls from relatives, all asking questions to which he had no answers.

Two months later, when Brandon was able to come home, his family was told that he had suffered irreversible brain damage, but that the extent of the resulting disabilities was unclear. The P.s left the hospital with the names of five different physicians to contact for appointments. In addition, they were told that Brandon would need physical therapy. It is no surprise that the P.s were overwhelmed by the daily care that Brandon required, and by the need to get service information, make appointments, and learn more about his disabilities.

This chapter discusses a philosophical context for early intervention programming that attempts to support families such as the P.s and enable them to develop their priorities for their children in a way that is consistent with overall family priorities, resources, and needs. Typical reactions of family members to the presence of a child with developmental delays is discussed, along with suggestions for professionals working with families or with specific family members in an early intervention capacity.

A PHILOSOPHICAL FRAMEWORK

"The importance of families as a context for studying early childhood development has been stressed by many theorists" (Silber, 1989, p. 10). Unfortunately, many early intervention services remain focused on the target child and involve the family in only limited ways. When interventionists try to affect the development of young children without making use of family strengths and helping families deal with their limitations, they may ignore a powerful agent of change and limit their possibility of success.

A family may be defined as:

any group of people who are related legally or by blood, or who are perceived to be family by the members. Such a definition includes those who are united by ties of marriage, blood, adoption, common-law marriage, support groups, communes, or religious communities. (Thomas, 1992, p. 36)

In the past, the traditional family, a married couple living with their children under age 18, was considered the norm. It is important to recognize that in today's society there are many common family structures. In addition to the traditional family structure, families may comprise: 1) single adult parents raising their children alone or living with other adults who may or may not be related to the children, 2) married or unmarried teenage parents raising their children with the assistance of their own extended families, 3) one or both parents raising their children in communal living arrangements, 4) married couples raising children from previous marriages, 5) single or married individuals raising foster children, and 6) single or married individuals raising adopted children (Becvar & Becvar, 1982; Hazel et al., 1988). In any of these cases, the adults may be raising typically or atypically developing children, or both. It is important to realize that "the [typical] nuclear family is not the only structure that rears healthy children and meets the emotional needs of its members" (Thomas, 1992, p. 36).

In addition to differences in structure, there are other family traits that need to be addressed by professionals attempting to provide family-centered services. For example: 1) families may prefer to take care of problems within the family, rather than work with professionals, schools, or agencies; 2) families may not live in the "mainstream" of community life, therefore they may feel isolated from information or services; 3) families may have different cultural or ethnic backgrounds from the majority of professionals functioning in the community, making the family's values different from those of service providers; and 4) families may place a special meaning on a child's illness or delay based on their culture and traditions (Hazel et al., 1988).

The personality characteristics of individual family members are varied, and this influences the ways that each member reacts to the idea of having a child with developmental delays in the family. These traits can be a source of strength for the family, or a limitation. In approaching a family system, it is important to think about the following characteristics of the individuals that make it up: 1) communication style—both verbal and nonverbal; 2) feelings—about oneself, about assumed responsibilities, and about what others think; 3) differences in energy level; and 4) life view—of one's own and of others' lives (Hazel et al., 1988; Thomas, 1992). Family members may also differ in their abilities and in their ways of expressing feelings, and their means of expression may depend on who is present. The cultural traditions of family members may also influence the way that feelings are expressed. With regard to a delayed child, one specific family member may assume the majority of responsibility for the child's care. This may be out of necessity, due to individual characteristics, or because the cultural background of the family dictates that this individual assume primary responsibility (Foster, 1986). In addition, family members may differ in personal self-esteem, feelings of competence regarding their ability to care for the child with special needs, and level of feelings of guilt over the child's problems. Some family members may feel a sense of shame or failure because of the child's delays, while others may not (Hazel et al., 1988).

Family members may have health problems, lowering their energy level and making it difficult for them to care for their own personal needs as well as those of the delayed child. They may be tired, depressed, or in need of healthcare themselves.

Some individuals may feel "in control" of their lives, while others may not feel that they have the ability to make positive changes in the family. Family members may also feel "unlucky" because of the presence of the delayed member (Hazel et al., 1988).

When early interventionists consider these different aspects of family life, their conceptualization of their profession is significantly broadened. One way to translate this broader role into an early intervention model is by incorporating a body of information known as family systems theory.

Family Systems Theory

Family systems theory recognizes that the family is a system and that actions affecting any one member affect all of the members (Minuchin, 1974). Families share some specific characteristics with all other types of systems: 1) the family is dynamic, it is constantly changing; 2) the family regulates itself to maintain homeostasis (in both routine daily functions and social/emotional issues); 3) the family operates according to the principal of equifinality—regardless of the initial source of the problem, the same patterns are repeatedly used by the family to maintain balance; 4) all family behavior, including symptoms, have positive functions for the family system; 5) every member of the family plays a part in the working whole; and 6) every action in the family system leads to reaction or feedback, although this is not necessarily a causal relationship (Becvar & Becvar, 1982; Thomas, 1992).

Viewed from the outside, the routines of families seem constant and ritualized; it may be difficult to recognize the changes that are constantly occurring. In reality, the system is always changing, or on the brink of change, as are its members. Even the composition and structure of the family itself are constantly changing. When attempting to work closely with a family, this is important to keep in mind. It is easy for an early interventionist to assume that a family is not acknowledging the limitations or needs of a delayed young child when, in reality, evidence of the delays is continually building in the minds of members and slowly leading to change. One example of this is Keri and her family:

> Keri is a young child with a severe congenital hearing impairment. For the first 1½ years of her life, her parents continued to believe that cochlear implants would give their daughter "normal" hearing. The physicians and health professionals explained many times that even in the best-case scenario, Keri would only hear environmental sounds, such as sirens. Even after both implants were in place, the parents continued to think that there would be additional improvement in Keri's hearing with time. After the implants were in place for 1 year, the parents were able to accept the many pieces of information and begin to make realistic goals for their daughter.

Family systems tend toward a state of homeostasis. Actions result in reactions aimed at balancing the family functioning. Some amount of disequilibrium is conducive for adjustment, and may be healthy in the face of a major change in the family system, such as the diagnosis of developmental delays in a young child. The best outcome from a systems theory perspective is that the family will experience some disequilibrium, leading to problemsolving in areas of concern, while still maintaining homeostasis in routines. Many of the situations that families with a young delayed child must face are new to them. Sometimes old coping styles may not be effective. For example:

> When John was born with spina bifida, his parents were both professionals working outside the home. One of the challenges faced by John's parents was the fact that the two had very different methods for coping with the grief and anger that they felt regarding John's disability. At first, one parent became over-involved in caregiving activities, while the other tried to deny the terrible disappointment that was felt. When this started to interfere with both their relationship and their work, John's parents were able to take some concrete steps to help solve some of the problems and maintain their daily lifestyle. They shifted responsibility for some of the caregiving and doctor visits to the less-involved parent, allowing the overinvolved parent to return to a more normal work schedule. The parent who was having difficulty expressing negative feelings joined a support group for parents with similar problems.

"Equifinality" refers to the propensity of individuals and/or families for using the same ingrained interactional patterns to solve most problems and return the family to equilibrium. When these reaction patterns do not work for a particular situation, the family remains in disequilibrium and discomfort. Thomas (1992) reports that the principle of equifinality often results in families seeking therapy. For example:

> Michelle was extremely premature and had many medical problems at the time of her birth. Her parents lived close to her paternal grandparents and had a history of depending on them to give advice and help with decisionmaking. When Michelle's grandfather had a heart attack within the 1st month of her life, he and his wife became less available as a source of support and advice to Michelle's parents. Both of Michelle's parents tried repeatedly to bring the grandparents into the decisionmaking process and daily caregiving routines, but it eventually became clear that they were unable to participate at the expected level. At this moment of great stress, Michelle's parents found themselves trying to utilize their past problemsolving mechanism. The results of such a state of disequilibrium could lead to either functional or dysfunctional behavior. In this case, Michelle's parents received assistance from a minister who was also a family friend. This individual took over some of the functions previously performed by the grandparents, such as listening to problems and giving advice. He was also able to facilitate the use of some new problemsolving strategies that benefited Michelle and her family.   .

Each repetitive behavior serves a function in the family system. This behavior has, in some way, returned the family system to homeostasis in the past. Even if a particular type of behavior seems nonproductive to an observer, it may be necessary for the family to try it before moving on to new solutions. For example, a family's denial of the long-term implications of their son's Down syndrome may be necessary in order for the family to deal with short-term needs. Trying to deal with both short- and long-term implications might be too overwhelming at a particular time. The behavior may also serve other functions for the family system, such as a protective function, or it may elicit help from outside of the family. According to Thomas (1992), the important question to ask is, "What positive function does this behavior serve for the entire family?" (p. 52).

The principal of wholeness refers to the notion that the whole is somehow greater than the sum of the parts. For example, when one member of the family system is away, he or she is still considered a member of the family. In early intervention this is often seen in situations in which an infant dies. The deceased child may continue to act as a family member, in the sense that the child may affect family decisions for a long time after death. An example is that of the R. family, who have a 2-year-old daughter who is developmentally delayed:

Mr. R. works 4 hours away from the town in which the rest of the family resides. He comes home twice a month for weekends with the family. Ms. R. does not work outside of the home and relies on her husband to take part in the family decisions. The early interventionists working with the R. family have learned that they must schedule decisionmaking meetings for times when Mr. R. is able to attend. He remains an important family member even though he is rarely present for routine caregiving or doctor's appointments.

It is also important for early interventionists to keep in mind that changing one member's behavior will have some impact on the entire system. Sometimes there are differences among family member's priorities for a child with delays. The time that an interventionist spends facilitating family strengths with one primary caregiver may have more impact than expected. For example:

Mary T., a 2½-year-old with cerebral palsy, lives in a two-generational family with her mother and grandmother, who share responsibility for her care. Mother and grandmother have different ideas regarding priorities for the child. Ms. T. wants to place the child in group care in order to return to high school, while her mother thinks that Ms. T. and Mary should be at home. Ms. T. feels that completing school will give her a better chance to support her child, while Mary's grandmother thinks that school isn't as important as caring for the baby. Early interventionists working with this family need to be aware that any support that they give to one member will have some impact on the entire system (positive and/or negative). It is important to keep this characteristic of systems in mind.

Two key ways in which the concepts of systems theory can be incorporated into early intervention are through family empowerment and family-centered care.

FAMILY-CENTERED CARE AS AN INTERVENTION PHILOSOPHY

The philosophy of family systems theory and the idea of family empowerment have been combined and implemented in the conceptual model known as family-centered care. "Empowerment implies that what you see as poor functioning [in families] is a result of social structure and lack of resources which make it impossible for existing competencies to operate" (Rappaport, 1984, p. 16).

Opportunities that create feelings of competence are called *enabling experiences* (Dunst, Trivette, Hamby, & Pollock, 1990). The implication is that:

the help seeker, learner, or client must attribute behavior change to his or her actions if one is to acquire a sense of control necessary to manage family affairs. It is not simply a matter of whether or not family needs are being met, but rather the manner in which needs are met that is likely to be both enabling and empowering. (Dunst, Trivette, & Deal, 1988, p. 4)

Family empowerment is an important part of the family-centered care model.

The philosophy of family-centered care has been further defined by the Association for the Care of Children's Health as a philosophy of care that recognizes and respects the pivotal role that the family plays in the lives of children with special needs. The major goal of this philosophy is to support families in their natural caregiving roles by building on unique individual and family strengths; it encourages promoting the family as a partner in the care of the child (Association for the Care of Children's Health, 1989). There are nine essential elements of family-centered care that apply to the early intervention setting:

1. Recognizing the family as a constant in the child's life, and intervention settings as temporary
2. Facilitating parent/professional collaboration in the care of the child; in the development, implementation, and evaluation of programs for the child; and in the development of intervention policy
3. Sharing information on the child's developmental status, behavior, and so forth in an unbiased, supportive manner
4. Implementing comprehensive policies and procedures that include emotional and financial services for families, as well as child-directed services
5. Recognizing the individuality of families, including their strengths and different patterns of coping
6. Understanding the developmental needs of delayed infants/ toddlers and incorporating them into the service-delivery system
7. Encouraging parent-to-parent support systems
8. Designing policies and procedures for comprehensive intervention systems in a manner that is flexible, accessible, and responsive to the unique needs of different families
9. Recognizing and respecting cultural differences

Family Reactions to Receiving Diagnosis

Families have many different reactions to the discovery of a child's developmental delay, but most go through a period of adjustment. Shock and denial, grief, anger or projection of blame, depression, guilt, and isolation are some of the reported reactions (see Table 1 for an in-depth description). It is important to note that these feelings are not mutually exclusive. Every individual does not feel each of these emotions, and they may not follow a specific hierarchy. One does not finish with one feeling and then go on to the next; instead, different emotions may return at various times. For example, some parents report the return of strong feelings of anxiety, guilt, and/or blame

Table 1.   Parental reactions to the diagnosis of developmental delay or disability

Denial   Parents who deny the existence of a child's disability feel threatened. Their security is unsure, and they are defending their egos or self-concepts. This is a difficult reaction for the professional to deal with. Time, patience, support, and information help these parents to see that much can be gained through helping children with disabilities realize their full potential.

Projection of blame   A common reaction is to project blame for the situation on someone or something else, such as a psychologist, teacher, or doctor. There may or may not be an actual basis for this criticism. Often parents' statements begin with "If only . . . " Again, patience, willingness to listen to the parent, and tact will help the professional deal with a potentially hostile situation.

Fear   The parents may not be acquainted with the cause or characteristics of the condition. They may have misfounded suspicions and erroneous information that causes anxiety or fear. Information, in an amount that the parent can handle, is the best remedy for fear of the unknown. A positive communication process helps the professional [and the parent] to decide when additional information should be provided.

Guilt   Feeling guilty that perhaps the condition is retribution for a misdeed or mistake is a reaction that is difficult to deal with. After genuine communication has been established, professionals can help by encouraging the grief-stricken parents to channel their energies into more productive activities.

Mourning or grief   Grief is a natural reaction to a situation that brings extreme pain and disappointment. Parents who have not been able to accept their child as a child with a disability, but, rather, look upon the child as disabled, may become grief-stricken. In this case it is necessary for the parents to go through a mourning period and start a healing process before they can learn about their child and how he or she can develop.

Withdrawal   The ability to withdraw and collect oneself is a healthy, necessary quality. It is only when one begins to shun others, avoid situations, and maintain isolation that it becomes potentially damaging.

Rejection   There are many reasons for, and many ways of exhibiting, rejection. They may be subtle, such as feigning acceptance, or they may be open and hostile. Some forms of rejection are: failing to recognize positive attributes, setting unrealistic goals, escaping by desertion, and presenting a favorable impression to others while inwardly rejecting the child.

Acceptance   The reaction of parents may be acceptance of the delay and acceptance of the child as an individual with unique strengths and limitations. Along with this comes acceptance of the family's role in the child's life.

Adapted from Berger (1987).

each time their child has a placement change or a new assessment. In addition, different family members may experience a wide range of emotions and may not have the same feelings at the same time.

Reactions of Fathers   Historically, the role of the father in families with a delayed child has been largely ignored. Typically, early interventionists have used the term *parents,* when in reality they have meant *mothers.* According to Allred (1992), there has been a great deal of misunderstanding and confusion regarding father's involvement in both family and early intervention activities. When interventionists attempt to make services more family oriented, it becomes important to learn more about fathers' roles. Conspicuously missing in the early intervention literature is any consistent evidence that fathers' behaviors have an impact on long-term outcomes for delayed young children. Allred (1992) recommends that early interventionists review literature from the field of child and family development that focuses on aspects of the dynamics of fathers in families.

Most literature on early studies of fathers' reactions to the birth or diagnosis of a delayed child tends to interpret these reactions from a psychoanalytic perspective (Love, Nauta, Coelen, Hewett, & Ruopp, 1976; Voysey, 1975). For example, research reported by Cummings (1976) indicates that fathers of children with mental retardation experience: 1) a greater level of psychological stress, 2) a relative lack of satisfaction from their other family relationships, 3) a higher score on an index of depression, and 4) a lower score on an index of self-esteem.

More recent research findings seem to interpret some fathers' behaviors as coping strategies useful in adaptation. For example, fathers' use of passive appraisal may be effective in allowing them to generate the energy necessary for adaptation (Allred, 1992). In addition, recent literature indicates that fathers use different coping mechanisms and exhibit lower stress levels than do mothers, and that fathers' acceptance of the delayed child is instrumental in family acceptance (Beckman & Bristol, 1987; Gallagher & Powell, 1989; McLinden, 1990).

There are two areas covered in the literature on fathers that seem particularly salient to early interventionists. The first relates to the understanding that there is no general consensus in the literature on what is normal and what is dysfunctional in families (Kazak & Clark, 1986). This means that professionals should be extremely careful about making such judgments and understand that behavior that is dysfunctional in one family may be functional in another (Allred, 1992). The second area is related to fathers' perceptions of family needs. In a study by Bailey and Simeonsson (1988), mothers reported twice as many family needs as fathers. Other similar studies indicated that fathers seem to report different needs than mothers. Implications for early intervention are: 1) that family assessments will be more representative if both parents are included in the assessment process and 2) that a possible reason for resistance to meeting "family goals" outlined in individualized family service plans may be related to fathers' disagreeing with them or having different priorities.

Reactions of Siblings   Siblings also seem to experience strong emotional reactions to the identification of developmental delay in a family member. In addition to the anger, guilt, and grief also experienced by parents, siblings may feel identification with the child, embarrassment, and resentment (Thurman, Cornwall, & Korteland, 1989). According to Gallagher and Powell:

> It is helpful to envision the effects of a child with a handicap on the sibling as a continuum, with very positive outcomes (i.e., acceptance and understanding) at one end and some negative outcomes (i.e., psychological disturbance) at the other. A sibling may have a very healthy, positive relationship at one time and yet at another time express some very negative behaviors and feelings toward the child with the handicap. (1989, p. 28)

Factors that may account for differences in these relationships include characteristics of the family, the child with disabilities, and the sibling without a disability as well as the family's interactional patterns. Characteristics such as family size, socioeconomic status, and parental attitudes and expectations all seem to affect sibling feelings toward the child with developmental delays. Studies suggest that when the sibling without a disability is considerably older than the child with developmental delays, he or she will be better adjusted (Simeonsson & Bailey, 1986). The particular type of disability does not appear to affect the relationship with the child without a disability, but the more severe the condition, the more adverse the effect seems to be. In addition, it seems that as the child with disabilities grows older, the nondisabled siblings experience more difficulties (Gallagher & Powell, 1989).

Child–Caregiver Interaction Patterns   A great deal of literature has explored the importance of the relationship between infants and their primary caregivers (Silber, 1989). Early attachment, disciplinary strategies, stimulation, and the effect of the child's functioning on the family are all relevant to the field of early intervention.

Attachment has been defined by Ainsworth, Blehar, Waters, and Wall (1978) as an emotional bond that permits the infant to use the caregiver as a secure base from which to explore. Results of several studies indicate that securely attached toddlers are more exploratory, enthusiastic, persistent, compliant, flexible, and have more positive affect (Arend, Gove, & Sroufe, 1979; Cassidy, 1986; Matas, Arend, & Sroufe, 1978). The results of one study of at-risk infants (Rauh, Achenbach, Nurcomb, Howell, & Teti, 1988) indicate that the promotion of sensitive transactions between parent and child through 11 1-hour sessions accounted for a significant difference in scores on the McCarthy Scales of Children's Abilities for as long as 4 years after the study. Guralnick (1989) hypothesizes that the continued improvement in these children was due to the natural evolution of learned interaction patterns as growth and development proceeded over the 4 years. Similar studies suggest that positive "changes in children's cognitive development were strongly associated with the quality of parent–infant interactions" (Guralnick, 1989, p. 7).

According to Bricker (1986), "asynchronous interactions between the parent and at-risk or handicapped children are likely to occur for a number of reasons" (p. 172). First, the parents are faced with the task of accepting the fact that their child may not be the one that they had envisioned. Instead, the child may look different, as in the case of children with Down syndrome, or act differently, as with those who have autism. The parents may feel strong emotions, such as anger at the situation, that may interfere with their ability to interact appropriately with the child. Specific parental characteristics that seem to facilitate positive child attributes are maternal responsiveness, parental warmth, and maternal involvement (Silber, 1989). For example, maternal involvement in the form of coordinated interactions in play and language seems to facilitate vocabulary growth (Thomasello & Farrer, 1986).

Characteristics of the child may also make interaction difficult. For example, a significantly premature infant may only have very short periods of alertness during which he or she can make eye contact with a parent. A child with visual impairments may not make eye contact or smile at the parent. Extreme irritability, inconsistent sleep patterns, and poor eating patterns are also examples of child characteristics that may interfere with positive interaction patterns.

It seems clear that the identification of a developmental delay in a family member results in additional stresses, challenges, and opportunities for all family members. These individuals may need help in marshaling the resources that they have available. Also, they may have to learn new skills and techniques in order to help their child develop, both in areas of delay or risk and in areas of strength. Some family members may need assistance in learning to interact with the child with special needs or to deal with their emotional reactions (Provence, 1990).

Families and Early Intervention

Many families choose to become involved with early intervention programs as one means of learning more about the special needs of their child. They may also want to develop new skills and techniques, as well as share information about their child. "Whether a child's differentness involves medical fragility, an identifiable disabling condition, or membership in a high risk group such as severely premature babies, parents . . . have urgent concerns about doing the right thing at the right time" (Healy, Keesee, & Smith, 1989, p. 1). There are many different activities that can provide assistance to families.

Family Support Activities   Professionals working with young children are well aware of the need to involve and support parents. A study by McLinden (1990) supports the need for individualizing plans for each family and "tailoring services to the needs of different family members" (p. 256). For example, mothers reported a greater frequency of negative effects on their time and well-being. Fathers indicated a lower frequency of the use of positive coping strategies. Both parents reported concerns about planning their child's future. These findings point to a need for: 1) assisting mothers in developing time-management skills; 2) facilitating the development of coping skills in fathers; 3) prioritizing community respite care as an important service that should be more widely available; 4) assisting families in locating child care services as requested; and 5) facilitating group discussion for parents about concerns over the future needs of their child with disabilities (including available and unavailable services, rational and irrational fears, etc.).

Recent attention to community-based, family-centered services for children with developmental delays suggests "the need for a closer look at home visiting programs as one mechanism to provide for a growing population of children who are eligible to receive services under PL 99-457" (Roberts & Wasik, 1990, p. 274). A number of national programs currently operate home visiting components or programs for broader populations of young children. The Administration for Children, Youth and Families funds a home component of Head Start (Love, Nauta, Coelen, Hewett, & Ruopp, 1976) and the Ford Foundation funds home visiting through Fair Start (Halpern & Larner, 1988). Roberts and Wasik (1990) provide a comprehensive review of home visiting programs serving young children with, or at at risk for, delays. They report on 643 programs serving children birth to 3 years old and their families. In the Roberts and Wasik (1990) review, program respondents reported the following services as being of primary importance: enhanced parenting skills (83%); child development skills (86%); parent coping (75%); emotional support to families (70%); information delivery to families (68%); and diagnostic services (68%) (p. 280).

There is little disagreement that the diagnosis of a child's disabling condition is a traumatic event for a family (De Bettencourt, 1987). For some children, the special needs are evident shortly after birth, as in the case of those with Down syndrome. Other families live through their child's early years with only the information that the child is at "high risk" for later developmental problems; confirmation of problems may come later if the child does not meet the typical developmental milestones. Regardless of the scenario, families must adjust to an unexpected reality (Thurman & Widerstrom, 1990). The information that a family's hopes and dreams for their new child may have to change can be devastating.

Involving Fathers   Helping fathers to become more involved in intervention programs may be beneficial to some families. One benefit of involving fathers in intervention activities is the possibility of the development of supportive relationships between fathers. Unfortunately, many fathers of children with delays seem to lack the types of relationships that can yield positive benefits for the family. The Association for the Care of Children's Health (ACCH Network, 1992) makes the following suggestions for facilitating a father's support group:

1. Build the group through needs assessments of the members and assurances that the goals will come from within the group.
2. Clarify the group's goals and purposes through the development of established group norms. Also, clarify time and length of meetings, confidentiality policy, member responsibilities, and rules for dealing with conflicts in values and ideas.
3. Begin each session with a brief statement from each father, including who he is, what his child's special needs are, and current information about his family's situation. Ending with individual statements about the value of the session may also be helpful.
4. Focus on feelings, rather than intellectualizing and debating. Do not be afraid to talk about grief, anger, depression, and sadness, which are all feelings that may be important to those who attend.
5. Guide interactions in ways that make it easier for men to talk, while gently closing completed topics. Avoid letting one member monopolize the conversation, and minimize blaming or complaining.
6. Encourage members to be active listeners.
7. When one person is discussing a concern, stay with the speaker until he is finished, rather than allowing others to divert the conversation to their similar situations.
8. Focus on the men attending, rather than on long stories involving past history or individuals who are absent.
9. Bring ideas together and complete one topic before going on to the next topic.
10. Empower members by sharing the leadership when others are able to facilitate.

11. Assist fathers in gaining information about their child's special needs and in locating helpful resources for their family.
12. Do not define success by the number of men who attend, instead, enjoy all who do participate.

A second suggestion for facilitating fathers' involvement in programming for their children was the development of "father's day" activities by the intervention program. According to Hietsch (1986), this type of program is effective in getting fathers into the center-based setting with their children for the purposes of interaction and observation and in starting ongoing involvement. This suggestion is easily translated to early intervention.

Assisting Siblings   Siblings of children with delays are a much-overlooked minority group. Too often, they merely receive orders regarding what they should be doing for the child with developmental delays, with little formal effort made to explain their roles (Stewart, Benson, & Lindsey, 1987). Lobato (1990) lists six major needs of siblings of children with disabilities:

1. Information on the child's condition, including how it is evaluated and treated
2. Open communication within the family about the condition and about family members' positive and negative experiences with it
3. Recognition by the parents of the sibling's own strengths and accomplishments
4. "Quality time" with parents on an individual basis
5. Contact and support from other siblings and families
6. Ways to cope with stressful events such as peer and public reaction, unexpected disruptions of family plans, and extra responsibilities

One of the most common strategies for helping siblings has been the use of discussion groups. The goals for such groups include: 1) allowing children to meet others in similar situations; 2) facilitating positive interactions with special educators, parents, and siblings with delays; and 3) assuring a forum for open expression of questions and opinions. Some sibling discussion groups are run parallel to parent discussion groups, and there are a few reports in the literature of joint groups. Parents of children who have participated in sibling discussion groups report that their children seemed better able to discuss related family issues.

Lobato (1990) suggests that single-session groups may not allow enough time for some children to meet their needs for information and support. Stewart et al. (1987) suggest a five-session discussion-group format for siblings of children with mental retardation, with sessions on: 1) introduction of general information on mental retardation; 2) the roles of persons with mental retardation in the community (information on long-term outcomes); 3) mental retardation and the family (impact on family members); and 4) feelings about one's sibling, and ending with 5) a field trip to a center-based program for children with disabilities. The authors suggest resource materials to be used with the discussion groups and encourage the use of role play to enhance discussion. Suggested role-play topics include typical situations such as explaining your sibling's special needs to a new friend being brought to the home for the first time.

A second strategy that has been reported as being helpful to many siblings is for intervention programs to provide periodic "tours" of program centers for siblings and extended family members. These are opportunities for siblings to visit programs and to "try out" special materials and equipment. Such tours may be effective as one part of a group of sessions or as separate activities.

Some studies have reported that older siblings can be effective in a teaching role for their siblings with disabilities. Swenson-Pierce, Kohl, and Egel (1987) report on studies showing positive results with sibling teachers in home, school, and camp settings. According to Lobato (1990), this teaching role can be appropriate because it is a natural one for siblings. One concern in using this strategy is the potential for the development of resentments between siblings. It appears that siblings who receive specific instruction in teaching techniques show the best benefits. In addition, the strategy requires close monitoring that may be impractical for some programs. It is suggested that sibling teaching strategies be included as a part of general family support programs.

Another way to support siblings is through a series of workshops. Lobato (1990) gives a detailed description of two different series of workshops, one designed for younger, and one for older, siblings. The series suggested for younger children includes six sessions on topics such as: disabilities, illness, and strengths; identifying positive and negative emotions; highlighting siblings' strengths and talents; and evaluating children's experiences. Sessions include activities such as: making family drawings, exploring adapted equipment, group story telling, and role play.

Parent Advocacy and Support Organizations   Advocacy can be defined as the pleading of the cause of another (Berger, 1987). Since very young children are unable to plead their own case, parents take on this responsibility, to varying degrees. Currently, many federal laws protect the rights of individuals with special needs, and understanding these rights and privileges has become a complicated job. Along with this comes the need for parents to understand certain aspects of the systems within which services are provided to their children, including state-of-the-art best practice and procedural safeguards (Binkard, 1985). A number of different agencies have been created to aid parents in this process. First, each state funds a private, nonprofit advocacy and protection agency (information on these agencies is available through state departments of education) to work with families of school-age children (over 3 years of age as of July 1991). In many states, these agencies are beginning to work with families of children with delays who are between birth and 3 years of age, as well.

In addition, there are several national organizations, such as the Mental Health Law Project, dedicated to fostering advocacy among parents of children with special needs. There are also a number of federally funded parent centers throughout the country that serve as information resources for families and professionals and as research institutions for studies on different aspects of family involvement. In addition, there are several national organizations devoted to assisting families with a member with a disability (Weissbourd & Patrick, 1988). While these organizations work with families of individuals of all ages, they may be especially helpful to families of young children by directing them to local groups or chapters of families in similar situations. Parent-to-Parent, for example, is a program that matches individual families with similar needs. A family with a child diagnosed as having a rare genetic syndrome might be matched with another family whose child has a similar or identical condition. Matches are also made according to care needs (e.g., home oxygen use, special feeding techniques) and/or parent concerns (i.e., disciplinary methods, strategies for developing trust funds). Some of these groups will also provide technical assistance and support to help individuals who wish to start a parents' group.

CONCLUDING COMMENTS

A central focus of PL 99-457 is family involvement in early intervention. Program models that call themselves family-centered, family-focused, or family-guided are becoming more numerous. Some data has been reported that supports positive relationships between child progress and the prioritizing of family needs as intervention objectives. When studies have failed to demonstrate this relationship there have been questions about the effectiveness of the type of parent involvement thus far investigated.

The strong current emphasis on families as being central to the intervention process raises some important general questions that relate to relevance, personnel training, and evaluation, such as: 1) Are there certain types of family priorities, needs, and concerns that are more appropriate to early intervention than others? 2) What are the competencies that early interventionists need in order to provide family services, and how will they acquire them? and 3) How can the field measure the effects of family objectives?

Most programs now accept family involvement as best practice, and PL 99-457 refers to a relationship between family services and the needs of the child with delays. But there seem to be many different opinions as to what extent and type of family involvement is appropriate. This is an important question for individual programs or systems to address as they formulate policies, procedures, and documentation. In order to have services that fit the philosophical framework of family-centered programming, policies, procedures, and program documentation must all reflect the program philosophy. For example, claiming to follow a philosophy of family-centered services, but making no provision for the involvement of a family-focused professional in service planning shows a disparity between philosophy and policy. So does policy that only allows programs to accept referrals from a physician. Programs without provisions allowing staff to attend evening meetings or services, when requested, do not facilitate family involvement. Documentation that is written in professional jargon may also hinder families from participating as full partners in their child's program.

Much has been written recently about the necessary competencies for early interventionists. Skills in working with families are included in most comprehensive preservice training programs. It is important that these future interventionists be exposed first-hand to programs that involve families as partners. Fieldwork in programs reflecting a family-centered philosophy is a critical part of preservice training.

For professionals who are already working in early intervention programs, the inclusion of family services represents a broadening of job responsibilities. These individuals may need ongoing involvement in programs in which family services are successfully provided in order to make the change from providing child-focused services to the inclusion of family services. Pairing professionals new to family services with professionals from successful programs of this type might be one way to foster new skills and strategies.

Researchers have cited the importance of measuring the development of family strengths and abilities as appropriate outcomes of intervention programs. Abilities to be measured might include parent perceptions of self-competence in parenting and advocacy and changes in caregiver–infant interaction patterns. Another area of importance is family satisfaction with the programs providing direct services. Unfortunately, the majority of funding agencies and programs continue to measure success by collecting data and using outcomes that emphasize child-focused goals in the areas of cognitive, language, social–emotional, adaptive, and motor skill development. While some of the family constructs are difficult to measure, if service providers are concerned with the provision of early intervention that is guided by the family and takes into account the concerns, resources, priorities, and culture of the family, then it is important to evaluate these areas, as well as child progress.

REFERENCES

Ainsworth, M., Blehar, M., Waters, E., & Wall, S. (1978). *Patterns of attachment: A psychological study of the strange situation.* Hillsdale, NJ: Lawrence Erlbaum Associates.

Allred, K. (1992). Fathers of young children with disabilities. *DEC Communicator, 18*(3), 6–7.

Arend, R., Gove, F., & Sroufe, L. (1979). Continuity of individual adaptation from infancy to kindergarten: A predictive study of resiliency and curiosity in preschoolers. *Child Development, 50,* 950–959.

Association for the Care of Children's Health. (1989, Spring). *Family Support Bulletin.* Author.

Association for the Care of Children's Health. (1992). Guidelines for Facilitating Father Support Groups. *ACCH Network, 9*(4), 2.

Bailey, D.B., & Simeonsson, R.J. (1988). Assessing needs of families with handicapped infants. *The Journal of Special Education, 22,* 117–127.

Beckman, P., & Bristol, M. (1987, December). *Stress and support in mothers and fathers of young handicapped children.* Paper presented at the National Early Childhood Conference on Children with Special Needs, Denver.

Becvar, R.J., & Becvar, D.S. (1982). *Systems theory and family theory.* New York: University Press of America.

Berger, E.H. (1987). *Parents as partners in education: The school and home working together* (2nd ed.). Columbus, OH.: Charles E. Merrill.

Binkard, B. (1985). A successful handicap awareness program—run by parents. *Teaching Exceptional Children, 23*(1), 12–16.

Bricker, D.D. (1986). *Early education of at-risk and handicapped infants, toddlers and preschool children.* Glenview, IL: Scott, Foresman and Co.

Cassidy, J. (1986). The ability to negotiate the environment: An aspect of child competence as related to quality of attachment. *Child Development, 57,* 331–337.

Cummings, S.T. (1976). The impact of the child's deficiency on the father: A study of the fathers of mentally retarded and chronically ill children. *American Journal of Orthopsychiatry, 46,* 246–255.

De Bettencourt, L.U. (1987). How to develop parent relationships. *Teaching Exceptional Children, 19*(2), 26–27.

Dunst, C.L., Trivette, C.M., & Deal, A.G. (1988). *Enabling and empowering families: Principles and guidelines.* Cambridge, MA: Brookline Books.

Dunst, C.L., Trivette, C.M., Hamby, D.M., & Pollock, B. (1990). Family systems correlates of the behavior of young children with handicaps. *Journal of Early Intervention, 14*(3), 204–218.

Foster, M. (1986). Families with young disabled children in family therapy. *Treating Young Children in Family Therapy, 4*(6), 62–72.

Gallagher, P.A., & Powell, T.H. (1989). Brothers and sisters: Meeting special needs, *Topics in Early Childhood Special Education 8*(4), 24–37.

Guralinck, M.J. (1989). Recent developments in early intervention efficacy research: Implications for family involvement in PL 99-457. *Topics in Early Childhood Special Education, 9*(3), 1–17.

Halpern, R., & Larner, M. (1988). The design of family support programs in high risk communities: Lessons from the Child Survival/Fair Start initiative. In D.R. Powell (Ed.), *Parent education as early childhood intervention: Emerging directions in theory, research and practice.* Norwood, NJ: Ablex.

Hazel, R., Barber, P.A., Roberts, S., Behr, S.K., Helmstetter, E., & Guess, D. (1988). *A community approach to an integrated service system for children with special needs.* Baltimore: Paul H. Brookes Publishing Co.

Healy, A., Keesee, P.D., & Smith, B.S. (1989). *Early services for children with special needs: Transactions for family support.* Baltimore: Paul H. Brookes Publishing Co.

Hietsch, D.G. (1986). Father involvement: No moms allowed. *Teaching Exceptional Children, 18*(4), 258–259.

Kazak, A.E., & Clark, M.W. (1986). Stress in families of children with myelomeningocele. *Developmental Medicine and Child Neurology, 28,* 220–228.

Kornblum, H., & Anderson, B. (1982). Acceptance reassessed—A point of view. *Child Psychiatry and Human Development, 12*(3), 171–179.

Lobato, D.J. (1990). *Brothers, sisters, and special needs: Information and activities for helping young siblings of children with chronic illnesses and developmental disabilities.* Baltimore: Paul H. Brookes Publishing Co.

Love, J.M., Nauta, M.J., Coelen, C.G., Hewett, K., & Ruopp, R.R. (1976). *National home start evaluation: Final report* (Contract No. 105-72-1100). Ypsilanti, MI: High Scope.

Matas, L., Arend, R., & Sroufe, L. (1978). Continuity of adaptation in the second year: The relationship between quality of attachment and later competence. *Child Development, 49,* 547–556.

McLinden, S.E. (1990). Mother's and father's reports of the effects of a young child with special needs on the family. *Journal of Early Intervention, 14*(3), 249–259.

Minuchin, S. (1974). *Families and family therapy.* Cambridge, MA: Harvard University Press.

Provence, S. (1990). Interactional issues: Infants, parents and professionals. *Infants and Young Children: An Interdisciplinary Journal of Special Care Practices, 3,* 1–7.

Rappaport, J. (1984). Studies in empowerment: Introduction to the issues. In J. Rappaport, C. Swift, & R. Hess (Eds.). *Studies in empowerment: Steps toward understanding and action.* New York: Haworth Press.

Rauh, V.A., Achenbach, T.M., Nurcomb, B., Howell, C.T., & Teti, D.M. (1988). Minimizing effects of low birth weight: Four year results of an early intervention program. *Topics in Early Childhood Special Education, 9*(3), 1–17.

Roberts, R.N., & Wasik, B.H. (1990). Home visiting programs for families with children birth to three: Results of a national survey. *Journal of Early Intervention, 14*(3), 274–284.

Silber, S. (1989). Family influences on early development. *Topics in Early Childhood Special Education, 8*(4), 1–23.

Simeonsson, R.J., & Bailey, D.B., Jr. (1986). Siblings of handicapped children. In J.J. Gallagher & P.M. Vietze (Eds.), *Families of handicapped persons: Research, programs, and policy issues* (pp. 67–77). Baltimore: Paul H. Brookes Publishing Co.

Stewart, D.A., Benson, G.T., & Lindsey, J.D. (1987). A unit plan for siblings of handicapped children. *Teaching Exceptional Children, 19*(3), 24–28.

Swenson-Pierce, A., Kohl, F.L., & Egel, A.L. (1987). Siblings as home trainers: A strategy for teaching domestic skills to children. *Journal of The Association for Persons with Severe Handicaps, 12*, 53–60.

Thomas, M.B. (1992). *An introduction to marital and family therapy: Counseling toward healthier families across the lifespan.* New York: Charles E. Merrill.

Thomasello, M., & Farrer, M. (1986). Joint attention and early language. *Child Development, 57*, 1454–1463.

Thurman, S.K., Cornwall, J.R., & Korteland, C. (1989). The liaison infant family team (LIFT) project: An example of case study evaluation. *Infants and Young Children: An Interdisciplinary Journal of Special Care Practices, 2*(2), 74–82.

Thurman, S.K., & Widerstrom, A.H. (1990). *Infants and young children with special needs: A developmental and ecological approach.* Baltimore: Paul H. Brookes Publishing Co.

Tulloch, D. (1983). Why me? Parental reactions to the birth of an exceptional child. *Journal of the Division for Early Childhood, 7*, 54–60.

Voysey, M. (1975). *A constant burden: The reconstitution of family life.* London: Routledge and Keegan Paul.

Weissbourd, B., & Patrick, M. (1988). In the best interests of the family: The emergence of family resource programs. *Infants and Young Children: An Interdisciplinary Journal of Special Care Practices, 1*(2), 46–54.

Collaboration and Service Coordination for Effective Early Intervention

Mary Beth Bruder
and Theresa Bologna

Polly is 18 months old and lives with her family in central Connecticut. She was born prematurely at a tertiary care hospital, the sole survivor of a set of triplets. Polly was hospitalized for 13 months following birth. Her medical and developmental conditions include:

Brain damage that resulted from spinal meningitis
Hydrocephalus, an enlargement of the head due to a buildup of fluid
within the brain (A shunt has been surgically inserted to drain
excess fluid from the cranial area.)
Episodes of congestive heart failure
Frequent infections that result in hospitalization
A dependency on oxygen
Self-abusive episodes, including severe head banging

As a result of these conditions, Polly and her family have been receiving a variety of services since she has been home, including:

Health care through her primary pediatrician
Occupational therapy once a week

103

Speech therapy once every other week
Physical therapy once a week
Home education through a regional education service center (RESC) twice a week
Sixteen hours per day of home nursing care
Medical supply vendors for special formulas and oxygen
Specialty care at a variety of clinics at the tertiary care hospital

Polly's family has numerous professionals in and out of their home on a regular basis. During the 5 months that Polly has been home she has received services from 5 therapists, 2 teachers, 10 nurses, and a hospital-based team composed of a physician, 2 nurses, a psychologist, a full range of therapists, and a social worker. Also assigned to her "case" are 2 social workers, 3 program supervisors, and 3 service coordinators from 3 separate agencies.

It is not surprising that Polly's parents are often caught in the middle of conflicts among the various professionals, who each seem to have different opinions about Polly's needs, appropriate treatments, payment options, and service schedules. For example, the family has three case managers. Each gave the family different information about eligibility for various public sources of funding, including the Medicaid waiver. As a result, their application for benefits was delayed and they had to pay several thousand dollars out-of-pocket for Polly's cost of care. Additionally, the nursing agency and the various therapists disagree about the amount of therapy Polly needs, resulting in a lack of cooperation between the agency and therapists. As a result, Polly's parents feel that the services that she receives are often the cause of confusion in their lives because there is no coordination among the service agencies and providers. The schedule for a typical week in their house looks like this:

Monday: 16 hours—nursing, teacher, supervisor, Department of Income Maintenance (DIM) case manager
Tuesday: 16 hours—nursing, occupational therapy, Department of Mental Retardation case manager
Wednesday: 16 hours—nursing, teacher, clinic visit at tertiary hospital, physical therapy
Thursday: 16 hours—nursing, physical therapy, vendor delivery, nursing supervisor, teacher
Friday: 16 hours—nursing, speech therapy, adaptive-equipment fitting at tertiary care hospital
Saturday: 16 hours—nursing
Sunday: 16 hours—nursing

Polly's parents have concluded that caring for her is not the primary cause of their stress, which they attribute instead to the multiple layers of fragmented services that cause so much havoc within their family. They are now seeking out-of-home placement for Polly because they feel that they have to put some order back into their lives. Neither feels "functional" with so many people in and out of their home. In Polly's case, one of the purposes of PL 99-457 (to reduce the likelihood of institutionalization) has not been realized.

Polly is typical of many infants and toddlers with severe disabilities. The parents of these children usually interact with a variety of agencies and programs in order to meet the unique intervention needs of their child. Unfortunately, when trying to gain access to these services, parents are confronted with a multitude of incomprehensible acronyms and an unwieldy maze of agencies that differ in priorities, mandates, geographic boundaries, and administrative structures (Dokecki & Heflinger, 1989; Featherstone, 1980; Rubin & Quinn-Curran, 1983).

The needs of infants and toddlers with disabilities have also created many challenges for service providers. Both federal legislation and recommended practice mandate that early intervention programs be family-centered, comprehensive, and community-based and -coordinated (Brewer, McPherson, Magrab, and Hutchins, 1989; McGonigel, Kaufmann, & Johnson, 1991), and state and local service agencies are presently struggling to develop such programs.

Most often, early intervention programs for infants and toddlers with disabilities consist simply of those services that are readily available. While the program may meet the needs of some families, other families may require a number of additional services that may be more difficult to access. This is especially true for those families who live in rural communities, where travel time to services may be more than an hour. For example, Polly's needs require her to participate in a hospital follow-up clinic, hospital- and home-based therapy, home health services (including equipment maintenance), and intervention program services from three agencies. These services are all limited in the type, frequency, and location of their delivery, and this dictates the options (or lack thereof) available to Polly's family. Additionally, the agencies providing the services have different goals, orientations, funding sources, and continuing eligibility requirements that further limit the availability of services. Although it is clear that few agencies have the resources to provide a complete continuum of services to deal with all of the issues that may affect an infant or toddler with disabilities and his or her family, services must be restructured in such a way as to maximize coordination and enhance, rather then inhibit, family functioning (Dunst & Trivette, 1989).

When examining the unique services required by Polly and her family, the immediate challenge is to identify the various agencies, professionals, and payment sources currently involved in the provision of early intervention services in the community. While interagency and multidisciplinary coordination may be the first step toward alleviating some of the stress that Polly's family experiences, the ultimate goal should be the collaborative development of an individualized family service plan (IFSP) to be carried out under the direction of the family. There are two keys to this goal: collaborative service delivery and family-centered services. The purpose of this chapter is to discuss the collaborative relationships required by Part H of IDEA, and, in particular, the interagency and multidisciplinary aspects of service provision.

EARLY INTERVENTION PROGRAM REQUIREMENTS

Part H of IDEA recognizes the fact that no one agency or service provider has all the knowledge and skills necessary to meet the multiple needs of families participating in early intervention. Many of the provisions of the law require both coordination and collaboration at the local, state, and federal level (Trohanis, 1989). For example, states that are participating in the federal program must initiate a number of collaborative planning and implementation activities. Among these are:

1. *The establishment of a statewide interagency coordinating council (ICC) composed of parents and representatives from relevant state agencies and services providers*   The reauthorization of PL 99-457 requires that these councils consist of between 15 and 25 members and that the chair *not* be from the lead agency. Councils may vary in how many agencies are represented, and at least 20% of the membership must be parents.
2. *The maintenance of a lead agency for general administration, supervision, and monitoring of programs and activities, including responsibility for carrying out the entry into formal interagency agreements and the resolution of disputes*   Approximately 21 states have chosen the Department of Education as their lead agency; others have chosen Departments of Health or Departments of Developmental Disabilities or Mental Retardation.
3. *The development of interagency and multidisciplinary models of service delivery for eligible infants, toddlers, and their families as specified in the*

IFSP, which is directed by the family   "Multidisciplinary" has been further defined by the U. S. Department of Education to mean efforts involving persons representing at least two disciplines.

4. *The appointment of a service coordinator to facilitate and ensure the implementation of the IFSP*   The service coordinator is responsible for the implementation of the IFSP and for ongoing coordination with other agencies and individuals to ensure the timely and effective delivery of services.

Inherent in these provisions is the concept of a statewide system of coordinated, comprehensive, multidisciplinary, interagency programs of early intervention services for infants and toddlers with disabilities and their families. This concept requires commitment by all service agencies and providers to cooperatively and collaboratively plan, implement, and evaluate services that enhance the capacity of families to meet the special needs of their child. It seems clear that the challenge to the service delivery system is to develop new interagency and multidisciplinary models of early intervention that meet the intent of the law, and, most importantly, the needs of families such as Polly's.

INTERAGENCY COLLABORATION: THE KEY TO PROGRAM DEVELOPMENT

The development of cooperative arrangements among agencies for the purpose of service delivery is a common strategy that has been used to improve service delivery (Shenet, 1982). Cooperative arrangements are required by many federal laws, and the desired outcome is the development of an interagency cooperative agreement. However, cooperative arrangements rarely result in improved services (Melaville & Blank, 1991). This is because cooperating agencies maintain their own autonomy, as well as their own philosophy and service goals, and these may not be appropriate for the target population. Unfortunately, this model tends to drive most initial attempts to organize services for young children with disabilities and their families.

In order to improve this situation, it has been suggested that the focus of interagency models should shift from cooperative arrangements among agencies to collaborations focused on joint service delivery. A collaborative strategy is called for in communities where the need and intent is to fundamentally change the way services are designed and delivered (Melaville & Blank, 1991). This requires that the involved agencies agree on a common philosophy and service goal that can only be achieved through joint agency activities. Part H of IDEA assists agencies in moving toward this model by embodying a philosophy of a service delivery system composed of 14 components that can only be achieved through the adoption of such activities (Trohanis, 1989). Furthermore, these components must be planned, implemented, and evaluated in such a way as to ensure interdependent, collaborative service delivery.

There are many benefits to collaborative service delivery models (Elder & Magrab, 1980), the most important being an improvement in service delivery to the target population. This occurs as a result of more efficient and effective use of services, providers, and funding streams across agencies (Audette, 1980; Bailey, 1984). These models also result in a reduction in service duplication (Garland & Linder, 1988; Healy, Keesee, & Smith, 1989). Lastly, collaborative efforts enable parents and service providers to efficiently locate and manage the services required by the family (Bailey, 1989a; Dunst & Trivette, 1988).

Unfortunately, collaborative early intervention service systems remain an elusive goal for many states. This is not surprising, considering that the service delivery system is composed of independent agencies, institutions, and organizations, each of which provides a specific service or function. As a result, each participating service provider has their own orientation toward the service system. For example, hospitals and health professionals view early intervention very differently from community-oriented agencies and professionals (Gilkerson, 1990). In order for divergent agencies to work together, many inherent barriers to the collaborative process must be identified and addressed. Some common barriers to interagency collaboration are listed in Table 1.

The Process of Collaboration

Under Part H of IDEA, interagency collaboration for the purpose of the design and delivery of early intervention services must occur at both the state and community level. Ideally, these collaborations will be closely aligned and allow for comprehensive service provision that benefits families and children.

There is no magic formula for developing interagency models, but a number of key ingredients have been identified (Elder, 1980a). In particular, Melaville and Blank (1991) have identified five variables that shape an effective interagency collaborative system, which are outlined below.

The Social and Political Climate for Change   A more favorable climate for collaboration occurs when the targeted service delivery issue is a priority for each of the service agencies. Often, however,

Table 1. Common barriers to interagency collaboration

COMPETITIVENESS BETWEEN AGENCIES
Turf issues
Lack of information about other agencies' functions
Political issues

LACK OF ORGANIZATIONAL STRUCTURE FOR COORDINATION
Differing philosophies
Independent goals
Haphazard team process
Lack of facilitator
Lack of monitoring and evaluation process
Lack of planning
Lack of power and authority to make and implement decisions

TECHNICAL FACTORS
Resources: staff, time, budget
Logistics: distance, geography

PERSONNEL
Parochial interests
Resistance to change
Staff attitudes
Lack of commitment to community needs
Questionable administrative support
Discipline-specific jargon and perspectives

there may be other factors contributing to the overall climate for change. For example, not all participating agencies may agree on the necessity for service improvement. There might be a higher priority, such as a budget shortfall, within one agency. Also, agencies may already have a history of competition or negative relationships. However, it seems clear that the federal legislation has created a need to prioritize collaboration, and this should facilitate the development of a favorable climate in which change can occur.

The Processes of Communication and Problemsolving Interagency collaborations rely on the adoption of a process to establish goals and objectives, clarify roles, make decisions, and resolve conflicts. The first step that has been identified as being necessary for collaborative arrangements to occur is the adoption of a common vision by all involved in the service delivery system. Part H of IDEA ensures that this will occur, because the legislation defines the vision for a collaborative statewide early intervention program. One difficulty in establishing this vision across the various agencies and programs involved in early intervention may be their differing interpretations of the adequacy of the existing system. This obstacle will only be overcome when specific processes are adopted by all participants to ensure open, continued communication, negotiation, and conflict management.

The Human Dimension   The people involved in the creation, development, and implementation of the interagency service system are a critical factor in the ultimate success of the collaborative model. Most important is an effective leader. A leader must be able to both establish and help sell the vision to all participants. He or she must also be able to translate the vision into the reality of service delivery. Second in importance is the competence and commitment of the other participants, both at the policymaking and service delivery levels; all should be provided access to support and training as their roles change with the development and implementation of a collaborative service delivery system.

The Policies that Support or Inhibit Interagency Collaboration   Each participating agency and program entering into an interagency collaboration has a set of rules and regulations that dictates their mandate, target population, budgetary operations, and service structure (including staffing patterns). Agencies and programs must be prepared to identify and share these policies with each other so that barriers to interdependent functioning can be identified and removed. Many existing agency and program policies will have to be evaluated and refined in order to comply with the collaborative requirements of Part H.

The Availability of Resources   Interagency collaborative efforts require new fiscal arrangements to ensure the development and delivery of services. Resources of all kinds (fiscal, staff, time, in-kind services) will have to be pooled to establish the most efficient system for the delivery of services. In an age of shrinking resources, interagency collaborations are often the only way to guarantee the development of an integrated service system. Early intervention is one area in which resources must be pooled and funding levels must be increased. Only then will states be able to implement services in conjunction with the spirit of Part H.

Lastly, a positive atmosphere of communication and trust among the participants must be maintained throughout the interagency collaborative process (Johnson & Johnson, 1987). This seems to occur when the focus of the collaboration is on the people involved, rather than on the individual agency and program requirements (Fisher & Brown, 1989). This focus should include both the consumers of the services (families and children) and the service providers. The collaborative vision can be defined as "relationship driven," as the participants focus on improving the services or system for people, rather than for agencies and programs. This collaborative model is at the very heart of early intervention under Part H of IDEA, and it must begin at the state level, through the ICC and the designated lead agency for service delivery (McNulty, 1989).

State Interagency Collaboration

The ICC has been established as a forum for statewide interagency communication and collaboration. The ICC in every state is responsible for assisting the lead agency to develop policies and procedures to enhance the implementation of a statewide, collaborative, comprehensive, family-centered early intervention system. The ICC can ensure the beginning of collaborative goal setting across participating agencies by sharing the philosophy and mandate of Part H of IDEA. This philosophy can begin to set the parameters for the development of a collaborate service system. The involved agencies must be able to identify the services that are common across them and then pool resources to jointly plan, implement, and evaluate new services. Finally, they must delegate individual agency responsibility for the outcomes of these joint efforts. The inclusion of parents on the ICC should ensure the family-centered nature of collaborative service provision. The responsibility for the actual interagency provision of services rests with the lead agency, though the conceptualization of any interagency collaborations should develop during the planning sessions of the ICC.

The role of the lead agency is to initiate collaborations with other state agencies involved in the provision of services to families and children. For this reason, the role of the lead agency must be facilitative, rather than dictatorial and isolationist. This attitude must be conveyed by all who represent the lead agency, since their role will be to display leadership during the implementation of a statewide collaborative service delivery system (Melaville & Blank, 1991).

As they build the statewide early intervention system, the most difficult task faced by the early intervention staff within the lead agency will be the need to adapt both their individual and collective styles in accordance with the diverse needs and styles of the representatives of other agencies. A collaborative climate must be maintained during the interagency process, and all agencies must feel free to contribute ideas and solutions, which are then to be jointly resolved.

A process for structuring interagency goal setting has been articulated by Magrab, Kazuk, and Greene (1981), and further refined by Hanson and Lynch (1989) and Hazel et al. (1988). This process begins with identification of a leader, either one independent person or a designated representative from an agency or project. A number of meetings will be required to complete the process. The following steps are necessary to reach the interagency goal:

1. *Service goals* are set.
2. *Time commitments* for interagency meetings are made by agency representatives, service providers, and consumers involved in the service system.

3. *A community profile* is developed to examine what services are currently in place.
4. *Service responsibilities, duplications, and gaps* among the providers are identified.
5. *The resources* (if any) that are available are identified.
6. *An action plan* is developed and implemented to address the service goal.
7. *An interagency agreement* (*or agreements*) is developed. This agreement should be in writing and be developed as part of the overall process.
8. *The outcome* is then evaluated in an ongoing, systematic fashion.

Unfortunately, when implementing this process, many service systems begin with the writing of an interagency agreement. To be functional, however, the agreement must reflect a dynamic and ongoing planning process that focuses on the primary needs of the target population, rather than on the existing service structure (Elder, 1980b). The primary purpose of the agreement should be the translation of policy into service delivery practice.

Developing state-level interagency collaborative services for early intervention may initially be problematic because of the breadth and scope of the possible collaborations that are required by Part H (McNulty, 1989). At the state-agency level, the absence of individual- and family-specific issues may also result in decisions being made based on abstract problems, which may not be effective. One remedy to this problem is to provide sample vignettes (e.g., those included in this chapter) from families who are involved in the service system to vividly illustrate the service issues to state-level participants. This methodology is becoming more widely used for instructional purposes, as well as for policy development (Kanter, 1989).

In Polly's situation, it would seem reasonable to suggest that some service issues could have been remedied if the state agencies involved had a collaborative policy for advising families on the need for, and availability of, financial assistance programs. The state agencies could also have provided guidance on the role of the many participating service agencies and possible reductions of personnel across them. Most importantly, agreements should have been developed to articulate the state's responsibilities (across agencies) to both the providers and to Polly's family for fiscal management and service-delivery options.

Community Interagency Collaboration

The IFSP is one of the most important provisions of the early intervention service system under Part H of IDEA. The process demands an open, nonstructured approach to family-centered early intervention services. As with interagency agreements, the IFSP can not be seen as the end in itself, but only as a means to an end. The family-centered nature of service delivery has been reinforced by the reauthorization amendments of 1991. A new provision has been adopted that defines the families' powers in the process. The bill specifies that the parent or guardian has the right to determine whether they, their infant or toddler, or other family member, will accept or decline each early intervention service.

Rather than concentrate on a specific form to use with the IFSP, the involved professionals must strive to collaboratively meet a family's priorities for their child. Again, as with interagency agreements, the challenge to the members of the service team is to develop relationships and focus on the needs of the persons involved, especially the family (Hall, 1980). Once a common philosophy is articulated, interdependent goals and practices can follow.

For example, in Polly's case, none of the involved agencies had ever had a meeting together. Furthermore, none had established any meaningful relationship with Polly's family. Perhaps the first step toward facilitating a more cohesive program for Polly would have been to organize a meeting of all the agency representatives and the family. The focus of the meeting could have been the family's self-identified resources and priorities. The various agency representatives could also have clarified their own roles and responsibilities to the family and to each other. This would have helped to facilitate the identification of gaps and duplications in service delivery, and allowed the family to identify the most appropriate services for themselves. The outcome of this meeting could have been the beginning of the IFSP process, and more importantly, the beginning of a relationship-driven collaboration between the family and the many service agencies.

SERVICE COORDINATION

An additional requirement of the IFSP process is the designation of a service coordinator. Historically, parents have had to assume the role of coordinating services for their child (Hazel et al., 1988). Part H of IDEA does not designate any one professional to assume this role, and the recent reauthorization acknowledges the rights of family members to fill this role (for themselves or others), if they obtain "appropriate training." The legislation defines the duties of the service coordinator:

> to assist and enable an eligible child and the child's family to receive the rights, procedural safeguards, and services that are authorized under the

state's early intervention program. Service coordinators are responsible for coordinating all services across agency lines and serving as the single point of contact in helping parents to obtain the services and assistance they need. (Mental Health Law Project, 1990)

The recognition of the need for service coordination stems from previous experience in social work and nursing. Professionals in these fields often worked in the capacity of managing a number of agency representatives who had an impact on the day-to-day functioning of people with developmental disabilities, mental illness, or complex medical needs (Rothman, 1991). As a result, these two disciplines may receive more training than others in the competencies necessary for service coordination. The demands of the early intervention system, however, require that members of each discipline involved in service delivery receive adequate preparation to fulfill both the spirit and intent of the law.

The regulations of Part H of IDEA do not establish discipline-specific requirements for service coordinators. Rather, the general qualifications for this position include:

1. Knowledge of early intervention legislation on a state and federal level
2. Knowledge of infants and toddlers with disabilities
3. Knowledge of available resources
4. Knowledge of the procedural safeguards available to families

The role of service coordinator is most critical to the implementation of the family-centered philosophy of the law. Rather than act on behalf of families, or as a restraint on optimal service provision, the service coordinator must facilitate the true intent of the law: to support families in their caregiving role (Dunst & Trivette, 1989). Service coordination must occur within a collaborative problemsolving partnership between the coordinator and family (Bailey, 1989a). The overall process includes the following activities:

(1) coordinating the performance of evaluations and assessments; (2) facilitating and participating in the development, review and evaluation of IFSPs; (3) assisting families in identifying available service providers; (4) coordinating and monitoring the delivery of available services; (5) informing families of the availability of advocacy services; (6) coordinating with medical and health providers; and (7) facilitating the development of a transition plan to preschool services, if appropriate. (Mental Health Law Project, 1990)

In a coordinated system, the family and child actively participate in a productive and constructive process that views the infant or toddler from their family's perspective (Hausslein, Kaufmann, &

Hurth, 1992); this is the ultimate goal of effective service coordination and collaborative service delivery (Dunst & Trivette, 1989).

The role of the service coordinator was apparently ignored in Polly's early intervention program. A service coordinator could help Polly's family manage the IFSP process. Furthermore, if the service coordinator was another parent, Polly's family could enjoy a supportive parent-to-parent relationship. Finally, a service coordinator could help Polly's family to identify and access those early intervention services and supports that would enhance, rather than undermine, their sense of family unity.

SERVICE DELIVERY COLLABORATION: THE KEY TO PROGRAM IMPLEMENTATION

While the success of program development efforts hinges on the effectiveness of interagency collaboration, service delivery must ultimately be implemented by individual service providers. There is no doubt that infants, toddlers, and their families require the services of professionals with a wide variety of skills (Bailey, 1989b). Personnel having medical expertise, therapeutic expertise, education and developmental expertise, and social service expertise are necessary to help establish and implement a viable intervention program. Part H of IDEA recognizes 12 separate professional disciplines that may be involved in service delivery (see Brown & Rule, chap. 9, this volume). In addition, the specific needs of the individual infant or toddler, the program emphasis, and the program location will also dictate personnel needs.

In Polly's situation, early intervention services were provided by professionals from several different agencies. Whether such services are provided through an inter- or intra-agency team, the personnel involved will have to adopt a team model to ensure effective collaborative service delivery (McCollum & Hughes, 1988). Those involved must be prepared to function in an optimum fashion to meet the family's self-identified needs related to the infant or toddler with a disability. The success of the interventions will depend on the manner in which the team functions.

The provisions of Part H of IDEA require that both the assessment and the IFSP be completed by a multidisciplinary team (representatives from at least two professional disciplines, and the family). However, transforming a group of individuals into a functional team requires much more than bestowing the label of a team on the group. A group of people becomes a team when their purpose and function are derived from a common philosophy with shared goals (Maddux, 1988). Table 2 lists the most important distinguishing characteris-

Table 2. Groups versus teams

Groups	Teams
Members think they are grouped together for administrative purposes only. Individuals work independently; sometimes at cross purposes with others.	Members recognize their interdependence and understand both personal and team goals are best accomplished with mutual support. Time is not wasted struggling over "turf" or attempting personal gain at the expense of others.
Members tend to focus on themselves because they are not sufficiently involved in planning the unit's objectives. They approach their job simply as a hired hand.	Members feel a sense of ownership for their jobs and unit because they are committed to goals they helped establish.
Members are told what to do rather than being asked what the best approach would be. Suggestions are not encouraged.	Members contribute to the organization's success by applying their unique talent and knowledge to team objectives.
Members distrust the motives of colleagues because they do not understand the role of other members. Expressions of opinion or disagreement are considered divisive and non-supportive.	Members work in a climate of trust and are encouraged to openly express ideas, opinions, disagreements and feelings. Questions are welcomed.
Members are so cautious about what they say that real understanding is not possible. Game playing may occur and communication traps may be set to catch the unwary.	Members practice open and honest communication. They make an effort to understand each other's point of view.
Members may receive good training but are limited in applying it to the job by the supervisor or other group members.	Members are encouraged to develop skills and apply what they learn on the job. They receive the support of the team.
Members find themselves in conflict situations which they do not know how to resolve. Their supervisor may put off intervention until serious damage is done.	Members recognize conflict is a normal aspect of human interaction, but they view such situations as an opportunity for new ideas and creativity. They work to resolve conflict quickly and constructively.
Members may or may not participate in decisions affecting the team. Conformity often appears to be more important than positive results.	Members participate in decisions affecting the team, but understand that their leaders must make a final ruling whenever the team cannot decide or an emergency exists. Positive results, not conformity, are the goal.

From Maddux, R.E. (1988). *Team building: An exercise in leadership.* Los Altos, CA: Crisp Publications; reprinted by permission.

tics of the two. There is a growing body of literature on the team-development process, and the scope of this chapter precludes an in-depth discussion of such.

Types of Team Models

The types of teams that typically function in early intervention have been identified as multidisciplinary, interdisciplinary, and transdisciplinary. While the transdisciplinary team model has been identified as the ideal for early intervention, other team models have also been identified and used for service delivery (Gibbs & Teti, 1990; Hanson & Lynch, 1989; McGonigel & Garland, 1988; Raver, 1991). A number of components that differentiate between types of teams have been identified, including the role of the family on the team, the mode of communication between team members, the role-clarification process, and the mode of intervention.

Multidisciplinary Teams   On a multidisciplinary team, the professionals represent their own discipline and provide isolated assessment and intervention services. This includes individual report writing, individual goal setting, and discipline-specific direct intervention with the child and/or family. The parent is invited to share information with the professionals, and the professionals in turn share the information from assessment, intervention, and follow-up with the family through an "informing" conference. There is minimal integration across disciplines, and the family are passive recipients of information about their child. This model makes it very difficult to develop coordinated, comprehensive programs for children and their families (McCormick & Goldman, 1979).

Interdisciplinary Teams   On an interdisciplinary team, each of the professionals carry out specific disciplinary assessments and interventions. The degree of communication between the professionals and the family represents a formal commitment to the sharing of information throughout the process of assessment, planning, and intervention (Bailey, 1984). However, the assessments and interventions are usually implemented by individuals representing separate disciplines. In many cases, the parents are active members of the team, but their input is generally considered secondary in importance to the material collected by the professionals.

Transdisciplinary Teams   On a transdisciplinary team, the members share roles and purposefully cross discipline boundaries. The communication style in this type of model involves continuous give and take between all the members of the team (especially the parents) on a regular, planned basis. Professionals from different disciplines teach, learn, and work together to accomplish a common set of service goals for a child and his or her family. The role differentiation between disciplines is defined by the needs of the situation, as opposed to discipline-specific characteristics. Assessment, intervention, and evaluation are carried out jointly by designated members of the team.

The primary purpose of the transdisciplinary approach is to pool and integrate the expertise of team members so that more efficient and comprehensive assessment and intervention plans and services can be provided (Hutchinson, 1978; Sailor & Guess, 1983). Other characteristics of the transdisciplinary team are joint team effort, joint staff development, and role release (McCollum & Hughes, 1988; Noonan & Kilgo, 1987; Woodruff & McGonigel, 1988).

Role release can be defined as a sharing and exchange of certain roles and responsibilities among team members (Lyon & Lyon, 1980; Orelove & Sobsey, 1991). Specifically, it involves a "releasing" of some functions traditionally associated with one's primary discipline. Effective implementation of the role-release process requires adequate sharing of information and training, as well as a willingness among participants to cooperate. Team members must have a solid foundation in their own discipline, combined with a recognition of the roles and competencies of the other disciplines represented on the team.

Role release may mean that one discipline implements intervention services traditionally associated with another discipline. However, team members continue to be recognized as the authority on their own primary discipline; role release is not role swapping. After techniques are appropriately taught to representatives of another discipline, these representatives must continue to be monitored or supervised by members of the authoritative discipline. The concept of role release also recognizes that parents and other family members have valuable expertise and must be considered a vital part of the service delivery team, and that their involvement in the team process must be actively encouraged by all team members.

In the transdisciplinary team model, the child's program is primarily implemented by a single person or a few persons. The role of the direct service provider is supported through the process of role release, with ongoing consultation provided by team members from various disciplines. In some programs, it is the teacher and program assistants who take on the major direct-service roles. Related-services support staff, most commonly therapists, often serve as consultants. This does not mean that therapists stop providing direct services to children. In reality, in order for therapists to be effective consultants, they need to maintain direct contact with the infant or toddler. The provision of indirect services should never be used as a strategy to justify the reduction of support staff.

There are four assumptions that govern the transdisciplinary team model:

1. Natural environments are the best place to assess and develop children's abilities.
2. Children should be taught clusters of skills needed for everyday living. These skills are best taught through natural routines and activities.
3. Discipline-specific goals and objectives should be implemented throughout the day and in all the settings in which the child functions.
4. Skills must be taught and reinforced in the settings in which they naturally occur. (Orelove & Sobsey, 1991, p. 15)

Although the transdisciplinary model may appear simple in concept, implementation of this approach can be difficult. Barriers to the implementation of the transdisciplinary approach tend to arise out of the differences between this model and the more familiar, traditional team structures. These barriers have been identified as philosophical and professional, interpersonal, and administrative (for a thorough discussion of these, see Orelove & Sobsey, 1991).

As with effective interagency service delivery models, collaboration is an inherent part of the transdisciplinary team approach. A transdisciplinary team is one in which the members perceive that they can achieve their own goal if, and only if, the other team members also achieve their respective goals. The collaborative team model may be described as a three-step process in which members: 1) develop positive interdependence (agreeing to do all that is in their power to achieve a mutually accepted goal); 2) practice collaborative skills; and 3) monitor and discuss their performance of collaborative behaviors (Fox et al., 1986).

The team that is providing services to Polly is made up of both inter- and intra-agency personnel. In order for them to provide transdisciplinary services, the members of the service team will have to collaboratively develop a service structure that accomplishes the IFSP goals while respecting the schedule and priorities of Polly's family. One practice that must be initiated by the service team is a regular meeting during which the various professionals can identify mutual goals and service strategies. Since the nurses are the professionals most often in contact with Polly, it seems reasonable to suggest that the nurses (along with the parents) assume the primary service delivery role. In this scenario, the therapists and teachers will monitor Polly, but focus most of their attention on the training and support of the nurses and parents through a consultation model. The key component in the success of this model will be the ability of the members to commit the time necessary to build relationships and encourage role release for the benefit of Polly and her family.

The Team Process

Whether developing an interagency collaborative agreement or a collaborative service delivery plan, the common denominator of effectiveness is the use of a functional process (Dyer, 1977). Unfortunately, service providers often lack the skills necessary to maintain a team process. These skills include the ability to overcome barriers, the motivation to accomplish the team's mission and goals, and the perseverance to maintain positive interactions (Starcevich & Stowell, 1990). Five factors that affect the development and maintenance of a team have been identified (Shonk, 1982). It is important for members to be aware of these factors and to understand how they influence team development and maintenance.

   1. Team Composition and Representation   There are many factors that influence the performance and development of the team. The program or agency affiliation of the members will exert a strong influence on the team process. For example, the resources available to the team will depend on the participating programs and/or agencies. These resources can include money, administrative support, and time. Teams with fewer resources will need to be more creative in identifying and implementing solutions.

   Additionally, the group's size and membership will affect collaborative outcomes. Different teams will have variations in structure, and all agencies and/or disciplines will not necessarily be represented on every team. The number of personnel and the variety of roles that they play may vary dramatically, depending on the needs of the child and his or her family and on the purpose of the team.

   2. Team Goals   Teams must devote time to identifying their goals and objectives. A truly effective team is made up of members who share responsibility for accomplishing common goals. An effective team will:

Have goals that are clearly understood and communicated to all team members   A collaborative philosophy or mission is the team's overall reason for existence and provides the team with a focus for its actions. A written statement of the collaborative philosophy will clearly delineate the team's direction. A team will function effectively to the extent that its philosophy and purpose is clear and agreed upon.

Have ownership of the goals and participate in setting them   All the team members (including the family) need to feel that their input is valued. This helps to ensure that the goals are clearly understood by everyone on the team.

Have goals that are operationally defined and measurable Goals must be written in such a way that everyone has a clear understanding of what is expected, and how attainment of the goal is to be determined and measured.

Share individual or personal objectives with one another Since teams are comprised of individuals, it is important to respect the human elements of any team.

3. Roles Within the Team The members of the team are unique individuals who each have different skills, knowledge, and personalities. In order for a team to be effective, each individual must have a clear role and identified responsibilities. Ambiguity is a major cause of conflict, therefore team members must continually clarify their current roles, including that of the leader.

In addition to the typical professional roles, responsibilities, and contributions of team members, there are other roles members will assume with regard to team development, maintenance, and problemsolving. These roles, or functions, as they are sometimes called, must occur within the group in order for the team to progress effectively.

To facilitate an effective team process, every team member has a responsibility to:

Share their expertise with other team members.

Offer recommendations for addressing service or child needs from their perspective or area of expertise.

Listen actively and use good communication skills, be clear and concise when reporting information, and avoid the use of jargon that other team members may not understand.

Recognize the contributions of other team members, and encourage the sharing of information.

Prepare the family for their role on the team and encourage their active participation.

4. Team Work Style The team's work style will affect the team's development and overall effectiveness. Effective team decisions will result from the use of a systematic problemsolving process. If a team's problemsolving process is haphazard, there is decreased likelihood that their decisions will be appropriate (Shonk, 1982). When a formalized, systematic process of problemsolving is applied, the probability of an effective outcome is increased. Systematic problemsolving will ensure that members are satisfied with and committed to the decisions that are made.

A variety of problemsolving models have been developed. For example, Project BRIDGE (Prentice & Spencer, 1986) has developed a five-step decisionmaking model for teams. It has been recommended that each step in the problemsolving process be used as a check point for teams to evaluate their ideas and practices in relationship or comparison to best practices for exemplary services in the field of early childhood special education. The steps include:

Problem formulation and information gathering   The problem must be described in clear and observable terms. Resources should be identified, and the team should focus on the facts, rather than opinions.

Generating proposals for solutions   As many alternatives as possible should be generated from all participants. Without being judgmental, the team must build positively on all suggestions.

Selecting alternatives and testing solutions   The team must judge the available resources, and evaluate the alternatives for attaining the solution. The team should decide whether or not the solution makes good use of the resources, is cost effective, and fits the needs and goals of the child and family.

Action planning and implementation   The team should assign specific responsibilities to individuals, determine timelines, and develop procedures for monitoring the plan. The plan should then be communicated to all relevant personnel.

Monitoring and evaluation   The team should determine how to judge the success of their decision. The team should select a unit of evaluation, decide how often to evaluate, and modify the plan as needed.

Problemsolving, as well as other team tasks, should take place during planned meetings, which are the hub of the team process. The team must work face-to-face in order to function, and the team meeting functions as a vehicle for facilitating the completion of the team's tasks and the achievement of its goals. The well-functioning team meets at regularly scheduled times, and all team members attend. Communication between the team members becomes a habit. An effective team meeting begins with a purpose or goal reflected in a written agenda, which should be distributed before the meeting so that team members can prepare to discuss the issues at hand. Rules should keep the meeting moving by establishing participants' roles and responsibilities (including those of a facilitator and a recorder), time frames for topics, and confidentiality policies. A meeting record should be kept to validate recommended actions and follow-up.

5. Team Membership   A team comprises individuals who are products of their past experiences and, consequently, bring different attitudes, values, and beliefs with them to the team. Individuals also bring expectations about the team: how it should function and what it should accomplish, for example. The personalities of the team members may ultimately determine the team's effectiveness.

Team leaders must adapt their style to meet the diverse needs and styles of the individuals who make up the group. The team leader should foster a climate in which all members feel free to contribute their ideas. In this atmosphere, the members can express differing viewpoints and proposed solutions.

Teams may have formal leaders who are assigned, appointed, or elected by group endorsement. Informal leaders may emerge because of their influence. The team may accept or propel a person into an informal leadership role for a number of reasons: his or her knowledge, skill, personal qualities, or because of the ineffectiveness of the formal leadership. Often, both types of leaders operate simultaneously. This can precipitate problems if the team members ignore the distinctions between informal and formal roles or misappropriate the functions of each. A team leader has a number of roles or functions with regard to a team's development. The main function of the leader is to focus the team on its collective responsibility, which is to ensure that collaborative early intervention services are delivered effectively.

As previously stated, the leadership role within an early intervention service delivery team should be assumed by the service coordinator. The service coordinator has responsibility for ensuring that the team members put aside their individual agendas in order to focus on the needs of the family and child. The service coordinator will have to facilitate the communication process so that team members develop mutual goals and strategies with the family. Communication is one skill that all team members will have to prioritize in order to develop an effective and functional team process.

CONCLUDING COMMENTS

Part H allows an opportunity for agencies, programs, and service providers to create an early intervention system that is built on a philosophy of collaborative service design and delivery. Families and service providers must strive to achieve the collaboration necessary to effectively implement early intervention programs that meet the needs of eligible children. Accomplishing this goal requires the adoption of both interagency and transdisciplinary models of service delivery.

In order to successfully implement a collaborative service-delivery model, both agencies and service providers will have to adopt a framework of group process. The process for both involves the establishment of a common vision or goal, the development of joint strategies for achieving the goal, and an ongoing system of collaborative activities. Above all, the collaborative process for both agencies and service providers should be relationship driven.

Hopefully, as states move toward full implementation of IDEA, experiences like those of Polly and her family will be eliminated. Polly did remain at home, and her parents did secure a model Medicaid waiver policy and begin to direct and limit the involvement of the many service providers. This all came about as a result of a parent-to-parent project that matched Polly's family with a parent of an older child who had needs similar to Polly's. The "veteran parent" took on the role of service coordinator after Polly's family requested assistance. Regular meetings among all the service providers were established, and a service delivery program and schedule were revised to meet the needs of the family. Most importantly, the providers communicated the issues surrounding Polly's care to their supervisors, who then began to formalize an interagency process to assist other children in situations similar to Polly's. Lastly, the state agencies involved in the provision of early intervention services began to communicate with each other about common areas of need and collaborative policy development.

REFERENCES

Audette, R.H. (1980). Interagency collaboration: The bottom line. In J.O. Elder & P.R. Magrab (Eds.), *Coordinating services to handicapped children: A handbook for interagency collaboration* (pp. 25–44). Baltimore: Paul H. Brookes Publishing Co.

Bailey, D. (1984). A triaxial model of the interdisciplinary team and group process. *Exceptional Children, 51*(1), 17–25.

Bailey, D. (1989a). Case management in early intervention. *Journal of Early Intervention, 13,* 120–134.

Bailey, D.B., Jr. (1989b). Issues and directions in preparing professionals to work with young handicapped children and their families. In J.J. Gallagher, P.L. Trohanis, & R.M. Clifford (Eds.), *Policy implementation and PL 99-457: Planning for young children with special needs* (pp. 97–132). Baltimore: Paul H. Brookes Publishing Co.

Brewer, E., McPherson, M., Magrab, P., & Hutchins, V. (1989). Family-centered, community-based, coordinated care for children with special health care needs. *Pediatrics, 83*(6), 1055–1060.

Dokecki, P.R., & Heflinger, C.A. (1989). Strengthening families of young children with handicapping conditions: Mapping backward from the "street level." In J.J. Gallagher, P.L. Trohanis, & R.M. Clifford (Eds.), *Policy Implementation & PL 99-457: Planning for young children with special needs* (pp. 59–84). Baltimore: Paul H. Brookes Publishing Co.

Dunst, C., & Trivette, C. (1988). *Protocol of resources and support scale.* Unpublished scale, Family, Infant and Preschool Program, Western Carolina Center, Morganton, NC.

Dunst, C., & Trivette, C. (1989). An enablement and empowerment perspective of case management. *Topics in Early Childhood Special Education, 8*(4), 87–102.

Dyer, W. (1977). *Team building: Issues and alternatives.* Reading, MA: Addison-Wesley.

Education of the Handicapped Act Amendments of 1986, PL 99-457. (October 8, 1986). Title 20 U.S.C. 1400 et seq: *U.S. Statutes at Large, 100,* 1145–1177.

Elder, J.O. (1980a). Essential components in development of interagency collaboration. In J.O. Elder & P.R. Magrab. (Eds), *Coordinating services to handicapped children; A handbook for interagency collaboration* (pp. 181–202) Baltimore: Paul H. Brookes Publishing Co.

Elder, J.O. (1980b). Writing interagency agreements. In J.O. Elder & P.R. Magrab (Eds.), *Coordinating services to handicapped children: A handbook for interagency collaboration* (pp. 203–242). Baltimore: Paul H. Brookes Publishing Co.

Elder, J.O., & Magrab, P.R. (Eds.). (1980). *Coordinating services to handicapped children: A handbook for interagency collaboration.* Baltimore: Paul H. Brookes Publishing Co.

Featherstone, H. (1980). *A difference in the family: Living with a disabled child.* New York: Penguin Books.

Fisher, R., & Brown, S. (1989). *Getting together: Building relationships as we negotiate.* New York: Penguin Books.

Fox, W., Thousand, J., Williams, W., Fox, T., Towne, P., Reid, R., Conn-Powers, M., & Calcagni, L. (1986). *Best educational practices '86: Educating learners with severe handicaps.* Burlington: University of Vermont, Center for Developmental Disabilities.

Garland, C., & Linder, T. (1988). Administrative challenges in early intervention. In J.B. Jordan, J.J. Gallagher, P.L. Hutinger, & M.B. Karnes (Eds.), *Early childhood special education: Birth to three* (pp. 5–27). Reston, VA: Council for Exceptional Children.

Gibbs, E.D., & Teti, D.M. (Eds.). (1990). *Interdisciplinary assessment of infants: A guide for early intervention professionals.* Baltimore: Paul H. Brookes Publishing Co.

Gilkerson, L. (1990). Understanding institutional functioning style: A resource for hospital and early interventions collaboration. *Infants and Young Children, 2*(3), 22–30. Rockville, MD: Aspen Publishers, Inc.

Hall, H.B. (1980). The intangible human factor: The most critical coordination variable. In J.O. Elder & P.R. Magrab (Eds.), *Coordinating services to handicapped children: A handbook for interagency collaboration* (pp. 45–62). Baltimore: Paul H. Brookes Publishing Co.

Hanson, M., & Lynch, E. (1989). *Early intervention: Implementing child and family services for infants and toddlers who are at-risk or disabled.* Austin, TX: PRO-ED.

Hausslein, E.B., Kaufmann, R.K., & Hurth, J. (1992). From case management to service coordination: Families, policymaking and Part H. *Zero to Three, 12*(3), 10–12.

Hazel, R., Barber, P. A., Roberts, S., Behr, S., Helmsetter, E., & Guess, D. (1988). *A community approach to an integrated service system for children with special needs.* Baltimore: Paul H. Brookes Publishing Co.

Healy, A., Keesee, P.D., & Smith, B.S. (1989). *Early services for children with special needs: Transactions for family support* (2nd ed.). Baltimore: Paul H. Brookes Publishing Co.

Hutchinson, D. (1978). The transdisciplinary approach. In J. Curry & K. Peppe (Eds.), *Mental retardation: Nursing approaches to care* (pp. 65–74). St. Louis: C.V. Mosby.

Johnson, D.W., & Johnson, F.P. (1987). *Joining together: Group theory and group skills* (3rd ed.). Englewood Cliffs, NJ: Prentice Hall.

Kanter, R.M. (1989, November–December). The new managerial work. *Harvard Business Review,* pp. 85–92.

Lyon, S., & Lyon, G. (1980). Team functioning and staff development: A role release approach to providing integrated educational services for severely handicapped students. *Journal of The Association for the Severely Handicapped, 5,*(3), 250–263.

Maddux, R.B. (1988). *Team building: An exercise in leadership.* Los Altos, CA: Crisp Publications.

Magrab, P., Kazuk, E., & Greene, L. (1981). *Community workbook for collaborative services to preschool handicapped children.* (Available from Georgetown University Child Development Center, 3800 Reservoir Rd., N.W., Washington, DC 20007.)

McCollum, J., & Hughes, M. (1988). Staffing patterns and team models in infancy programs. In J.B. Jordan, J.J. Gallagher, P.L. Hutinger, & M.B. Karnes (Eds.), *Early childhood special education: Birth to three* (pp. 129–146). Reston, VA: Council for Exceptional Children.

McCormick, L., & Goldman, R. (1979). The transdisciplinary model: Implications for service delivery and personnel preparation for the severely and profoundly handicapped. *AAESPH Review, 4,* 152–162.

McGonigel, M., & Garland, C. (1988). The individualized family service plan and the early intervention team: Team and family issues and recommended practices. *Infants and Young Children, 1*(1), 10–21.

McGonigel, M.J., Kaufmann R.K., & Johnson, B.H. (Eds.). (1991). *Guidelines and recommended practices for the individualized family service plan.* Washington, DC: National Early Childhood Technical Assistance System (NEC*TAS) and Association for the Care of Children's Health (ACCH).

McNulty, B.A. (1989). Leadership and policy strategies for interagency planning: Meeting the early childhood mandate. In J.J. Gallagher, P.L. Trohanis, & R.M. Clifford (Eds.), *Policy implementation & PL 99-457: Planning for young children with special needs* (pp. 147–168). Baltimore: Paul H. Brookes Publishing Co.

Melaville, A.I., & Blank, M.J. (1991). *What it takes: Structuring interagency partnerships to connect children and families with comprehensive services.* Washington, DC: Education and Human Services Consortium.

Mental Health Law Project. (1990). *Early intervention advocacy network: Notebook.* Mental Health Law Project, January, 1990.

Noonan, M., & Kilgo, J. (1987). Transition services for early age individuals with severe mental retardation. In R. Ianacone & R. Stodden (Eds.), *Transition issues and directions* (pp. 25–37). Reston, VA: Council for Exceptional Children.

Orelove, F.P., & Sobsey, D. (1991). *Educating children with multiple disabilities: A transdisciplinary approach* (2nd ed.). Baltimore: Paul H. Brookes Publishing Co.

Prentice, R.R., & Spencer, P.E. (1986). *Project Bridge; decision-making for early services: A team approach.* Illinois: American Academy of Pediatrics.

Raver, S.A. (1991). *Strategies for teaching at-risk and handicapped infants and toddlers.* New York: Macmillan Publishing Company.

Rothman, J. (1991). A model of case management: Toward empirically based practice. *Social Work, 36*(6), 520–528.

Rubin, S., & Quinn-Curran, N. (1983). Lost, then found: Parents' journey through the community service maze. In M. Seligman (Ed.), *The family with a handicapped child: Understanding and treatment* (pp. 63–94). New York: Grune & Stratton.

Sailor, W., & Guess, D. (1983). *Severely handicapped students: An instructional design.* Boston, MA: Houghton Mifflin.

Shenet, M.A. (1982). *State education coordination efforts: Summary.* (Project Rep. No. 1449). Washington, DC: Urban Institute.

Shonk, J.H. (1982). *Working in teams: A practical manual for improving work groups.* New York: AMACOM.

Starcevich, M., & Stowell, S. (1990). Team effectiveness questionnaire. In M. Starcevich & S. Stowell, *Teamwork: We have met the enemy and they are us.* Bartlesville, OK: The Center for Management and Organization Effectiveness.

Trohanis, P.L. (1989). An introduction to PL 99-457 and the national policy agenda for serving young children with special needs and their families. In J.J. Gallagher, P.L. Trohanis, & R.M. Clifford (Eds.), *Policy implementation & PL 99-457: Planning for young children with special needs* (pp. 1–18). Baltimore: Paul H. Brookes Publishing Co.

Woodruff, G., & McGonigel, M. (1988). Early intervention team approaches: The transdisciplinary model. In J.B. Jordan, J.J. Gallagher, P.L. Hutinger, & M.B. Karnes (Eds.), *Early childhood special education: Birth to three* (pp. 163–181). Reston, VA: Council for Exceptional Children.

Woodruff, G., McGonigel, M., Garland, C., Zeitlin, S., Chazkel-Hochman, J., Shanahan, K., Toole, A., & Vincent, L. (1985). *Planning programs for infants.* Chapel Hill: University of North Carolina.

Curricula for Early Intervention

Susan R. Sandall

This chapter addresses two major topics in the design and delivery of early intervention for infants and toddlers. The first is the development and use of the individualized family service plan (IFSP). The purpose of the plan is to allow the family and the rest of the early intervention team to plan and work together to identify existing resources and methods of reaching the family's goals. The second set of issues concerns the design and implementation of intervention activities to meet goals for enhancing the infant's or toddler's development. These are issues of curriculum content and methods.

THE INDIVIDUALIZED FAMILY SERVICE PLAN

An Overview

The IFSP, required by PL 99-457, serves as the driving force behind early intervention. A sample IFSP is provided in Appendix A at the end of this chapter. Each plan is individually tailored to meet the needs of the young child and his or her family. The law and regulations that provide guidance for developing IFSPs explicitly acknowledge the family as the central focus of early intervention policies and practices. That is, families are the context within which early intervention efforts take place, families participate in the assessment and intervention process, and families make decisions for and about themselves and their child with a disability. Dunst and his colleagues (1991) argue that the IFSP process and product should be family-centered, not simply family-focused. Family-centered intervention is described as "a combination of beliefs and practices that define particular ways of working with families that are consumer-driven and competency enhancing" (Dunst, Johanson, Trivette, & Hamby, 1991, p. 115).

The degree to which the process of developing and implementing a family plan is positive and supportive is largely determined by the attitudes and skills of the early intervention professionals. A national task force developed the following set of principles to guide the IFSP process:

Infants and toddlers are uniquely dependent on their families for their survival and nurturance. This dependence necessitates a family-centered approach to early intervention.

States and programs should define "family" in a way that reflects the diversity of family patterns and structures.

Each family has its own structure, roles, values, beliefs, and coping styles. Respect for and acceptance of this diversity is a cornerstone of family-centered early intervention.

Early intervention systems and strategies must reflect a respect for the racial, ethnic, cultural, and socio-economic diversity of families.

Respect for family autonomy, independence and decision making means that families must be able to choose the level and nature of early intervention's involvement in their lives.

Family/professional collaboration and partnerships are the keys to family-centered early intervention and to successful implementation of the IFSP process.

An enabling approach to working with families requires that professionals reexamine their traditional roles and practices and develop new practices when necessary—practices that promote mutual respect and partnerships.

Early intervention services should be flexible, accessible, and responsive to family-identified needs.

Early intervention services should be provided according to the normalization principle—that is, families should have access to services provided in as normal a fashion and environment as possible and that promote the integration of the child and family within the community.

No one agency or discipline can meet the diverse and complex needs of infants and toddlers with special needs and their families. Therefore, a team approach to planning and implementing the IFSP is necessary. (McGonigel, 1991, p. 9)

Components of the IFSP

The IFSP is a written document developed by a multidisciplinary team, including the parents or guardians, that comprises the following components:

1. A statement of the infant's or toddler's present levels of physical development (including vision, hearing, and health status), cognitive development, communication development, social or emotional development, and adaptive development, based on acceptable, objective criteria
2. A statement of the family's resources, priorities, and concerns relating to enhancing the family's capacity to meet the developmental needs of their infant or toddler with a disability
3. A statement of the major outcomes expected to be achieved for the infant or toddler and family, and the criteria, procedures, and timelines to be used to track progress and to determine whether modifications or revisions of the goals or services are necessary
4. A statement of specific early intervention services necessary to meet the needs of the infant or toddler and the family, and of the necessary frequency, intensity, and method of delivering services
5. A statement of the natural environments in which early intervention services shall appropriately be provided
6. The projected dates for initiation of services and the anticipated duration of such services
7. The name of the service coordinator, who is a member of the profession most immediately relevant to the infant's, toddler's, or family's needs, or who is otherwise qualified to carry out all applicable duties, who will be responsible for the implementation of the plan and for coordination with other persons and agencies
8. The steps to be taken to support the transition of the toddler with a disability to services provided by public school districts

Further regulations (Federal Register, Department of Education, 34 CFR, Part 303) elaborate on the IFSP requirements specified in PL 99-457 itself. In addition, PL 102-119, in reauthorizing Part H of PL 99-457, makes changes in the requirements for IFSPs, both in terms of the language of the law and in the addition of another component to the IFSP document, the requirement that services be provided in natural environments.

Development of the IFSP

The development of the IFSP is a cooperative effort. Team members generate accounts of the child's current level of functioning. Multiple sources and methods are used to gather this information and to describe the child's abilities, interests, and qualities (see McLean & McCormick, chap. 3, this volume). Parents and other family members add important information based on their intimate knowledge of the child. A careful and accurate description of the child's strengths and needs leads to a discussion of important and meaningful goals or outcomes. The effects of the services and supports provided will ultimately be evaluated in relation to the description of the child's level of functioning at the time that the IFSP is composed.

With the concurrence of the family, the IFSP may also include a statement of the family's resources, priorities, and concerns. A variety of methods are useful in gathering this information, including checklists and needs surveys, informal conversations, and focused interviews (Bailey & Simeonsson, 1988). Summers and her colleagues (1990) found that families generally prefer an informal and relaxed approach to information gathering. The purpose of this process is to assist the family in identifying their hopes and dreams for their child and themselves and in discovering the ways that they can attain these hopes and dreams. The sharing of family information should arise out of trust between team members. Because this component of the IFSP is potentially intrusive, it is voluntary, and may change and expand over time as trust and confidence are established among team members.

From this sharing of information by the team, the process proceeds to a delineation of target outcomes. Outcomes are positive statements of the changes that team members want to see for the child and family. They are written in easily understood terms and include a description of what is to occur during service delivery and of what is expected as a result of these actions. Deal, Dunst, and Trivette (1989) suggest that outcomes be written as "in order to" statements, capturing both the process and the expected outcome. Some examples of acceptable outcome statements are:

Tony will develop more mature eating skills in order to eat at the dinner table.

Mr. and Mrs. Whitley will find an afternoon babysitter for Brian so that Mrs. Whitley can return to her job.

Maria will use single words to request actions or things.

Jermaine will creep forward on his hands and knees in order to move around the house or yard.

Someone will be identified to go with Mrs. De Palma to the doctor's appointments so that she can better understand Michelle's medical problems.

As outcomes are generated, the discussion expands to include identification of the resources, strategies, and actions necessary for the accomplishment of those outcomes. Contributions to this discussion should include the family's knowledge of their own resources, strengths, and preferences; the professionals' knowledge of child development and specialized intervention methods; and the team's knowledge of community resources. Outcomes and actions should be prioritized; the plan itself should include specification of the agreed-upon criteria, procedures, and timelines. Additional components of the written plan are descriptions of the specific services and supports to be provided and of the planned frequency, intensity, and methods of delivering these services and supports. The settings for intervention are also to be specified. Appendix A, a sample IFSP, illustrates these components. Additional examples of IFSPs and descriptions of the process can be found in McGonigel, Kaufman, and Johnson (1991).

The name of the service coordinator also appears on the IFSP. The primary responsibilities of this individual are to identify, procure, coordinate, and evaluate services and supports. Thus, the service coordinator must be knowledgeable about the legalities of early intervention and the availability of services. This individual should also be skilled in such areas as bargaining, negotiating, and mediating. However, the service coordinator is not to supplant the family by making decisions for them or taking the place of existing supports, and a parent may, in fact, be the service coordinator for their own or another family. An effective service coordinator builds on a family's capabilities, shares new information and skills as needed, and strengthens the family's own role in identifying, procuring, coordinating, and evaluating services (Bailey, 1989; Dunst, 1989).

A final element of the IFSP document is a plan to support the child's transition to preschool services at age 3 if the child continues to be eligible for special services. This component is designed to ensure the smooth continuation of services and supports. Planning for transition should also be incorporated into the IFSP process (Kilgo, Richard, & Noonan, 1989).

A number of safeguards are in place to guarantee that an individualized plan is written and implemented in a timely manner for each eligible infant and family; the plan must be written within 45 days of determination of eligibility. With parental consent, early intervention services may begin immediately upon the determination of eligibility. In this situation, an interim IFSP, with the name of the service coordinator and a description of immediate services, is composed and signed. The multidisciplinary assessment and IFSP must still be completed in 45 days.

The IFSP process follows the general sequence outlined above. The steps and activities involved in composing the IFSP are interconnected. The process should be flexible and responsive to an individual family's situation. Families may differ in almost every aspect of the process, such as the amount of their participation and the time spent on specific topics and activities. The nature of the outcomes and actions generated will certainly be specific to each family.

Use of the IFSP

The IFSP maps the route for early intervention. It must be reviewed every 6 months, and it is recommended that the plan be used and reviewed even more frequently. Families have repeatedly told professionals and researchers that they want IFSPs to be dynamic plans that truly reflect their own family's situation and that can be adjusted to address changes in the family's situation (Able-Boone, Sandall, Loughry, & Frederick, 1990; Summers et al., 1990). Deal et al. (1989) provide an example of a flexible format for developing and using IFSPs in this manner.

An IFSP is a plan for an individual child and family. In the remainder of this chapter, the focus widens to the master plan, or comprehensive curriculum, and to strategies for individualizing intervention in accordance with this plan.

EARLY INTERVENTION CURRICULA

Early intervention programs share a common goal: to promote the development of infants and toddlers who either have disabilities or are at risk for developmental difficulties. As noted above, early intervention programs must have a strong family focus. There is growing evidence that such efforts have broad-based effects on child, parent, and family functioning (Dunst et al., 1991; Simeonsson & Bailey, 1990).

The definition of the promotion of infant and toddler development can be further expanded to include maximizing the child's self-esteem, problemsolving capabilities, and behaviors that lead to greater independence. The curriculum is the master plan of activities and experiences designed to help reach these goals. By definition, curriculum includes both what to teach (content) and how to teach (methods). Exemplary early intervention curricula include a number of necessary components: a philosophical framework, a scope and sequence, sound instructional methods, a variety of activities and experiences, methods of promoting generalization, strategies for the use of the physical environment, systems for adapting to unique needs, and methods for data collection and use.

Philosophical Framework

The activities and experiences provided for infants and toddlers should flow from a sound philosophical framework. This framework underlies the nature and conduct of the early intervention enterprise. Effective intervention programs explicitly state their framework in terms of the role of the infant, of the family and other caregivers (including teachers and therapists), and of the environment. Early intervention curricula are influenced by child development research and changing theoretical perspectives, and the perspectives described below have been particularly influential.

The Maturational Perspective   This perspective is closely associated with the work of Arnold Gesell (Gesell, 1925; Gesell & Ilg, 1949). His careful observations of young children provided the basis for his own developmental schedules and numerous assessment tools that followed. This perspective emphasizes biologically determined maturation and views development in terms of a linear model. Early experiences are designed to permit the infant to act on his or her innate tendencies toward self-expression. The interventionist's role is to create the warm, positive atmosphere that sets the stage for age-appropriate enrichment activities.

The Behavioral Perspective   This perspective emphasizes the effects of the environment and of environmental manipulations on development and learning. Associated with the work of Skinner (1974) and others, this perspective has exerted a strong influence on intervention efforts, especially in special education. This perspective has also influenced infant research that has documented infants' learning capabilities and contingency awareness. In terms of intervention, the goal is to teach the child skills and information that are considered useful and valuable. The interventionist carefully organizes the learning environment and sequences activities to maximize the acquisition of targeted behaviors, and children are reinforced for the production of those behaviors.

The Interactional Perspective   This perspective views biological and environmental factors as mutually influencing one another. For the child, this interaction results in the continual reorganization of mental structures. This perspective is typically associated with the work of Piaget (1952), who put forth the principle of the infant as an interactive organism. Varied experiences are provided to allow infants to initiate interactions and to actively experiment, and these experiences are carefully sequenced to promote development. The interventionist organizes the social and physical environment to engage and challenge the infant.

Sameroff and Chandler (1975) expanded on the notion of mutual influences. They describe the "transactional" effects of familial, social, and environmental factors on human development. Their conceptualization of the transactional perspective has had a major influence on intervention efforts, heightening awareness of environmental factors and of the importance of socially responsive environments.

The Ecological Perspective   This perspective, developed by Bronfenbrenner (1979), has also influenced early intervention and infant curricula. Infants are viewed as living and developing as members of different ecological settings. In terms of intervention efforts, the adult must recognize the multiple contexts and interrelationships of infant and family life and must also be aware of the direct and indirect effects of intervention and other systemic changes. From this perspective, the infant is not the sole focus of intervention; the ecological settings must also change to support the infant's existing capabilities, to enhance the development of new capabilities, and to buffer stressful events. The infant is viewed as a dynamic and interactive learner. The interventionist mediates systems-level change. Intervention efforts built on this perspective attend to the goodness-of-fit between the infant and the environment (Thurman & Widerstrom, 1990).

In adopting and stating a philosophical framework, early interventionists are making decisions about what, and how, to teach. In reviewing and selecting published curricula, one should look for a clear statement of philosophy, as an explicit philosophy is crucial for cohesiveness and continuity (Bricker, 1989).

Scope and Sequence

Scope refers to the spectrum of goals of a curriculum. The scope of infant curricula is based on developmental theory and includes the typical developmental accomplishments of infancy and toddlerhood, which are stated as long-term goals. These goals are further broken down into short-term or intermediate objectives, which are then sequenced in some fashion. Dependent on the philosophical framework of their designers, curricula differ in their relative emphasis on developmental products or processes, in the functionality of goals and objectives, and in the breadth of curricular content.

Traditionally, curricular contents are grouped into developmental domains: motor (gross and fine), cognitive, communicative, social–emotional, and adaptive. While such demarcations may be useful for organizational purposes, they may not convey the interrelated and interdependent nature of the different facets of early development (Berkeley & Ludlow, 1989). Lewis (1984) suggested that early intervention practices should incorporate the principle that development proceeds from undifferentiated (interrelated) to differentiated skills. Curricular content should reflect the various interconnections inherent in early development. Interventionists are responsible for implementing services in such a way that the infant develops and learns integrated, meaningful behaviors.

Early relationships and the nature of caregiving environments are critical to development. The scope of infant curricula must reflect this through the inclusion of such important content areas as caregiver–infant interaction and social–communicative behavior. Content should be directed toward assisting infants to initiate and maintain interactions with their parents and other social partners.

The developmental-domains approach may not fully capture the range of important content areas for infants and toddlers. Other critical areas to be included in a comprehensive curriculum include additional areas of infant growth and development such as self-regulation and nutrition, and process issues such as transition from early intervention services. Furthermore, comprehensive curricula include a conceptualization of family involvement.

Useful infant curricula provide interventionists with sequences of behaviors or activities. The purposes are to foster positive developmental change and to provide appropriate learning challenges to the child. Traditionally, curriculum developers have borrowed these sequences from the maturational or developmental-milestones model as presented on norm-referenced tests. Dunst (1982) identified several potential pitfalls of using this approach: items on infant tests may be ordered in particular ways for psychometric reasons, rather than as representations of developmental progressions; once behaviors are placed in a linear sequence, interventionists may presume that all behaviors must be taught in that sequence; developmental milestones do not necessarily present sequences for teaching, and may be irrelevant for children with disabilities (Bailey & Wolery, 1984); and placement of behaviors in linear sequences may further exacerbate the potential risk of teaching discreet and nonintegrated behaviors. There are also alternative paths of development (Fisher, 1980) that some children with developmental disabilities undoubtedly may follow to reach developmental and/or adaptive outcomes.

Bricker (1989) advises that curricula developers use developmental theory as a framework for specifying long-term goals, short-term objectives, and intervention sequences. She warns, however, that these should be viewed as general guidelines. Interventionists must expect that infants will demonstrate their own developmental progressions, and must respond to individual children and their unique family contexts. Curricular sequences help interventionists to organize and plan intervention, but rigid adherence to particular sequences may be counterproductive.

Instructional Methods

Infant curricula differ in both the specificity and types of instructional methods used. In this section, the focus is on methods that involve planned interaction between adult and infant; modifications of the physical environment are described in a later section.

Early interventionists need to be familiar with a variety of instructional methods in order to meet the needs of children. These methods should result in developmental progress and mesh with the cultural beliefs and values of the child's family and community. Bailey and McWilliam (1990) specify four characteristics of good instructional methods: they are effective, efficient, functional, and normalized.

The philosophical framework of the curriculum determines which instructional methods are used. The maturational perspective is associated with enrichment activities. The behavioral perspective is associated with direct-instruction methods. The interactional and ecological perspectives are associated with a variety of both responsive and active-learning techniques. A selection of instructional methods are described below. Standard names for these methods are not always used in the literature. The reader will also note that these methods are not entirely distinct; there is some commonality across them.

Enrichment   Inasmuch as the adult assumes a largely supportive and nurturing role, the methods associated with this approach are not instructional per se. Rather, the adult sets the stage for development by providing a stimulus-rich environment and age-appropriate toys and activities. The infant sets the pace, and play and self-expression are encouraged.

Direct Instruction   The methods involved in direct instruction include specification and systematic analysis of objectives, sequencing of learning steps, and systematic reinforcement of the targeted objective, or approximations of the objective, as specified in the learning steps. Activities and learning tasks are generally teacher-directed.

Incidental Teaching   Incidental teaching is a naturalistic instructional method in which targets are preselected and prompts are used in a particular sequence. It involves the arrangement of the environment to evoke the child's attention. The interventionist uses this child-selected incident to respond to the child's initiation, to elaborate, and to reinforce the child's use, or attempted use, of the targeted behavior (Hart, 1985). Incidental teaching is one of the procedures used in an approach called milieu teaching. Milieu teaching is a set of naturalistic procedures that involves environmental arrangements and the use of specific strategies (e.g., modeling, time delay) in everyday exchanges (Warren & Kaiser, 1986). These procedures have been used primarily to teach language and communication behaviors.

Activity-Based Intervention   This method is "a child-directed, transactional approach that embeds intervention on children's individual goals and objectives in routine, planned, or child-initiated activities, and uses logically occurring antecedents and consequences to develop functional and generative skills" (Bricker & Cripe, 1992, p. 40). It is designed to take advantage of natural events and routines in an objective and measurable way. It is similar to other naturalistic strategies, but has been used with a wider range of target behaviors and with groups of young children as well as individuals.

Response-Contingent Learning   These methods have as a specific purpose to enable infants to learn that their behaviors have an impact on the environment (Brinker & Lewis 1982; Dunst & Lesko, 1988). The infants, in effect, "learn to learn." These methods are based on the principle that infants who partake of opportunities for response-contingent learning are competent learners. The procedures are developed through careful observation and planning for individual children. The interventionist does not directly elicit the behavioral target; the infant must first perform the behavior, after which the consequence is consistently provided. This focus on responsiveness differentiates these procedures from those that put the adult in the role of stimulator of infant behavior.

All of the methods described above focus rather directly on the infant's behavior and behavioral change. The following procedures focus on caregivers, as well as infants, and also take into account the possible indirect effects of intervention.

Parent–Infant Interaction   Parent–infant interaction has received a great deal of attention in recent years. Many of the responsive and interactional procedures previously described are useful when the aim is balanced, positive, productive parent–infant interaction, rather than particular infant behaviors. Interventions that focus on parent–infant interaction are known by a variety of names, including social-reciprocity interventions, interactive coaching, partnerships, turntaking, and relationship-focused interventions. These methods share some common features; they each involve encouraging social exchanges, following the child's lead, taking turns, and elaborating on the interaction. Some sources of information on parent–infant interaction intervention are: Bromwich (1981), Calhoun, Rose, and Prendergast (1991), Fraiberg (1971), Hanson and Krentz (1986), Hussey-Gardner (1988), MacDonald and Gillette (1989), Mahoney and Powell (1986), Manolson (1983), and McCollum and Stayton (1985).

Social Support   Social support refers to social networks, including persons and institutions, and resources, including information and materials provided to families. There are formal sources of support, such as professionals and agencies, and also informal sources, including family, friends, and coworkers. Using an ecological and social-systems framework, Dunst, Trivette, and Deal (1988) reconceptualized early intervention as encompassing many types of support, such as respite care, talking with a friend, receiving information on job training or child development, and a host of other types of assistance. Direct intervention aimed at the infant is just one piece of a much larger picture. Dunst and Trivette (1990) report evidence from their research that social support can be an effective form of early intervention that enhances family well-being and lessens the impact of distress.

Experiences and Activities

An additional characteristic of an early intervention curriculum is the inclusion of activities and ideas as learning experiences. Infants are active and interactive learners; they thrive on social experiences. And the caregiving environment plays a crucial role in their development.

Early development occurs primarily within the social context. It makes sense, therefore, that learning experiences should be highly social, and should promote social behaviors. In particular, curricula should take advantage of and seek to promote positive interactions between infants and their significant, consistent social partners. The importance of intervention activities that promote caregiver–infant interaction has been repeatedly described for a variety of intervention settings, including NICUs (e.g., Gottwald & Thurman, 1990), homes (e.g., Barrera, Rosenbaum, & Cunningham, 1986), and centers (e.g., Rose & Calhoun, 1990).

Infants and toddlers and their caregivers participate in a number of routines throughout the day. Some of these fulfill a particular need, such as feeding, diapering, and bathing. Some interactions are specifically playful. Other routines occur at the numerous transition points during the day, such as getting up from a nap or getting ready to go outside. Individual objectives can often be naturally embedded into these routines and transitions. Doing so increases the probability that targeted behaviors are functional and meaningful for the infant and for the parent or caregiver. This process also incorporates natural conditions to set the occasion for and to support targeted behaviors. Furthermore, the use of natural routines probably increases the number of teaching and learning opportunities. It should be apparent that the effective use of naturally occurring routines does not simply happen, but requires careful planning.

Activities and experiences should also promote the infant's engagement or active involvement with the environment. Engagement refers to the amount of time a child spends in developmentally and contextually appropriate behavior (McWilliam, 1991). Activities and experiences that promote engagement capture the infant's attention and interest, match the infant's level of competence, and maintain the infant's interest in order to promote development. In addition, activities and experiences must be accessible to the infant. Some young children cannot or will not engage with the environment independently, so curricula must include procedures to help children to initiate and sustain interactions. Since infants and toddlers have their own unique interests and preferences, curricula should include a wide variety of activities and experiences that are appropriate for the age and capabilities of infants. Also, a range of activities and experiences that elaborate and extend the infant's attention should be provided.

It is both possible and preferable to integrate objectives from different domains into the same activity or routine. In this way, the infant is viewed as a whole person, and development is viewed as an integrated process. The infant's individual objectives can be effectively combined to optimize teaching and learning. Consider the following episode with Eddie and his father:

Eddie is in his infant seat and his father is preparing to feed him some cereal. As dad sits down, he taps the spoon on the bowl. Eddie gazes at his father. Dad asks, "Ready to eat?" and Eddie wiggles. Dad scoops some cereal into the spoon and brings it toward Eddie's mouth. Eddie takes the cereal off the spoon with his lips and tongue. Dad says, "Mmm, that's some good cereal." Eddie wiggles and moves his arms. Dad asks, "Would you like some more?" and scoops more cereal onto the spoon.

In this small caregiving activity, we see that several of Eddie's current objectives have been included: using upper lip movements to take food off of a spoon, turning and looking toward a sound, initiating and maintaining interactions with adults, and making beginning reaching movements.

Interventionists should have a variety of activities and experiences available to them. In reviewing and selecting infant curricula, users should consider such issues as range, variety, and social aspects of activities, use of natural routines, promotion of active engagement, and integration of multiple objectives into activities.

Generalization

Another standard by which we evaluate infant curricula is the degree to which they promote the generalization of targeted behaviors. Generalization occurs when a behavior learned in one situation is used in another (Kazdin, 1975). Generalization can occur across settings, (e.g., home, child care center, park), people (e.g., mother, grandmother, occupational therapist), and across other conditions, such as materials and directions.

A consistent and troubling finding in the research literature is the poor rate of generalization of newly acquired behaviors to functional, less-structured settings by individuals with disabilities (Guess, Sailor, Keogh, & Baer, 1976; Stokes & Baer, 1977; Warren, Rogers-Warren, Baer, & Guess, 1980). Consequently, effective curricula must include procedures for ensuring the generalization of behaviors.

According to Bailey and McWilliam (1990), functional procedures promote generalization. Many of the procedures described above are functional and are useful both for the acquisition of new behaviors and for generalization. The selection of functional, meaningful behaviors as targets of instruction is a first step in planning for generalization. If the behavior is truly functional, the infant will have any number of opportunities to practice and use the behavior across settings, people, and materials. In addition, Bricker (1989) notes that targeted behaviors should reflect conceptual or response classes, rather than singular, highly specific behaviors. Other effective generalization strategies include the provision of teaching and learning opportunities in natural environments and the use of materials, examples, people, and cues that are commonly available. Distributed practice also contributes to generalization (Holvoet, Guess, Mulligan, & Brown, 1980), and the use of naturally occurring routines and events allows for distributed practice.

The Physical Environment

The description of critical content and strategies has thus far focused on the social aspects of early intervention, but the physical environment also plays an important role. The physical environment includes furnishings, materials, toys, and equipment, and the organization, scheduling, and use of these items.

The quality of the environment affects infant development (Elardo & Bradley, 1981; Wachs, 1979), and research shows that manipulation of the environment can affect child behavior and influence child engagement (Dunst, McWilliam, & Holbert, 1986). Furthermore, environmental manipulations represent relatively unobtrusive and natural interventions. As such, these types of interventions may be considered normalized procedures.

Basic environmental supports include organization of the physical space and schedule to decrease confusion and increase predictability. The broad range of environmental manipulations in the NICU has included such procedures as reduction of noise, light, and activity to promote self-regulation by preterm infants (Gottfried & Gaiter, 1985), positioning of highly interesting materials to promote communication (McCollum & Stayton, 1985), and selection of toys to elicit mastery behaviors (Jaeger, Meidl, & Hupp, 1989).

The physical environment can be designed or modified to create opportunities for infants to initiate and to learn that their actions can have external consequences. Such responsive and contingent environments lead to continued interactions and further learning opportunities (Brinker & Lewis, 1982; Dunst, Cushing, & Vance, 1985). Provision of response-contingent settings entails more than allowing access to interesting toys or materials. Infants must have actual opportunities to act or to manipulate a toy. This may require careful placement or positioning or the use of adapted switches. Many readily available infant toys, such as rattles, chime balls, and busy boxes provide immediate and contingent feedback. Jaeger et al. (1989) and Langley (1985) provide some useful formats for assessing and using toys.

In reviewing and evaluating infant curricula, the interventionist should consider the attention given to the physical environment and the provision of strategies for effectively using the physical environment to foster development and learning.

Curricular Adaptations

Recommended practice guidelines in early intervention encourage methods that promote the delivery of services and supports in locations close to the family (McGonigel et al., 1991). Such locations include homes, child care centers, nurseries, special centers, and many other settings. The core curriculum for programs that deliver services and supports close to the family must also be broad enough to address the needs of infants and toddlers of varying abilities. Furthermore, curricula must be adaptable enough to meet the unique needs of individual infants and toddlers with developmental difficulties.

A variety of supports and resources will facilitate the process of adapting and individualizing a core curriculum. These include access to specialists who provide consultation and technical assistance, availability of highly specialized curricula, and use of broad-based curricula that are adaptable for infants with sensory, motor, health, or other specialized needs. Sparling (1989) suggests that early interventionists work as a team to embed narrow-spectrum (highly specialized) curricula within broad-spectrum (comprehensive) curricula.

The needs of children and early interventionists could be met, at least in part, if developers of curricula provided strategies and suggestions for adaptations. Fewell and Sandall (1983), for example, offer general guidelines for making such modifications for young children with hearing, vision, or motor disabilities.

Data Collection and Evaluation

Another necessary component of an effective and useful infant curriculum is a set of procedures for collecting and using data. Such procedures are used to monitor change and evaluate the effects of the intervention. High-quality early intervention programs regularly monitor the effects of their efforts. Chapter 10 of this volume provides more extensive information on evaluation.

A number of methods are available for collecting infant data. Selection of a particular method will be based on consideration of the objective or outcome, the skills and preferences of the interventionists, and the resources available. Regardless of the method, data should be collected regularly and systematically.

Anecdotal records are written notes made by the interventionist or parent. Notes include factual accounts of activities, experiences, and the infant's performance, but may also include subjective or interpretive information. Anecdotal records are generally written from memory following a session or visit. This reliance on memory may be a limitation, but careful notetaking can be very useful for recounting the last session and planning for the next.

Interventionists may also use developmental checklists as a way of collecting data and monitoring progress. Developmental checklists are lists of skills or behaviors that represent important indicators of developmental change. Such checklists are generally easy to use; the interventionist usually records the infant's performance by simply checking off the item or recording the date the behavior was observed. Since checklists may be sequences of skills or behaviors drawn from the developmental milestones perspective, some of the same limitations described for this perspective apply here as well. The checklist can also be constructed to represent a logical teaching sequence.

Permanent product samples that may be useful for infants and toddlers include audiotapes, videotapes, and still photographs. Permanent product samples should be collected at regular intervals in order to document change. For example, audiotapes of a toddler, recorded every month or so during a storybook activity, would help to document changes in the child's verbal behavior. Permanent products often provide valuable illustrations of progress, but their use can be time consuming and more expensive than other methods.

Performance data are counts or timings of specified behaviors, based on direct observation. Since the data are based on direct observations, they provide objective information on the young child's meaningful and functional use of the behavior. As with the other methods, performance data must be collected often to be useful in making instructional decisions and monitoring change.

Further information on monitoring change in children may be found in Bricker and Cripe (1992) and in Wolery, Bailey, and Sugai (1988).

The data-collection systems outlined above focus on infants and toddlers. Similar methods may be appropriate for monitoring change in family outcomes. However, some methods may be discomforting for families; family self-report may be sufficient for this component of the IFSP. Goal-attainment scaling has also been used to evaluate progress in both infant and family IFSP outcomes (Bailey & Simeonsson, 1988; Dunst, Leet, & Trivette, 1988).

Child-performance data is used to make individual decisions about the effects of the intervention, and collectively, such information can be used to make decisions about the effects of a program for groups of children. Program-evaluation data should be linked to the goals of the program. Data should not be limited to child performance, but also should include records, careful descriptions, satisfaction surveys, family reports, and a host of other methods that assist in answering evaluation questions. For more information on program evaluation, see Bickman and Weatherford (1986).

Technology

Technology applications for very young children are limited but growing. PL 100-407, the Technology-Related Assistance for Individuals with Disabilities Act of 1988, is expected to have a major impact on research and development efforts for individuals of all ages, including infants and toddlers.

Technology applications can provide young children with tools for play and for daily living, including the critical communicative function. Furthermore, technology can provide access to many traditional early childhood activities. Most technological interventions have been designed for children with sensory or physical disabilities, but other young children may benefit as well. Technology can allow young children opportunities for play, socialization, and language learning, and can help them to learn to independently manipulate the environment (Behrmann, Jones, & Wilds, 1989). Matching technology with a child's needs and abilities is sometimes difficult. Each child must be individually assessed to determine potential benefits and to identify the appropriate methods and devices.

There are a number of skills that appear to be necessary to access much of the available hardware and software. Two of these are a reliable and consistent motor movement and some knowledge of cause and effect. Luckily, these and other basic skills can be taught without expensive computers and technological devices. Battery-operated toys, for example, can be adapted to be operated by a switch (Burkhardt, 1980, 1982). Switches require activation, but this does not always mean pressing the switch with one's hand; switches can be activated with pressure from other body parts, by eye blinks, breath puffs, or with the voice. Battery-operated toys can be used to teach cause and effect, and can be incorporated into interactive play to facilitate communication and cognitive development (Hutinger, Mietus, Robinson, Weaver, & Whitaker, 1986; Musselwhite, 1986).

Microcomputer technology has also been used to help infants with developmental delays in contingency learning (Brinker & Lewis, 1982; Sullivan & Lewis, 1990). The intervention involves the use of a microcomputer, specialized software, and adaptive toys. The participating infants have demonstrated positive emotional behavior, increased attention, and improved learning, memory, and self-regulation.

Augmentative communication is another important technology application. Recent advances provide the means for young children with disabilities to actively participate in the communication process. A variety of augmentative communication devices and computers with peripherals are available even for very young children. Again, the selection of equipment and communication options is complicated and individualized.

There are many potential benefits to the use of technology with young children. Technology intervention should be integrated with the individual goals for a child and with the goals for the early intervention program as a whole. That is, technology should be used as a means to maximize a child's ability to learn to become independent.

CONCLUDING COMMENTS

In a very real sense, early intervention program personnel construct their own comprehensive curriculum. This is a team effort. Two crucial components of this process are the clear specification of the program's goals and a statement of the program's philosophy. These should be consistent with recommended guidelines for services and practices that strengthen families, recognize and support diversity, and are also effective, efficient, and normalized.

"Early intervention" refers to a wide range of activities. The shared goal is to enhance the infant's development and learning. Thus, a critical piece of the master plan of any early intervention program is that which focuses directly on the procedures for meeting goals and objectives—the infant curriculum.

Many infant curriculum and activity guides are commercially available. Early intervention personnel must be careful and thoughtful consumers. Reviews of selected infant curricula are provided in Appendix B, at the end of this chapter. Selection guidelines are based on breadth of content; inclusion of sequences and multiple activities; applicability to young children with developmental delays, rather than only to children with specific conditions; and attention to the components described in this chapter. Early intervention personnel are encouraged to review the many other available curricula and activity guides to construct a master plan that matches the philosophy of their program and addresses the concerns of the children and families with whom they work.

Early interventionists are engaged in the important work of designing and implementing appropriate and effective services and supports for infants and families. This work requires not just knowledge and skill, but a spirit of cooperation that ensures that families and team members work together. In this chapter, guidelines for the development of both individual plans and a master plan have been provided. These plans should include only sound and effective procedures that meet the needs of infants and their families.

REFERENCES

Able-Boone, H., Sandall, S.R., Loughry, A., & Frederick, L.L. (1990). An informed, family-centered approach to Public Law 99-457: Parental views. *Topics in Early Childhood Special Education, 10*(1), 100–111.

Bailey, D.B. (1989). Case management in early intervention. *Journal of Early Intervention, 13*, 120–134.

Bailey, D.B., & McWilliam, R.A. (1990). Normalizing early intervention. *Topics in Early Childhood Special Education, 10*(2), 33–47.

Bailey, D.B., & Simeonsson, R.J. (1988). *Family assessment in early intervention.* Columbus, OH: Charles E. Merrill.

Bailey, D.B., & Wolery, M. (1984). *Teaching infants and preschoolers with handicaps.* Columbus, OH: Charles E. Merrill.

Barrera, M.E., Rosenbaum, P.L., & Cunningham, C.E. (1986). Early home intervention with low-birth-weight infants and their parents. *Child Development, 57*, 20–33.

Behrmann, M.M., Jones, J.K., & Wilds, M.L. (1989). Technology intervention for very young children with disabilities. *Infants and Young Children, 1*(4), 66–77.

Berkeley, T.R., & Ludlow, B.L. (1989). Toward a reconceptualization of the developmental model. *Topics in Early Childhood Special Education, 9*(3), 51–66.

Bickman, L., & Weatherford, D. (1986). *Evaluating early intervention programs for severely handicapped children and their families.* Austin, TX: PRO-ED.

Bricker, D. (1989). *Early intervention for at-risk and handicapped infants, toddlers, and preschool children.* Palo Alto, CA: VORT Corp.

Bricker, D., & Cripe, J.J.W. (1992). *An activity-based approach to early intervention.* Baltimore: Paul H. Brookes Publishing Co.

Brinker, R., & Lewis, M. (1982). Making the world work with microcomputers: A learning prosthesis for handicapped infants. *Exceptional Children, 49,* 163–170.

Bromwich, R. (1981). *Working with parents and infants: An interactional approach.* Austin, TX: PRO-ED.

Bronfenbrenner, U. (1979). *The ecology of human development: Experiments by nature and design.* Cambridge: Harvard University Press.

Burkhardt, L.J. (1980). *Homemade battery powered toys and educational devices for severely handicapped children.* College Park, MD: Author.

Burkhardt, L.J. (1982). *More homemade battery devices for severely handicapped children with suggested activities.* College Park, MD: Author.

Calhoun, M.L., Rose, T.L., & Prendergast, D.E. (1991). *Charlotte Circle intervention guide for parent–child interactions.* Tucson, AZ: Communication Skill Builders.

Deal, A.C., Dunst, C.J., & Trivette, A.M. (1989). A flexible and functional approach to developing Individualized Family Support Plans. *Infants and Young Children, 1*(4), 32–43.

Dunst, C.J. (1982). Theoretical bases and pragmatic considerations. In J.D. Anderson (Ed.), *Curricula for high risk and handicapped infants* (pp. 13–23). Chapel Hill, NC: TADS.

Dunst, C.J. (1989, October). *Case management practices in early intervention.* Paper presented at the International Conference on Children with Special Needs, Division for Early Childhood, Minneapolis.

Dunst, C.J., Cushing, P.J., & Vance, S. (1985). Response-contingent learning in profoundly handicapped infants: A social systems perspective. *Analysis and Intervention in Developmental Disabilities, 5,* 33–47.

Dunst, C.J., Johanson, C., Trivette, C.M., & Hamby, D. (1991). Family-oriented early intervention policies and practices: Family-centered or not? *Exceptional Children, 58*(2), 115–126.

Dunst, C.J., Leet, H., & Trivette, C.M. (1988). Family resources, personal well-being, and early intervention. *The Journal of Special Education, 22,* 108–116.

Dunst, C.J., & Lesko, J. (1988). Promoting the active learning capabilities of young children with handicaps. *Early Childhood Intervention Monographs, 1.* Morganton, NC: Family, Infant and Preschool Program, Western Carolina Center.

Dunst, C.J., McWilliam, R.A., & Holbert, K. (1986). Assessment of preschool classroom environments. *Diagnostique, 11,* 212–232.

Dunst, C.J., & Trivette, C.M. (1990). Assessment of social support in early intervention programs. In S. Meisels & J. Shonkoff (Eds.), *Handbook of early childhood intervention* (pp. 326–349). New York: Cambridge University Press.

Dunst, C., Trivette, C., & Deal, A. (1988). *Enabling and empowering families.* Cambridge, MA: Brookline Books.

Education of the Handicapped Act Amendments of 1986, PL 99-457. (October 8, 1986). Title 20, U.S.C. 1400 et seq: *U.S. Statutes at Large, 100,* 1145–1177.

Elardo, R., & Bradley, R. (1981). The Home Observation for Measurement of the Environment: A review of research. *Developmental Review, 1,* 113–145.

Fewell, R.R., & Sandall, S.R. (1983). Curricular adaptations for young children: Visually handicapped, hearing impaired, and physically impaired. *Topics in Early Childhood Special Education*, 2(4), 51–66.

Fisher, K. (1980). A theory of cognitive development: The control and construction of hierarchies of skills. *Psychological Review*, 87, 477–531.

Fraiberg, S. (1971). Intervention in infancy: A program for blind infants. *Journal of the American Academy of Child Psychiatry*, 10, 381–405.

Gesell, A. (1925). *The mental growth of the preschool child*. New York: Macmillan.

Gesell, A., & Ilg, E. (1949). *Child development: An introduction to the study of human growth*. New York: Harper and Row.

Gottfried, A.W., & Gaiter, J.L. (1985). *Infant stress under intensive care: Environmental neonatology*. Baltimore: University Park Press.

Gottwald, S.R., & Thurman, S.K. (1990). Parent–infant interaction in neonatal intensive care units: Implications for research and service delivery. *Infants and Young Children*, 2(3), 1–9.

Guess, D., Sailor, W., Keogh, W., & Baer, D.M. (1976). Language development programs for severely handicapped children. In N.G. Haring & L.J. Brown (Eds.), *Teaching the severely handicapped* (Vol. 1, pp. 301–326). New York: Grune & Stratton.

Hanson, M.J., & Krentz, M.S. (1986). *Supporting parent–child interactions: A guide for early intervention program personnel*. San Francisco: San Francisco State University, Department of Special Education.

Hart, B. (1985). Naturalistic language training techniques. In S.F. Warren & A. Rogers-Warren (Eds.), *Teaching functional language* (pp. 63–88). Austin, TX: PRO-ED.

Holvoet, J., Guess, D., Mulligan, M., & Brown, F. (1980). The Individual Curriculum Sequencing Model (Part II): A teaching strategy for severely handicapped students. *Journal of The Association for Persons with Severe Handicaps*, 5, 337–351.

Hussey-Gardner, B. (1988). *Understanding my signals*. Palo Alto, CA: VORT Corporation.

Hutinger, P., Mietus, S., Robinson, L., Weaver, K., & Whitaker, K. (1986). *ACCT (Activating Children Through Technology) curriculum*. Macomb, IL: Western Illinois University.

Individuals with Disabilities Education Act Amendments of 1991, PL 102-119. (October 7, 1991). Title 20, U.S.C. 1400 et seq: *U.S. Statutes at Large, 105*, 587–608.

Jaeger, J., Meidl, D., & Hupp, S. (1989). *Exploring the world through play*. Department of Educational Psychology, University of Minnesota.

Kazdin, A.E. (1975). *Behavior modification in applied settings*. Homewood, IL: The Dorsey Press.

Kilgo, J.L., Richard, N., & Noonan, M.J. (1989). Teaming for the future: Integrating transition planning with early intervention services for young children with special needs and their families. *Infants and Young Children*, 2(2), 37–48.

Langley, M.B. (1985). Selecting, adapting, and applying toys as learning tools for handicapped children. *Topics in Early Childhood Special Education*, 5(3), 101–118.

Lewis, M. (1984). Developmental principles and their implications for at-risk and handicapped infants. In M.J. Hanson (Ed.), *Atypical infant development* (pp. 3–24). Austin, TX: PRO-ED.

MacDonald, J.D., & Gillette, Y. (1989). *ECO: A partnership program (kit)*. Chicago, IL: Riverside Press, Inc.

Mahoney, G., & Powell, A. (1986). *Transactional Intervention Program (TRIP): A child centered approach to developmental intervention with young handicapped children.* (Monograph No. 1). Farmington, CT: Pediatric Research and Training Center, University of Connecticut School of Medicine.

Manolson, A. (1983). *It takes two to talk: A Hanen early language parent guide book.* Toronto: Hanen Early Language Resource Centre.

McCollum, J.A., & Stayton, V.D. (1985), Infant/parent interaction: Studies and intervention guidelines based on the SIAI model. *Journal of the Division for Early Childhood, 9*(2), 125–135.

McGonigel, M.J. (1991). Philosophy and conceptual framework. In M.J. McGonigel, R.K. Kaufmann, & B.H. Johnson (Eds.), *Guidelines and recommended practices for the individualized family service plan* (2nd ed., pp. 7–14). Bethesda, MD: Association for the Care of Children's Health.

McGonigel, M.J., Kaufman, R.K., & Johnson, B.H. (Eds.). (1991). *Guidelines and recommended practices for the individualized family service plan* (2nd ed.). Bethesda, MD: Association for the Care of Children's Health.

McWilliam, R.A. (1991). Targeting teaching at children's use of time: Perspectives on preschoolers' engagement. *Teaching Exceptional Children, 23*(4), 42–43.

Musselwhite, C.R. (1986). *Adaptive play for special needs children: Strategies to enhance communication and learning.* San Diego: College Hill Press.

Piaget, J. (1952). *The origins of intelligence in children.* (M. Cook, Trans.). New York: International Universities Press.

Rose, T.L., & Calhoun, M.L. (1990). Project profile: The Charlotte Circle Project: A program for infants and toddlers with severe/profound disabilities. *Journal of Early Intervention, 14,* 175–185.

Sameroff, A., & Chandler, M. (1975). Reproductive risk and the continuum of caretaking casualty. In F.D. Horowitz, M. Hetherington, S. Scarr-Salapatek, & M. Siegel (Eds.), *Review of child development research* (Vol. 4, pp. 187–244). Chicago: University of Chicago Press.

Simeonsson, R.J., & Bailey, D.B. (1990). Family dimensions in early intervention. In S.J. Meisels, & J.P. Shonkoff (Eds.), *Handbook of early childhood intervention* (pp. 428–444). Cambridge: Cambridge University Press.

Skinner, B.F. (1974). *About behaviorism.* New York: Alfred A. Knopf.

Sparling, J.J. (1989). Narrow- and broad-spectrum curricula: Two necessary parts of the special child's program. *Infants and Young Children, 1*(4), 1–8.

Stokes, T.R., & Baer, D.M. (1977). An implicit technology of generalization. *Journal of Applied Behavior Analysis, 10,* 341–367.

Sullivan, M.W., & Lewis, M. (1990). Project profile: Contingency intervention: A program portrait. *Journal of Early Intervention, 14,* 367–375.

Summers, J.A., & Dell'Oliver, C., Turnbull, A.P., Benson, H.A., Santelli, E., Campbell, M., & Siegel-Causey, E. (1990). Examining the individualized family service plan process: What are family and practitioner preferences? *Topics in Early Childhood Special Education, 10*(1), 78–99.

Technology-Related Assistance for Individuals with Disabilities Education Act of 1988, PL 100-407. (August 19, 1988). Title 29, U.S.C. 2201 et seq: *U.S. Statutes at Large, 102,* 1044–1065.

Thurman, S.K., & Widerstrom, A.H. (1990). *Infants and young children with special needs: A developmental and ecological approach* (2nd ed.). Baltimore: Paul H. Brookes Publishing Co.

Wachs, T.D. (1979). Proximal experience and early cognitive-intellectual development: The physical environment. *Merrill-Palmer Quarterly, 25*, 3–41.

Warren, S.F., & Kaiser, A.P. (1986). Incidental language teaching: A critical review. *Journal of Speech and Hearing Disorders, 51*, 291–299.

Warren, S.F., Rogers-Warren, A., Baer, D.M., & Guess, D. (1980). Assessment and facilitation of language generalization. In W. Sailor, B. Wilcox, & L. Brown (Eds.), *Methods of instruction for severely handicapped students* (pp. 227–258). Baltimore: Paul H. Brookes Publishing Co.

Wolery, M., Bailey, D.B., & Sugai, G.M. (1988). *Effective teaching: Principles and procedures of applied behavior analysis with exceptional students.* Newton, MA: Allyn and Bacon.

Appendix A

Sample Individualized
Family Service Plan

INDIVIDUALIZED FAMILY SERVICE PLAN

Section 1. Identifying Information

Child's Name: David Conway   Date of Birth: 1-20-91

Address: 1298 N. Jackson #12   Phone: 427-2111

_____   County/School District: District 23

Medicaid/Insurance Company and Number: Lincoln HMO

Parent(s) or Legal Guardian(s):

(1) Name: Patrice Conway   Phone: 427-2111

Address: 1298 N. Jackson #12

(2) Name: Darrell Conway   Phone: 838-4488

Address: Rt. 2 Box 1270, Downingtown

Section 2. Service Coordination

Name of Service Coordinator:

Valerie Howard   Phone: 555-3223

IFSP Date	Initiation Date	Review Date
3-26-92	4-2-92	9-1-92

Section 3. Staffing

INTERVENTION PLANNING TEAM

Team Members	Title	Date
Patrice Conway	Mother	3-7, 3-15-92
Darrell Conway	Father	3-19-92
Valerie Howard	Early interventionist	3-7, 3-15-92
Christine Moreno	Physical Therapist	3-15-92
Sherry Costa	Speech Therapist	3-15-92
Michael Taggert	Social Worker	3-15, 3-19-92

Section 4. Child/Family Strengths and Concerns

Name: __David Conway__

Present Levels of Functioning	Strengths	Needs
__CHILD__ Assessed at Seaside on 3-15-92; home visit on 3-7-92. Assessments used: Bayley Scales of Infant Development, Play Assessment Scale, REEL, behavioral observations. Medical/health report from Dr. Fred Kemble. All results in assessment report.	David explores with eyes, hands, and mouth, vocalizes vowel sounds and sounds of displeasure, protest, rolls, pushes up in prone, sits with help. Knows mom, dad, and sister. General health is good. Vision and hearing normal.	David is fussy and difficult to satisfy. He isn't able to maintain body positions to play. He gets easily agitated. Team expressed concerns over his feeding skills.
__FAMILY__ Mother - Patrice Father - Darrell Sister - Rachel, 3 years Mother participated in multidisciplinary assessment. Father spoke with social worker before the IFSP meeting.	Resources Patrice is the primary caregiver. She and her sister share babysitting. Darrell sees the children on the weekend. Darrell is employed. He pays the rent on the apartment and lives at his parent's house.	Concerns Both parents are concerned about David's fussiness and overall delays. Patrice also said that Rachel needs more attention. Darrell would like more information on David's development and care.

Section 5. Early Intervention Services

Type of Service	Begin Service	End Service	Frequency	Intensity	Location	Method	Payor	Provider & Discipline
Home Visits	4-10-92	Continuing	1 visit per week	1½ hours	Home	Home visit	State	Seaside Early Intervention-Education
Physical Therapy	4-6-92	Continuing	1 session per week	45 min.	Doctors Hospital	Individual therapy	Lincoln HMO	Doctors Hospital-Phys. Therapy
Speech Therapy	4-10-92	Continuing	Consultation as requested		Seaside	Consultation	State	Seaside-Speech therapy
Feeding Evaluation	TBA				St. Mark's Hospital	Evaluation	Lincoln HMO	St. Mark's-Feeding clinic
Social work Family support	4-10-92	Continuing	1 contact per month	2 hours per group	ARC	Fathers group	no cost	Fathers group-ARC

SUMMARY OF CURRENT STATUS:
David will continue to receive Physical Therapy at Doctors Hospital. Home visits will be provided by The Seaside Early Intervention Program. David usually spends his time at home or with his aunt for babysitting. Home visits may include babysitting group after David becomes more comfortable. Team will consult with each other once a week to plan. Teacher/Service coordinator is responsible for planning meetings.

Section 6. Child and Family Outcomes

CHILD

Page 4 of 10

Child's Name: David Conway

Date of Plan: 3-26-92

MAJOR OUTCOMES	STEPS TOWARD MAJOR OUTCOMES	PROCEDURES	TIMELINES/ STATUS	COMMENTS/ STATUS
David will smile and make vocalizations during play and caregiving to show that he is happy, pleased, satisfied.	1. Coo and make other positive sounds during play with mom.	Team will identify good positions, activities, + times.	Achieved ___ Modified ___ Made Progress ___ Initiated ___ 1. 4-2-92	Team will discuss progress weekly.
	2. Coo, smile, and make other positive sounds during play with others.	Use turn-taking strategies during home visits.		
	Criteria: to parents' satisfaction	Videotape play at home when comfortable.		

Section 6. Child and Family Outcomes

Child's Name: __David Conway__

CHILD

Page __5__ of __10__

Date of Plan: __3-26-92__

MAJOR OUTCOMES	STEPS TOWARD MAJOR OUTCOMES	PROCEDURES	TIMELINES/ STATUS	COMMENTS/ STATUS
David will receive a feeding evaluation at St. Mark's Hospital by the end of August, 1992	1. Make referral and appointment by end of April.	Service Coordinator will contact family doctor to assist with referral.	Achieved / Modified / Made Progress / Initiated	
	2. Receive evaluation by end of August.	Service Coordinator will attend evaluation with family.		
	3. Act on recommendations.	Schedule review meeting when report received.		

Section 6. Child and Family Outcomes

CHILD

Child's Name: __David Conway__

MAJOR OUTCOMES	STEPS TOWARD MAJOR OUTCOMES	PROCEDURES	TIMELINES/ STATUS	COMMENTS/ STATUS
David will improve his balance and strength in his upper body so that he can sit by himself and play with toys.	1. Sit with head up when held at lower trunk or hips. 2. Sit while using his arms for support. 3. Sit with head up and hands free for play. Criteria: will sit by himself and play for 2-3 minutes.	Physical therapist will provide direct therapy, information, + modeling. Home visitor will help David practice during her visits. Use toys and activities that David likes.	Achieved Modified Made Progress Initiated 1. 4-2-92	

Section 6. Child and Family Outcomes   FAMILY

Page 7 of 10

Child's Name: David Conway

Date of Plan: 3-26-92

MAJOR OUTCOMES	STEPS TOWARD MAJOR OUTCOMES	PROCEDURES	TIMELINES/STATUS	COMMENTS/STATUS
Darrell will participate in ARC father's group with David in order to learn more about David's development and care.	1. Provide schedule of father's group meetings. 2. Talk with contact father from group. 3. Attend father's group.	Social worker will discuss father's group and activities with Darrell and put another father in touch with Darrell.	Achieved Modified Made Progress Initiated	

Page _8_ of _10_

Date of Plan: 3-26-92

Section 6. Child and Family Outcomes

FAMILY

Child's Name: David Conway

MAJOR OUTCOMES	STEPS TOWARD MAJOR OUTCOMES	PROCEDURES	TIMELINES/ STATUS	COMMENTS/ STATUS
Rachel will attend a play group or recreation program so that she has some special time with other children.	1. Identify low-cost play groups or recreation programs.	Social worker and teacher will provide names of programs.	Achieved / Modified / Made Progress / Initiated	
	2. Make phone calls and visit programs.	Mother will talk to friends and neighbors to find play group.		
	3. Locate play group or program by beginning of summer.	Mother will make phone calls and visits.		

Section 7. Transition Plan

Child: David Conway   Expected transition date: January, 1994

Coordinator: Valerie Howard   Target receiving site: _____

Reason for transition: Not applicable. David will be eligible for Seaside Early Intervention for the coming year.

Transition Event	Person Responsible	Dates Achieved

1. Parents informed of possible options

2. Receiving agencies contacted

3. Parents visit agencies

4. Transition conference to determine appropriate placement

5. Transfer of records

6. Written transition plan developed

7. Placement

8. Follow-up

Section 8. IFSP Team

Family:

I had the opportunity to participate in the development of this IFSP. I understand the plan, and I give permission to the Seaside Early Intervention Program to carry out the plan with me, leading toward the agreed upon outcomes.

Patrice Conway   _Jane O Conway_   _3/24/92_
Parent(s)/Legal Guardian(s)   Date

I had the opportunity to participate in the development of this IFSP. I do not agree with this plan and I do not give my permission to the _____to carry out the plan.

_____

Parent(s)/Legal Guardian(s)   Date

Other IFSP Meeting Participants:

The following individuals participated in the development of the IFSP. Each person understands and agrees to carry out the plan as it applies to their role in the provision of services.

Valerie Howard   _Michael Taggart_

Christine Moreno   _____

Sherry Costa   _____

The IFSP was developed with telephone consultation from the following people:

Fred Kemble, M.D.

Appendix *B*

Reviews of Selected Infant Curricula

The Carolina Curriculum for
Infants and Toddlers with Special Needs, Second Edition (1991)
by
Nancy M. Johnson-Martin, Kenneth G. Jens, Susan M. Attermeier,
and Bonnie J. Hacker

Publisher:

Paul H. Brookes Publishing Co.
P.O. Box 10624
Baltimore, MD 21285

Philosophical Framework:

This is a developmentally based curriculum with content drawn from norm-referenced tests, and from the work of Piaget and Uzgiris and Hunt. Instructional methods are based on a behavioral perspective. The curriculum does not assume normal development across domains or across all children with disabilities. Additional content was provided by the authors and other content specialists.

Scope and Sequence:

The curriculum is aimed at young children with disabilities functioning in the birth to 24-month age range. There are 26 areas of development, which represent finer breakdowns of the traditional areas of cognitive, communicative, adaptive, and fine and gross motor skills. Each area is broken down into behaviors, and behaviors are broken down into logical teaching steps.

Instructional Methods:

Direct instruction is the primary method.

Experiences and Activities:

A directed activity is provided for each behavior. Some behaviors include additional activities, but the number of activities is limited. Information on incorporating learning experiences into daily routines is provided.

Generalization:

Learning steps provide for the use of behaviors across materials and situations. Teaching-procedures section provides suggestions for various materials. Behaviors are functional.

Physical Environment:

Some suggestions for using the physical environment are incorporated into the guidelines for using consequences effectively.

Adaptations:

There are some suggestions within the teaching procedures for working with children with visual impairments. The curriculum includes a helpful chapter on motor development. Adaptations for children with motor impairments are also included in teaching procedures.

Data Collection:

Curriculum includes an assessment log for determining entry level and monitoring progress. An individual activity-sheet format is provided that includes space for the regular collection of infant performance data.

Developmental Programming for
Infants and Young Children (1981)
by
D. Sue Schafer and Martha S. Moersch

Publisher:

University of Michigan Press
839 Greene Street
Ann Arbor, MI 48109

Philosophical Framework:

The curriculum is based on a developmental model; developmental milestones form the basis for much of the curricular content. Piagetian theory is incorporated into the cognitive section.

The social–emotional section is based on attachment theory and ego development.

Scope and Sequence:
Materials include a guide for assessment and implementation (Volume 1), an assessment profile (Volume 2), and a set of activities (Volume 3). Volumes 1, 2, and 3 are designed for young children with disabilities and include behaviors that typically develop over the birth to 36-month age range. Domains covered are: perceptual/fine motor, cognition, language, social/emotional, self-care, and gross motor. Within domains, activities are arranged to correspond to age ranges. Within each age range there are short-term goals and suggested activities. Developmental sequences are used.

Instructional Methods:
General teaching strategies incorporate direct instruction methods into playful activities and routines. Techniques similar to incidental teaching are also encouraged.

Experiences and Activities:
A number of learning activities are provided for each objective. Some activities are numbered and sequenced and are intended to be presented in that order. Other activities are not numbered. Activities can be incorporated into home and center settings.

Generalization:
Curriculum does not provide specific attention to generalization. Use of typical activities and routines and a variety of materials should promote generalization. Use of activities, rather than discrete teaching trials, is encouraged.

Physical Environment:
Curriculum does not provide specific attention to use of the physical environment. Use of high-interest toys and materials is encouraged.

Adaptations:
Adaptations (if needed) are provided for children with motor, vision, and hearing impairments for each objective.

Data Collection:
Materials include a developmental assessment tool that is to be used for initial assessment and quarterly reviews of progress. Strategies for data collection on a daily or weekly basis are not provided.

Assessment, Evaluation, and Programming System
for Infants and Children: Volume 1,
Measurement for Birth
to Three Years (1993)
edited by
Diane Bricker,
and
Assessment, Evaluation, and Programming System
for Infants and Children: Volume 2,
Curriculum for Birth
to Three Years (1993)
edited by
Juliann Cripe, Kristine Slentz, and Diane Bricker

Publisher:
Paul H. Brookes Publishing Co.
P.O. Box 10624
Baltimore, MD 21285

Philosophical Framework:
The curriculum is based on a developmental model with the curricular content implemented with methods based on behavioral learning principles. The curriculum also incorporates a transactional perspective, as reflected in its attention to the interaction between child and the social/physical environment.

Scope and Sequence:
The Assessment, Evaluation, and Programming System has a number of components, including assessment intruments, parent evaluation forms, IEP/IFSP goals, procedures concerning family needs and outcomes, curriculum, and progress forms. The infant curriculum is designed for young children with disabilities and those at risk. The age range is 1 month to 3 years. Domains included are: fine motor, gross motor, adaptive, cognitive, social–communication, and social. Each domain is broken down into strands that organize related groups of behaviors. Each strand contains a series of long-range goals, and these goals are broken down into a series of training objectives and programming steps that represent logical instructional sequences.

Instructional Methods:
This curriculum uses activity-based instruction, and procedures for using these methods are provided first for each objective. Direct instruction methods (prompts and cues) are also given, should these be needed for some children.

Experiences and Activities:
Multiple sample activities are provided for each objective. Activities are suitable for both home and center. Attention is given to using typical or authentic activities and routines.

Generalization:
Several strategies are incorporated to increase generalization. Objectives are generalizable, functional behaviors. Activity-based instruction is built on incorporating objectives into natural activities and routines. Suggestions are provided for concurrent teaching to encourage combining objectives into activities.

Physical Environment:
Suggestions for environmental arrangements and materials are provided for each objective.

Adaptations:
Adaptations or precautions for children with sensory or motor impairments are provided for some objectives.

Data Collection:
Assessment Level I is used for initial assessment and monitoring progress. Regular (weekly or daily) monitoring of performance is recommended, and strategies are provided in supplemental materials.

HICOMP Curriculum (1983)
by
Sara J. Willoughby-Herb and John T. Neisworth

Publisher:
Merrill Publishing Company
1300 Alum Creek Drive
Columbus, OH 43216

Philosophical Framework:
The curricular content is based on developmental milestones. The behavioral perspective underlies the intervention strategies.

Scope and Sequence:
The curriculum is aimed at young children who are developmentally delayed. The age range covered is from birth to 5 years. The curriculum covers 4 domains: communication, own care, motor, and problem solving. Each domain is broken down into subdomains, within which objectives are sequenced developmentally.

Instructional Methods:
The primary methods are direct instruction strategies, including shaping, modeling, prompting, and so forth.

Experiences and Activities:
A developmental activities handbook provides activities for each objective. Activities include games, naturally occurring events, and specifically designed learning tasks.
Generalization:
The curriculum provides a section on generalization. Recommended generalization strategies are teaching in different settings and using varied instructions and materials.
Physical Environment:
Specific recommendations for use of the physical environment are not given.
Adaptations:
Recommendations for adapting activities for children with sensory or motor disabilities are not given.
Data Collection:
The curriculum includes an assessment for initial placement in the curricular sequences and a format for monitoring progress. Specific techniques and formats for daily or weekly data collection are also provided.

Infant Learning (1981)
by
Carl J. Dunst

Publisher:
DLM/Teaching Resources
One DLM Park
Allen, TX 75002
Philosophical Framework:
The author describes his approach as a neo-Piagetian perspective of sensorimotor development. Furthermore, it represents an ecological perspective with attention given to behaviors that are meaningful and useful and to the interaction of child and environment.
Scope and Sequence:
The focus is on cognitive and linguistic development. The curriculum was designed primarily for young children with disabilities. The intervention framework is organized into three levels (adaptive actions, coordinated actions, and contingency awareness). Each level contains a matrix of intervention strategies and intervention domains (covering sensorimotor domains, communication, and social play). Examples are provided to help inter-

ventionists plan in ways that incorporate behaviors, levels of intervention, and domains (or context) of intervention. Organization is sequential and hierarchical.

Instructional Methods:
Intervention strategies are provided that encourage interaction and response-contingent learning.

Experiences and Activities:
A variety of activities and experiences are provided. Use of common materials and games is encouraged. Social activities are emphasized.

Generalization:
Several strategies are incorporated to facilitate generalization. Behaviors are meaningful and functional. Activities are designed to use natural routines and common materials.

Physical Environment:
The context for development and learning is emphasized. Naturalistic situations and settings are used.

Adaptations:
Adaptations for children with sensory or motor disabilities are not given.

Data Collection:
The Uzgiris and Hunt Scales are used for initial assessment. No strategies are given for daily or weekly data collection.

Partners: Early Partners
for Low-Birth-Weight Infants (1984)
by
J. Sparling, I. Lewis, S. Neuwirth
and
Partners for Learning: Birth to 24 Months (1984)
by
J. Sparling and I. Lewis
and
Partners for Learning: 24–36 Months (1984)
by
J. Sparling and I. Lewis

Readers are also referred to the following article: Sparling, J., Lewis, I., Ramey, C.T., Wasik, B.H., Bryant, D.M., & Lavange, L.M. (1991). Partners: A curriculum to help premature, low birthweight infants get off to a good start. *Topics in Early Childhood Special Education*, 11(1), 36–55.

Publisher:

Kaplan Press

P.O. Box 609

Lewisville, NC 27023

Philosophical Framework:

This multipart curriculum is developmental and interactional. The developmental perspective incorporates knowledge of preterm and early childhood development.

Scope and Sequence:

The curriculum was developed for high-risk, preterm infants. Early Partners includes the following target areas: cues from the baby, sleep/wake states, calming, levels of stimulation, interaction/communication, muscle tone, eye–hand coordination, and independent handling and manipulation. Partners for Learning covers 23 child development areas drawn from the broad areas of cognitive/fine motor, social and self, motor, and language. Areas are developmentally sequenced and arranged for cyclical use.

Instructional Methods:

This curriculum uses a naturalistic instructional model that incorporates behavioral principles. The adult teaching skills are: preparing, attending, modeling, supporting, prompting, rescuing or revising, and building or elaborating.

Experiences and Activities:

Activities are presented as games that can be implemented by parent, home visitor, or center-based teacher. Games are to be integrated into daily life. Games/activities are presented on cards containing simple text and illustrations. Positive caregiver–child interaction is stressed.

Generalization:

Methods to support generalization include naturalistic teaching techniques and the integration of activities into daily life.

Physical Environment:

Information is provided on organizing the environment and using the activities within various locations.

Adaptations:

There are no particular adaptations for children with unique needs. However, Early Partners is aimed at premature infants.

Data Collection:

An assessment instrument for recording developmental status, determining entry level, and recording progress is included. A cumulative record sheet is used to record the activities used by a child. Methods for daily/weekly monitoring of child performance are not included.

Intervention in the Neonatal Intensive Care Unit

S. Kenneth Thurman

Since the 1970s, the treatment of critically ill infants in neonatal intensive care units (NICUs) has become commonplace in the United States. NICUs are staffed by a variety of highly skilled professionals who have specialized training in the care and treatment of these infants. The implementation of PL 99-457 has mandated the provision of services to these infants and their families beginning at birth. Thus, it is important for the practitioner involved in early intervention services to begin to understand the nature and workings of the NICU. This chapter provides the reader with an overview of the physical and social environment of the NICU and the implications of each of these for infants. In addition, the roles of various professionals in providing services in the NICU are described. Next, the chapter focuses on different medical conditions that affect these infants and the means by which those conditions are treated. The chapter ends with a discussion of developmental and behavioral interventions, with par-

The author would like to acknowledge Dr. Eileen Tyrala, Director of Newborn Services, Temple University Hospital, for her review of and suggestions for this chapter.

ticular attention paid to the need for these services to be family-centered.

THE NICU ENVIRONMENT

The history of neonatal intensive care began around the turn of the twentieth century with the work of Etienne Tarnier and Pierre Budin in Paris. These physicians developed the first incubators for infants, which were modeled on those used by zoos for young animals (Sammons & Lewis, 1985). These pioneers were the first to recognize that premature infants have difficulty with temperature control and feeding and that they are more susceptible to disease and infection. These same issues are of central importance in the treatment of premature infants today.

During the 1920s, Dr. Julian Hess established the first special care nursery for premature infants in the United States at the Sarah Morris Hospital in Chicago (Sammons & Lewis, 1985). The babies that he treated were routinely kept in incubators and were given oxygen to aid their respiration. Visitation was strictly controlled, and a number of policies were put into place to help decrease the probability of infection. Not until the 1970s did visitation policies ease so that parents could regularly visit their infants during their hospitalization.

By the mid-1970s NICUs had become commonplace in major teaching hospitals. Technology had been developed for more aggressive and specialized treatment of these infants. In addition, neonatology emerged as a recognized subspeciality within pediatrics. With this coming of age, NICUs began to treat smaller and smaller infants, as well as those with more severe illnesses and anomalies. Today, the NICU is a highly technical and sophisticated environment dedicated exclusively to the care and survival of critically ill newborns. NICUs are graded according to the level of care they provide. A Level I NICU is equipped to achieve resuscitation and stabilization of newborns. In the cases of unexpectedly small or sick babies, this would be prior to their transfer to a Level II or Level III facility. The Level I facility is also equipped for ultrasound, fetal heart-rate monitoring, radiology, and laboratory services on a 24-hour basis. Level I NICUs may provide continuing care for relatively minor problems, but they primarily provide care for convalescing babies who have returned from Level II or Level III facilities. The Level II NICU is prepared to care for small newborns with a moderate degree of illness. Some Level II hospitals have intensive care facilities, while others manage low birth weight (LBW) newborns who are otherwise normal. The Level III NICU provides comprehensive perinatal services, research and educational support, data collection, and evaluation of new technologies. The Level III NICUs differ markedly from Level II facilities and are equipped to serve critically ill infants or those with illnesses that are more complex or difficult to diagnose.

Special Equipment

Figure 1 shows the complex and technological nature of a typical NICU. These units are active 24 hours a day and often give the uninformed visitor an impression of chaos and disorganization. In reality, however, they are highly organized and staffed by well-trained professionals who specialize in the care of the critically ill newborn.

Sophisticated monitoring and treatment devices are employed to help assure that each infant in the NICU is given the utmost in care. Figure 2 shows some of the special equipment that is employed in

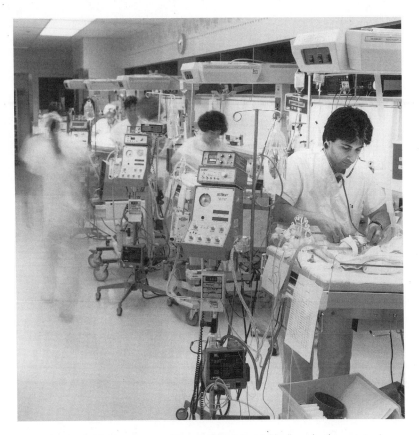

Figure 1. The NICU environment. (Photograph by Robert Coldwell; used with permission.)

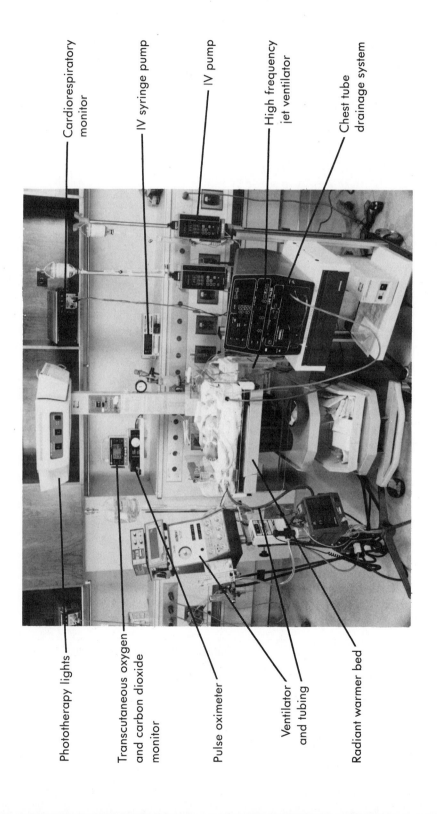

Figure 2. Some of the special equipment employed in the NICU. (Photograph by Robert Coldwell; used with permission.)

Cardiorespiratory monitor

IV syringe pump

IV pump

High frequency jet ventilator

Chest tube drainage system

Photothphy lights

Transcutaneous oxygen and carbon dioxide monitor

Pulse oximeter

Ventilator and tubing

Radiant warmer bed

treating premature infants. Each device has a specialized function, and each is employed based on the needs of a particular infant.

Warmer Bed   Since premature infants often have difficulty maintaining adequate body temperature, they may require the assistance of a warmer bed. The warmer bed provides radiant heat to the infant and is controlled by a sensor attached to the baby's skin. If the baby's temperature drops below a healthy level, the heat from the warmer increases. The warmer bed also has the advantage of providing open access to the infant, so that necessary medical and caregiving procedures can be carried out efficiently. When infants improve, they are moved to isolettes or incubators that provide continuous circulation of warm air to help maintain body temperature. Finally, when the infants are able to maintain their own temperature, they are moved to a regular bassinet, like those found in the typical newborn nursery.

Cardiorespiratory Monitor   Premature babies are often subject to lapses in breathing of more than 15 or 20 seconds, a condition called *apnea*. Often, apnea is accompanied by a significant decrease in heart rate, usually to less than 100 beats per minute, known as *bradycardia*. Either of these conditions can be life-threatening to an infant. Cardiorespiratory monitors are used to continuously assess an infant's respiration and heart rates. The monitor is attached to the skin by means of an electrode. If respiration stops for more than a few seconds, or if the heart rate falls too low, an alarm will sound, alerting NICU staff that the infant requires immediate attention.

Blood-Gas Monitors   In order to determine whether an infant's respiration is adequate, NICU staff must monitor not only the baby's breathing, but also the amount of oxygen in the blood. This may be done by drawing small amounts of blood from the infant and testing the blood directly, but blood gases can also be continually assessed through the use of a transcutaneous oxygen analyzer or a pulse oximeter. The transcutaneous oxygen analyzer provides continuous analysis of arterial oxygen tension, the pulse oximeter continuously measures oxygen saturation. Both are useful when the newborn is unstable and requires frequent changes in the level of oxygen administered.

Ventilator   Many preterm babies have lungs that are not mature enough to sustain adequate breathing independently. These babies must be placed on ventilators or respirators to maintain sufficient blood-oxygen levels. The respirator is attached by means of a tube placed into the infant's throat and trachea, and can be set to control the percentage of oxygen delivered to the infant, as well as the number of respirations per minute. A more recent advance is the *jet ventilator*, which can be set to breathe for a baby through several hundred rapid-pulsed breaths per minute, thus avoiding extreme expansion of the lungs. Jet ventilators are found only at selected hospitals and require specially trained staff to assure their proper use.

Intravenous (IV) Pumps   IV pumps are used to control the amount of medication or nutrients given to the infant through a tube attached to a vein. These tubes may be attached by a needle into one of the veins of the scalp, feet, or hands, or they may be attached by means of a catheter directly into a major vessel, such as the umbilical or jugular vein. Alarms on the pumps will sound when the flow of fluids is interrupted.

Chest Tubes and Suction Chambers   Often, the pressure applied to a premature infant's lung through the use of mechanical ventilation will cause it to develop a hole, which results in a leak, leading to a *pneumothorax*, or collapsed lung. When this occurs, the neonatologist will insert a tube into the infant's chest, which is then attached to a special suction chamber. This suction chamber removes air from the chest cavity so that the collapsed lung can reinflate.

Phototherapy Lights   Both premature and full-term infants have decreased liver function at birth. When this happens a substance called *bilirubin*, produced during the breakdown of red blood cells, which is normally metabolized by the liver, can build up in the system, causing the baby to become jaundiced. Left uncorrected, increased bilirubin levels can lead to permanent damage to an infant's nervous system. When the blood-bilirubin level is increased, the infant is placed under phototherapy lights, which, through the skin, cause a photochemical reaction that decreases the toxicity of the bilirubin. When phototherapy lights are in use, the infant's eyes are protected by covering them with cotton pads.

Environmental Neonatology

As the discussion above suggests, the physical environment of the NICU is replete with technical apparatus that is critical to maintaining infants and sustaining their lives. The application of this technology is not without negative consequence, and it is employed with the assumption that its benefits outweigh its costs. The emerging field of *environmental neonatology* (Gottfried & Gaiter, 1985; Wolke, 1987) focuses on studying the effects of the NICU environment on the infant. Wolke (1987) defines environmental neonatology as "the study of newborn special care units and their impact on the medical and developmental status of sick infants" (p. 17).

Noise   The machines that are used to treat infants in NICUs can create an environment that is quite noisy. Gottfried (1985) reported that the mean sound level in the NICU that he studied was 77.4 dB and at times reached a level as high as 109 dB. Low-frequency sounds were characterized as having the highest intensities. Lawson and Turkewitz (1985) reported a mean sound level of 72.2 dB in the NICU they studied. Wolke (1986) reported somewhat lower (i.e., 60–69 dB) average sound levels in a British NICU. When infants are placed in an incubator, their sound environment is somewhat different than that of the NICU in general. First of all, only low-frequency sounds tend to penetrate the walls of the incubators. Since human speech is often in a higher frequency range, it can be masked or obscured by the incubator. Gottfried (1985) reports the mean noise level within the incubator as being 81.1 dB. He attributes this higher noise level to the incubator's constantly running motor. Furthermore, throughout his observations, Gottfried found that nonspeech sounds were present 100% of the time, speech sounds were present 92.2% of the time, and the radio was on 79.4% of the time.

Although there is no firm evidence that noise levels in the NICU lead to permanent hearing loss in infants, the acoustic environment does have some effect. First, as several authors (Gottfried, 1985; Gottfried et al., 1981; Wolke, 1987) have indicated, infants have no control over the sounds in the NICU, nor are they able to easily match a sound with its source. Thus, the sources, intensities, types, and fluctuations in sound are all outside of the infant's control. While, to some extent, this may also be the case with all newborns and young infants, their environments are generally much less noisy, and, typically, the children are more easily able to link sounds with their sources. Wolke (1987) has speculated that babies hospitalized in NICUs may be less able to associate a particular voice with a particular face, since they do not have the opportunity to do this with the frequency of a newborn reared at home. Lawson and Turkewitz (1985) have also suggested that the constancy of sound in the NICU may impede the infants' opportunities "to form an association between a particular sound and its visual and tactile referents" (p. 168). Wolke (1987) also points out that these "infants are exposed to the described noises for weeks and sometimes months" (p. 168). He asserts further that "the noise and sound is [sic] not under the control of the infant and cannot be avoided by the infant, a classical learned helplessness situation" (p. 26).

Lawson and Turkewitz (1985) present data showing a relationship between speech in the room and the state of the infant in neonatal intensive care. They report a correlation of −.54 between the infant state of quiet sleep and speech sounds in the room. At the same time, correlations indicated a moderate relationship ($r = .47$) between speech in the room and infant quiet awake state. Peabody and Lewis

(1985) have indicated that the noise levels in the typical NICU are intense enough to wake infants from sleep. They suggest that "hospital personnel eliminate unnecessary noise, including radios, in the nursery. . . . [and that] more carefully controlled studies are needed to evaluate the effects of this environmental factor on the outcome of preterm and sick infants" (p. 205).

Light   Another environmental factor in the NICU is light. Like noise, light can be a constant in the NICU, and there is often little variation in the level of light. Glass, Avery, Subramaniou, Keys, Sostek, and Friendly (1985) report that the intensity of light has increased markedly in NICUs since the 1960s, and they present evidence to suggest that the light levels found in NICUs may be a contributing factor in retinal damage in very low birth weight infants. There is also speculation that the continuous bright lights of the NICU interfere with the establishment of natural diurnal rhythms. Gottfried (1985) reports an average illumination in the NICU of 530 lumen/m². This figure is somewhat higher than the 200 lumen/m² that Mann, Haddow, Stokes, Goodley, and Rutter (1986) reported. Although infants' eyes are patched to protect them from the light, especially during sessions of phototherapy, this practice is not without side effects. Rao and Elhassani (1981), for example, report that eye patches can cause distortions of the face, corneal injury, or conjunctivitis. Since the full extent of the effects of high levels of light is not known, Wolke (1987) suggests that lighting in the NICU be flexible, and reduced when possible. He also suggests that infants be protected from direct sunlight and that light levels be altered to simulate day and night rhythms.

Touching and Handling   In order to be treated, babies in the NICU must be touched and handled. Much of this touching is related to the medical maintenance of the infant. Jones (1982) presents data that indicate that ill and premature infants are given both medical and general care at rates that are as much as eight times higher than their full-term well peers. Murdoch and Darlow (1984) reported that babies under 1500 grams in their study received a mean of 234 procedures that involved handling in a 24-hour period. On average, this would mean that infants are being handled about once every six minutes. While much of this handling is necessary to ensure proper care of the infant, data from other researchers suggests that handling may disrupt sleep patterns (Gabriel, Grote, & Jonas, 1981) and physiological states (Gorski, 1984; Gorski, Hole, Leonard, & Martin, 1983; Murdoch & Darlow, 1984) and may be related to increases in intraventricular hemorrhage (IVH) (Volpe, 1990). Much of the touching and handling of infants in the NICU can be done in clusters spread out at intervals (Lawhon & Melzar, 1988). By using a clustering technique, some of the adverse effects of handling may be reduced. In summary, Wolke (1987) has suggested that "there is a bad fit between the infant's need for behavioural [sic] and physiological organization and the handling in the NICU. . . . Furthermore, the sicker the infant, the more adverse are the procedures and the higher the stress for the baby" (p. 30).

Social Aspects of the NICU Environment

The complexity of the NICU environment does not end with its physical features. The NICU is also a complex social environment. Of importance are not only the social interactions between the infants and their caregivers, but also the social environment among the caregivers themselves.

In the mid-1970s, largely due to the work of Klaus and Kennell (1976), interest began to focus on bonding between hospitalized newborns and their mothers. It was hypothesized that the separation brought about by hospitalization interfered with the development of the bonding, or initial attachment between a mother and her infant. Although later research has not clearly substantiated this position, the work of Klaus and Kennell can be credited with establishing the need for concern about the social interactions and environments of infants in NICUs.

A number of studies have suggested that there is relatively little social contact between parents and infants during NICU hospitalization. According to Jones (1982), about 90% of the touching an infant receives in the NICU comes from individuals other than the baby's parents. Linn, Horowitz, Buddin, Leake, and Fox (1985) reported that mothers were seen interacting with their NICU-confined infants less than 5% of the time, on average. It must be pointed out that these data were collected only during daytime hours, rather than during the evening, when parents are more likely to visit.

Jones (1982) reports that NICU staff were in contact with infants with respiratory distress 22% of the time, those with surgical problems 28.5% of the time, and those with complex histories 30.7% of the time. These figures are for personal contact only, and include contact for medical or general care. In contrast, she reports that total staff contact with infants in the term nursery amounted to 13.3% of the time the infant spent there. Mother–infant contact time totalled .9%, .2.9%, 2.9%, and 23.3% (including the time when infants were taken to the mother's room for feeding), respectively, for these four groups of infants. Total parental contact time was even lower, being .7%, .7%, and 2.5% for the three groups of NICU babies. Jones reports that no direct contact was noted between fathers and their infant in the full-term nursery, but that no data were available for fathers' visits in mothers' rooms, where contact may have occurred. As previously noted, much of the contact and interaction between the infant and the environment is not within his or her control (Linn et al., 1985). Thus, not only is the infant's social environment rather limited in the NICU, but the infant's control of that environment is also severely restricted. Marton, Dawson, and Minde (1980) reported that premature infants received a little over 8 minutes of contact per hour from NICU staff. They further note that most of this contact was devoted to medical procedures, rather than to strictly social interaction.

Gottwald and Thurman (1990) have recently discussed parent–infant interaction within the context of the NICU. They conclude that relatively little research has been done in this area, notwithstanding its importance. They point to the link between social interaction and infant arousal, cautioning that "caregivers must respond to an infant's need for frequent respites from active interaction [and] they must tailor their interaction style so that infants can integrate new behaviors" (p. 5). They suggest that a number of factors may affect the nature of the parent–infant interaction in the NICU, including medical status, degree of prematurity, and neurological integrity. Parental factors include: stress and emotional reactions, altered roles in caring for the infant, psychological well-being, and degree of social support. NICU factors include: noncontingent stimulation in the environment, medical interventions, lack of privacy, and flow of activity.

Parental visits can be infrequent, especially if a family lives some distance from the hospital (Rosenfield, 1980). Early visits may also be of a tenuous nature (Minde, Marton, Manning, & Hines, 1980). These early visits have also been characterized as less active, with mothers preferring to simply look at, rather than interact with, their infants (Minde et al., 1978). Minde, Marton, et al. (1980) also report that mothers with a higher degree of well-being, as measured by psychiatric interview, were more assertive in their interactions with their infant, as compared to mothers who had lower states of well-being. Furthermore, these authors suggest that mothers who interact more actively with their infants during NICU hospitalization continue to do so during their baby's first 3 months at home.

The interaction of fathers with their infants in the NICU has also been examined by several researchers. Marton, Minde, and Perotta (1981) indicated that mothers talk more to their infants than do fathers during visits to the NICU. Furthermore, their data suggest that infants in the NICU behave differently toward their mothers and fathers. Thurman and Korteland (1989) have reported that fathers are more disengaged from their infants during NICU visits than are mothers. In addition, they interact with their infant in a more remote fashion than do mothers, who were more affectionate. Finally, these authors present evidence suggesting that both mothers and fathers will communicate more with their infants during NICU visits when they are visiting individually, rather than as a couple.

In another study, Levy-Shiff, Shari, and Molgari (1989) examined parent–infant interaction when infants were transferred from the intensive care unit to the transitional care unit. On initial transfer, mothers exhibited more caregiving, talking, and holding behavior than fathers. However, by the time of discharge, these differences had disappeared. Data indicated that mothers also took on more caregiving responsibility than fathers, who played with and stimulated the infants more.

Professional Roles in Neonatal Intensive Care

Providing care to critically ill newborns requires the skills and talents of professionals from a variety of disciplines. Each of these disciplines makes a unique contribution to the care and treatment of the infant. The typical NICU will be staffed by professionals from pediatrics; nursing; social work; physical, occupational, speech-language, and respiratory therapies; and infant developmental specialists.

Pediatrics   The physicians who work in NICUs are all pediatricians who have a subspecialty (e.g., neonatology, cardiology, pulmonary, or infectious disease). By far, most of the physicians working in the NICU are neonatologists. These physicians are first trained as pediatricians and then receive additional training in the diseases of the newborn. The overall responsibility for the treatment of any infant in the NICU at a large teaching hospital lies with the attending neonatologist. She or he oversees the medical interventions and provides direction to the house staff (pediatric residents) and fellows (physicians who have completed their pediatric training and are learning to be neonatologists), and to nursing staff. At community hospitals with NICUs, there may be only attending physicians, in which case these doctors would provide direction to nursing personnel. As Marshall, Roberts, and Walsh (1985) suggest, the role of the attending neonatologist is to "be as supportive [of other staff] as possible while maintaining the highest possible standards of care" (p. 242).

Other pediatric subspecialists may also be called upon to provide intervention to infants in the NICU. For example, a pediatric cardiologist will become a member of the treatment team if an infant has a cardiac anomaly. An infectious-disease specialist may be involved in determining what type of infection an infant has, or a pediatric surgeon may be called upon to do a resection on a baby with an intestinal blockage. Jurisdictional disputes can sometime arise between neonatologists and other subspecialists, but as Marshall et al. (1985) point out, these problems can usually be worked out among the parties involved or with the help of the respective department chairs.

Nursing   Nursing staff are the backbone of any NICU. Most NICUs, especially Level IIIs, require a large number of nurses to maintain an appropriate level of care. Marshall et al. (1985) point out that the nursing staff of the NICU may account for as much as 25% of the nursing staff of an entire children's hospital. The neonatal nurse is the primary caregiver for the infant in the NICU. Nurses are responsible for monitoring each infant's functioning, responding to crises, and for feeding, bathing, diapering, and nurturing infants. Nurses may also provide the main link to the parents and are often the ones available to parents to answer questions or interpret information. In addition, an experienced neonatal nurse may be integral to the training of medical students, residents, and even neonatology fellows. It is often the nurse who will first notice a symptom in a baby and the need to make an appropriate response to it, whether that be some immediate action or consultation with a physician. Many neonatal nurses are now seeking advanced training and are becoming neonatal nurse practitioners or clinical nurse specialists, thus expanding their roles. With this advanced preparation, these nurses can take on a greater role in patient management, administration, and staff development. Although nurses must still work under the direct supervision of a physician, it is clear that their roles within the NICU are expanding and that they are increasingly in a position to make and implement independent decisions regarding the care and treatment of critically ill newborns.

Social Work   Most larger NICUs have at least one social worker who is responsible for providing services to families with hospitalized infants. Marshall et al. (1985) have suggested that social workers

> often . . . can identify problems [with communication among staff and families] before a physician is aware of them. . . . [In addition,] social workers can also help by providing insight into . . . families. . . . [but,] perhaps the most valuable service that the social worker can provide is listening to the neonatologist as a true professional friend who has no medical or nursing responsibilities and thus may have a unique perspective. (p. 243)

In this context, listening does not mean following orders, but rather acting as a sounding board or providing a fresh perspective. Social workers are available to families to provide support and to identify community resources and services that they may want. Social workers can help families by making referrals or, in some cases, providing direct counseling to reduce the stress that families often experience as a result of their baby's hospitalization. Social work intervention can also be invaluable in the event of an infant's death. In this situation the social worker may be helpful both to family members and to staff, who have often formed strong attachments to infants. Unfortunately, many hospitals do not have a full-time social worker assigned only to the NICU. Thus, social work services may not be as readily available as the ideal would allow. Furthermore, even when a full-time social worker is available, she or he often functions in relative isolation from the other NICU staff. Social workers are seen as the professionals who handle the emotional needs of the family and are often perceived as doing this in isolation from the rest of the NICU staff. As will be discussed later, a more family-centered approach to service within the NICU would include the belief that this separateness does not represent best practice.

Related Therapies   Related therapies include physical, occupational, speech-language and respiratory therapy, and audiology. Each of these groups of professionals, when available, is in a position to make a unique contribution to the treatment of infants in the NICU. However, these professionals may not always be available. In addition, it may be the case that, while a hospital employs a range of therapists, they might not have specific expertise in pediatrics or in working with ill infants. This is more likely in a general care hospital, rather than a children's hospital that specializes in pediatric populations.

Physical Therapists   Physical and occupational therapists are both concerned with motor function. However, the physical therapist is typically more concerned with gross motor function and posture, whereas the occupational therapist concentrates more on fine motor function and sensory integration. Physical therapists may provide suggestions on how to best position an infant in the isolette so as to reduce tension in the limbs. They may also suggest exercises to develop muscle strength or reduce spasticity in the limbs. Recent literature (e.g., Schneider & Chasnoff, 1987; and Schneider, Griffith, & Chasnoff, 1989) suggests that the expertise of a physical therapist can be particularly important in the treatment of infants who are hospitalized due to prenatal exposure to cocaine.

Occupational Therapists   Like a physical therapist, an occupational therapist would also be concerned with positioning of the infant. However, this type of positioning would be more directed at allowing the infant to relate to his or her sensory environment. The occupational therapist would provide techniques that would help a baby to integrate different stimuli from a single source (e.g., a face and a voice). As discussed earlier, the nature of the NICU environment is not always conducive to the development of these abilities in infants. The occupational therapist might also provide exercises that would expose infants to various stimuli in a much more controlled fashion than typically occurs in the NICU, thus, helping to counterbalance the somewhat hectic, noncontingent nature of this environment.

Speech-Language Therapists   Speech-language therapists would typically bring their expertise to bear in two specific areas: feeding and parent–infant interaction. The speech-language therapist would also provide techniques that would aid the infant in sucking and swallowing and enhance oral motor development. It should be pointed out that in some cases the occupational therapist might also concentrate on these skills. The speech-language therapist can also provide valuable input to parents regarding their interaction with their infant. They can help parents recognize cues that their infant is demonstrating that suggest that the child is ready for interaction or, conversely, that he or she is ready to stop interacting. The speech-language therapist can also help parents respond in a more contingent way to their infant's cues once they have come to recognize them.

Audiologists   Audiologists also play a role in the NICU. During hospitalization, several factors may negatively affect an infant's hearing (e.g., antibiotics, intraventricular hemorrhage). As a result, it is important to assess the hearing of these infants prior to discharge. At most NICUs, an audiologist is available to perform a test referred to as a Brainstem Auditory Evoked Response or BAER. This test measures brainstem activity through an electrode placed on the infant's head to determine whether or not the nervous system is responding to auditory stimuli. If hearing loss is detected, the audiologist is available to work with physicians and speech-language therapists in suggesting interventions and treatments that may be beneficial to the infant.

Respiratory Therapists   The role of the respiratory therapist is somewhat different than that of the other therapists. These professionals are concerned with the maintenance and adjustment of the ventilators that are used to support an infant's respiration. They help assure that the equipment is working properly and that the prescribed settings are maintained. They may also assist in procedures that help facilitate an infant's breathing.

Infant Developmental Specialists   These professionals have just recently begun to join the NICU staff. Typically, they will have degrees in psychology or special education with specialized training in working with infants who are at risk or who have disabilities. They will focus on many of the same areas as the other therapists, but will often be able to integrate the information into a unified intervention plan such as an individualized family service plan (IFSP). As has recently been discussed by Krehbiel, Munsick-Bruno, and Lowe (1991), IFSPs can be a useful tool in helping to ensure that an infant's developmental as well as medical needs receive attention. It should be stressed, however, that many of the developmental interventions provided by physical, occupational, and speech-language therapists, as well as those provided by infant developmental specialists, can only be implemented when the baby has achieved a reasonable level of medical stability. In addition to being available within the NICU, the infant developmental specialist can also provide information to parents as they prepare to take the baby home. If a baby is to receive community-based early intervention services, the infant developmental specialist can also act as liaison to these programs by sharing information about an infant's developmental needs.

The NICU as a Work Environment

Regardless of the discipline or role, working in a NICU can create a high degree of stress. This is especially true for physicians and nurses who are confronted on a daily basis with significant crises that often require immediate decisions that can determine whether a particular infant lives or dies. Sammons and Lewis (1985) have summarized some of the challenges and expectations that confront NICU staff. Some of these challenges are self-created, but others are clearly determined by the hospital, or even by society as a whole. Challenges faced by the NICU staff include:

Long hours of intense effort in restricted surroundings
Acquisition of complicated technical skills
Uncertainties over optimal therapy and unexpected harm from new techniques
Ethical dilemmas
Dealing with their own intense emotional reactions and those of the parents and infants
Coping with infants whose rapidly changing condition demands immediate correct decisions and rapid intervention
Frequent frustration because of the inability to accurately define prognosis (p. 102)

In addition to these challenges, NICU staff must also learn to deal with the death of an infant, both as it affects them and as it affects the family. As Marshall et al. (1985) suggest, it is important for those working in the NICU to provide mutual support to each other by becoming what they refer to as "professional friends" or to have a colleague to depend on (Glass, Gretz, Fisher, & Speaks, 1985). If NICU staff does not receive enough emotional support, the stresses of the environment can become unbearable and can lead to high rates of staff burnout, increased turnover, reduced job satisfaction, and impaired job performance (Duxbury, Armstrong, Drew, & Henly, 1984; Duxbury, Henly, & Armstrong, 1982; Glass et al., 1985; Gribbons & Marshall, 1982; Jacobson, 1978; and Norbeck, 1985). Anyone choosing to work in a NICU will be confronted with a number of significant challenges and frustrations, but they can also be the recipients of significant rewards.

MEDICAL CONDITIONS AND INTERVENTIONS

Obviously, if an infant is hospitalized in the NICU, it is because of some serious medical condition. While infants are most often placed in NICUs because of prematurity, many other medical conditions can lead to their hospitalization, including: evidence of prenatal asphyxia, neonatal infection (e.g., herpes, syphilis), prenatal drug exposure, signs of neurological insult (e.g., seizures), congenital anomalies (e.g., heart defects, myelomeningocele), genetic disorders (e.g., Down syndrome, Trisomy 18, cri-du-chat syndrome), or because of maternal conditions such as diabetes or toxemia. NICUs, especially those at large regional teaching hospitals, are equipped to provide treatment for a wide variety of medical conditions and typically have a number of highly skilled physicians and nurses who, in addition to neonatologists, can bring their subspecialty expertise to bear in intervention with critically ill infants. It is beyond the scope of this chapter to discuss in detail the treatments that are given for each of the many specific conditions that can affect the newborn. The interested reader who wants more information on medical treatment is advised to consult Klaus and Fanaroff's (1986) *Care of the High-Risk Neonate* (3rd ed.) or Avery and Taeusch's (1984) *Schaeffer's Diseases of the Newborn* (5th ed.).

Medical treatment of the preterm infant is directed at increasing the chances of survival of the infant by instituting interventions that compensate for prematurity. To achieve this, neonatologists use a variety of specialized medical techniques and closely monitor the infant's physiological state. The means by which the infants are monitored are discussed above. Based on the continuous information that physicians and nurses gather, individual treatment regimens are developed for each baby. Thus, each infant receives individualized attention to his or her respiration, circulation, nutrition, blood pH balance, hydration, temperature maintenance, and neurological function. In essence, the role of the neonatologist is to create a simulation of the womb that will support the infant until a level of maturity roughly equivalent to 39–40 gestational weeks is reached.

There are a number of complications that can arise in the treatment of preterm infants. A preterm infant is one who is born at less than 37 gestational weeks, and is thus not fully developed. This prematurity increases the infant's vulnerability, which, in turn, increases the risk to the infant. Because of the infant's vulnerable status, treatment itself becomes an additional source of risk. Many of the complications experienced by premature infants during the course of their hospitalization are the direct result of treatment. Complications that arise as a function of treatment are referred to as *iatrogenic*. Thus arises the tenuous balance in the care and treatment of preterm infants. Left untreated, many of these infants would die. At the same time, treatment often leads to complications to which the neonatologist must be responsive, and ironically, these complications can themselves lead to the death of the infant. Thus, the medical treatment of the premature infant, especially those under 30 weeks of gestation, becomes an individually determined balancing act designed to help ensure the survival of the infant while minimizing the complications associated with treatment. The following paragraphs provide a description of some iatrogenic complications and their treatment. The reader should keep in mind that one infant may experience all of these complications while another may experience none of them.

Bronchopulmonary Dysplasia

Bronchopulmonary dysplasia (BPD) results from long-term ventilation and exposure to oxygen of infants who need assistance with their breathing. Many infants who are born prematurely have inefficient lungs, due to the lack of a substance called surfactant, and suffer from a condition known as *respiratory distress syndrome*, or RDS. Recent advances in the development and use of artificial and natural surfactant have led to improvements in the respiratory status of preterm infants. Even with this advance, however, many infants will still require mechanical ventilation assistance (Merritt et al., 1986). It is the use of ventilation that leads to the development of BPD or chronic lung disease. Most infants who remain on a ventilator for more than a week or so experience some level of BPD. Those infants who are still ventilated at the end of the first month of life are at highest risk of developing significant damage to the lung, with implications for impaired lung function lasting for months or even years. BPD has been characterized as the development of fibrosis in some portions of the lung and collapse in other sections, conditions that are identified through x rays:

> Overall the lungs are usually hyperexpanded and have poor elasticity. These children appear stressed. They look worried, and their eyes tend to bulge out. Their skin color is very reactive and, when stressed, readily turns shades of blue. They have difficulty feeding and they tend to be more

sensitive and reactive to stimulation than other premies. (Sammons & Lewis, 1985, p. 342)

Sammons and Lewis point out that infants with BPD are often treated with diuretics to reduce fluid buildup in the lungs. Because of their nutritional difficulties, they are also fed diets high in calories. These babies may also be suctioned frequently and given chest physical therapy to reduce secretions. Sometimes, bronchodilators are prescribed to help improve respiratory function. In addition, one multisite study has suggested that surfactant replacement at birth can reduce the incidence of BPD and lower the mortality rate (Morley, 1987). Other studies, however, have failed to demonstrated similar results (e.g., Hobar et al., 1989), but these were based on a single dose of surfactant, rather than the multiple doses administered in other studies (e.g., Shapiro & Nutter, 1988).

Necrotizing Enterocolitis

Necrotizing enterocolitis (NEC) is a complication that occurs in as many as 15% of all NICU admissions (Klaus & Fanaroff, 1986), although other authors have suggested a rate of incidence in the 3%–5% range (Sammons & Lewis, 1985). NEC can be a serious, even life-threatening, complication. NEC is characterized by the death or necrosis of a portion of the bowel wall, and may result from a viral or bacterial infection, or from insufficient blood flow to the bowel. It also more commonly appears after the infant receives food by mouth. Symptoms of NEC include "temperature instability, lethargy, abdominal distention, and retention of feedings" (Klaus & Fanaroff, 1986, p. 138). Treatment of NEC includes cessation of feeding and administration of broad-spectrum antibiotics. If the NEC progresses to the point that actual perforation of the bowel occurs, then surgery is required to resect a section of the bowel (Klaus & Fanaroff, 1986; Sammons & Lewis, 1985).

Infection and Sepsis

Infection and sepsis are the results of the relative immaturity of the infant's immune system, coupled with exposure to bacterial and viral agents. The infant may develop a localized infection, such as a urinary tract infection, or the infection may be systemic—it may infect the bloodstream and spread throughout the body—in which case it is called sepsis. As Sammons and Lewis (1985) suggest, "infection continues to be one of the major problems in neonatal intensive care" (p. 348). Many of the treatment procedures used with preterm infants involve the placement of tubes and catheters into the body. With the introduction of each tube, there is a possibility of exposing the infant to microorganisms that can lead to infection. Once the symptoms of infection or sepsis become evident (e.g., temperature abnormalities, lethargy, vomiting, changes in muscle tone), it is necessary to determine the agent responsible for the infection before treatment can be instituted. The exact disease agent is determined by blood test and then, if bacterial, treated with the appropriate antibiotic. In the case of viral infections, interventions may be more focused on the treatment and relief of symptoms, since antibiotics are not effective in eliminating viral infections. In a sense, the best treatment of infections in the NICU is their prevention. To this end, a number of techniques are employed, including the use of sterile materials and, most importantly, hand washing to reduce the incidence of infection and sepsis. In spite of these precautions, some infants in NICUs are inevitably going to develop infections.

Intracranial Hemorrhage

Intracranial hemorrhage refers to bleeding inside the skull or bleeding directly into the ventricular system of the brain. The most common type of intracranial hemorrhage in premature infants is the *intraventricular hemorrhage* (IVH) (Sammons & Lewis, 1985, p. 363). IVH most likely results from the immaturity of the blood vessels and their response to changes in blood pressure and intravascular blood volume. Depending on the severity of the bleeding, IVH can have long-term neurological consequences. IVH may not cause any clinical signs, but can sometimes result in sudden changes in the infant's condition, especially the occurrence of neurological signs. IVH is typically confirmed through ultrasound or CAT scan. The severity of IVH is graded from one through four, with four being the most severe (Papile, Burstein, Burstein, & Koffler, 1978). Treatment involves monitoring the infant and reducing intracranial pressure, if necessary. Most studies have suggested a relationship between severity of IVH and later developmental outcome (Krishnamoorthy, Shannon, De-Long, Todres, & Davis, 1979; Papile, Munsick, Weaver, & Peca, 1979; Shankaran, Slovis, Bedard, & Poland, 1982). As with infections, the best treatment for IVH lies in its prevention. Dramatic decreases in the incidence of IVH have occurred over the past 15 years, which is probably related to improvements in neonatal care. Studies of several drugs (e.g., phenobarbital, ethamsylate, and indomethacin) as well as vitamin E administered postnatally have indicated that they may play some role in reducing the incidence of IVH (Volpe, 1990), but this has not been proven conclusively. Volpe (1990) also suggests that IVH can be prevented by medical management that maintains cerebral blood flow at a constant level. Sammons and Lewis (1985) have discussed two other types of intracranial hemorrhage. The *subarachnoid hemorrhage*, which occurs outside the brain and is typically not of clinical significance, and the *subdural hemorrhage*, which if not properly treated can cause compression of the brain and subsequent brain damage.

Retinopathy of Prematurity

Retinopathy of prematurity (ROP), which has historically also been referred to as *retrolental fibroplasia* (RLF), is a condition that is common among premature infants, especially those weighing under 1,000 grams (Sammons & Lewis, 1985). ROP has been related to the exposure of the immature blood vessels of the retina to oxygen tensions that lead to vasoconstriction of, and subsequent decreased blood flow to, the retina. In an early collaborative study, ROP was related to the length of time a baby received oxygen, as well as the concentration of oxygen to which the infant was exposed (Kinsey, Jacobus, & Hemphill, 1956), although the factors leading to ROP are still not fully understood (Sammons & Lewis, 1985). E. Glass et al. (1985) have also suggested a link between the levels of light in the nursery and ROP. As with infection, the best treatment for ROP is prevention—monitoring blood oxygen and keeping it at the lowest possible level while still allowing adequate oxygen delivery to the brain. Neonatologists are challenged in "providing enough oxygen to prevent brain damage while avoiding even transient abrupt peaks that may contributed to RLF [ROP]" (Sammons & Lewis, 1985, p. 372). After severe ROP occurs, a surgical procedure called cryosurgery has been used to reduce the effects on the retina, and thus minimize vision loss (Cryotherapy for Retinopathy Cooperative Group, 1988). There is also some evidence that vitamin E may help prevent ROP, although this therapy has been accompanied by major complications (Urrea & Rosenbaum, 1989). Hansen and McClead (1990) have concluded that "an effective means for the prevention and treatment of ROP remains to be found" (p. 184).

DEVELOPMENTAL AND BEHAVIORAL INTERVENTIONS

As the medical treatment of infants in NICUs has become more sophisticated, awareness has simultaneously developed that other types of interventions, which are more behavioral and developmental in orientation, might also benefit these babies. Over the past 20 years, various interventions have been designed that are focused on the developmental and behavioral state of the infant. These interventions range from those that are based on very specific techniques (e.g., Katz, 1971; Korner, Kraemer, Haffner, & Cosper, 1975) to those that are more focused on the infant as part of a greater system (e.g., Thurman, Cornwell, & Korteland, 1989).

Sensory Stimulation

During the 1960s and 1970s, most of the intervention studies carried out in the NICU focused on direct stimulation of the infant (Bennett, 1987, 1990; DeSocio & Ensher 1986; Field, 1986). These interventions included those that provided: 1) visual stimulation, such as decorations on the side of the isolette or mobiles; 2) auditory stimulation, such as recordings of the maternal voice or heart beat, music boxes, or singing; 3) tactile stimulation, such as nonnutritive sucking, massaging, flexing, and positioning; and 4) vestibular-kinesthetic stimulation, such as rocking and oscillating waterbeds. Many of the studies conducted during this time combined sensory modalities, rather than relying on a single one. Bennett (1990) has suggested that the rationales for these sensory interventions "were (1) to compensate for intrauterine experiences lost as a result of premature birth and (2) to correct for the presumed sensory deprivation associated with prolonged care in the disruptive neonatal intensive care environment" (p. 34). As noted above, this latter assumption has been challenged (Linn et al., 1985). In addition, Gorski et al. (1983) and Long, Philip, and Lucey (1980) have presented data that suggest that indiscriminate handling of sick neonates can lead to physiological distress characterized by hypoxia, apnea, bradycardia, and vomiting. Table 1, which is taken from Bennett (1987), summarizes some representative studies that have used various sensory interventions with infants in the NICU. Additional studies employing similar strategies are reviewed and summarized in Masi (1979) and in DeSocio and Ensher (1986). The interested reader is urged to consult these sources.

Virtually every published study that has provided some type of stimulation to hospitalized newborns has shown an effect that may be considered positive (e.g., more rapid weight gain, shorter hospitalizations, decreased episodes of apnea and bradycardia). Bennett (1987) has therefore suggested that "one is almost forced to conclude that practically any early intervention protocol can be expected to yield at least some benefits in some measured area of performance" (p. 106). It is important to point out that most of these studies were conducted with relatively healthy premature infants with birth weights exceeding 1,000 grams (Bennett, 1990). The generalizability of these results to less healthy and lower birth weight infants is questionable. In addition, it should be noted that many of the effects found in these studies were of a short-term nature, and differences between experimental and control infants were rarely still noted at 1 year of age (Bennett, 1987).

Table 1. Neonatal developmental intervention studies

Reference	Nature of intervention	Intervention parameters	Setting	Role of parents
A. Auditory stimulation only (2)				
Katz (1971)	Tape-recorded mother's voice via a speaker placed in the incubator	Tape recorder was activated for 5-minute segments, six times daily, at 2-hour intervals; regimen began on fifth day of life and continued until the infant's gestational age at the completion of the regimen was 36 weeks	Neonatal Intensive Care Unit	None, except for mother recording her voice
Segall (1972)	Tape-recorded mother's voice via a speaker placed in the incubator	Tape recorder played every day for a single period of 30 min until the infant reached 36 weeks gestational age	Neonatal Intensive Care Unit	None, except for mother recording her voice
B. Tactile stimulation only (1)				
Powell (1974)	Extra handling from simple touching to prolonged holding	Maternal handling began after 3 days of age at least 3 times weekly; nursing handling began after 3 days of age for a 20-min period twice daily until birthweight regained and then once daily until discharge	Neonatal Intensive Care Unit	Mothers provided the handling stimulation for one experimental group
C. Vestibular-kinesthetic stimulation only (1)				
Korner et al. (1975)	Oscillating waterbed which replaced the mattress conventionally used in incubators	Infants were placed on the waterbed on either the third, fourth, or fifth postnatal day and remained for 7 total days	Neonatal Intensive Care Unit	None
D. Auditory and vestibular-kinesthetic stimulation (3)				
Barnard (1973)	Oscillating bed plus tape recorded heart beat	Infants received both stimulations together during the 33rd and 34th weeks of gestational age for a 15-min period each hour	Neonatal Intensive Care Unit	None

Child characteristics	Experimental design	Outcome measures	Results
62 premature infants between 28–32 weeks gestational age; infants with severe neurological or physiologic disturbances excluded	Infants assigned on a sequential basis, according to birth order, into either an experimental group (31) or control group (31); post only comparisons	At 36 weeks gestational age, developmental level assessed by the Rosenblith Modified Graham Behavior Scale which measures general maturation, audiovisual response, muscle tension, and irritability	1. E Group scored significantly ($p < .01$) higher than C Group in general maturation (including both motor and tactile-adaptive development), auditory and visual function, and optimal muscle tension 2. No group differences in irritability
60 premature infants between 28–32 weeks gestational age; infants with severe problems at birth excluded	Each infant randomly assigned to either experimental (30) group and then paired with another infant of same sex and ethnicity, thus forming 30 pairs of infants; post only comparisons	At 36 weeks gestational age, heart rate measurements were recorded in response to a variety of auditory stimuli (white noise, mother's voice, unfamiliar female voice)	1. E Group demonstrated significantly ($p < .05$) greater amount of increase in heart rate (suggesting increased autonomic responsivity) than C Group in response to white noise during quiescence 2. E Group responded with a significantly ($p < .01$) greater decrease in heart rate during crying to both mother's voice and unfamiliar female voice 3. Nonsignificant trend to decelerate heart rate more to mother's voice than to unfamiliar female voice
36 black singleton infants between 1000 and 2000 g birthweight; severe problems excluded	Each infant randomly assigned to one of three groups: maternal experimental group (11), nurse experimental group (13), or control group (12); post only comparisons	Brazelton-Cambridge Newborn Scales administered between 4 and 12 days of age; Bayley Scales of Infant Development at 2, 4, and 6 months corrected age; Maternal Behavior Ratings of mother–child interaction	1. Handled infants regained birthweight faster (trend); no growth differences later 2. Handled infants scored higher on BSID at all follow-up visits, some significant at $p < .05$ 3. No differences in maternal behavior or infant development between maternal and nurse experimental groups
21 premature infants with gestational age ≤ 34 weeks and birthweight <2000 g; severe problems excluded	Random assignment to either experimental group (10) or control group (11); pre- and postcomparisons	Mean daily heart rate, respiratory rate, temperature, weight, incidence of vomiting, and incidence of apnea	1. Significantly ($p < .01$) less apnea in experimental group 2. No other significant differences
15 premature infants between 28–32 weeks gestational age; severe problems excluded	Assignment to either experimental group (7) or control group (8); pre- and postcomparisons	Behavioral rating scale of activity to observe sleep/wake behavior; maturation on Dubowitz gestational age assessment; weight gain	1. E Group showed significantly ($p < .001$) greater gain in quiet sleep, while C Group actually showed a decline 2. E Group showed significantly ($p < .01$) greater drop in active awake state 3. E Group showed a trend of greater neurological maturation 4. No differences in corrected weight gain

(continued)

Table 1. (continued)

Reference	Nature of intervention	Intervention parameters	Setting	Role of parents
Burns et al. (1983)	Oscillating waterbed plus tape recorded intrauterine sounds of a pregnant woman	Infants received both of these stimulations on a continuous basis for 4 weeks beginning on the fourth postnatal day	Neonatal Intensive Care Unit	None
Kramer & Pierpoint (1976)	Rocking waterbed plus tape recorded simulated heartbeat and a female voice	Infants were placed on the waterbed at 2–7 postnatal days for the duration of stay in the incubator. Mechanical rocking of the waterbed occurred one hour prior to each feeding; playing of the recorded heartbeat and voice occurred during the rocking	Neonatal Intensive Care Unit	None

E. Tactile and vestibular-kinesthetic stimulation (3)

Reference	Nature of intervention	Intervention parameters	Setting	Role of parents
Rice (1977)	Stroking and massaging plus rocking, holding, and cuddling	Structured, sequential, cephalocaudal progression of stroking and massaging the infant's nude body administered for 15 min, 4 times daily for a total duration of 30 days, beginning the day the infants came home from the hospital; following each stroking treatment, infant was rocked, held, and cuddled for another 5 min; each infant had about 120 total treatments	Home	Mothers administered the intervention following training by nurses
Rosenfield (1980)	Stroking with a variety of textured materials plus stretching and folding of extremities, torsion of the trunk, and rocking	Intervention begun when infant clinically stable at an average of 2.5 weeks of age. Involved two 20-min periods daily and was administered inside the incubator	Neonatal Intensive Care Unit	None
White & Labarba (1976)	Rubbing plus flexing the arms and legs (passive kinesthetic stimulation)	Within 48 h after birth, infants received both stimulations in 15-min periods every hour for 4 consecutive hours; intervention continued through the end of the 11th day; rubbing included the infant's neck, shoulders, arms, legs, chest, and back; infants remained in incubators during stimulation	Neonatal Intensive Care	None

Child characteristics	Experimental design	Outcome measures	Results
22 premature infants between 28–32 weeks gestational age; severe problems excluded	Random assignment to either experimental group (11) or control group (11); pre- and postcomparisons	Growth parameters, state organization observations, and Brazelton Neonatal Behavioral Assessment Scale	1. E Group demonstrated significantly ($p < .05$) greater drop in active sleep 2. E Group scored significantly ($p < .05$) better in motoric organization and state organization on the Brazelton Scale 3. No differences in growth parameters
20 premature infants of <34 weeks gestational age; severe problems excluded	Random assignment to either experimental group (11) or control group (9); post only comparisons	Growth parameters, neurologic status, Brazelton Neonatal Behavioral Assessment Scale	1. E Group gained significantly ($p < .01$) more weight and increased their head circumference significantly ($p < .01$) greater 2. No significant differences in neurologic status or Brazelton Assessment
29 premature infants ≤37 weeks gestational age; severe problems excluded	Random assignment to either experimental group (15) or control group (14); pre- and postcomparisons	Assessment at 4 months age with growth parameters, neurological evaluation, and Bayley Scales of Infant Development	1. E Group showed significantly ($p < .05$) greater weight gain, but no differences on length or head circumference gains 2. E Group showed significantly ($p < .05$) more mature performance on certain neurological reflexes and reactions 3. E Group scored significantly ($p < .05$) higher on the Bayley Mental Scale, but not on the Motor Scale
78 premature infants of <1500 g birthweight	Random assignment to either experimental or control group; groups similar with respect to birthweight, gestational age, duration of hospitalization, race, sex, and maternal demographic variables; pre- and postcomparisons	State rating system and maternal visiting frequency	1. E Group demonstrated significantly ($p < .001$) more optimal, i.e., more awake and alert, state organization 2. E Group mothers demonstrated significantly ($p < .01$) higher visitation rates
12 premature infants ≤36 weeks gestational age and lowest SES group; severe problems excluded	Random assignment to either experimental group (6) or control group (6); pre- and postcomparisons	Weight gain, feeding volume, temperature, heart rate, respiratory rate, frequency of voiding and stooling	1. E Group demonstrated significantly ($p < .001$) greater rate of weight gain and volume of formula ingested 2. No significant differences in any other physiological measures

(continued)

Table 1. (continued)

Reference	Nature of intervention	Intervention parameters	Setting	Role of parents
F. Multimodal sensory stimulation (2)				
Leib et al. (1980)	Visual (mobile), tactile (rubbing, soothing), vestibular-kinesthetic (rocking), and auditory (talking, singing, music box)	Stimulations administered during feeding times; during intermediate care period, visual and tactile (5 min) procedures done inside incubator; during convalescent care period, all stimulations performed in open crib	Neonatal Intensive Care Unit	None
Scarr-Salapatek & Williams (1973)	Special room in the nursery. Visual (mobile, human faces), tactile (handling, patting), vestibular-kinesthetic (rocking), and auditory (talking)	Nursery staff in the special room is instructed to provide as much of these stimulations as possible to approximate optimal home care conditions; patterned visual experience included mobiles both inside and outside the incubator; as soon as possible, infants were removed from the incubator during feedings for rocking, talking, and "playing;" this consisted of eight ½-h stimulation sessions daily	Neonatal Intensive Care Unit with weekly home visitation throughout first year of life to encourage continuation of stimulation program	None during hospitalization; mediators of continued stimulation during infancy

During the 1980s, thinking regarding behavioral and developmental intervention in the NICU began to shift. In part, this occurred because research began to demonstrate, as noted above, that certain types of stimulation could cause distress for infants (Gorski et al. 1983). This research set the stage for the development of approaches that were more considerate of the fragile state of the infant, one specific example of which was the approach developed by Als et al. (1986). Bennett (1990) notes that:

> the specific components of this environmental neonatology model include reduction of excessive environmental stimulations (e.g., light, noise, traffic), minimal handling protocol, use of facilitative positioning, promotion of self-regulation and state control, timing of daily routines to match readiness, and parent support and behavioral observation training. (p. 36)

This approach emphasizes teaching nurses to use individualized plans based on each infant's status and state.

Parent-Interactional Approaches

Another approach to intervention in the NICU evolved during the 1980s and paralleled other developments in early intervention, with a

Child characteristics	Experimental design	Outcome measures	Results
28 premature infants with birthweights between 1200 and 1800 g; severe problems excluded; all middle-class white	First 14 infants meeting selection criteria assigned to control group. Following discharge of last control infant, next 14 elligible infants assigned to experimental group; pre- and postcomparisons	Hospital weight gain; Brazelton Neonatal Behavior Assessment Scale prior to discharge; Bayley Scales of Infant Development at 6 months age	1. No significant differences in weight gain 2. No significant changes in neonatal behavioral assessment 3. E Group scored significantly ($p <$ .001) higher on both Bayley Mental and Motor Scales at 6 months
30 consecutively born premature infants with birthweights between 1300 and 1800 g; all lowest SES, black	Alternate assignment to either experimental group (15) or control group (15); pre- and postcomparisons	Brazelton Cambridge Newborn Scales before and after hospital stimulation phase; Cattell Infant Intelligence Scale at 1 year of age; weight gain	1. E Group showed significantly greater weight gain in the nursery 2. E Group showed significantly superior Brazelton performance after stimulation, whereas C Group had been somewhat superior before stimulation began 3. E Group showed significantly ($p <$ .05) higher Cattell scores at 1 year

From Bennett, F.C. (1987). The effectiveness of early intervention for infants at increased biological risk. In M.J. Guralnick and F.C. Bennett (Eds.), *The effectiveness of early intervention for at-risk and handicapped children* (pp. 79–112). Orlando: Academic Press; reprinted with permission.

focus on parent–child interactions and relationships. In some instances, these programs placed emphasis on the provision of emotional support (e.g., Minde et al., 1980). In others, emphasis was placed on helping mothers to understand their infants' states and to be more responsive to them, both in social interaction and in the initiation of caregiving activities (Rauh, Achenbach, Nurcombe, Howell, & Teti, 1988; Resnick, Armstrong, & Carter, 1988; Resnick, Eyler, Nelson, Eitzman, & Bucciarelli 1987; Widmayer & Field, 1981). Yet a third approach has been to combine stimulation of the infant with teaching the mother how to read her baby's cues and provide appropriate stimulation (Brown et al., 1980). While the studies just cited report on interventions that were employed, at least in part, while the infants were still hospitalized, similar approaches have been instituted after the infants have been discharged (e.g., Barrera, Rosenbaum, & Cunningham, 1986; Bromwich & Parmelee, 1979; Field, Widmayer, Stringer, & Ignatoff, 1980). Most recently, the Infant Health and Development Program (1990) has demonstrated the effectiveness of using a specific home-based, parent-mediated teaching approach with low birth weight infants for 1 year after their discharge from the hospital. This home-based intervention was followed by a center-based program for an additional 2 years. The results of this multisite investigation revealed significant Stanford Binet IQ differences in higher birth weight (>2,000g) infants who received intervention, as compared to controls. However, no such differences were found between experimental and control groups of infants weighing less than 2,000 grams.

Transition from NICU to Home

Pearl, Brown, and Meyers (1990) have recently defined transition "as the passage of the child [and the family] from one set of service circumstances to another" (p. 41). These authors point to the importance of medical, developmental, and family issues in the transition process. Medical issues may include linking the family with a home healthcare agency, providing information on the infant's medical needs to the local primary care pediatrician or family physician, and making provisions for visits to medical specialists, therapists, and follow-up clinics. If the infant is sent home on a respirator or heart or apnea monitor, it is necessary that the proper arrangements be made with the agencies providing this equipment and that parents be fully aware of how to use and maintain the equipment.

Developmental issues that might arise during the transition process center on determining the infant's needs for early intervention services. At a minimum, these would include screening and, if indicated, further assessment and evaluation. If the infant is eligible for early intervention services, then the transition planning should include referral to the appropriate early intervention programs. It is also important at this point to provide for service coordination, which is required under the provisions of federal and state laws.

Family issues center around the development of support mechanisms that will facilitate the family's ability to cope. Some families have large and readily available support systems, while others have rather limited ones. In this latter case it may be necessary for professionals to step in and fill the gap so that families will experience lower levels of stress as the infant approaches the time for discharge and joins the family at home. Transition planning may require even greater thought and effort when an adolescent or a substance-abusing parent is being served.

Pearl et al. (1990) have suggested a five-component comprehensive model for helping to ensure smooth transitions for infants and their families as they move from the NICU to their home:

1. Preparation and outreach for the health community through on-going educational activities
2. Incorporation of community professionals into the NICU rounding team
3. Comprehensive information on regional resources for follow-up, early intervention services and related services
4. Family-centered transitional planning and support services
5. Interdisciplinary follow-up, including evaluation and monitoring of NICU graduates. (p. 48)

Bruder and Cole (1991) have described Project Connect, which was specifically "designed to improve and expand the implementation of coordinated, family-centered, community-based practices for families transitioning from hospital to home care" (pp. 41–42). The project adopted a parent-to-parent approach that links parents together for the purpose of providing mutual support and understanding, as well as sharing information regarding services and child development. Bruder and Cole (1991) suggest that a smooth transition is accomplished through the development of a discharge/transition summary coupled with a continuing care plan. These documents can serve as the basis of an IFSP, if necessary. Tables 2 and 3 identify the

Table 2. Components of discharge summary

Medical history
  maternal history
  infant's birth history
  infant's neonatal history
  diagnosis/prognosis
Infant's current medical needs
  equipment
  medications
Infant's needs for growth and development
  feeding and growing
  sleeping
  behavioral observations
Assessment of family function
  participation in infant's care
  psycho-social support network
  the home environment
  financial situation
Assessment of family needs
  needs for information
  needs for training
  needs for support
Community services
  well baby health care
  community health nursing agencies
  early intervention services

From Bruder, M. B., and Cole, M. (1991). Critical elements of transition from NICU to home and follow-up. *Children's Health Care, 20,* 40–49; reprinted with permission.

Table 3.   Components of a continuing care plan

Demographic/background information
  child status/prognosis
  medical history/care providers/payment source
  family members
  transportation needs
  equipment needs
  cultural needs
Community services
  care coordinator (if other than family), agency communication system
  health care provider(s), location, phone number, payment source
    primary
    specialty
    neonatal follow-up
  early intervention services, provider, location, frequency, phone numbers
  community health services, provider, frequency, phone number
Fiscal management
  public sources of funding
    application
    assistance to apply
  private sources of funding
    application
    assistance to apply
Family support needs
  formal services, method, outcome
    financial assistance
    respite provider
    care child provider
    parent groups
    transportation
    translation
    training (e.g., rights and responsibilities, equipment maintenance, fiscal man-
      agement)
  informal
    identification of network
    facilitation of network
    parent to parent

From Bruder, M. B., and Cole, M. (1991). Critical elements of transition from NICU to home and follow-up. *Children's Health Care, 20,* 40–49; reprinted with permission.

components of a discharge summary and a continuing care plan, as provided by Bruder and Cole (1991).

Family-Centered Services in the NICU

An emerging approach to early intervention services is a family-centered approach, which is based on the premise that services to the infant are meaningfully provided only within the context of the entire family. In essence, services are rendered to the entire family, and each family decides which kinds and levels of services it desires. Emphasis is also placed on developing better fit within the family ecology (Thurman & Widerstrom, 1990). The application of family-centered approaches to neonatal intensive care have only very recently been described (Thurman et al., 1989).

The hospitalization of a newborn infant in a NICU clearly sets the stage for increased levels of stress and anxiety in virtually any family. Families are first confronted with the highly technical environment described at the beginning of this chapter. In addition, the fate of their infant is often uncertain, and they may also live a good distance from the hospital, making communication and visitation more difficult. Moreover, premature delivery, by cutting pregnancy short, does not provide parents with all of the time that they may have anticipated to prepare for their baby's arrival. As Thurman (1991) has suggested:

> All of these conditions lead to the need to provide services in the NICU which are family-centered rather than primarily infant centered as has most often been the case. This is not to suggest that the medical and developmental needs of the infant should be de-emphasized but rather that the emotional and psychological needs of families must be given equal concern and that the infant's needs be interpreted within the family context. (pp. 34–35)

According to Thurman (1991) adherence to several guiding principles is necessary if family-centered services are to be provided in NICUs. The principles that he suggests are the need to:

1. Establish and maintain adaptive fit within the family and between the family and the service delivery system
2. Provide services based on family identified needs and desires
3. Foster family independence and empowerment while providing a stable ongoing support system and
4. Recognize that families are complex, dynamic and ever changing systems. (p. 35)

Thurman (1991) goes on to describe physical and functional organizational changes that can be made in NICUs to facilitate the development of a family-centered approach. Accommodations for families should be provided, including sleeping and bathroom facilities. Such space might also be used to teach parents the skills required to attend to an infant's ongoing medical needs (Rushton, 1990). "In addition it is necessary to make provisions for family privacy, such as curtains which can be drawn between isolettes and quiet pleasantly-decorated side rooms for [conferences with service providers or] breast feeding" (Thurman, 1991, p. 37). Rocking chairs and other seating should be provided in the NICU, and staff should refer to individual infants by name and by the proper gender.

Functional organizational changes addressed by Thurman (1991) speak to the development of a unit approach, rather than one that is departmental. In a unit organization, each staff member would have line responsibility to the director of the NICU, who might or might not be a neonatologist. In contrast, in the more traditional departmental organization, each professional is responsible to his or her own respective department head. A unit structure can help facilitate the development of team function, which is also critical in establishing and maintaining a family-centered approach. As discussed above, effective discharge and transition planning is important in the implementation of a family-centered approach. Finally, Rushton (1990) has suggested that primary nursing or the assignment of a case manager provides the continuity important in maintaining a family-centered approach. Furthermore, she asserts that "assigning a consistent attending physician for infants and children with long-term ICU admissions can avoid the periodic changing of the guard" (p. 77), and thus facilitate greater continuity of service for the family.

A recent description of an ecologically oriented family-centered model based in a NICU has been provided by Thurman et al. (1989). They describe the Liaison Infant Family Team (LIFT) project, which operated using the guidelines provided above. LIFT services were based on the premise that families whose infants received neonatal intensive care should themselves receive intensive support and services. LIFT services began within 24 hours of the infant's hospitalization and continued until families no longer felt the need for them. Typically, services remained in place until the child was a toddler. The LIFT model also helps to establish continuity of services for families, the importance of which is discussed above.

Brown, Pearl, and Carrasco (1991) have suggested that family-centered care within NICUs is an important new trend in service delivery. They conclude that:

> family-centered care expectations for improved communication and partnership with families are being realized in some [NICU-based] model demonstration programs at this time. Ecological concepts of family empowerment and "goodness of fit" are beginning to influence the service delivery system, but remain little known and accepted. The unique challenges that families find in the NICU setting make it an important site for family-centered care. (p. 55)

CONCLUDING COMMENTS

This chapter describes the complexity of the care and treatment of critically ill newborns in a NICU. In addition, the roles of various professionals in the delivery of services within the NICU are elucidated, and a number of behavioral and developmental interventions are described. Finally, the rationale and parameters for establishing a family-centered approach to services in the NICU are provided. With the implementation of both federal and state mandates to provide services, beginning at birth, to infants who are at risk or disabled and their families, it is clear that, more and more, the NICU will become the site where early intervention begins. For most professionals working in early intervention, the NICU still represents a new, and perhaps somewhat intimidating, setting in which to work. But the challenges and excitement of working within a NICU can be great if one gains insight into the needs of infants and families who are served in this setting. Hopefully, this chapter provides a basis for beginning to develop this insight.

REFERENCES

Als, H., Lawhon, G., Brown, E., Gibes, R., Duffy, F.H., McAnulty, G., & Blickman, J.G. (1986). Individualized behavioral and environmental care for the very low birth weight preterm infant at high risk for bronchopulmonary dysplasia: Neonatal intensive care unit and developmental outcome. *Pediatrics, 78,* 1123–1132.

Avery, M.E., & Taeusch, H.W., Jr. (1984). *Diseases of the newborn* (5th ed.). Philadelphia: W.B. Saunders.

Barrera, M.E., Rosenbaum, P.L., & Cunningham, C.E. (1986). Early home intervention with low-birthweight infants and their parents. *Child Development, 57,* 20–33.

Bennett, F.C. (1987). The effectiveness of early intervention for infants at increased biological risk. In M.J. Guralnick & F.C. Bennett (Eds.), *The effectiveness of early intervention for at-risk and handicapped children* (pp. 79–112). Orlando: Academic Press.

Bennett, F.C. (1990). Recent advances in developmental intervention for biologically vulnerable infants. *Infants and Young Children, 3*(1), 33–40.

Bromwich, R.M., & Parmelee, A.H. (1979). An intervention program for preterm infants. In T.M. Field, A.M. Sostek, S. Goldberg, & H.H. Shuman (Eds.), *Infants born at risk: Behavior and development* (pp. 389–411). Jamaica, NY: SP Medical and Scientific Books.

Brown, J.V., LaRosa, M.M., Aylward, G.P., Davis, D.J., Rutherford, P.K., & Bakeman, R. (1980). Nursery-based intervention with prematurely born babies and their mothers: Are there effects? *Journal of Pediatrics, 97,* 487–491.

Brown, W., Pearl, L.F., & Carrasco, N. (1991). Evolving models of family-centered services in neonatal intensive care. *Children's Health Care, 20,* 50–55.

Bruder, M.B., & Cole, M. (1991). Critical elements of transition from NICU to home and follow-up. *Children's Health Care, 20,* 40–49.

DeSocio, D.A., & Ensher, G.L. (1986). Intervening in intensive care nurseries. In G.L. Ensher & D.A. Clark (Eds.), *Newborns at risk: Medical care and psychoeducational intervention* (pp. 190–214). Rockville, MD: Aspen Publishers, Inc.

Duxbury, M.L., Armstrong, G.D., Drew, D.J., & Henly, S.J. (1984). Head nurse leadership style with staff nurse burnout and job satisfaction in NICUs. *Nursing Research, 33,* 97–101.

Duxbury, M.L., Henly, G.A., & Armstrong, G.D. (1982). Measurement of nurse organization climate of NICUs. *Nursing Research, 31*, 83–88.

Field, T.M. (1986). Interventions for premature infants. *Journal of Pediatrics, 109*, 183–191.

Field, T.M., Widmayer, S.M., Stringer, S., & Ignatoff, E. (1980). Teenage, lower class mothers and their preterm infants: An intervention and developmental follow-up. *Child Development, 51*, 426–436.

Gabriel, M., Grote, B., & Jonas, M. (1981). Sleep–wake patterns in preterm infants under two different care schedules during four day polygraphic recording. *Neuropediatrics, 12*, 366–373.

Glass, B., Gretz, J., Fisher, L., & Speaks, S. (1985). A nurse colleague program: One solution to nurse turnover. *Neonatal Network, 3*, 16–21.

Glass, E., Avery, G.B., Subramaniou, K.N.S., Keys, M.P., Sostek, A.M., & Friendly, D.S. (1985). Effect of bright light in the hospital nursery on the incidence of retinopathy of prematurity. *New England Journal of Medicine, 313*, 401–404.

Gorski, P.A. (1984). Premature infant behavioral and physiological responses to caregiving intervention in the intensive care nursery. In J.D. Call, E. Galenson, & R. L. Tyson (Eds.), *Frontiers in infant psychiatry* (pp. 142–169) New York: Basic Books.

Gorski, P.A., Hole, W.T., Leonard, G.H., & Martin, J.A. (1983). Direct computer recording of premature infants and nursery care: Distress following two interventions. *Pediatrics, 72*, 198–203.

Gottfried, A.W. (1985). Environment of newborn infants in special care units. In A.W. Gottfried & J.L. Gaiter (Eds.), *Infant stress under intensive care: Environmental neonatology* (pp. 23–54). Baltimore: University Park Press.

Gottfried, A.W., & Gaiter, J.L. (Eds.). (1985). *Infant stress under intensive care: Environmental neonatology.* Baltimore: University Park Press.

Gottfried, A.W., Wallace-Lande, P., Sherman-Brown, S., King, J., Coen, C., & Hodgman, J.E. (1981). Physical and social environment of newborn babies in special care units. *Science, 214*, 673–675.

Gottwald, S.R., & Thurman, S.K. (1990). Parent–infant interaction in neonatal intensive care units: Implications for research and service delivery. *Infants and Young Children, 2*(3), 1–9.

Gribbons, R., & Marshall, R. (1982). Nurse burnout in a NICU. In R.E. Marshall, C. Kasman, & L.S. Cape (Eds.), *Coping with caring for sick newborns* (pp. 123–145). Philadelphia: W.B. Saunders.

Hansen, N.B., & McClead, R.E. (1990). Advances in neonatal intensive care to improve long-term outcome. In S.M. Pueschel, & J.A. Mulick (Eds.), *Prevention of developmental disabilities* (pp. 179–187). Baltimore: Paul H. Brookes Publishing Co.

Hobar, J., Soll, R., Sutherland, J., Kotagal, U., Philip, A., & Kessler, D. (1989). Multicenter randomized placebo controlled trial of surfactant. *New England Journal of Medicine, 320*, 959–965.

Infant Health and Development Program. (1990). Enhancing the outcomes of low-birth weight, premature infants: A multi-site randomized trial. *Journal of the American Medical Association, 263*, 3035–3042.

Jacobson, S. (1978). Stressful situations for neonatal intensive care nurses. *American Journal of Maternal/Child Nursing, 3*, 144–150.

Jones, C.L. (1982). Environmental analysis of neonatal intensive care. *Journal of Nervous and Mental Disease, 170*, 130–142.

Katz, V. (1971). Auditory stimulation and developmental behavior of the premature infant. *Nursing Research, 20,* 196–201.

Kinsey, V., Jacobus, J., & Hemphill, F. (1956). Retrolental fibroplasia: Cooperative study of retrolental fibroplasia and the use of oxygen. *AMA Archives of Ophthalmology, 56,* 481–485.

Klaus, M.H., & Fanaroff, A.A. (1986). *Care of the high-risk neonate* (3rd ed.). Philadelphia: W.B. Saunders.

Klaus, M.H., & Kennell, J.H. (1976). *Parent–infant bonding.* St. Louis: C.V. Mosby.

Korner, A.F., Kraemer, H.C., Haffner, M.E., & Cosper, L.M. (1975). Effects of waterbed flotation on premature infants: A pilot study. *Pediatrics, 56,* 361–367.

Krehbiel, R., Munsick-Bruno, G., & Lowe, J.R. (1991). NICU infants born at developmental risk and the individualized family service plan. *Children's Health Care, 20,* 26–33.

Krishnamoorthy, K.S., Shannon, D.C., Delong, G.R., Todres, I.D., & Davis, K.R. (1979). Neurologic sequelae in the survivors of neonatal intraventricular hemorrhage. *Pediatrics, 64,* 233–237.

Lawhon, G., & Melzar, A. (1988). Developmental care of the very low birth weight infant. *Journal of Perinatal Neonatal Nursing, 2*(1), 56–65.

Lawson, K., & Turkowitz, G. (1985). Relationships between the distribution and diurnal periodicities of infant state and environment. In A.W. Gottfried & J.L. Gaiter (Eds.), *Infant stress under intensive care: Environmental neonatology* (pp. 157–170). Baltimore: University Park Press.

Levy-Shiff, R., Shari, H., & Molgari, M.B. (1989). Mother-and-father–preterm infant relationship in the hospital preterm nursery. *Child Development, 60,* 93–102.

Linn, P.L., Horowitz, F.D., Buddin, B.J., Leake, J.C., & Fox, H.A. (1985). An ecological description of neonatal intensive care unit. In A.W. Gottfried & J.L. Gaiter (Eds.), *Infant stress under intensive care: Environmental neonatology* (pp. 83–112). Baltimore: University Park Press.

Long, J.G., Philip, A.G., & Lucey, J.F. (1980). Excessive handling as a cause of hypoxemia. *Pediatrics, 65,* 203–207.

Mann, N.P., Haddow, R., Stokes, L., Goodley, S., & Rutter, N. (1986). Effect of night and day on preterm infants in a newborn nursery: Randomised trial. *British Medical Journal, 293,* 1265–1267.

Marshall, R.E., Roberts, J.L., & Walsh, J.H. (1985). The impact of the environment on the NICU caregiver: Perspectives of the nurse, pediatric house officer, and academic neonatologist. In A.W. Gottfried & J.L. Gaiter (Eds.), *Infant stress under intensive care: Environmental neonatology* (pp. 227–250). Baltimore: University Park Press.

Marton, P.M., Dawson, H., & Minde, K. (1980). The interaction of ward personnel with infants in the premature nursery. *Infant Behavior and Development, 3,* 307–313.

Marton, P., Minde, K., & Perotta, M. (1981). The role of the father of the infant at risk. *American Journal of Orthopsychiatry, 51,* 672–679.

Masi, W. (1979). Supplemental stimulation of the preterm infant. In T.M. Field, A.M. Sostek, S. Goldberg, & H.H. Shuman (Eds.), *Infants born at risk: Behavior and development* (pp. 367–387). New York: SP Medical and Scientific Books.

Merritt, T.A., Hallman, M., Bloom, B.T., Berry, C., Bernirschke, K., Sahn, D., Key, T., Edwards, D., Jarvenpaa, A.L., Pohjavuori, M., Kankaanpaa, K.,

Kunnas, M., Paatero, H., Raploa, J., & Jaaskelainen, J. (1986). Prophylactic treatment of very premature infants with human surfactant. *New England Journal of Medicine, 315,* 785–790.

Minde, K.K., Marton, P., Manning, D., & Hines, B. (1980). Some determinants of mother–infant interaction in the premature nursery. *Journal of the American Academy of Child Psychiatry, 19,* 1–21.

Minde, K.K., Trehub, S., Corter, C., Boukydis, C., Celhoffer, L., & Marton, P. (1978). Mother–infant relationships in the premature nursery. *Pediatrics, 61,* 373–379.

Morley, C.J. (1987). Ten center trial of artificial surfactant in very premature babies. *British Medical Journal, 294,* 991–996.

Murdoch, D.R., & Darlow, B.A. (1984). Handling during neonatal intensive care. *Archives of Disease in Childhood, 59,* 957–961.

Norbeck, J.S. (1985). Perceived job stress, job satisfaction and psychological symptoms in critical care nursing. *Research in Nursing and Health, 8,* 253–259.

Papile, L., Burstein, J., Burstein, R., & Koffler, H. (1978). Incidence and evolution of subependymal and intraventricular hemorrhage: A study of infants with birth-weights less than 1500g. *Journal of Pediatrics, 92,* 529–534.

Papile, L.A., Munsick, G., Weaver, N., & Peca, S. (1979). Cerebral intraventricular hemorrhage (CVH) in infants under 1,500 grams: Developmental follow-up at one year. *Pediatric Research, 92,* 529–534.

Peabody, J.L., & Lewis, K. (1985). Consequences of newborn intensive care. In A.W. Gottfried & J.L. Gaiter, *Infant stress under intensive care: Environmental neonatology* (pp. 199–226). Baltimore: University Park Press.

Pearl, L.F., Brown, W., & Meyers, M.K.S. (1990). Transition from the neonatal intensive care unit: Putting it all together in the community. *Infants and Young Children, 3*(1), 41–50.

Rao, H.K.M., & Elhassani, S.B. (1981). Iatrogenic complications of procedures performed on the newborn. *Perinatology/Neonatology, 5,* 23.

Rauh, V.A., Achenbach, T.M., Nurcombe, B., Howell, C.T., & Teti, D.M. (1988). Minimizing adverse effects of low birth weight: Four-year results of an early intervention program. *Child Development, 59,* 544–553.

Resnick, M.B., Armstrong, S., & Carter, R.L. (1988). Developmental intervention program for high-risk premature infants: Effects on development and parent–infant interaction. *Journal of Developmental and Behavioral Pediatrics, 9,* 73–78.

Resnick, M.B., Eyler, F., Nelson, R., Eitzman, D.V., & Bucciarelli, R.L. (1987). Developmental intervention for low birth weight infants: Improved early developmental outcome. *Pediatrics, 80,* 68–74.

Rosenfield, A.G. (1980). Visiting the intensive care nursery. *Child Development, 51,* 939–941.

Rushton, C.H. (1990). Family-centered care in the critical care setting: Myth or reality? *Children's Health Care, 19,* 68–78.

Sammons, W.A.H., & Lewis, J.M. (1985). *Premature babies: A Different beginning.* St. Louis: C.V. Mosby.

Schneider, J.W., & Chasnoff, I.J. (1987). Cocaine abuse during pregnancy: Its effects on infant motor development—A clinical perspective. *Topics in Acute Care Trauma and Rehabilitation, 2,* 59-69.

Schneider, J.W., Griffith, D.R., & Chasnoff, I.J. (1989). Infants exposed to cocaine in utero: Implications for developmental assessment and intervention. *Infants and Young Children, 2*(1), 25–36.

Shankaran, S., Slovis, T.L., Bedard, M.P., & Poland, R.L. (1982). Sonographic classification of intracranial hemorrhage: A prognostic indicator of mortality, morbidity, and short-term neurologic outcome. *Journal of Pediatrics, 100,* 469–475.

Shapiro, D., & Nutter, R. (1988). Controversies regarding surfactant replacement therapy. *Clinics in Perinatology, 15,* 891–901.

Thurman, S.K. (1991). Parameters for establishing family-centered neonatal intensive care services. *Children's Health Care, 20,* 34–39.

Thurman, S.K., Cornwell, J.R., & Korteland, C. (1989). The Liaison Infant Family Team (LIFT) Project: An example of case study evaluation. *Infants and Young Children, 2*(2), 74–82.

Thurman, S.K., & Korteland, C. (1989). The behavior of mothers and fathers toward their infants during neonatal intensive care visits. *Children's Health Care, 18,* 247–251.

Thurman, S.K., & Widerstrom, A.H. (1990). *Infants and young children with special needs: A developmental and ecological approach* (2nd ed.). Baltimore: Paul H. Brookes Publishing Co.

Urrea, P.T., & Rosenbaum, A.L. (1989). Retinopathy of prematurity: An ophthalmologist's perspective. In S. Isenberg (Ed.), *Eye in infancy* (pp. 428–456). Chicago: Yearbook Medical Publishers, Inc.

Volpe, J.J. (1990). Intraventricular hemorrhage in the premature infant. In S.M. Pueschel & J.A. Mulick (Eds.), *Prevention of developmental disabilities* (pp. 197–215). Baltimore: Paul H. Brookes Publishing Co.

Widmayer, S.M., & Field, T.M. (1981). Effects of Brazelton demonstrations for mothers on the development of preterm infants. *Pediatrics, 67,* 711–714.

Wolke, D. (1986, July). *The neonatal intensive care environment: Developmental support for preterm infants.* Paper presented at the International Symposium on The Biopsychology of Parent–Infant Communication, Lisbon, Portugal.

Wolke, D. (1987). Environmental and developmental neonatology. *Journal of Reproductive and Infant Psychology, 5,* 17–42.

Developmental Follow-Up of At-Risk Infants

Lynda F. Pearl

Improved survival of neonates at high risk has now been described in this country and abroad (Cooper & Kennedy, 1989; Hack, Fanaroff, Avrog, & Merkatz, 1979). An important issue in improving the physical and mental health of children is the development and implementation of effective follow-up procedures for young children thought to be at high risk for later developmental delays. There are two broad purposes of follow-up: 1) to identify individual children and families in need of intervention, and 2) to identify high-risk factors that appear to predict later developmental delays. Implicit in both of these purposes is the goal of referring identified children into a system of direct intervention services aimed at normalizing development to the greatest degree possible.

Research efforts in the 1970s and 1980s have attempted to identify specific high-risk characteristics that appear to be determinants of later developmental performance. Studies of single risk factors and conditions are discussed in this chapter, along with the concept of multiple risk factors. A range of models for follow-up and risk assessment that starts in the hospital setting and transfers with the family into the home community is described. Along with better definitions of high-risk factors have come suggestions for different methods of service delivery to different high-risk populations. A variety of different follow-up models are presented. Some of the models presented, such as those designed for working with children who are HIV positive or have been prenatally exposed to drugs, follow families so intensely that they can also be considered intervention systems. Others develop a centralized listing of all children with a specific condition who reside within a political area and refer families to a wide variety of different service providers.

LONG-TERM FOLLOW-UP RESULTS FOR HIGH-RISK INFANTS

In each decade of this century, there have been significant reductions in infant mortality, particularly in the first four weeks of life . . . The most dramatic reduction in neonatal mortality has been since 1970 with a drop in mortality from 15.1 per 1,000 in 1970 to 8.4 per 1,000 in 1980. (Waldstein, Gilderman, Taylor-Hershel, Prestridge, & Anderson, 1982, p. 7)

The decline in mortality rates is credited primarily to the development of the neonatal intensive care unit (NICU). As neonatal medicine has saved larger numbers of extremely premature and sick infants, the area of high-risk follow-up research has become a new frontier in pediatrics. Table 1 lists some common conditions that merit follow-up.

Many of the children discharged from NICUs are at risk for later developmental delays, due to the factors surrounding their birth and early development. These children are discharged when they are medically stable, but enter community hospitals or their home com-

Table 1. Common criteria for inclusion in high-risk follow-up

One or more of the following:

Medical conditions
Birth asphyxia
Meconium aspiration
Intraventricular hemorrhage
Severe respiratory distress syndrome
Severe bronchopulmonary dysplasia
Perinatal seizures
Hyperbilirubinemina requiring several exchange transfusions
Sepsis
Meningitis
Significant congenital abnormalities

Other clinical conditions
Low birth weight (less than 2,500 g)
Infants small for gestational age
5-minute Apgar score of four or less
Significant neurological problems
Psychosocial problems (maternal substance abuse, family psychiatric problems, etc.)
Conditions for which there is no precedent
Chromosomal abnormalities
Significant vision and hearing impairment

munity to continue healing. This healing process can take months or even years. Discharge from the NICU does not mean that recovery is complete (Pearl, Brown, & Myers, 1990). While some children's medical and developmental conditions seem to be resolved in early childhood, other children continue to show delays in development or long-term medical problems into their school years. Also, some children who seem to have resolved their problems in early childhood later show evidence of learning difficulties.

A major focus of research in this area has been the examination of risk factors and their later developmental outcomes through longitudinal research designs. This type of research presents some significant challenges for professionals attempting to determine which single risk factors act as accurate predictors of later development. A great deal of the focus has been on determining predictive relationships between specific early medical conditions and later developmental delays. Several serious challenges make this type of research difficult.

The difficulty of assembling a homogeneous sample is one of these challenges. In order to establish prediction, researchers need to isolate the key variables to the greatest degree possible so that their effects can be measured. Unfortunately, infants with high-risk medical conditions (i.e., extreme prematurity) rarely have only one diagnosis or disease condition, but, rather, tend to have many interrelated problems. The researcher is thus faced with a dilemma. If he or she chooses to study infants who have only the target condition, the sample size may be very small, leading to the loss of some degree of generalizability. In addition, the normal attrition rate in any long-term study usually lowers the sample size over time, which also affects statistical analyses. If the investigator chooses to study a more typical population of infants with the target condition *and* the various associated conditions, then the results may be affected by the fact that the subjects may be dissimilar or the related conditions may be the true causes of the results.

An additional concern relates to the problem of interpreting longitudinal research in a changing technological climate. Studies that follow children for long periods of time may take many years from implementation to the dissemination of results. According to Carran, Scott, Shaw, and Beydouin (1989) most longer high-risk follow-up studies currently being reported that were done in the United States involve children born at least a decade ago. Within this time, the changes in technology have been so great as to make some study results somewhat outdated. For example, results of studies done with a population of extremely premature infants prior to the development of mechanical ventilation would be difficult to generalize now that this technology has become commonplace. A similar phenomenon is the widespread use of artificial surfactant for infants diagnosed as having respiratory distress syndrome. In an effort to achieve more generalizable research results and address some of these issues, large collaborative studies using multiple sites have been initiated, and data from these sites is being compiled.

Studies of high-risk newborns have concentrated on several "higher incidence" subgroups, including low birth weight infants (as well as those who are small for gestational age [SGA]), infants with specific syndromes or diseases, and infants who have been prenatally exposed to drugs. An additional group that evokes a great deal of concern is that made up of infants with a positive diagnosis for HIV. Each of these subgroups will be discussed in terms of research perspectives and findings.

Low Birth Weight Infants

Of the high risk groups, infants with low birth weight are one of the most frequently studied. Low birth weight has been defined as less than 3,500 g (approximately 5½ lbs), and very low birth weight as less than 1,500 g (approximately 3 lbs). Recently, some researchers have also defined a subgroup of extremely low birth weight infants as those weighing less than 1,000 g (approximately 2 lbs). Low birth weight has been implicated as a possible cause of mild disabilities in later childhood, although there is no clear understanding of how direct the link may be (Carran et al., 1989; Kitchen et al., 1980).

The general pattern of outcomes for infants with low birth weights in the twentieth century is described by Hack et al. (1979). Initially (prior to 1940), care for these infants was primarily the responsibility of the obstetrician. Control of environmental temperature, avoidance of infection, and fostering of the mother–child bond were the primary goals of care. While newborn mortality rates were high, long-term follow-up results were remarkably good (Hess, 1953).

Between 1940 and 1960, treatment of low birth weight infants

. . . was punctuated by many setbacks, often resulting from well intentioned but misdirected therapeutic interventions. Retrolental fibroplasia [now called retinopathy of prematurity] was produced by the overuse of oxygen, and starvation hypoglycemia, dehydration, and jaundice resulted from an inappropriate delay in initiating feeding . . . Compounding such therapeutic misadventures, was an imposed isolation of the premature infants that separated the infant from the mother and family.(Hack et al., 1979)

Developmental-outcome studies of children with low birth weight show that high percentages of children with later disabilities were found in studies of cohorts born between 1940 and the 1960s. Drillien, Thomson, and Burgoyne (1980) found that 60% of the children with low birth weight whom they followed later showed disabilities, while Lubchenco (1980) reports a 68% disability rate. Many studies from this period lack control groups of typically developing children, and treatment groups of low birth weight infants include those who were small for gestational age, as well as typical-size premature babies. As a result, the use of the long-term data for comparative purposes is limited.

In the 1970s and 1980s, new medical techniques developed rapidly. These included more effective treatment of asphyxia through earlier intubation, mechanically aided ventilation, active ways to correct metabolic acidosis, and better methods of monitoring oxygen administration. At the same time, perinatal advances allowed for better monitoring of fetal growth and development. One result of these new approaches was a decrease in neonatal mortality and morbidity (Rawlings, Reynolds, & Stewart, 1971).

Long-term follow-up studies from the 1970s to the early 1990s show increased survival and positive outcome rates for small infants. Research studies seem to use subject groups that are increasingly better-defined. For example, Blackman (1988) reviews the specific effects of inadequate oxygenation of the brain at birth on later developmental outcomes for preterm infants. His sample is subdivided into preterm infants and infants who experience neonatal seizures. He concludes that research shows that the "relationship between low Apgar scores and poor developmental outcomes is particularly weak for preterm infants, whose immature nervous systems may be more tolerant of temporary oxygen deprivation than those of full-term infants" (Blackman, 1988, p. 10). Infants who were subject to newborn seizures appear to function significantly below the norm in the areas of verbal, perceptual, and pre-academic skills as preschoolers (Blackman, 1988). Janowsky and Nass (1987) have followed mildly asphyxiated full-term infants up to age 5. They have found that these infants have a high probability of delay on the Early Language Milestone Scale at age 2. Infants born weighing under 1,000 g are showing fewer severe early medical problems (Breslau, Klein, & Allen, 1988; McCormick, 1989); however, they continue to be very vulnerable to cognitive and neurological disorders as they get older (How, Bill, & Sikes, 1988).

Long-term studies on the developmental outcomes of low birth weight have concentrated on determining major deficits in intelligence and school performance (Affleck, Tennen, & Rowe, 1991). Many studies focusing on low birth weight infants end in early childhood, while others follow children into school but examine only educational outcomes or milder forms of morbidity (Campbell, Leib, Vollman, & Gibson, 1989). The results of one study by Carran et al. (1989) divided infants into normal, low, and very low birth weight groups and followed them to ages 8 through 12. Carran's results showed no significant differences in medical problems between groups. Results demonstrate that there is an increasing rate of morbidity in lower birth weight populations. Perhaps the most important finding is that infants from low income homes who are between 1,500 and 2,500 grams are at greatly elevated risk of mild learning disabilities as compared to their normal birth weight peers. Other recently reported studies of very low birth weight infants show the majority of subjects with typical intelligence, but with a significant subgroup experiencing school failure, low achievement-test scores, and a higher chance of being diagnosed with learning disabilities (Affleck et al., 1991; Lefebvre, Bard, Veilleux, & Martel, 1988; Saigal, Rosenbaum, Stoskopf, & Milner, 1982). In addition, there is evidence that low birthweight infants show a higher-than-average incidence of aggressive and/or hyperactive behaviors both in the preschool and school years (Raugh, Achenbach, Nurcombe, Howell, & Teti, 1988; Breslau et al., 1988).

Infants Small for Gestational Age

A subgroup of infants with low birth weight are those who are small for gestational age (SGA). Infants are considered to be SGA, or small for date, if their birth weight is less than the 10th percentile for gestational age (Sell & Brazelton, 1980). Fitzhardinge and Steven (1972) studied infants who were below the 3rd percentile in weight at birth and found that their most rapid period of growth occurred in the first 6 months of life. At 6 years, the children's mean weights still remained between the 10th and 25th percentile. The same essential pattern was recorded for height, with the largest gains being made in the first 6 months. "Children who eventually attained normal height were those who grew the most during the first year of life" (Sell & Brazelton, 1980, p. 110). Children also seemed to retain the same relative proportions between height, weight, and head circumference throughout early childhood. It is important to note that while infants who were SGA remained smaller than average, the majority had measurements within the normal range (Kumar, Anday, Sacks, Ting, & Delivoria-Papadopoulas, 1980).

In addition to determining outcomes for physical characteristics, there has been interest in whether slower growth in utero leads to slower postnatal intellectual development. Parkinson, Wallis, and

Harvey (1981) studied 60 infants who were SGA and used ultrasound techniques to determine the gestational age at which head growth slowed down. They found that infants whose head growth had slowed before 26 weeks had lower developmental quotients at age 4 and 5 than did infants whose head growth slowed after that point. When the same children were followed up at age 9, similar differences continued to be recorded. Ounsted, Mour, and Scott (1983) studied 221 SGA infants and 244 average-for-date infants to determine differences in developmental rates at age 4. The results were similar to those of the Parkinson et al. study (1981).

Infants with Congenital Disease Conditions

The research in this area has concentrated on specific conditions found more commonly in newborns, such as intraventricular hemorrhage, bronchopulmonary dysplasia, respiratory distress syndrome, and asphyxia. Many of these conditions occur most often in premature infants, so the research may be confounded by the impact of low birthweight and prematurity on the specific disease condition.

Intraventricular hemorrhage (IVH) is a condition in which swelling or bleeding occurs in the ventricles of the brain. "Infants who are under 34 weeks of gestational age, and who weigh less than 1,500 grams, and who experience respiratory failure requiring ventilator support are at increased risk for suffering . . . IVH" (Saylor, Levkoff, & Elksnin, 1989, p. 87). Hemorrhages are graded as to severity from Grade I to IV according to the following criteria:

Grade I: Bleeding confined to the subependymal germinal matrix.
Grade II: Bleeding extends into the ventricals, but there is no ventricular dilation.
Grade III: Bleeding extends into the ventricals and there is ventricular dilation.
Grade IV: Massive bleeding into the ventricals occurs and dilation is profound. (Saylor et al., p. 88)

Most research has seemed to indicate that infants who sustain the higher-grade hemorrhages (Grade III–Grade IV) have poorer developmental outcomes in later early childhood (Bagnato & Neisworth, 1989; Taeusch & Yogman, 1987). Since the area affected in a grade IV hemorrhage is traversed by the motor and sensory pathways (Saylor et al., 1989), the most common areas in which delays appear in these cases are the motor, sensory, and cognitive areas of development (Taeusch & Yogman, 1987). Recent technological developments have provided the ability to detect and follow children with less severe bleeding (Grade I–Grade II). This has led to questions regarding the developmental outcomes for these children.

For infants with respiratory distress syndrome (RDS) at birth, the developmental outcomes have been more positive. Research appears to indicate that when infants sustain RDS without the complications of very low birth weight or IVH, the prognosis for later development is very good (Hack et al., 1979; Janis, Cummins, & Davis, 1979). The exception to this seems to be children with bronchopulmonary dysplasia, which is a complication of RDS:

> Bronchopulmonary dysplasia (BPD) causes complex changes in the lungs of newborn infants after prolonged mechanical ventilation. BPD can have a widely varied course in different children and a wide range of severity depending on the infant. Only a relatively small population of infants with BPD remain technology-dependent beyond the period of their initial hospitalization. (Ahmann & Lipsi, 1991, p. 71)

Delays in development may be due to inadequate sensory stimulation (because of extended hospitalization), poor nutrition, perinatal, and/ or neonatal events (Goldson, 1984). Infants with BPD show significantly lower scores on the Bayley Scales of Development at age 2. Also, these children seem to have a higher percentage of abnormal findings in the motor area when assessed by a physical therapist at age 2 (Field, Widmayer, Stringer, & Ignatoff, 1980).

Recent commercial use of artificial surfactant may reduce the percentage of children with severe BPD, due to a reduced need for mechanical ventilation. Neonatal researchers are currently in the process of evaluating the impact of artificial surfactant products.

Infants Who Have Been Prenatally Exposed to Drugs

The National Institute on Drug Abuse estimates that over 5 million women of childbearing age are using illegal substances (Mangano, 1991). The National Association on Perinatal Addiction Research and Education (Mangnano, 1990) estimates that 375,000 drug-exposed infants were born in 1987. It is estimated that 1 million of these mothers were abusing cocaine. The President's Drug Control Strategy estimates that 100,000 cocaine-exposed infants are born each year (Office of the Inspector General, 1990a). Another source (Tyler, 1992), estimates that "the incidence of prenatal exposure to illicit substances in the U.S. is 11% of live births. However, this estimate is based on random sampling. Not all infants and mothers are screened at the time of birth and delivery" (p. 706).

The problem of prenatal drug exposure has been occurring since biblical times; in Judges 13:14, Samson's mother was warned not to drink alcoholic beverages during her pregnancy. In the United States, it was not until the latter part of the 20th century that fetal alcohol syndrome was described (Tyler, 1992). In the 1960s, the medical profession began to identify and address complications associated with prenatal drug exposure, and in the 1970s, researchers started to evaluate the developmental problems related to the condition. The emphasis of this early research was on the consequences of heroin and methadone exposure, because the subjects were primarily heroin-addicted women entering treatment programs to obtain methadone.

Research today shows that the problem of prenatal drug exposure includes the abuse not only of illicit drugs, but also of alcohol, nicotine, and prescription drugs. In addition, although a user may have a "drug of choice," there is usually multiple-drug use. Furthermore, illicit drugs are rarely pure, and users often don't know the dosage or the elements used to dilute the dose (Russel & Free, 1991; Tyler, 1992). Drug-abusing mothers are also at high risk for developing AIDS, because they often engage in behaviors, such as sharing needles, that lead to transmission of this disease. According to the Office of the United States Inspector General (1990b) it may be very difficult to separate cocaine-addiction problems from AIDS problems.

Drug testing of mothers in labor is inconsistent from hospital to hospital. Most private hospitals do not test, while some public hospitals perform random testing and some only test women who self-report. Many tests can detect cocaine in the system for only a short period (hours) after use. For this reason, practitioners recommend that toxicology screenings should be combined with a good medical and social history, as well as a neurobehavioral evaluation of the infant (Tyler, 1992). There is a possibility that current drug screening policies, or the lack of them, may only lead to identification of mothers who are heavy users. It is possible that research today is focusing on one end of the continuum, with a significant number of children who react less severely to the effects of drug exposure remaining unidentified and unfollowed (Frank, 1990).

Prenatal drug exposure places the fetus at risk for many medical problems. Children seem to be affected to differing degrees, however:

> exposure to alcohol or illicit drugs during any trimester of pregnancy is detrimental to the developing fetus to some degree. In the first trimester, the developing fetus is most susceptible to malformations of major organs . . . In the second and third trimesters, the problems brought by drug exposure can be more subtle and less readily apparent. (Tyler, 1992, p. 706)

Fetal growth is often poor, with higher possibilities of miscarriage, smaller infants, and premature birth. If the infant is born prematurely, then he or she is subject to all of the complications associated with early birth as well (e.g., chronic respiratory problems, intracranial hemorrhaging leading to cerebral palsy or cognitive deficits).

In addition, infants and children with a history of prenatal drug exposure show many abnormal developmental signs. As infants, they
may be irritable, difficult to console, or very lethargic for extended
periods. Later, these children may develop problems related to poor
impulse control or self-regulation (e.g., short attention span, difficulty changing activities, poor ability to interact socially, behavior
problems). Infants often have recurring tremors of the arms and legs
that may present later as difficulties in motor dexterity, speech production, or writing. These children are also at higher risk for vision
and hearing impairment. When neural damage or repeated middle
ear infections lead to oral motor difficulties, causing poor speech and
hearing impairment, the result can be major communication problems (Tyler, 1992).

Many infants who have been prenatally exposed to crack cocaine
go unidentified. This may occur for two reasons: there is no typical
reaction to exposure, and testing technology is limited. Symptoms
may differ widely. While 18% of babies prenatally exposed to crack
are born prematurely, many others are full-term and are discharged
as normal newborns. Myers, Olson, and Kaltenbach (1992) state that
there is presently no conclusive information on the precise effects of
prenatal exposure to cocaine. One recent review of research (Neuspiel & Hamel, 1991) seems to indicate that the only findings substantiated across studies are that infants exposed to cocaine are at greater
danger of being younger and smaller at birth. Prenatal exposure to
cocaine may also lead to birth defects, low birth weight, neurological
and respiratory problems, small head size, poor feeding, and higher
risk of sudden infant death syndrome. There is also some indication
of hemorrhaging in the frontal lobes and basal ganglia during pregnancy (Chasnoff, 1990; Frank, 1990). In addition, most experts believe
that significant numbers of these infants will have long-term developmental delays, although the full range of effects remains unknown. It
is difficult to separate the impact of social risk factors such as poverty,
medical risk factors such as poor maternal nutrition, or the effects of
other drugs such as alcohol or marijuana, from cocaine exposure
(Frank, 1990).

Experience with other potential developmental insults during
pregnancy has shown that the critical determinants of outcome are
often not severity of prenatal insult, but the quality of the postnatal
experience. The typically chaotic lifestyle of the drug abuser is not
conducive to the healthy development of a child. These children are
rarely exposed to consistent, nurturing caregiving (Gregorchik, 1992).
Continued drug abuse in the families of drug exposed infants jeopar-
dizes the quality of their environment and experiences. The risks may

be both pharmacological and social (Frank, 1990). For example, infants of mothers who continue to use cocaine may intoxicate their infants through their breast milk, and passive inhalation of cocaine has been reported to be related to childhood seizures. The quality of infant experience may vary with the amount of continued drug use.

A serious lack of drug treatment programs that will accept a pregnant drug abuser is reported throughout the literature (Chasnoff, 1990; Miller, 1989; Office of the Inspector General, 1990a, 1990b). While the number of female users seems to be on the increase, there are few treatment programs designed for women, and those that are available have only limited space. Lubinski (1990) reports that fewer than 50 programs nationwide have the capacity to serve pregnant women or women and their dependent children. When follow-up services are available, the cost is extremely high because of the wide range of services that are needed by children and families. For example, "The Florida Department of Health and Rehabilitation estimates an annual cost of over $40,000 per child to get crack babies ready for school" (Office of the Inspector General, 1990a, p. 3).

According to testimony in front of the Senate Subcommittee on Children, Family, Drugs, and Alcoholism, "expanded access to a continuum of treatment programs for all addicted persons and especially pregnant women and mothers is absolutely essential" (Coletti, 1990). Also in testimony before the Senate Subcommittee on Children, Family, Drugs, and Alcoholism, the president of Operation PAR (parental awareness and responsibility), a program serving drug-abusing women, states that the solution lies in providing community-based services (Coletti, 1990). Short-term goals for community programs should include: education and training for professionals, outreach to mothers, specialized services to the affected child, access to prenatal health care, and substance-abuse treatment. Long-term goals should include specialized training for child care providers working with drug-exposed children, more training of educators and administrators in recommended practices for educating drug-exposed children, and promotion of cooperation among child welfare, social services, schools, and communities in planning and implementing programs for this population (Coletti, 1990).

Infants with HIV Diagnoses

HIV, the virus that causes acquired immunodeficiency syndrome (AIDS), has gradual and progressive effects on the human body's defense mechanism, and eventually renders the person defenseless to fight off opportunistic infections and malignancies. The spectrum of the disease ranges broadly from asymptomatic, to enlarged lymph nodes and immunocompromise without disease, to symptomatic disease with infection. Most infected children are likely to have acquired this infection from HIV-positive mothers or through contaminated blood or blood by-products (Conlon, 1992). Mothers who have the HIV-positive antibodies transfer them to their newborn. For the majority of these infants, the antibodies measured between birth and 15 months are those passed on by the mother. The children usually show no symptoms of disease during this time. But if antibodies and/or disease symptoms persist after 15 months, the child is likely to be infected with the virus (Howard, Beckwith, Rodning, & Kropenske, 1989). Approximately 50% of the infants of HIV-positive mothers will also be HIV-positive.

Children of color have been particularly affected by the AIDS epidemic:

> While African-American children constitute 15% of all children in the U.S., they represent 53% of all childhood AIDS cases. A similar disparity is found among Latino children. They make up 10% of our nation's children, but comprise 25% of all pediatric AIDS cases. (Crossings, 1991/1992)

Typical symptoms of HIV infection include small size for age; failure to thrive; swelling of lymph glands; pneumonia; recurrent viral, bacterial, and other opportunistic infections; and thrush (Rendon, Gurdin, Bassi, & Weston, 1989).

Even the short-term outcomes for infants testing positive for HIV are problematic, because many of these infants have no home to be discharged into. Often, the parents are too ill or disorganized to care for the children at home, and, as a result, the child remains in the hospital. The term *boarder babies* has been applied to this group of children. According to Gurdin and Anderson (1991), in New York City during the mid 1980s, over 300 babies per month remained in the hospital beyond the point of medical necessity simply because they had nowhere to go. The foster-care system has had difficulty finding placements for HIV-positive infants in most states; one example of a foster care follow-up program for children who are HIV positive is provided at the end of this chapter.

Environmental Risk Factors

Family processes play a critical role in the moderation of biological risk factors such as those discussed above (Silber, 1989). There is some indication that the influence of environmental factors may be heightened for young children at biological risk for later delay (Crnic, Greenberg, Ragozin, Robinson, & Basham, 1983). For example, Crnic,

Greenberg, and Slough (1986) indicate that their recent research findings show family factors accounting for more than one-half of the variance in the intellectual performance of preterm infants. The child who has been prenatally exposed to drugs and comes from a dysfunctional family living in poverty has many negative family factors that may lead to poorer developmental outcomes. Working with typically developing young children, Brazelton (1981) expressed the view that socioeconomic status and parental education level may be among the most accurate predictors of later development. According to Kochanek and Buka (1991), research has shown that early identification of children at high risk for poor later development must be based not only on information on biological insults, "but also [on] the social and familial environment within which a child interacts" (p. 12). This leads to an understanding of the complexity of risk analysis, which involves multiple factors entering into a determining formula.

Multiple Risk Factors

While some single factors may appear to have significant short-term effects on development, long-term adverse effects are predicted most accurately when multiple risk factors are analyzed together. Research has identified several single factors that seem to have a significant negative impact when they are one of a group of factors present in an individual. Table 1 provides a list of criteria commonly recorded in follow-up studies. Parental mental illness, parental substance abuse, child abuse, and homelessness all appear to increase the risk status of any young child. Many of these risk factors are interrelated. For example, the addition of economic deprivation significantly increases a child's risk for poorer developmental outcomes because it is associated with some of the single factors listed above.

In general, research seems to indicate that the specific combination of risk factors is less important than the total number of risk factors found. It appears that for many high-risk infants, later developmental outcomes are a function of "several continuous and cumulative vulnerabilities or benefits that interact to depress or enhance intellectual potential" (Ensher & Clark, 1986, p. 145). Use of multiple-risk factor analysis has been proposed as an alternative to single-factor predictors. Central to this concept is the understanding that these multiple risk factors must be derived from both biological and social variables. According to Kochanek and Buka (1991), this means that identification models must include data collection on "biological and developmental circumstances as well as family needs, strengths, resources, support systems and the quality and quantity of the child/parent relationship" (p. 12).

COMPONENTS OF DEVELOPMENTAL FOLLOW-UP

The refining of multiple-factor models is a complex and ongoing process. As a result, the development of follow-up assessment and intervention models is often based on the different theoretical frameworks and professional interests of the participants. This is an important factor for those engaged in the review of follow-up models. The components and direction of follow-up models may be specifically related to the researchers' conceptualization of the multiple variables that affect later development. In addition, different disciplines have traditionally focused on different areas of development. For example, follow-up programs administered by hospital perinatal units tend to follow a medical model and emphasize the medical aspects of development. Other programs may emphasize the importance of sensory integration or of the language or cognitive aspects of development, or of family functioning, depending on the orientation of the participants.

Recently, there has been increased interest in follow-up models that are interdisciplinary in orientation and staffing and broader in conceptualization. According to Parmelee and Cohen (1985), when developing an interdisciplinary follow-up model, it is important to consider the diverse interests of each of the different professionals and families involved, understanding that neonatologists, pediatricians, community service providers, and families may all have different perspectives on the components of an appropriate follow-up program.

Follow-up programs are generally designed to meet one or more of the following objectives: 1) to provide ongoing support for the family, 2) to smooth the transition for the infant and family, 3) to direct the family toward appropriate community resources, 4) to meet specific training goals for students and professionals, 5) to research specific questions, 6) to provide ongoing secondary care of infants after discharge, and 7) to provide quality-control information for the intensive care nursery (Fitzhardinge, 1987; Pearl et al., 1990). All of these are appropriate reasons for following children.

In order to achieve the purposes of follow-up models listed above, some general components that should be present are: 1) an understanding of trends in early development (e.g., discontinuity, transient abnormalities, use of the normal developmental sequence for children with certain conditions); 2) appropriate transitional services during the move from hospital to home community; 3) a range of available follow-up services; 4) a focus on family-centered services; 5) adequate collaboration with community services; and 6) the means to evaluate the services provided.

Early Developmental Trends

The typical early-development pattern is not one of even, continuous growth. Instead, growth and development show discontinuity, characterized by spurts and slower periods. In addition, there are some common transient atypical patterns that appear in infancy but resolve themselves in early childhood. For example, some infants between 4 and 8 months develop high muscle tone which typically diminishes by 18 months of age. The fact that development is not a smooth progression supports the need for ongoing, continuous follow-up throughout the early years. The appropriate interval for follow-up may not be the same for all children and should be based on the needs of the child and family.

Transition

The transition from the hospital to the home community setting is an important one with many challenges for follow-up programs. "Even when transition is a sign of progress, such as the transition from the NICU to the home, the change can be unsettling" (Healy, Keesee, & Smith, 1989, p. 107). Addressing medical, developmental, and family issues is critical to the success of a follow-up program. Medical issues include: 1) ongoing medical education for primary-care physicians in order to enhance continuity of care; 2) individualized planning for families through the mechanism of discharge planning; 3) provision of a "medical home" for each family; and 4) coordination of specialty care. Developmental issues include: 1) facilitating the shift from a medical focus to a broader developmental focus, 2) providing access to information on community services through a single point of entry, 3) facilitating the sharing of appropriate information between hospital and community service providers, and 4) building the capacity of communities to provide follow-up within the local area.

The transition period can be used to provide opportunities to build the confidence of family members. Some suggestions for building confidence include:

1. Developing an individualized written transition plan for each family. If the child is eligible for services under Part H of IDEA, this plan may also be the family's IFSP.
2. Encouraging parents to participate in the discharge planning process, which should reflect their concerns and priorities.
3. Organizing and encouraging parents to participate in a "rooming-in" program prior to discharge. During rooming in, the parents should have the opportunity to care for their child in a supportive

environment. NICU staff should make every effort to help the parents develop feelings of confidence and independence.

4. Providing an opportunity for family members to learn infant CPR and basic care skills before discharge. (If they wish to do so, parents should be allowed to bring an additional person who will become a caregiver for the child to planning meetings, training sessions, and rooming-in programs.)

5. Organizing support groups available to parents, siblings, and extended family members while the target child is in the NICU. Some families may wish to talk to another parent who has had similar experiences or who has a child with a similar condition. When families do not wish to meet with a support group while the child is still in the hospital, it is important to provide some mechanism for later contact.

6. Providing videotaped reviews of medical procedures for viewing at home. These reviews may be tapes taken during rooming in or may be commercially available tapes.

7. Establishing interdisciplinary follow-up programs that focus on both the medical/developmental condition of the child and on family functioning. (Typically, such clinics focus only on the child.)

8. Including as part of the follow-up team a professional from the NICU who is known to the family. This provides the team with perspective and can be very reinforcing for the family if the child is growing and developing well (Pearl et al., 1990).

Range of Follow-Up Services

Considering the many high-risk conditions and their differing impacts on young children, the differences in resources within geographic areas, and the different needs of families, it seems clear that an important characteristic of effective follow-up for high-risk infants is program flexibility. Most programs recognize that the type and intensity of service needs differ among children and families and may change for any given family over time.

Programming that allows for different levels of service intensity may be more effective in meeting the needs of a wide range of families. Three levels of service that seem to be appropriate for comprehensive programs are:

Level 1—continuous intense early intervention that includes a comprehensive individualized plan, is provided by an interdisciplinary team, and includes service coordination

Level 2—intensive, interdisciplinary intervention services, including service coordination, during the infant/toddler period, with services tapering off at 2–3 years, and with periodic monitoring continuing into the school period

Level 3—continuous periodic monitoring throughout the early childhood period

Some of the necessary services may be provided by collaborating agencies, rather than by the follow-up program. The relationship between agencies and the importance of collaboration among community agencies is critical to the success of this type of program.

Collaboration with Community Services

The concept of interagency collaboration received considerable attention during the 1970's and 80's, with a growing recognition that the parallel, non-coordinated activities of many human service agencies dealing with young children . . . with disabilities resulted in a "patchwork quilt" of services. As a result, the notion developed that service agencies should work together to tackle such problems as (1) duplication of services and simultaneous gaps in services; (2) poor coordination among agencies offering interrelated and possible interdependent services; (3) diminishing financial resources to support human services programs that are similar or involve the same populations; and (4) poor accessibility of services, particularly in cases when recipients needed multiple forms of assistance. (Peterson, 1991, p. 89)

At the same time, the predominant philosophy of early childhood special education included the belief that interagency collaboration was a necessary ingredient for comprehensive early intervention with young children and their families. These trends are reflected in Part H of IDEA, which makes interagency collaboration an integral part of the service system for infants and toddlers with special needs.

Follow-up programs for high-risk infants are unique in that they include two teams. Beginning in the tertiary hospital, program members may be involved with the specialists providing neonatal intensive care, including neonatologists, specialized nurses and nurse practitioners, respiratory therapists, pediatric nutritionists, and various medical specialists, such as pediatric surgeons and cardiologists.

As the child and his or her family move home, the follow-up program team often interacts with a second team of community service providers. These professionals come from different disciplines and provide a wide range of services such as home health nursing, home-based early intervention, speech-language therapy, and functional vision training. Because they are often linked with early medical services, follow-up programs have an important contribution to make to the collaborative process. Access to medical information such as hospital discharge summaries, insight into the early medical problems that the child experienced, and consultation on later medical questions are examples of information that follow-up programs may be able to bring to community service teams because of their involvement with the medical and developmental teams. This link is important in providing continuity of care.

Family-Centered Follow-Up Services

Follow-up programs should support families by providing information and training. The principles of family-centered care, including respect, information delivered clearly and without jargon, empowerment, and enablement, can be implemented at all levels of the follow-up program. These principles should be incorporated into the services provided to infants and toddlers at high risk from the time that these children are identified to the end of their involvement with follow-up.

Families can guide programs by informing professionals about their priorities, concerns, and resources. For example, many programs ask families to complete a battery of assessments that gather information on resources, previous training, respite care, transportation, and financial needs. The wholesale application of these assessments without first establishing family concerns or problems is inconsiderate and inappropriate, and may be considered intrusive. Techniques to informally determine, with the family's help, exactly which assessments from the general battery are needed may help to tailor program services to family issues. One technique for determining general areas of need is the focused interview (Slentz & Bricker, 1992).

Some additional things that programs can do to keep the focus on the family include:

1. Developing policies, procedures, and documentation that maintain the type of family-focused message that the program team wishes to convey. If one of these components is "at odds" with this message, there will be difficulty keeping the program focused on families.
2. Acknowledging that the infant or toddler at high risk plays many roles in addition to that of a child with special needs, such as those of son/daughter, sibling, and young child. Each of these roles is important and may need to be fostered.
3. Asking parents if there are any other things that the child is doing or not doing that concern them. Sometimes a parent has a serious concern that is never mentioned, simply because no one asks. For

a further discussion of the principles of family-centered care, see Chapter 4 of this volume.

4. Incorporating follow-up needs into the individualized family service plan.

Evaluation of Services

Evaluation is an important component of all service delivery systems, including follow-up programs. Both formative and summative data can be collected and used to make program decisions. Summative evaluation relates to specific measurable outcomes, such as the amount of child progress in various developmental areas, or weight gain and other physical changes. Formative evaluation examines the ongoing workings of a program. Some examples of formative evaluation questions include: Were specific program timelines met? What was the profile of program strengths and weaknesses as seen by parents? What were identified on a needs assessment as areas in which staff training was needed?

Many follow-up programs are administered by hospitals, but take place, at least in part, in the community. Others are performed by community-based agencies, but involve a significant amount of work within the hospital setting. This may mean that in order to get relevant information, follow-up programs need to use evaluatiᵥ techniques different from those typically used by the rest of their agency. In addition, these programs require working with members of different disciplines, all of whom are traditionally evaluated in different ways. For example, the evaluative procedures used for physicians in a hospital are very different from those used to evaluate early interventionists within publicly administered agencies.

Specific Models for Follow-Up Services

A variety of different models for following infants and toddlers at high risk have been developed. Some of the more common ones, such as the interdisciplinary clinic, the high-risk register, and the large-scale referral/tracking system, are discussed below. Specific examples of programs are given, along with a description of services. In addition, some examples of comprehensive programs serving special populations are presented. The two special populations served in these examples are those of children with positive diagnoses for HIV and those who have been prenatally exposed to drugs. These examples have been included because of the increasing numbers of children with these problems being identified.

Interdisciplinary Follow-Up Clinics

Traditionally, hospital NICU's have followed their graduates by having them periodically visit an interdisciplinary clinic. Because of their medical affiliation, many of these clinics utilize a medical, rather than an educational, model. Often associated with research projects, these clinics vary in organizational structure and in the frequency, intensity, and duration of follow-up that they provide. Clinics also vary greatly in staffing patterns and settings.

The organization and staffing of follow-up clinics is usually interdisciplinary, with different numbers and types of disciplines represented. Typical disciplines represented might include: 1) medical professionals (a pediatrician, neonatologist, developmental pediatrician or pediatric nurse practitioner, or public health or pediatric nurse); 2) an early development specialist (a developmental psychologist or early childhood special educator); 3) developmental therapists (occupational, physical, and/or speech-language therapists); 4) an audiologist; 5) a family-focused professional (a family therapist or social worker); and 6) a pediatric nutritionist. The clinic may be organized for screening in each area, with referrals made for more in-depth testing, or it may provide assessment batteries as well as screening. One interesting variation provides scheduled screening in communities throughout the service area and refers children identified as needing more assessment to a central site for in-depth testing. The concept is similar to nursing triage, which is a familiar part of many medical service models.

There has been a great deal of variation in the frequency and length of follow-up. The typical clinic is organized to provide longitudinal follow-up through scheduled visits. For example, the Northeast Tennessee Regional Perinatal Center administers a follow-up clinic that commonly sees children at 2, 6, 12, 18, and 24 months of age (Pearl et al., 1990). At present, there seems to be agreement that follow-up should continue over time, but no specific preferred interval for scheduled assessments is clearly delineated in the research.

The setting for follow-up has usually been a hospital or public health department. Recently, some programs have developed traveling teams that visit specific locations at scheduled times. These groups may meet in many different types of settings.

High-Risk Registers

High-risk registers are listings of individuals with specific conditions for the purpose of follow up and/or data collection. Most are administered by a public agency. The goal of the registry usually relates to service provision, rather than research. One example is the Florida

Abuse Registry (Gregorchik, 1992). In 1987, the Florida Health and Rehabilitation Services Substance-Abused Newborns Regulation required all birthing places to provide information on any baby suspected of being a victim of substance abuse. According to Gregorchik (1992), in 1988–1989, 10,425 infants were added to the registry because of suspected or confirmed prenatal exposure to drugs. The Palm Beach County Health Department and Rehabilitative Services are currently engaged in a follow-up study of this population.

Large-Scale Tracking Programs

These types of programs attempt to track a large number of infants/toddlers who are at risk for later problems. The mechanism for getting information is usually a checksheet or interview protocol completed by the parent. One example of an instrument suitable for large-scale tracking of high-risk infants or toddlers is the Infant Monitoring Questionnaires (Bricker & Squires, 1989). This instrument is comprised of a series of protocols for different-age children (4–36 months). The questionnaires are completed by parents and returned to a central location, where they are analyzed. When questionable results are received, the parents are notified and arrangements are made for further assessments. The Watch Me Grow Program (M. Summerfelt, personal communication, 1992) is using the Infant Monitoring Questionnaires to follow a high-risk population. Supporting Families, a program described below, utilizes this instrument along with other sources of information.

EXAMPLES OF SPECIFIC PROGRAM MODELS

South Carolina Services Information System (SCSIS)

As the variety of services and service delivery models has grown, information and referral has become an issue. It is often difficult for families to find available services or to determine available service choices:

> The multitude of services available and the complex requirements of these services create a situation in which it is not feasible for an individual or service provider to be aware of all specialized community services. Consequently, information and referral (I&R) in today's society requires a professionally operated service dedicated to providing information. (Mayfield-Smith, Yajnik, & Wiles, 1990, p. 69–70)

The two major functions of a formalized I&R system are: 1) linking people in need with available, appropriate services and/or resources; and 2) assisting in long-range systematic planning using the data on the system to identify gaps in services (Levenson, 1981; Mayfield-Smith et al., 1990). This process may vary from simply identifying a service provider to maintaining ongoing contact with a family to help them negotiate the maze of different services and agencies. In addition, an organized I&R system may keep data on requested services that are unavailable in specific geographic areas.

I&R staff face the problem of constantly updating, adding, and deleting services. Services may utilize a print directory, but advances in computer technology make computer I&R systems possibilities for many areas. One such system operated in South Carolina by the Center for Developmental Disabilities is the South Carolina Services Information System (SCSIS). According to Mayfield-Smith et al. (1990), this is a computer-based I&R system that provides information in response to telephone requests. The requests come in over a toll-free number that is advertised in the communities served. SCSIS serves individuals of all ages who have special needs, as well as the families of infants and toddlers who require I&R services. Information specialists answer calls and discuss needs with clients. Often, multiple needs are discovered as the conversation continues. Transportation and financial assistance are two needs discussed, along with service referrals. If the services do not exist, the request is documented. State planners may utilize this data when reporting on service gaps.

The SCSIS database lists over 60,000 services in South Carolina and responds to over 400 calls per month. Several other states have adopted the South Carolina system for I&R (Mayfield-Smith et al., 1990).

Supporting Families

Supporting Families serves families in the rural southern Appalachian area of Tennessee. This project is a collaborative effort of the Center for Early Childhood Learning and Development, East Tennessee State University; the Association for Retarded Citizens of Washington County; and the Northeast Tennessee Regional Perinatal Center, Quillen College of Medicine, East Tennessee State University. The project is funded through the State of Tennessee Developmental Disabilities Planning Council. Families with children who are at risk for developmental delay due to established, environmental, or biological risk factors are eligible for Supporting Families. Families with infants who have terminal diagnoses are also eligible for services. The purpose of Supporting Families is to help enable families to better care for their at-risk infant through the provision of family-centered services. The program resulted from the medical, educational, and advocacy communities' acknowledgment of the lack of transitional services for children moving from the tertiary hospital to the community hospital and to the home community, and of intensive in-home services that were focused on empowering families to work on issues and concerns that affect all members, including the target infant. The three parts of the program are: developmental tracking for at-risk infants; family services; and community awareness. A tracking system is available for all interested families using the Infant Monitoring Questionnaires (Bricker & Squires, 1989). This is a parent-report system in which parents are mailed a developmental questionnaire when their child is ages 4, 8, 12, 16, 20, 30, and 36 months. Parents indicate whether their child can or cannot perform each item. Studies of the effectiveness of the questionnaires show that they provide a low-cost method of screening large numbers of at-risk children. This tool also has the benefit of involving the parents in the screenings, which builds information on child development and may stimulate some training activities.

As part of its family services component, Supporting Families provides assistance in obtaining general child care instruction; medical information and information on nutrition; transportation to doctor's appointments (for the target child); locations of child care facilities for children with special needs; applications for financial assistance; and advice on housing, budgeting, and other subjects. The program helps families to access all available community resources and provides additional help as requested. One emphasis of the program is the formation of a friendship between the family members and the family liaison assigned to them.

The community services component is focused on encouraging collaboration and joint efforts among agencies. This includes informing the families of infants who are back-transported to community hospitals about available support services.

The program is staffed by a coordinator who is responsible for receiving and coordinating referrals from two tertiary hospitals. The coordinator initiates services and meets with families while their child is still hospitalized and attends discharge-planning meetings for referred families. A transitional plan is developed for each family. Each of the eight counties covered by one of the tertiary hospitals has a family liaison working with the program. Families living in the vicinity of the tertiary hospital may begin services with their family liaison prior to discharge. Due to the extremely rural nature of the area, many families live far from the tertiary unit. In these cases, the local family liaison will take over services at the time of discharge to the home or back-transport to a community hospital.

Liaison Infant Family Team Project (LIFT)

The Liaison Infant Family Team Project (LIFT) started as a model demonstration project funded for 3 years by the Handicapped Children's Early Education Program of the United States Office of Special Education Programs. Services are provided at Bryn Mawr Hospital's neonatal intensive care unit and administered through Temple University's Department of Special Education (Philadelphia). According to the model, services to families can begin as early as 24 hours after admission to the NICU and can continue for as long as the family desires them. Individual program plans are developed, implemented, and monitored for each family. Services include in-hospital visits for families and assistance with transition of the child and family into the home community. The guiding principals of the program are:

> *Adaptive fit:* Interventions should be designed to increase the adaptive fit (i.e., a mutual acceptance between individuals who comprise a social system).
>
> *Family-driven services:* The needs and desires of the family should dictate the type and extent of service responses; help is given in response to and congruent with family-identified needs.
>
> *Family empowerment:* Families should develop independence from service providers and be empowered to get their own needs met; families should gain a sense of confidence and control in decisionmaking.
>
> *Family dynamism:* Families are complex and ever changing systems whose needs, resources, and styles of functioning respond to environmental events. (Thurman, Cornwall, & Korteland, 1989, p. 78)

The staff include an interdisciplinary team of four professionals with the following roles:

1. *Infant coordinator*—enhancing infant–parent interactions, performing developmental assessment, developing specific interventions and assisting families in carrying them out, and consulting with community intervention projects on the target child's program (educational psychologist specializing in infancy)

2. *Family coordinator*—providing support to families, assessing and promoting the development of adaptive fit between infant and family (counseling psychologist specializing in family therapy)

3. *Liaison coordinator*—determining appropriate community resources with families and linking families with these resources (hospital social worker)

4. *Team coordinator*—monitoring the development of team functioning and coordinating team activities (neonatal nurse practitioner)

Important features of this project are: the early and continued involvement with the family throughout the hospitalization, individualized planning, interdisciplinary team approach, focus on family-centered services, and transition into the home community.

Operation PAR

Operation PAR (parental awareness and responsibility) is a comprehensive service system for drug abusers, located in St. Petersburg, Florida (Coletti, 1990). In recent years, the program has focused on the needs of addicted women and their children and pregnant abusers. The services include a system of programs available to families as appropriate to their special needs. The following are offered:

1. *Maternal Substance Abuse Intervention Team*—This team works in conjunction with the public health and justice systems to identify, assess, refer, follow-up, and track cases of maternal drug abuse. The team also provides education for community professionals.
2. *Child Development and Family Guidance Center*—This program provides therapeutic child care services for infants and children of substance abusers, age 2 months to 5 years. The program provides case management, parent education, and support groups, as well as direct intervention services for the children.
3. *PAR Village*—This is a new program that will represent a partnership between the program, local community, and county and federal government. The program provides a special living situation within a therapeutic community setting, where women will be able to receive treatment and have their children with them. Mothers will receive quality long-term residential services and children will receive developmental child care and counseling.
4. *Education/Networking Services*—PAR provides community education and public awareness activities. The program coordinates conferences and networks related to substance abuse and is actively involved in research projects focusing on the effects of cocaine use on pregnancy and child development.

The Shields for Families Projects

The Shields for Families Projects are located in the Watts community of Los Angeles. Shields consists of three nonresidential programs for drug and alcohol abusing women and their drug-exposed newborns and other high-risk children. There are also three support programs administered through Shields. The goals of Shields are: to increase the number of substance-abusing women seeking prenatal care; to help maintain these women in medical and drug treatment; to assist them in maintaining their biological families through re-parenting and parent skill building; and to increase the number of infants cared for in their biological families in both center- and home-based settings (Babies and Cocaine, 1990).

The following programs are described as part of the Shields Projects:

1. *Project Support* offers regular group counseling on a long-term basis, home visits, and therapeutic child care to drug-using and recovering women and their drug-exposed infants. The project is based at the King/Drew Medical Center and receives referrals from the newborn nurseries. This is the least intensive of the programs administered by Shields. Since 1988, 400 women and 800 children have received these services.

2. *The Eden Infant, Child, and Family Development Center* is the most intensive of the outpatient programs offered by Shields. It provides comprehensive, long-term developmental services to drug-exposed newborns and their families. Families make a commitment to participate in services for as long as 3 years. Home-based services and a Cocaine Anonymous support group are part of the therapeutic and family rebuilding services offered. The Eden Center has served 50 women and 175 children since its start.

3. The Children's Ark is a crisis-intervention nursery and educational respite program that serves drug-exposed infants, their mothers, and siblings up to age 4. This is a short-term program aimed at preventing child abuse and the removal of children from the biological family by assisting with crisis resolution and providing therapeutic services. Referrals come through the Los Angeles Department of Social Services, and since its start, Ark has served over 24 families, including 70 children.

4. *Shields Family Day Treatment Center* is a new program that started in 1990. It is a comprehensive outpatient family drug treatment and parenting program for drug-abusing pregnant women and women with young children.

In addition to the major programs, Shields also offers these support programs:

1. *The Maternal Psychological Profiles Project* is a brief assessment tool used within the Shields projects to determine clients' social and educational functioning, general life skills, psychological status, and vocational strengths and weaknesses. Individualized service plans are generated based on these profiles and other data.

2. *The High Energy Resources and Opportunities* (HERO) program is a drug and alcohol prevention program for early adolescents age

7–15 whose mothers participate in other Shields programs. HERO provides programming after school and weekends. Activities focus on the development of self-esteem, conflict resolution, and self-acceptance. The activities also help children to develop an understanding of parents' drug or alcohol abuse. Children and their families may receive individual, small group, or family counseling through the HERO program.

3. *The Prenatal Outreach Program* is available to all Shields participants and is aimed at reducing or eliminating drug use during pregnancy. It assists participants in locating and utilizing prenatal care and provides education on the effect of drugs on the unborn child and the family.

Leake and Watt Child Placement Agency

The Leake and Watt Child Placement Agency was developed by Leake and Watt's Children's Home at the request of New York City and state officials. Its purpose is the development of appropriate, specialized, trained foster homes for infants and children diagnosed as HIV positive. Specialized foster families are recruited specifically for the purpose of caring for these infants. The following criteria are used in identifying families: 1) there can be no other foster children in the home and no biological children under 6 years of age (due to the risk of infecting the infant with HIV); 2) all family members must accept the medical explanation for HIV transmission and be willing to care for the child; 3) the family must realize that there will be frequent illnesses, many medical appointments, the possibility of developmental delay, and eventual death; 4) a family member or designated relative must be in the home at all times to provide care to the child; 5) caring for the foster child must be a high priority, and the family must be willing to work with the agency as team members; and 6) it is highly recommended that at least one member of the family have knowledge of basic medical principals and treatment (Gurdin and Anderson, 1991).

Potential infants are chosen as a result of medical, developmental, and psychological assessments to determine their appropriateness for the program, and efforts are made to keep each child with his or her biological family before placement is considered. Prospective foster families have pre-placement visits with the children. The project staff includes: a project director, foster family recruiter, nurses, and social workers. Social workers carry a caseload of approximately 12 children, and nurses carry a caseload of approximately 15. Staff members are on call 24 hours a day, every day. Critical links have been established with major medical institutions serving this population and with the city welfare administration and the New York State Department of Social Services.

Program services are aimed at locating and retaining specialized foster homes for children diagnosed as HIV positive. Initial services to foster families are educational in nature and are provided on a one-to-one basis by project nurses or social workers. Support groups are also available for foster families, and the project provides foster families with the equipment and materials necessary to care for the children (e.g., clothes, furniture, diapers). Medical care is provided through a pediatric AIDS clinic at a medical center. Respite care is seen as a critical service related to long-term retention of foster families.

The program currently serves 90 children in 64 foster homes, and no foster families have withdrawn to date. The Leake and Watts program is also providing outreach services to other agencies administering foster care for children diagnosed as HIV positive. The following outreach services are offered: an information hotline, a consultation service, an educational outreach initiative, regional support groups for foster parents, a newsletter for foster families, a publication on guidelines for foster placement of HIV positive children, and public awareness activities (Gurdin & Anderson, 1991).

CONCLUDING COMMENTS

Despite recent legislation and great advances in medical technology, early intervention models, and comprehensive training for interventionists, some important concerns remain to be addressed by early intervention professionals involved in follow-up of infants at high risk. Methodological problems have been cited in many of the early follow-up studies. An important contribution of the more methodologically sophisticated second-generation research studies is their examination of the impact of many different types of variables (e.g., child and family characteristics, program features, child and family goals) on later development. Also important is the recognition that researchers must examine each study with regard to the specific conditions under which the outcomes occurred and the specific population being studied (Guralnick, 1989).

Other concerns seem to consistently re-appear in the literature and represent important considerations for those conducting future research. These include: the need to develop effective models that present a wide range of service alternatives and utilize the skills of professionals from different disciplines; the importance of synthesizing new research results from different disciplines in order to translate this information into practice; the change of focus from child-centered to family-centered services, taking into account the unique resources, concerns, and priorities of individual families; the acknowledgement of the importance of long-term follow-up, including organized transitions that help families to respond to their changing needs over time as their child changes settings (e.g., from NICU to community hospital, to home community, to intervention programs, to school).

A major goal for researchers conducting follow-up studies of infants at high risk is to use the data that they gather to create interventions that match the needs, goals, and priorities of each child and family. This match is both complex and dynamic, and represents an important challenge for early interventionists from many different fields.

REFERENCES

Affleck, G., Tennen, H., & Rowe, J. (1991). *Infants in crisis: How parents cope with newborn intensive care and its aftermath.* New York: Springer-Verlag.

Ahmann, E., & Lipsi, K.A. (1991). Early intervention for technology-dependent infants and young children. *Infants and Young Children: An Interdisciplinary Journal of Special Care Procedures, 3*(4), 67–77.

Babies and cocaine: New challenges for educators. (1990). Alexandria, VA: LRP Publications.

Bagnato, S.J., & Neisworth, J.T. (1989). Neurodevelopmental outcomes of early brain injury: A follow-up of fourteen case studies. *Topics in Early Childhood Special Education, 9*(1), 72–89.

Blackman, J.A. (1988). The value of Apgar scores in predicting developmental outcome at age five. *The Journal of Perinatology, 8*, 206–210.

Blackman, J.A. (1989). The relationship between inadequate oxygenation of the brain at birth and developmental outcome. *Topics in Early Childhood Special Education, 9*(1), 1–13.

Brazelton, T.B. (1981). Introduction. In C.C. Brown (Ed.), *Infants at risk: Assessment and intervention—an up-date for healthcare professionals and parents.* Skillman, NJ: Johnson & Johnson.

Breslau, N., Klein, N., & Allen, L. (1988). Very low birthweight: Behavioral sequelae at nine years of age. *Journal of the American Academy of Child Psychiatry, 27*, 605–612.

Bricker, D., & Squires, J. (1989). The effectiveness of parental screening of at-risk infants: The infant monitoring questionnaires. *Topics in Early Childhood Special Education, 9*(3), 67–85.

Campbell, P.H., Leib, S.A., Vollman, J., & Gibson, M. (1989). Interaction pattern and developmental outcome of infants with severe asphyxia: A longitudinal study of the first years of life. *Topics in Early Childhood Special Education, 9*(1), 1–13.

Carran, D.T., Scott, K.G., Shaw, K., & Beydouin, S. (1989). The relative risk of educational handicaps in two birth cohorts of normal and low birthweight disadvantaged children. *Topics in Early Childhood Special Education, 9*(1), 1–13.

Chasnoff, I. (1990). Congressional Testimony for National Association for Perinatal Addiction Research and Education. In *Babies and cocaine: New challenges for educators*. Alexandria, VA: LRP Publications.

Coletti, S.D. (1990). Testimony before U.S. Senate Subcommittee on Children, Families, Drugs, and Alcoholism. In *Babies and cocaine: New challenges for educators*. Alexandria, VA: LRP Publishers.

Conlon, D.J. (1992). New threats to development: Alcohol, cocaine, and AIDS. In M.L. Batshaw & Y.M. Perret, *Children with disabilities: A medical primer* (3rd ed.). Baltimore: Paul H. Brookes Publishing Co.

Cooper, C.C., & Kennedy, R.D. (1989). An update for professionals working with neonates at risk. *Topics in Early Childhood Special Education, 9*(3), 32–50.

Crnic, K., Greenberg, M., Ragozin, A., Robinson, N., & Basham, R. (1983). Effects of stress and social support on mothers of premature and full-term infants. *Child Development, 54*, 209–217.

Crnic, K., Greenberg, M., & Slough, N.M. (1986). Early stress and social support influences on mother's and high-risk infant's functioning in late infancy. *Infant Mental Health Journal, 7*, 19–48.

Crossings: Bridging the gap in care for children with AIDS. (1991, Fall/1992, Winter). *ACCH Network*, p. 5.

Drillien, C.M., Thomson, A.J.M., & Burgoyne, K. (1980). Low-birthweight children at early school-age: A longitudinal study. *Developmental Medicine and Child Neurology, 22*, 26–47.

Ensher, G.L., & Clark, D.A. (1986). *Newborns at risk: Medical care and psychoeducational intervention*. Rockville, MD: Aspen Publications.

Field, T., Widmayer, S., Stringer, S., & Ignatoff, E. (1980). Teenage, lower class, black mothers and their preterm infants: An intervention and developmental follow up. *Child Development, 51*, 526–531.

Fitzhardinge, P.M. (1987). Follow-up studies of the high-risk newborn. In G.B. Avery (Ed.), *Neonatology: Pathophysiology and management of the newborn*. London: J.B. Lippincott.

Fitzhardinge, P.M., & Steven, E.M. (1972). The small for date infant: ii. Neurological and intellectual sequelae. *Pediatrics, 50*, 50–57.

Frank, D.A. (1990). Infants of substance abusing mothers: Demographics and medical profile. In *Babies and cocaine: New challenges for educators*. Alexandria, VA: LRP Publications, Inc.

Goldson, E. (1984). Severe bronchopulmonary dysplasia in the very low birthweight infant: Its relationship to developmental outcomes. *Journal of Developmental Behavioral Pediatrics, 5*, 165–168.

Gregorchik, L.A. (1992, May). The cocaine-exposed children are here. *Phi Delta Kappan*, pp. 709–711.

Guralnick, M.J. (1989). Recent developments in early intervention efficacy research: Implications for family involvement in PL 99-457. *Topics in Early Childhood Education, 9*(3), 1–17.

Gurdin, P., & Anderson, G.R. (1991). Specialized foster care for children with HIV. In N.J. Hochstadt & D.M. Yost (Eds.), *The medically complex child: The transition to home care*. London: Harwood Academic Publishers.

Hack, M.B., Fanaroff, C.B., Avrog, A.M.B., & Merkatz, I.R. (1979). The low birthweight infant: Evaluation of a changing outlook. *The New England Journal of Medicine, 301*(21), 1162–1165.

Healy, A., Keesee, P.D., & Smith, B.S. (1989). *Early services for children with special needs: Transactions for family support* (2nd ed.). Baltimore: Paul H.

Brookes Publishing Co.

Hess, J.H. (1953). Experience gained in a thirty year study of prematurely born infants. *Pediatrics, 11,* 425–434.

Horowitz, F.D. (1987). *Exploring developmental theories: Toward a structural/behavioral model of development.* Hillsdale, NJ: Lawrence Erlbaum Associates.

How, E., Bill, J., & Sikes, D. (1988). Very low birthweight: A longterm developmental impairment. *International Journal of Behavior Development, 11,* 37–67.

Howard, J., Beckwith, L., Rodning, C., & Kropenske, V. (1989). The development of young children of substance abusing parents: Insights from seven years of intervention and research. *Zero to Three, 9,* 5.

Janis, R.A.K., Cummins, M., & Davis, P.A. (1979). Infants of very low birthweight: A 15 year analysis. *Lancet,* June 23, 1979, 1332–1335.

Janowsky, J.S., & Nass, R. (1987). Early language development in infants with cortical and subcortical brain injury. *Developmental and Behavioral Pediatrics, 8*(1), 3–7.

Kitchen, W.H., Ryan, M.M., Rickards, A., McDougall, A.B., Billson, F.A., Keir, E.H., & Naylor, F.D. (1980). A longitudinal study of very low birthweight infants: IV. An overview of performance at eight years of age. *Developmental Medicine and Child Neurology, 22,* 172–188.

Kochanek, T.T., & Buka, S.L. (1991). Using biologic and ecologic factors to identify vulnerable infants and toddlers. *Infants and Young Children: An Interdisciplinary Journal of Special Care Practices, 4*(1), 11–25.

Kumar, S.P., Anday, E.K., Sacks, L.M., Ting, R.Y., & Delivoria-Papadopoulas, K. (1980). Follow-up studies of very low birthweight infants (1,250 grams or less) born and treated within a perinatal center. *Pediatrics, 66*(3), 438–444.

Lefebrve, F., Bard, H., Veilleux, A., & Martel, C. (1988). Outcome at school age of children with birthweight of 1,000 grams or less. *Developmental Medicine and Child Neurology, 30,* 170–180.

Levenson, R.W. (1981). Information and referral services. In G.N. Specht (Ed.), *Handbook of social services.* Engelwood Cliffs, NJ: Prentice Hall.

Lubchenco, L.O. (1980). Gestational age, birth weight, and the high-risk infant. In C.C. Brown (Ed.), *Infants at risk: Assessment and intervention: An update for health care professionals and parents.* Johnson & Johnson Baby Products Company.

Lubinski, C. (1990). Addressing the impact on women, children and families. In *Babies and cocaine: New challenges for educators.* Alexandria, VA: LRP Publications.

Magnano, M.F. (1991). Testimony before the U.S. Senate Subcommittee on Children, Families, Drugs, and Alcoholism. In *Babies and cocaine: New challenges for educators.* Alexandria, VA: LRP Publications.

Mayfield-Smith, K., Yajnik, G.G., & Wiles, D.L. (1990). Information and referral for people with special needs: Implications for the central directory of Public Law 99-457. *Infants and Young Children, 2*(3), 69–78.

McCormick, M. (1989). Longterm follow-up of infants discharged from neonatal intensive care units. *Journal of the American Medical Association, 261,* 1767–1772.

Miller, G. (1989). Addicted infants and their mothers. *Zero to Three.*

Myers, B.J., Olson, H.C., & Kaltenbach, K. (1992). Cocaine exposed infants: Myths and misunderstandings. *Zero to Three, 13*(1), 1–5.

National Association for Perinatal Addiction Research and Education. (1990, October). Innocent addicts: High rates of prenatal drug abuse found. *ADAMHD News*.

Neuspiel, S.C., & Hamel, S.C. (1991). Cocaine and infant behavior. *Journal of Developmental and Behavioral Pediatrics, 12*, 55–64.

Office of the Inspector General. (1990a). *Crack babies: Selected model practices* (U.S. Government Report No. OEI-03-89-01542). Washington, DC: U.S. Government Printing Office.

Office of the Inspector General. (1990b). *Crack babies* (U.S. Government Report No. OEI-03-89-01540). Washington, DC: U.S. Government Printing Office.

Ounsted, M.K., Mour, V.A., & Scott, A. (1983). Small-for-dates babies at the age of four: Health, handicap, and developmental status. *Early Human Development, 3*(4), 243–258.

Parkinson, C., Wallis, S., & Harvey, D. (1981). School achievement and behavior of children who were small-for-dates. *Developmental Medicine and Child Neurology, 23*, 41–50.

Parmelee, A.H., & Cohen, S.E. (1985). Neonatal follow-up services for infants at-risk. In S. Harel & N.J. Anastasiow (Eds.), *The at-risk infant: Psycho/socio/medical aspects* (pp. 269–273). Baltimore: Paul H. Brookes Publishing Co.

Pearl, L.F., Brown, W., & Myers, M.K.S. (1990). Transition from neonatal intensive care unit: Putting it all together in the community. *Infants and Young Children, 3*(1), 41–50.

Peterson, N.L. (1991). Interagency collaboration under Part H: The key to comprehensive, multidisciplinary, coordinated infant/toddler intervention services. *Journal of Early Intervention, 15*(1), 89–105.

Raugh, V., Achenbach, T., Nurcombe, B., Howell, C., & Teti, D. (1988). Minimizing adverse effects of low birthweight: Four year effects of an early intervention program. *Child Development, 59*, 544–553.

Rawlings, G., Reynolds, E.O.R., & Stewart, A. (1971). Changing prognosis for low birthweight infants. *Lancet, 1*, 516–519.

Rendon, M., Gurdin, P., Bassi, J., & Weston, M. (1989). Foster care for children with AIDS: A psychosocial perspective. *Child Psychiatry and Human Development, 19*, 256–269.

Russel, F.F., & Free, T.A. (1991). Early intervention for infants and toddlers with prenatal drug exposure. *Infants and Young Children: An Interdisciplinary Journal of Special Care Procedures, 3*(4), 78–85.

Saigal, S., Rosenbaum, P., Stoskopf, B., & Milner, R. (1982). Follow-up of infants 501–1,500g birthweight delivered to residents of a geographically defined region with perinatal intensive care facilities. *Journal of Pediatrics, 100*(4), 606–613.

Saylor, C.F., Levkoff, A.H., & Elksnin, N. (1989). Premature infants with intraventricular hemorrhage: A need for early intervention. *Topics in Early Childhood Special Education, 9*(8), 86–98.

Sell, E.J., & Brazelton, T.B. (1980). *Follow-up of the high risk newborn—A practical approach*. Springfield, IL: Charles C Thomas.

Silber, S. (1989). Family influences in early development. *Topics in Early Childhood Special Education, 8*(4), 1–23.

Slentz, K.L., & Bricker, D. (1992). Family-guided assessment for IFSP development: Jumping off the family assessment bandwagon. *Journal of Early Intervention, 16*(1), 11–19.

Taeusch, H.D., & Yogman, M.W. (Eds.). (1987). *Follow-up management of the high-risk infant.* Boston: Little, Brown.

Thurman, S.K., Cornwall, J.R., & Korteland, C. (1989). The Liaison Infant Family Team (LIFT) Project: An example of case study evaluation. *Infants and Young Children, 2*(2), 74–82.

Tyler, R. (1992, May). Prenatal drug exposure: An overview of associated problems and intervention strategies. *Phi Delta Kappan,* 705–708.

United States Office of the Inspector General. (1990). *Crack babies.* Washington, DC: Government Printing House.

United States Office of the Inspector General. (1990). *Crack babies: Selected model practices.* Washington, DC: Government Printing House.

Vohr, B.R., & Hack, M. (1982). Developmental follow-up of low-birth-weight infants. *Pediatric Clinics of North America, 29*(6), 1441–1454.

Waldstein, A., Gilderman, D., Taylor-Hershel, D., Prestridge, S., & Anderson, J. (Eds.). (1982). *Issues in neonatal care.* Western States Technical Assistance Resources.

Woodruff, G., Sterzin, E.D., & Hanson, C. (1989). Serving drug-involved families with HIV infection in the community. *Zero to Three* (National Center for Clinical Infant Programs), *9,* 5.

Personnel and Disciplines in Early Intervention

Wesley Brown
and Sarah Rule

One essential feature of effective early intervention services is that they be provided by qualified personnel who meet standards established by the state. In addition, recommended practices in early intervention require that the services be comprehensive and transdisciplinary. Achieving these key elements is a serious challenge to professionals involved in the planning of direct service systems for young children with developmental delays and their families.

In this chapter, specific personnel issues related to early intervention are discussed, including: definitions of key terms and personnel groups addressed in Part H of IDEA and roles for common participating disciplines; personnel standards and state regulations; state standards, licensure, and certification; the roles of professional organizations in training within disciplines; service coordination—a role for all disciplines; the inclusion of parents in training; paraprofessionals in early intervention; and continuing professional development for interventionists.

KEY TERMS AND PERSONNEL GROUPS

Multidisciplinary coordination between personnel was mandated for early intervention services because no single agency, group, or discipline could meet all of the needs of eligible children and their families. According to Part H, this requires the coordinated efforts of a wide range of personnel groups, including: 1) audiologists, 2) early childhood special educators, 3) nutritionists, 4) nurses, 5) occupational therapists, 6) physicians, 7) psychologists, 8) physical therapists, 9) social workers, 10) speech-language pathologists, and 11) vision specialists. Service providers in all categories deliver various early intervention services and consult and interact with parents, other service providers, and community agencies. Most are involved in informing and assisting parents and others with the provision of services, and many participate in the multidisciplinary team's assessment of the child and his or her family and in the development of integrated goals and outcomes for the individualized family service plan (IFSP).

While no discipline is excluded from providing early intervention services, the 11 specified above are to be actively involved in the provision of early intervention services in every state. The Part H regulations define a discipline as a specific occupational category that: 1) provides early intervention services to children and their families, 2) has been established or designated by the state, and 3) has a required scope of responsibility and degree of supervision. The Part H provisions for multidisciplinary assessment and the development of the IFSP by a multidisciplinary team focus on the shared responsibility for these program components among multiple disciplines and have major implications for the staffing of early intervention programs.

"Multidisciplinary" is defined in Part H as the involvement of two or more disciplines or professions in the provision of integrated and coordinated services, including evaluation and assessment activities and the development of the IFSP. It is rare that a single discipline would work independently of other disciplines or service areas in the provision of early intervention.

DISCIPLINARY ROLES AND
SERVICE AREAS IN EARLY INTERVENTION

This section contains mission and role information collected from sources from numerous disciplinary and professional groups, including a series of papers evolving from work at the Frank Porter Graham Child Development Center and various planning projects related to Part H, especially the work completed in Tennessee. Table 1 provides direct and comparable information about the disciplines. Additional information about professional organizations is presented later in the chapter.

Table 1. Disciplines in early intervention

Audiologist

Audiology services

Identifying children with auditory impairment using at-risk criteria and appropriate audiologic screening techniques
Determining the range, nature, and degree of hearing loss and communication functions through the use of audiologic evaluation procedures
Referring children with auditory impairments for medical and other services necessary for their habilitation or rehabilitation
Providing auditory training, aural rehabilitation, speech-reading, and listening-device orientation and training
Providing services for the prevention of hearing loss
Determining the need for individual amplification, including selecting, fitting, and dispensing appropriate listening and vibrotactile devices
and evaluating the effectiveness of those devices

Audiologist's roles

To determine auditory function and characteristics of hearing losses
To assess and monitor middle ear function
To assist in the identification of risk factors that contribute to hearing loss
To determine the relationship of auditory function and communicative development
To recommend appropriate amplification and/or assistive communication devices
To assist in determining the presence of significant developmental delays and provide appropriate referral
To implement strategies for parent education, guidance, and counseling
To disseminate information about intervention within the community
To monitor the stability of hearing loss, the effectiveness of interventions, and family adjustment
To implement intervention plans
To serve as service coordinator for selected infants with hearing impairments and their families

Early childhood special educator

Early childhood special education services

Designing learning environments and activities that promote the acquisition of skills in a variety of developmental areas, including cognitive
processes and social interaction
Curriculum planning, including the planned interaction of personnel, materials, and time and space, that leads to achievement of the goals in
the individualized family service plan
Providing families with information, skills, and support related to enhancing the skill development of the child
Working with the child to enhance development

(continued)

Table 1. (continued)

Early childhood special educator's roles

To conduct screening and child-find programs
To asess children's developmental competence
To plan and provide developmental intervention/services
To coordinate interdisciplinary services
To integrate and implement interdisciplinary team recommendations
To assess family needs and strengths
To plan and implement family support services or training
To coordinate services from multiple agencies
To evaluate program implementation and effectiveness of overall services for young children and their families
To advocate for children and families
To provide consultation to other professionals, families, and other caregivers
To work effectively as a team member

Nutritionist

Nutrition services

Conducting individual assessments in:
1. nutritional history and dietary intake
2. anthropometric, biochemical, and clinical variables
3. feeding skills and problems
4. food habits and food preferences
Developing and monitoring appropriate plans to address the nutritional needs of children
Making referrals to appropriate community resources to achieve nutrition goals

Nutritionist's roles

To develop nutrition care plans through assessments of nutritional status, food intake, eating behavior, and feeding skills
To coordinate nutrition services and contribute to individualized family service plans
To serve as a team member and provide case management services, consultation, and technical assistance
To provide preventive nutrition information, services, guidance, and early intervention
To make referrals to community resources

Nurse

Nursing services

Assessing health status for the purpose of providing nursing care, including the identification of patterns of human response to actual or potential health problems

Providing nursing care to prevent health problems and promote optimal health and development

Administering medications, treatments, and regimens prescribed by a licensed physician

Nurse's roles

To identify infants and toddlers with disabilities or at risk

To assess physiological, psychological, and developmental characteristics of the child and the family

To work with parents and caregivers to meet basic health and daily-care needs of the child

To enhance the child and family's abilities to cope with the disability

To recommend, plan, and/or implement interventions to improve the child's health/developmental status

To develop medical plans to treat underlying causes of medical or developmental problems and/or help parents to implement the plan

To serve as a case manager/care coordinator

To recommend necessary services or programs and collaborate on follow-up plans

Occupational therapist

Occupational therapy services

Performing identification, assessment, and intervention to address functional needs related to adaptive skills, play, and sensory, motor, and postural development

Adapting the environment to the child's needs and selecting, designing, and fabricating assistive and orthotic devices to facilitate development and promote the acquisition of functional skills

Preventing or minimizing the impact of initial or future impairment, delay in development, or loss of functional ability

Occupational therapist's roles

To work with families to assess children's developmental levels, functional performance, sensory processing, and adaptive responses

To assess family–infant interactions and environment as they relate to the development of the child

To collaborate with families in developing and implementing occupational therapy intervention to enhance sensory function, motor skill, cognition, communication, social–emotional development, and adaptive/coping abilities of infants and toddlers with special needs

To recommend adaptation to the environment and to select, design, and fabricate assistive seating and orthotic devices that promote functioning and interaction with the environment

To provide services to prevent secondary sensory, motor, cognitive, and social–emotional problems

(continued)

249

Table 1. (continued)

To work with families and other caregivers to enhance caregiving and an understanding of how to optimize the child's functional abilities

To collaborate and consult with other early intervention team members and family service providers

To provide care-management services, including advocacy, coordination, information gathering, and linking families with community resources and services

To evaluate the effectiveness of occupational therapy services and contribute to the evaluation of interdisciplinary outcomes

Physician

Medical services

Assessing, synthesizing, and imparting information; providing health education and family support; and teaching family members to care for the special needs of a child with disabilities

Physician's roles

To provide services to the child, including assessment, provision of a "medical home," comprehensive medical care, diagnosis, treatment, and referral

To consult in community settings on diagnosis, treatment, and so forth.

To advocate for a healthy child and family and appropriate health care

To instruct caregivers

Psychologist

Psychological services

Administering psychological and developmental tests and other assessment procedures

Interpreting assessment results

Obtaining, integrating, and interpreting information about child behavior and child and family conditions related to learning, mental health, and development

Planning and managing a program of psychological services, including psychological counseling for children and parents, family counseling, consultation on child development, parent training, and education programs

Psychologist's roles

To assess the developmental/psychological/behavioral characteristics, needs, and resources of children and/or families

To plan and provide psychological/developmental interventions for infants and families

To coordinate interdisciplinary efforts, consult with families and professionals, serve as case manager when appropriate, and evaluate interventions

Physical therapist

Physical therapy services

Screening of infants and toddlers to identify movement dysfunction

Obtaining, interpreting, and integrating information appropriate to program planning in order to prevent or alleviate movement dysfunction and related functional problems

Providing services to prevent or alleviate movement dysfunction and related functional problems

Physical therapist's roles

To screen and assess for motor-skills, neuromuscular, musculoskeletal, cardiopulmonary, oral motor, feeding, and general-developmental dysfunction

To design, implement, monitor, evaluate, and modify therapeutic interventions

To identify family strengths, needs, and priorities and develop family recommendations and monitor their implementation

To participate in interdisciplinary planning, consult, refer, and provide case management

To recommend and/or fabricate adaptive equipment and mobility devices

To recommend and/or implement environmental modifications

To teach handling, positioning, and movement techniques to facilitate motor functioning and posture

Social worker

Social work services

Making home visits to evaluate a child's living conditions and patterns of parent–child interaction

Preparing a psychosocial developmental assessment of the child within the family context

Providing individual and group counseling for parents and other family members and appropriate social skillbuilding activities for the child and parents

Working with those problems in the home, community, or any center where early intervention services are provided that affect the impact of early intervention services

Identifying, mobilizing, and coordinating community resources and services to enable the child and family to receive maximum benefit from early intervention services

Social worker's roles

To build partnerships with families of infants and toddlers with disabilities in order to facilitate active participation in early intervention services

To assess families' basic needs for food, housing, clothing, and so forth, and to see that those needs are met

To provide a psychosocial assessment of the infant/toddler in the family context, using home visits to evaluate strengths, resources, and parent–child interactions

(continued)

251

Table 1. (continued)

To investigate allegations of mistreatment and provide protective services for children
To provide crisis intervention services linking families to support and helping them to better manage crises
To provide social work services, such as counseling, training, child management, and skill building, to strengthen families
To provide case management services, family advocacy, consultation with professionals on family and social factors, team participation, and group services
To monitor, document, and evaluate social work services and provide follow-up over time

Speech-language pathologist

Speech-language pathology services

Identifying children with communicative or oral pharyngeal disorders and delays in development of communication skills, including the diagnosis and appraisal of specific disorders and delays in those skills
Referring children with communicative or oral pharyngeal disorders or delays in the development of communication skills for medical or other professional services necessary for their habilitation or rehabilitation; and rehabilitation or prevention of communicative or oral pharyngeal disorders and delays in the development of communication skills

Speech-language pathologist's roles

To screen, assess, and diagnose communication and oral-motor abilities in the context of overall development with other professionals and the family
To recommend, plan, coordinate, implement, manage, reassess, and evaluate appropriate therapeutic intervention programs with families and other professionals
To provide information, consult, and collaborate with family members and other professionals regarding the identification, assessment, and treatment of oral-motor and communication skills

Vision specialist

Vision services

Evaluating and assessing visual functioning, including diagnosis and appraisal of specific visual disorders, delays, and abilities
Referring children with visual functioning disorders for medical or other professional services necessary for their habilitation or rehabilitation
Providing communication-skills training, orientation and mobility training for all environments, visual training, independent living skills training, and additional training necessary to activate visual motor abilities

Vision specialist's roles

To perform assessment procedures, including functional vision assessments, interpretation of eye reports, determination of the relationship of development and visual loss, recommendations for appropriate services or specialized evaluations, and determination of eligibility
To develop appropriate intervention strategies and plans for visually impaired children and to work with families in implementing the intervention strategies to minimize developmental risks
To serve as case manager, coordinate interdisciplinary services, and provide information for families and professionals

Adapted from Bailey (1989).

Audiologists   Audiologists provide and coordinate services to children with auditory impairments, including early identification of the problem and comprehensive management of potential communication disabilities. Audiologists must complete a master's program that is appropriately accredited and approved. They perform coursework in the basic communication processes, including anatomic and physiological bases for the normal development and use of speech, language, and hearing. They also study linguistic and psycholinguistic variables related to normal development and the use of speech, language, and hearing. Graduate studies include the areas of speech and language disorders, auditory assessment, and habilitation. Audiologists also complete a variety of field experiences in speech–language pathology and audiology.

Early Childhood Special Educators   Early childhood special educators are involved in preparing environments for infants and preschoolers with disabilities that facilitate the children's development of social, motor, communicative, adaptive, cognitive, and behavioral skills and that enhance their self-concept and sense of competence, control, and independence. These professionals work directly with infants and toddlers with disabilities and their families. ECSE represents a specialized area of special education, and certification or licensure in this area is available through either undergraduate or graduate preparation. While training programs may focus on either the preschool period or the infant and toddler period, few states require differential certification for these two areas.

Nutritionists   Nutritionists maximize the health and nutritional status of infants and preschoolers through developmentally appropriate nutrition services within the family and community environments. They develop and implement nutrition-care plans and participate in interdisciplinary team activities in early intervention. Licensed dietitians/nutritionists complete approved baccalaureate or post-baccalaureate programs. They also complete studies in human nutrition, food and nutrition, dietetics, or food-systems management.

Nurses   Nurses diagnose and treat actual and potential human responses to illness. For infants and preschoolers with disabilities, this means promoting the highest health and developmental status possible and helping families to deal with changes in their lives resulting from the child's disability. Registered nurses complete a course of study in an approved school of nursing. The minimum degree is generally an associate's. However, some nurses are graduates of nondegree, hospital-based programs and others complete a bachelor's program to receive their R.N. license.

Nurses complete studies in biological and physical sciences, behavioral sciences, and nursing, and are trained in maternity nursing, the care of infants and children, promotion and maintenance of health, prevention and detection of illness, and restoration of health. They also have experience with disease prevention, health-problem management, developmental and family issues, community and home-based services, and multidisciplinary teamwork, and their education also includes a variety of laboratory experiences.

Occupational Therapists   Occupational therapists promote a child's independence, mastery, and sense of self-worth and self-confidence in their physical, emotional, and psychosocial development. These services are designed to help families and other caregivers improve children's functioning within their environments. Therapists use a developmental framework in assessing the following domains: play, adaptive skills, sensorimotor, posture, fine-motor manipulation, and oral-motor feeding. Purposeful activity is then used to expand the child's functional abilities in these areas.

There are two levels of practice within occupational therapy (Hanft & Humphry, 1989). A certified occupational therapist assistant (COTA) is generally prepared through an associate's degree program, while some complete a nondegree, 1-year certificate program. A registered occupational therapist (OTR) enters the field with a bachelor's degree or a postbaccalaureate certificate or master's degree.

Physicians   Physicians identify children at risk and, by providing health care services, assist families in the promotion of the optimal health, growth, and development of their infants and young children. Physicians must graduate from an accredited medical school and complete an approved residency (pediatricians complete an approved pediatric residency program). Families often turn first to their physician for information and assistance when they are concerned about the development of their child. Physicians are very interested in seeing that each child with special needs has a *medical home*. The medical home concept requires that each child have a regular physician to provide primary care, detect difficulties, support parents, and coordinate services needed by the child and family. This is quite different than medical care that is only provided when there is a significant, acute medical problem for which assistance is provided in an emergency clinic or other short-term care setting.

Psychologists   The psychologist's mission is to develop a comprehensive picture of child and family functioning and to identify, implement, and evaluate psychological interventions. Psychologists have completed doctoral-level training and have some practical experience in psychology. They are trained in research, statistics, and measurement skills, and complete extensive study on the biological, cognitive-affective, and social bases of behavior. They generally have specialty training in psychological assessment, consultation, and intervention procedures. Master's-level graduates in psychology are also licensed in various ways by many states to provide different psychological services. Psychological "examiners," for example, may conduct assessments and provide other services under the supervision of a psychologist. Finally, school psychologists complete approved training programs to prepare them for practice in school settings.

Physical Therapists   The mission of physical therapy is to enhance the sensorimotor development, neurobehavioral organization, and cardiopulmonary status of infants with, or at risk for, developmental delays. Physical therapists graduate from an accredited program and are licensed by their state. They are trained to determine the physical therapy needs of individuals referred for treatment.

Social Workers   The purpose of social work in early intervention is to improve the quality of life of infants and toddlers and their families. Social workers are prepared through several levels of academic training. Certified Master Social Workers complete a master's-level or higher training program accredited by the Council on Social Work Education. Master Social Workers who have completed 2 full years of clinical experience after receiving their degree may seek licensure for the independent practice of social work. Social workers should have a broad understanding of cultural and social diversity, allowing them to more fully understand human behavior and social environments. School social workers are specifically prepared to carry out social work practice in school settings.

Speech-Language Pathologists   The mission of the speech-language pathologist (SLP) is to promote children's oral-motor functioning and communication skills in the context of social interactions in school and in the community. Speech-language pathologists complete an approved master's program in speech pathology. They complete coursework in the basic communication processes, including study of the anatomic and physiological bases for the normal development and use of speech, language, and hearing. They also study linguistic and psycholinguistic variables related to normal development and use of speech, language, and hearing. Graduate studies include the areas of speech and language disorders and auditory assessment and habilitation. SLPs also have extensive field experience in audiology and speech-language pathology.

Vision Specialists   The mission of the vision specialist is to provide and coordinate services to children with visual disabilities in order to prepare them to function competently in a variety of settings and to assist them to develop compensatory skills that will enable independent functioning. Vision specialists complete an approved program in visual impairment. They develop a knowledge of disabling conditions and an ability to evaluate and instruct individuals with visual impairments.

PERSONNEL STANDARDS AND STATE REGULATIONS

PL 102-119 mandates that each state establish standards to regulate the various disciplines. Appropriate professional requirements for providing early intervention are defined as those that are based on the highest requirements in the state applicable to the profession or discipline to which a person belongs and that include suitable qualifications for personnel providing early intervention services to children and their families who are served by state, local, and private agencies. The highest requirements in the state applicable to a profession or discipline are the highest entry-level academic degree needed for any state-approved or -recognized certification, licensing, registration, or other comparable requirements that apply to a particular profession or discipline. A qualified service provider is one who has met state-approved or -recognized certification, licensing, registration, or other comparable requirements that apply to the area in which the person is providing early intervention services.

Standards, Licensure, and Certification

While the new law requires that early intervention personnel meet the highest applicable standards for their discipline, few states have defined those standards for all disciplines providing service to infants and young children with disabilities. Bruder, Klosowski, and Daguio (1989) surveyed Part H coordinators and national professional organizations on standards for special education, physical therapy, occupational therapy, speech pathology, audiology, nursing, medicine, nutrition, psychology, and social work. Predictably, all states were reported to have specialization requirements for medical doctors, physical therapists, nurses, and psychologists who serve children. However, only 23 states had requirements for special educators who serve children from birth to 3 years or from birth onward, and only 20 had standards for nutritionists who serve these populations. Standards for each of the other four disciplines were defined by more than 23, but less than 50, states. States will obviously require considerable time and resources to define standards for these disciplines in order to comply with the law. At a time when there are growing personnel shortages across disciplines, setting standards to ensure that personnel will be appropriately qualified without excluding present personnel who are competent remains an important challenge.

Content of Standards

Changes in (or the creation of) standards resulting from Part H will differentially affect the disciplines involved. It is likely that changes in licensure for pediatricians will be minimal, while special educators in many states will, for the first time, be expected to meet standards for services provided to infants and toddlers with disabilities. Although states will determine the final form that standards take, many professionals advocate developing core standards that are applicable across disciplines. The California Early Intervention Personnel Study Project (Hanson & Brekken, 1991) has recommended that early intervention standards recognize four levels of personnel, independent of their disciplines: early interventionists, early intervention assistant, specialized consultant, and special/technical assistant. A team composed of professionals from various disciplines recommended a set of standards that all early interventionists must meet. Early intervention assistants would be required to meet some of these standards. Specialized consultants would be expected to have additional training in particular areas, and special/technical assistants would work in narrowly defined supportive roles not requiring mastery of all standards. The standards were configured in five basic areas: child development, family involvement, assessment, developing and implementing individualized intervention program plans, and professional-interaction skills.

Not all states will develop early intervention standards that are applicable across disciplines. However, it is likely that many will adopt a common core of standards. Given the multidisciplinary emphasis of the law, standards that address teaming, for example, will be critical, regardless of the interventionist's professional discipline. Moreover, in light of the important role that paraprofessionals have played in delivering services to infants and toddlers with special needs, certain core standards should also apply to personnel without degrees in early intervention programs.

CONTENT OF TRAINING
TO MEET PROFESSIONAL STANDARDS

Recommendations about the training needed to prepare early intervention personnel derive from a number of sources, including surveys (e.g., Bailey, Palsha, & Simeonsson, 1991) and professional study groups. Fenichel and Eggbeer (1991) suggest that there are certain content-independent issues pertinent to all personnel preparation: 1) there is a "framework of concepts common to all disciplines concerned with infants, toddlers, and their families" (p. 58); 2) personnel in training need to observe and interact with young children and families; 3) individualized supervision should be provided to personnel during preparation; and 4) there must be support from colleagues from various disciplines.

Core Training

Four content areas identified as standard in training are discussed below: working with families, teaming, infant development, and service coordination. These are examples of areas that should be addressed in core training for all early intervention personnel, and they are typical of the content that is required regardless of one's role.

Working with Families   A number of competencies are required to provide family-centered service, to understand the interactions between family members and a child with disabilities, and to help families enhance their child's development. The law clearly emphasizes services to families of young children with disabilities, but current training does not necessarily address this issue. McCollum and Thorp (1988) surveyed early intervention practitioners in Illinois and learned that only 52% had contact with families during their preservice training. Bailey et al. (1991) surveyed professionals in two other states. They found that social workers and nurses rated their skills in working with families higher than did personnel from other disciplines, suggesting that training in this area varies across professions. Experience was not a determinant in ratings of skills in family-centered service.

Education to make early intervention personnel culturally competent is critical to extending service to all populations. Planning and providing this education logically requires constituents of culturally diverse populations who can help personnel to understand the interaction between their culture and participation in intervention. Hanson, Lynch, and Wayman (1990) describe how cultural values, which influence how families view disabilities, and differences in family structures affect acceptance of intervention activities. They suggest that services can be flexible in response to differing cultures, rather than rigid in deference to agency structures and routines. Changes in service patterns, however, are predicated on staff development activities that foster an understanding of cultural variations.

Various arrangements for providing training that includes preservice experience with families have been explored. Rowan, Thorp, and

McCollum (1990) devised an interdisciplinary practicum for students in speech and language pathology and in special education. Master's-level students, supervised by doctoral students, serve parents and their young children in community-based play groups. This experience prepares students to help families enhance their young children's development. In so doing, it is consistent with Fenichel and Eggbeer's (1991) suggestion that preservice preparation include opportunities to work with infants and families. Special Education students at Utah State University complete a practicum in the homes of families that include young children with disabilities. Their supervisors are university personnel, including parents of children with disabilities (Rowland, Sanders, Rule, Fiechtl, & Fodor-Davis, 1991). No single practicum can address all of the skills required for effective partnership with families, but preservice experience with families is an important component of personnel preparation.

Teaming   Chapter 5 of this volume, by Mary Beth Bruder and Theresa Bologna, is devoted to collaboration and coordination in early intervention and explains role variations in service delivery. Given the various professional disciplines that may provide service, it is apparent that professionals must be prepared to act as members of a team. Transdisciplinary teaming has been addressed in inservice training for special educators (Beninghof & Singer, 1992), but is equally important in other disciplines. The settings and nature of the intervention may vary from neonatal intensive care units and hospital outreach programs (Cooper & Kennedy, 1989; Kaplan-Sanoff & Nigro, 1988; Pearl, Brown, & Myers, 1990) to resource services for parents who serve as primary interventionists for their own children (Timm & Rule, 1981). However, there is a consistent need for all team members, including parents, to act in a supportive manner.

The practicum described by Rowan et al. (1990) is one model for providing cross-disciplinary training. Others include practicum placements in interdisciplinary service programs and preservice training by faculty from various disciplines (Rule, Huntington, Riall, & Fiechtl, 1988). As with working with families, there are a host of competencies necessary for effective teaming, but practical experience is always an important component of training.

Typical and Atypical Infant Development   An understanding of typical and atypical infant development is critical to working with infants and toddlers. McCollum, McLean, McCartan, and Kaiser (1989) recommend content in this area for early childhood special educators. Much of this content, however, is also applicable to other disciplines, for example: 1) the biological and environmental factors and medical conditions that place a child at developmental risk and the interventions that may address these risks; 2) typical development across domains and the influences of social and physical contexts, family, community and culture; and 3) the nature of various disabilities and their impact on the family and child. This foundation of knowledge is critical in formulating early intervention service.

Service Coordination   Service coordination or case management must be provided to all families receiving early intervention. To be effective, the interventionist must thoroughly understand: 1) the laws, regulations, and state and local policies affecting the provision of services; 2) the services available in the community (and, sometimes, the state and region) and how to access them; and 3) how to act as an advocate for families and children. In addition, early interventionists must possess well-developed interpersonal skills, including effective listening and appropriate assertion, in order to link families with the services that they desire. Training must develop these skills and areas of knowledge.

The Comprehensive System of Personnel Development (CSPD)

States are required to ensure that early intervention personnel have access to the experiences necessary to help them meet and maintain professional standards. While states may rely on institutions of higher education to supply personnel with basic qualifications, they must also develop a system to recruit and retain qualified personnel. There are three major challenges in developing this system. First, in states in which a lead agency other than Education is responsible for services to families and children from birth to 3 years, there is a need to develop a consistent system of personnel development across Education and the Part H lead agency. This is particularly challenging because the Part H lead agency will probably need to provide personnel development activities applicable to more disciplines than the education system has traditionally addressed. A comprehensive system of personnel development (CSPD) plan allows participating agencies to share resources and minimize obstacles for participating personnel.

Second, it is desirable for the CSPD to be integrated with personnel-development activities across agencies and institutions. For example, if inservice education provided by the lead agency is a cooperative venture with institutions of higher education, there may be opportunities to accredit the inservice education. This may allow participating personnel to accrue credit applicable to advanced degrees or upgraded credentials, as well as meet the requirements of the lead agency. Moreover, cooperative endeavors are another way to spread personnel-development resources. North Carolina has adopted a competency-based approach to certification for early intervention

(Bennett, Watson, & Raab, 1991). This system affords personnel a number of ways to acquire the training necessary to demonstrate competencies. These include higher-education courses and inservice training offered by the lead agency. This model is applicable to the development of CSPDs in other states.

The third challenge—not independent of the first two—is finding the financial resources to support the comprehensive system of personnel development. The U.S. Department of Education, Office of Special Education and Rehabilitative Services, Division of Personnel Preparation, has funded inservice training projects that can be important components of state systems of personnel development. Cooperative efforts between state agencies providing early intervention and university-based training programs have greatly enhanced state CSPD efforts. Such endeavors require cooperation between the coordinators of services for infants, toddlers, and school-age children, the preschool representative of the state Office of Education–funded CSPD training agency, institutions of higher education, and project staff. The pooling of resources makes education affordable and accessible for practicing personnel. Such projects have provided the impetus for the development of coordinated CSPD activities between the state agencies responsible for services to infants, toddlers, and preschool children with disabilities.

The Roles of Professional Organizations in the Development of Specializations

Many professional organizations have recognized the need to define and teach competencies to members of their discipline who serve young children with disabilities. Through committees and task forces, professional organizations have served as a catalyst for action. These organizations have sponsored work such as the definition of standards, development of certification and/or licensing procedures, and of exemplary training programs. Finally, professional organizations play a role in one of the four critical areas cited by Fenichel and Eggbeer (1991): they support members who have a common interest in early intervention. The examples cited below are not exhaustive, but, rather, are typical of the influence that professional organizations can exert in responding to the need for trained early intervention personnel.

Speech-Language Pathology and Nutrition The American Speech-Language-Hearing Association (ASHA)'s Committee on Speech-Language Service Delivery with Infants and Toddlers (cited in Rowan et al., 1990) has described services and the roles of speech and language pathologists who provide early intervention services.

ASHA has sponsored training for early intervention personnel through meetings and conferences. A number of professional organizations have influenced specialty training for nutritionists. The American Dietetic Association (ADA) Commission on Accreditation, which sets the requirements for personnel preparation, is considering a pediatric specialization. An active group of university-affiliated programs that provide interdisciplinary training have developed *Guidelines for Nutrition Training* (Thompson & Smith, cited in Baer, Blyler, Cloud, & McCamman, 1991) that combine multidisciplinary and discipline-specific competencies. The Society for Nutrition Education, the ADA, members of the American Association on Mental Retardation, and the American Public Health Association, who have an interest in nutrition services for children with disabilities, have played roles in making nutritionists aware of families' needs for assistance (Baer et al., 1991).

Social Work Preparation of social workers is addressed by the Council on Social Work Education, which develops standards for programs that offer the master's in social work (MSW) degree. At present, few of the 89 accredited programs offer coursework pertinent to individuals with disabilities or to infants (Nover & Timberlake, 1989). However, Nover and Timberlake describe one model training project that has developed curriculum materials pertinent to early intervention, which were used in the program for the National Catholic School of Social Work. Because the Council on Social Work Education accreditation standards provide for areas of concentration within the discipline, curricula developed by model training projects can be incorporated into training delivered by institutions of higher education. Thus, while the professional organization has not developed standards for preparation of social workers for early intervention roles, their approach to accreditation accommodates this preparation if institutions of higher education choose to address this specialization.

Occupational Therapy Like the social work profession, training program accreditation standards for occupational therapists are set by a professional organization, the American Occupational Therapy Association (AOTA); their Education Essentials define standards. Accreditation of personnel preparation programs is the joint responsibility of the AOTA and the American Medical Association Committee on Allied Health and Accreditation. Unlike certification in some other professions, they recognize two levels—the registered occupational therapist and the certified occupational therapist assistant. The standards for accreditation of training set by the professional organizations are important, since only 38 states have their own standards for the practice of occupational therapy. Through a survey funded by a personnel preparation grant from the Office of Special Education and Rehabilitative Services, the AOTA compiled a description of early intervention practices and defined needs for continued personnel preparation (AOTA, 1988). Moreover, the AOTA has addressed early intervention practice in publications, workshops, and symposia.

Nursing   Nurses are prepared to specialize at the master's or doctoral level. The opportunity to specialize in early intervention varies across programs. Standards for nurses who serve children with disabilities have been developed by the Nursing Division of the American Association of University Affiliated Programs and the American Association on Mental Deficiency. These may serve as guidelines for programs that prepare nurses to practice early intervention.

Special Education   The Division for Early Childhood of the Council for Exceptional Children has endorsed content for personnel preparation programs that lead to early childhood special education certification (McCollum et al., 1989). It recommends two levels of certification: a generalist level addressing service to children from birth through 5 years and a specialist level focusing on either early intervention or preschool service delivery. Like other organizations, the Division for Early Childhood has promoted personnel preparation through its journal, sponsorship of professional conferences, and advocacy at the local, state, and federal levels.

Service Coordination—A Role Common to All Disciplines

While most disciplines perform such functions as assessment and intervention planning in relation to their specialization, virtually all disciplines have viewed the newly developing function of service coordination as an area in which they can assume responsibility and provide expertise. Most professionals consider themselves prepared to provide family assistance and consultation. The Part H regulations have defined service coordination as the activities carried out by a service coordinator to assist and enable an infant or toddler and his or her family to receive the rights, procedural safeguards, and services that are authorized to be provided under the state's early intervention program. As such, service coordination activities include: 1) coordinating evaluations and assessments; 2) facilitating and participating in the development, review, and evaluation of individualized family service plans; 3) assisting families in identifying available service providers; 4) coordinating and monitoring the delivery of available services; 5) informing families of the availability of advocacy services; 6) coordinating with medical and health providers; and 7) facilitating the development of a transition plan to preschool services, if appropriate.

Service coordinators are persons who have demonstrated knowledge of and understanding about the infants and toddlers eligible for services under Part H. They must also understand the provisions of Part H and the nature and scope of services available under the state's early intervention program, including the system of payments for services.

The Inclusion of Parents in Personnel Training

The role of parents in personnel preparation is no less important than their roles in formulating IFSP's and in service delivery. Parents can serve as mentors, assist in the development of standards for personnel, and help to design systems of inservice and preservice education. Parents in Vermont and other states have had a role in these endeavors for some time (Bryan et al., 1988). In other states, and in some programs within those states (see Rowland et al., 1991), the benefits of parental input are only beginning to be realized. It is sufficient to say that parents can communicate their needs, feelings, and reactions to services provided by professionals better than anyone else. Omission of their input at any level of personnel preparation leaves a void that may adversely affect early intervention services.

Paraprofessionals in Early Intervention

Paraprofessionals make a valuable contribution to early intervention, not only in the context of home visiting, as has been mentioned, but also in other patterns of service delivery. Attention to the competencies that should be required of paraprofessionals and to the means of providing education for these personnel have been addressed in some states but not others. The proposed California standards (Hanson & Brekken, 1991) provide a model for states that have yet to define training and certification procedures.

Paraprofessionals are well-established members of early intervention service teams, serving in roles that vary from home visiting to conducting group activities in center-based services. Their effectiveness has been demonstrated in a number of studies. For example, in 1974 Schortinghuis and Frohman examined the roles of paraprofessionals who delivered home-based services using the Portage model. They compared gains in small groups of children served by paraprofessionals with gains in those served by professionals and found no differences. The authors noted that these paraprofessionals participated in intensive systematic training. Moreover, their roles included not only independent service delivery but also ½ day per week of service delivery with a professional. This study raises issues that are quite current: the training and role descriptions for paraprofessional intervention team members.

At the state level, paraprofessional personnel development issues include defining standards and, as required by PL 102-119, provision for training as part of the comprehensive system of personnel development. The proposed California standards (Hanson & Brekken, 1991) represent one state's efforts to address these issues.

The provision of training has often been relegated to the local level. Service delivery programs have developed and implemented their own training procedures. Many include joint inservice training for professionals and paraprofessionals, recognizing the value of training team members together. However, this training can no longer be solely the responsibility of local agencies. Fortunately, there are resources to assist states, such as model projects that address systems to prepare paraprofessional early intervention personnel. For example, the federally funded First Start program at the Colorado Health Sciences Center developed a training-the-trainers program to equip professionals to train paraprofessionals who serve families of children who are chronically ill or have disabilities (Krajicek, Thrornam, & Moore, 1985). Personnel from a number of states have participated in this training and subsequently trained paraprofessionals in their own states. The National Resource Center for Paraprofessionals in Education and Related Services, Center for Advanced Study in Education, City University of New York, offers a network for those engaged in paraprofessional training. They sponsor an annual conference and publish a newsletter, *New Directions*.

A critical issue for statewide systems is the development of a career ladder that not only prepares paraprofessionals for one role, but helps them obtain further education. The Maine Paraprofessional Training Project (Dunn & Magioncalda, 1990), for example, has developed an associate's degree program for paraprofessionals who deliver special education or related service. Alaska has a four-stage program to certify early childhood teachers; paraprofessionals can advance through all levels or obtain intermediate credentials (e.g., an associate's degree after completing the third level). Similar programs for early intervention personnel should be part of statewide systems.

The roles of paraprofessionals on early intervention teams will remain an issue for local service providers, since each may configure services somewhat differently. Roles that facilitate team members' work together (as mentioned in regard to the Portage project) not only facilitate communication but also provide the opportunity for team members to provide mutual help and support. Roles in which team members observe each other and provide frequent feedback assist all personnel in developing and maintaining skills.

Continuing Personnel Development for Interventionists

Fenichel and Eggbeer (1991) are among the writers who have noted that personnel development is not a one-time activity, but a lifelong issue. The advances in technology that affect early intervention, the medical developments that affect the survival and health of infants, the changing cultural and demographic patterns in the country, and the evolving role of the family in society all affect the provision of early intervention service. Preservice training is only the beginning of personnel development if those who practice early intervention are to deliver effective services. Hence, planning and innovation in personnel development activities for early interventionists must be a continual process, and they must occur at the federal, state, and local levels to meet the immediate challenges presented by the passage of PL 99-457 and the continuing challenges inherent in the delivery of quality services.

CONCLUDING COMMENTS

Enabling children and families to receive optimal, responsive early intervention services requires an extensive delivery system in each community of our nation. While the success of this system is dependent on a multitude of factors, perhaps none is more important than having sufficient numbers of qualified personnel. Because of the requisite comprehensive and coordinated nature of services and the cross-disciplinary approach required, early intervention services now require new and evolving family-centered approaches. Such changes present great philosophical and operational challenges to the disciplines and to the individuals practicing within them. Training and education programs that produce sufficient numbers of personnel will ensure the provision of services to all infants and toddlers with, or at risk for, disabilities, but, more importantly, professionals themselves must take responsibility for ensuring that the quality of these services is maintained.

REFERENCES

American Occupational Therapy Association. (1988). *Survey of Occupational Therapists and Early Intervention.* Rockville, MD: Author.
Baer, M.T., Blyler, E.M., Cloud, H.H., & McCamman, S.P. (1991). Providing early nutrition intervention services: Preparation of dietitians, nutritionists, and other team members. *Infants and Young Children, 3*(4), 56–66.

Bailey, D.B. (1989). Issues and directions in preparing professionals to work with young handicapped children and their families. In J.J. Gallagher, P.L. Trohanis, & R.M. Clifford (Eds.), *Policy implementation and PL 99-457: Planning for young children with special needs* (pp. 97–132). Baltimore: Paul H. Brookes Publishing Co.

Bailey, D.B., Palsha, S.A., & Simeonsson, R.J. (1991). Professional skills, concerns, and perceived importance of work with families in early intervention. *Exceptional Children, 58*(2), 156–165.

Beninghof, A.M., & Singer, A.L.T. (1992). Transdisciplinary teaming: An in-service training activity. *Teaching Exceptional Children, 24*(2), 58–61.

Bennett, T., Watson, A.L., & Raab, M. (1991). Ensuring competence in early intervention personnel through personnel standards and high quality training. *Infants and Young Children, 3*(3), 49–51.

Bruder, M.B., Klosowski, S., & Daguio, C. (1989). *Personnel standards for ten professional disciplines serving children under P.L. 99-457: Results from a national survey.* Farmington, CT: Division of Child and Family Studies, Department of Pediatrics, University of Connecticut Health Center.

Bryan, M., Bishop, K.K., Bricker, D., DiVenere, N., Sanchez, R., & Yoder, D. (1988, July). *Personnel preparation, practices, and standards.* Paper presented at Partnerships for Progress II, Washington, DC.

Cooper, C.S., & Kennedy, R.D. (1989). An update for professionals working with neonates at risk. *Topics in Early Childhood Special Education, 9*(3), 32–50.

Dunn, L., & Magioncalda, M. (1990). The Maine (statewide) paraprofessional training project. *New Directions, 11*(3), 1–2.

Education of the Handicapped Act Amendments of 1986, PL 99-457. (October 8, 1986). Title 20, U.S.C. 1400 et seq: *U.S. Statutes at Large, 100,* 1145–1177.

Fenichel, E.S., & Eggbeer, Z. (1991). Preparing practitioners to work with infants, toddlers, and their families: Four essential elements of training. *Infants and Young Children, 4*(2), 56–62.

Hanft, B.E., & Humphry, R. (1989). Training occupational therapists in early intervention. *Infants and Young Children, 1*(4), 54–65.

Hanson, M.J., & Brekken, L.J. (1991). Early intervention personnel model and standards: An interdisciplinary field-developed approach. *Infants and Young Children, 4*(1), 54–61.

Hanson, M.J., Lynch, E.W., & Wayman, K.I. (1990). Honoring the cultural diversity of families when gathering data. *Topics in Early Childhood Special Education, 10*(1), 112–131.

Individuals with Disabilities Education Act Amendments of 1991, PL 102–119. (October 7, 1991). Title 20, U.S.C. 1400 et seq: *U.S. Statutes at Large, 105,* 587–608.

Kaplan-Sanoff, M., & Nigro, J. (1988). The educator in a medical setting: Lessons learned from collaboration. *Infants and Young Children, 1*(2), 1–10.

Krajicek, M., Thrornam, C., & Moore, C.A. (1990). First start: Training paraprofessionals to care for young children with special needs. *New Directions, 11*(3), 2–3.

McCollum, J., McLean, M., McCartan, K., & Kaiser, C. (1989). Recommendations for certification of early childhood special educators. *Journal of Early Intervention, 13*(3), 195–211.

McCollum, J.A., & Thorp, E.K. (1988). Training of infant specialists: A look to the future. *Infants and Young Children, 1*(2), 55–65.

Nover, A.R., & Timberlake, E.M. (1989). Meeting the challenge: The educational preparation of social workers for practice with at-risk children (0–3) and their families. *Infants and Young Children*, 2(1), 59–65.

Pearl, L.F., Brown, W., & Myers, M.K.S. (1990). Transition form neonatal intensive care unit: Putting it all together in the community. *Infants and Young Children*, 3(1), 41–50.

Rowan, L.E., Thorp, E.K., & McCollum, J.A. (1990). An interdisciplinary practicum to foster infant–family and teaming competencies in speech language pathologists. *Infants and Young Children*, 3(2), 58–66.

Rowland, C., Sanders, C., Rule, S., Fiechtl, B., & Fodor-Davis, J. (1991, November). *Practicum with infants and families: A course description and evaluation*. Paper presented at the Teacher Education Division of the conference of the Council for Exceptional Children, Charlotte, NC.

Rule, S., Huntington, L., Riall, A., & Fiechtl, B. (1988, November). *Training early childhood special educators: Responses to the need by a university-affiliated program and a department of special education*. Paper presented at the Eleventh Annual Teacher Education Division of the conference of the Council for Exceptional Children, Salt Lake City, UT.

Schortinghuis, N.E., & Frohman, A. (1974). A comparison of paraprofessional and professional success with preschool children. *Journal of Learning Disabilities*, 7(4), 62–64.

Timm, M.A., & Rule, S. (1981). A cost effective parent-implemented program for young handicapped children. *Early Child Development and Care*, 7, 147–163.

Program Evaluation in Early Intervention

Scott Snyder
and Robert Sheehan

Program evaluation is the process of systematically gathering, synthesizing, and interpreting reliable and valid information about programs for the purpose of aiding with decisionmaking. This definition sets the parameters for discussion within this chapter.

The number of intervention programs for infants and toddlers with disabilities and their families has increased markedly since the early 1970s. The importance of intervention with these populations has been formalized by Part H of IDEA. If services mandated by this law are to achieve their full potential, program evaluation must be incorporated as a routine and influential component of intervention. Implementing a program for infants with disabilities and their families is a complex endeavor that requires frequent monitoring, feedback, and corrections in order to promote quality service provision. This chapter is based on the assumption that for intervention programs to operate optimally, individuals and groups with investments in these programs must regularly gather data on the operations and outcomes of such programs and then ensure that this information is used to make appropriate decisions.

Program evaluation consists of five sequential components. First, the purpose of the evaluation is determined. This component consists of: 1) determining the questions about the program that need to be answered, 2) being aware of the decisions that will be made based on the answers to the questions, and 3) identifying the audience who will need to receive and act on the results of the evaluation. Second, a methodology for answering the questions (e.g., means of determining the sources of information; procedures for gathering, storing, analyzing, and interpreting information) is formulated. The specific methodology used for the evaluation will be based on the nature of the questions being asked (descriptive, comparative, or relational) and the resources (e.g., time, budget, material, technology, expertise) available to answer them. Third, to ensure that the methodology is feasible, timelines for data collection and analysis and report preparation are established; budget allocations for the evaluation are made; and responsibilities for key personnel are assigned. Questions and methods are adjusted to comply with management constraints. Fourth, the evaluation and management plans are implemented (and modified as needed). Finally, results are reported in a manner that is congruent with the needs of audiences and decisionmakers. The goal of this chapter is to provide the reader with an introduction to these components of the evaluation process.

DETERMINING THE PURPOSE OF EVALUATION

Unlike research designed to advance science, program evaluation is undertaken primarily to assist in answering questions on specific aspects of a program in order to enable decisionmaking. The range of questions that can be answered through an evaluation process in programs for infants and toddlers with disabilities is very broad. This section of the chapter will discuss key individuals involved in determining program evaluation questions and the way in which the focus of a program evaluation is determined.

Key Individuals in Evaluation

In any program evaluation there are three groups of key players who influence the focus of evaluation: program participants and stakeholders, evaluators, and decisionmakers. A single individual can be a member of more than one of these groups. Program participants and stakeholders are individuals who have an investment in a program. In programs for infants and toddlers with disabilities, this group includes the children served by the program (regardless of whether the child does or does not have a disability), the families of these infants and toddlers, program administrators, program staff, related service providers, community leaders, representatives from schools and other agencies, and state administrators of Part H.

Evaluators are those individuals or teams who have primary responsibility for facilitating, coordinating, planning, conducting, and reporting the results of a program evaluation. Program evaluators may either be internal program staff assigned the responsibility of evaluation or external consultants with specific training in program evaluation. The decision to use internal or external evaluators typically depends on the nature of the decisions to be made, the evaluation skills of internal staff (if local staff have sufficient training and experience, there will be little need for external evaluators), and the availability of resources and funds (while external evaluators may be highly skilled, the costs of their services may be prohibitive, in light of the limited budgets under which most early intervention programs operate). Most decisions about improving program operations can be made by internal evaluators, while decisions concerning renewing or terminating a large program typically require external experts. External evaluators for programs serving infants with disabilities and their families should have considerable expertise in evaluation methodology and early intervention. External evaluators are frequently required by federal funding sources (e.g., model demonstration programs). While internal evaluators may be any program staff assigned the responsibilities for planning and conducting the evaluation, the authors recommend that such individuals or teams have some training in program evaluation, limit their efforts according to their own level of qualification, have the authority to facilitate data collection, and not have a direct investment in the outcome of the evaluation.

Decisionmakers are those individuals who are ultimately responsible for deciding on the focus of an evaluation, influencing the evaluation while it is in process, and making decisions about a program based on evaluation information. These decisionmakers (typically program administrators, administrative boards, or state-level administrators) have the power to influence the allocation of resources that enable evaluations, to make decisions based on evaluation information, and to implement (or obstruct) actions in response to decisions.

Methods of Focusing Evaluation Questions

There are three primary methods of focusing evaluation questions (i.e., identifying specific evaluation questions that are worth pursuing):

1. Autocratic determination by the decisionmaker
2. Determination by internal program personnel
3. Determination by all stakeholders

When decisionmakers have clear and well-defined questions that they want addressed so that they can make specific decisions about a program, the decisionmaker may choose to do little more than inform others of the evaluation. Each state's lead agency for Part H assumes this autocratic role when mandating the collection of information on service provision. At other times, program personnel (interventionists, related service providers, second-level administrators, staff-development personnel) may be empowered to suggest questions that might become the focus of an evaluation. Yet another, and more comprehensive, procedure for identifying program evaluation questions is for the decisionmaker to solicit from stakeholders suggestions regarding program evaluation objectives. Given the range of backgrounds, values, and motivations held by these distinct groups, the process of identifying evaluation questions relevant to all stakeholders is often challenging. Using group processes (e.g., focus groups, Delphi surveys), evaluation objectives can be prioritized according to the consensus within and between groups of stakeholders, the importance of the objective in serving the program mission, and immediacy of need. Again, even though this process yields recommendations from stakeholders, decisionmakers typically have the final responsibility for determining which particular evaluation is undertaken.

The program evaluator (or evaluation team) serves to facilitate the identification of relevant objectives by working with decisionmakers and/or stakeholders to identify appropriate evaluation objectives. The level of influence that an evaluator has over the objectives of an evaluation varies with factors such as the evaluator's familiarity with the program or decisionmaker, the evaluator's previous experiences as a practitioner, administrator, and evaluator for infant and toddler programs, and the decisionmaker's experience with program evaluation and evaluators. The evaluator should not impose an evaluation agenda on decisionmakers or stakeholders, but should instead facilitate the identification of relevant objectives to meet the decisionmaking needs of the program.

Regardless of the source of the evaluation questions, we recommend focusing on only those evaluation questions that:

1. Can assist in selecting between clearly defined decision alternatives,
2. Have the commitment of the decisionmaker to take action as a result of the information gathered, and
3. Can be adequately addressed, given logistical constraints (e.g., available time, money, and personnel).

We use a simple rule in arriving at a final list of questions; in cases in which decisionmakers are unsure of how the answers to an evaluation question could guide decisionmaking, the question is not included in the evaluation. Simply stated, when in doubt about the utility of a question, delete the question from the evaluation.

Program evaluation questions generated by the various contributors can be categorized according to the general type of decision that each assists in making. There are five general types of decisions served by program evaluation questions:

1. Front-end decisions
2. Program-process decisions
3. Impact decisions
4. Cost decisions
5. Ecological decisions

Table 1 illustrates the ranges of decisions within each of these broad categories. It is important that program-evaluation questions be paired with decisions for two major reasons. First, as systematic inquiry in any program results in some disruption of services or reallocation of resources, it is essential that the evaluation yields information that warrants these costs. Information that assists with making important and defensible decisions concerning a program is likely to justify the moderate costs of gathering it. The second reason for pairing questions with decisions is that the type of decision to be made influences the methodology appropriate to the evaluation. The next section of this chapter examines the relationship between decision type and methodology.

PROGRAM EVALUATION METHODOLOGY

For each of the five types of decisions in Table 1, there is an appropriate type of program evaluation. Front-end decisions are served by

Table 1. Decision types and examples

Decision type	Example
Front-end	It needs to be decided if there are unmet needs within the community, if the program can hope to meet such needs, and how the program might best fulfill them.
Program process	It needs to be decided whether any changes are needed in order to comply with standards.
Impact	It needs to be decided in what ways the program is and is not successful and what has to be done to make it successful.
Cost	It needs to be decided if (or how) the cost of services that are being provided can be justified.
Ecological	It needs to be decided if the program is making the contribution to the community that it was intended to make. If it is not, it must be decided how the program can better contribute.

needs assessment, program-process decisions by program monitoring, impact-related decisions by impact evaluation, cost decisions by cost-evaluations, and ecological decisions by ecological analysis. This section will describe in detail the first three of these general types of evaluation in terms of: 1) the types of questions and decisions served by each type of evaluation, 2) potential sources of information for answering each type of question, 3) procedures for gathering and analyzing such information, and 4) a case illustration for each type. The section concludes with briefer discussions of the final two types of evaluations.

Needs Assessment

Needs assessment is typically conducted to study unmet needs for services within a community (i.e., a discrepancy between actual and desired conditions) and determine the availability of resources to adequately meet such needs. Such analysis can be conducted to inform decisions about either implementing a new program or expanding an existing program. Needs assessment can be concerned with either immediate needs and resources or predicted future needs and resources. Needs assessments within infant programs are prompted by: 1) parents interested in new or expanded services for their children or for themselves; 2) medical personnel concerned about the availability of comprehensive services for infants with, or at-risk for, developmental disabilities; 3) community service professionals aware of existing or anticipated community-wide gaps in services to families; 4) advocacy coalitions committed to ensuring the availability of services for constituents; or 5) administrators and staff of early intervention programs or schools who wish to ensure comprehensive and integrated service delivery.

Questions and Decisions for Needs Assessment   Needs assessment addresses descriptive questions, such as: What are the needs of this community for services to infants and toddlers with disabilities and their families? What resources are currently available and/or currently used to meet these needs? Is there a discrepancy between needs and resources? At what rate and in what ways are the needs and resources in this community likely to change in the future? These questions serve to facilitate decisions about: 1) whether there is sufficient need to implement a new or expanded program for infants and toddlers with disabilities and their families, 2) how best to use existing or potential resources to meet this need, and 3) how the community must prepare to meet needs in the future.

Information Sources and Procedures for Needs Assessment
Information concerning unmet, undermet, and projected needs with-

in a community is typically collected through surveys and interviews of parents of infants and toddlers with disabilities, stakeholders, and community service providers, and/or through examination of extant demographic data, incidence figures, medical trends (e.g., increases in the numbers of babies who are born HIV-positive, drug exposed, or with low birth weight), population projections, and rates of usage for existing programs. The surveys and interviews ask respondents about their perceptions of the needs of infants and toddlers with disabilities and their families, which needs are and are not adequately met within the community, where needs are currently being met, and recommendations concerning settings in which needs can be met with existing resources. These surveys are typically developed by interested stakeholders. Hanson and Lynch (1989) provide the Needed Resources Worksheet, a schema for surveying stakeholders about duplications, gaps, and priorities for services in a community.

Additional information can be derived from census data available from state or county government agencies, state education agencies, and local programs. Such information serves to clarify where and at what rate eligible infants and toddlers and their families are currently receiving services and to predict how many infants and toddlers are likely to be eligible within the catchment area, both currently and in the near future. If, based on such data, a judgment is made that substantial needs are not being sufficiently met by existing resources, the feasibility of meeting such needs must be studied. First, available and potential resources (e.g., funding, materials, space) should be identified through such sources as community contacts and grant searches. Second, proposals for meeting the needs with the available and potential resources should be considered. Finally, if a judgment is made that the proposed plan can adequately meet the identified needs, specific funding alternatives should be pursued as needed. The reader interested in more information on needs assessment is referred to McKillip (1987).

Needs Assessment Case Example   For example, needs assessment conducted by a southeastern Arc (the Association for Retarded Citizens of the United States) interested in expanding existing preschool services to infants and toddlers may reveal that: 1) based on the most recent census data, of the approximately 3,000 children between birth and age 3 living in the service area there are, based on a projected 2.5% eligibility rate, an estimated 75 infants and toddlers who would be eligible for services under the state's eligibility criteria; 2) given that the population in the catchment area is growing more rapidly than that in other areas of the state, it is projected that this estimate will grow by approximately five children per year for the next 5 years; 3) approximately 30 infants within the service area are currently receiving some services through independent therapists, related service agencies, and a regional university affiliated program; and 4) surveys and interviews of parents and service providers support the necessity of more services to adequately meet the needs of unserved or underserved infants and families. Examination of resources available to meet these needs may show that the state is offering five $30,000 competitive grants to fund service delivery to infants with disabilities and their families (but such projects must demonstrate a replicable model). The Arc might also have a preschool center, full-time administrator, half-time secretary, and a variety of intervention resources and assistive devices. After gathering information about existing programs serving similar needs, client populations, contexts, and budget restrictions, the advisory board of The Arc may decide to submit a proposal for a combined center-based and home-based program to serve 20 infants and toddlers on a rotating basis and provide weekly parent support/training sessions at the center.

Program Monitoring

Program monitoring involves the ongoing assessment of program operation for the purposes of assessing compliance with internal and external standards. In both externally motivated and internally motivated monitoring, various components of infant programs can be evaluated, including public awareness, child find, multidisciplinary factors, IFSP development, case management, program implementation, family involvement, due process, staff development, coordination of resources, transition, payment for services, and program administration.

Questions and Decisions for Program Monitoring As externally motivated (compliance-focused) monitoring and internally motivated monitoring serve somewhat different purposes, the questions and decisions of the two approaches will be considered separately. The fundamental question addressed by external monitoring is: "To what extent is the program functioning according to externally imposed guidelines, delivery projections, or contracted plans?" Decisions that are made based on answers to this question influence the allocation of funds, accreditation/approval of the program as a service delivery source, or the provision of staff-development or technical assistance. Externally motivated monitoring is requisite to documentation for Part H of IDEA, the entitlements that are enabled by the law, and necessary demonstration of accountability on state and federal grants.

Internal monitoring assists in facilitating internal accountability and program improvement. In addition, the extensive descriptions of infants, families, service providers, service provision, intervention and management models, budget expenditure, resource allocations, and so forth, are essential for a program to be adequately understood and replicated. While internal monitoring is also concerned with the same questions of compliance discussed above, it also addresses a variety of other questions, including:

1. To what extent are services congruent with the program's specified intervention model or curriculum?
2. To what extent is the program being administered in a manner congruent with a specified organizational management/supervision theory?
3. To what extent are program components carried out with prescribed procedures, on schedule, and with efficient use of resources?
4. To what extent are staff performing roles and responsibilities consistent with expectations?
5. What are the direct and indirect program expenditures incurred during a given period of time?
6. To what extent are program components carried out in a manner congruent with best practices?
7. To what extent are the clients for whom this program was developed actually receiving services?
8. What are the reasons for unexpected departures from pre-established expectations for 1 through 7 above?

The fundamental decisions informed by answering such internal program monitoring questions are: 1) is there a need to correct or improve program operations, and 2) if so, how can this be achieved?

Sources and Procedures for Program Monitoring Programs serving infants with disabilities and their families are typically responsible for collecting and reporting data on service delivery and program management to state education agencies (SEAs) or federal agencies who allocate funds or accredit programs. Published state guidelines for the implementation of Part H of IDEA and regulations for external grants are common sources of standards guiding external monitoring of programs for infants and toddlers with disabilities. The data typically required by such agents (i.e., mandated in Part H of IDEA) include: the number of infants and toddlers served, by age; services received; program setting; the number of service delivery staff, by performance area; expected federal, state, and local funds; the number of eligible infants and toddlers on the waiting list; and the areas of service in need of improvement. Such data are typically reported to the lead agency of each state using a common format for all agencies serving the target population within the state. All sites should regularly monitor and update their records concerning these data in order to increase reporting efficiency.

States may also monitor program compliance with other components of Part H, such as the requirements for IFSPs. This monitoring is likely to be done by representatives of the state's lead agency for Part H while conducting an announced site visit. During the visit, the representative may examine existing records, interview staff, meet with parents, and observe service delivery in order to identify areas of compliance and noncompliance.

Internal program monitoring is typically conducted by periodically and systematically comparing desired operations to actual administrative activities and delivery of service. Service activities that may be monitored include public awareness, child find, multidisciplinary assessment, IFSP development and review, service delivery, service coordination, family involvement, coordination of resources, and transitioning. Administrative activities that may be monitored include program management, supervision, staff development, program funding, budget management, and ensuring payment for services and due process compliance. Many evaluations of the past have given inadequate attention to the description of the programs under investigation. The lack of adequate documentation reduces what is known about program variations and about how such variations effect program outcomes.

Process evaluation (Stufflebeam, 1983) or discrepancy evaluation (Provus, 1971) are related models used in program monitoring. Both models fundamentally involve: 1) establishing standards for program functions, 2) describing current program functions, and 3) comparing actual practices of standards. The first step in the process is formulating clear (i.e., unambiguous and operationalized) statements of expectations or standards for all targeted service and administrative activities. Some typical examples of written documentation of established standards useful for internal monitoring are: policy, procedure, and service delivery manuals of local programs; job descriptions; program operating objectives; descriptions of models for guiding intervention and administrative practices; legal criteria of Part H; budget details; and short- or long-term funding plans. Supplemental interviews with administrators can serve to clarify or expand the evaluator's understanding of other desired, but unwritten, operational processes. Such standards serve to answer the question: "Is our program operating as expected?"

Stakeholders and decisionmakers may also be interested in answers to the question: "Is our program operating in a manner consistent with best practices in the field?" The published criteria for best practices in the field provide another source of standards for comparison. Such guidelines may provide a better assessment of the "quality" of the service delivery than is provided by most internally developed manuals. An example of published standards is provided by Judith Carta and her colleagues (Carta, Schwartz, Atwater, & McConnell, 1991) who propose seven general factors that they believe are important for appropriate practice:

1. "A range of services that vary in intensity based on the needs of the children" (p. 4)
2. "Individualized teaching plans consisting of goals and objectives that are based on a careful analysis of the child's strengths and weaknesses, and on skills required for future school and non-school environments" (p. 5)
3. Multisource and multisetting assessments of sufficient frequency to monitor children's progress toward their individual objectives
4. Instructional approaches that are effective, efficient, functional, and normalized (see also Bailey & McWilliam, 1990)
5. Instructional approaches that result in high levels of active engagement
6. A focus on strengthening the abilities of families "to nurture their children's development and promote normalized community adaptation" (p. 7)
7. Systematic efforts to determine if individual children are making progress toward stated objectives

Program personnel can use these guidelines by asking, for each general guideline: "To what extent are program practices consistent with this standard? What specific things do we do that comply with this standard? What things do we do that are not consistent with this standard? How can we better integrate these standards into our practices?" The literature provides similar standards for more specific components of infant and toddler programs. For example, Johnson, McGonigel, and Kaufman (1989, in press) have provided guidelines for recommended practices concerning IFSPs. The Division of Early Childhood of the Council for Exceptional Children has completed a study to define the indicators of recommended practices in a variety of program processes (DEC Task Force, 1993). These indicators should be useful not only in planning intervention programs but also in internally monitoring programs for infants and toddlers with disabilities and their families.

After standards are determined (e.g., Part H regulations, internal policy statements, recommended-practice guidelines), a procedure is implemented for recording information in a manner that will allow evaluators to compare existing practices to the particular standards of concern. Typical procedures for describing program practices include logs, rating scales, checklists, surveys or interviews, and naturalistic descriptions. Logs are brief daily records used to monitor the frequency and characteristics of regularly occurring events (e.g., phone calls requesting information about a program, referrals, attendance, efforts of a program to increase public awareness, home-visitation records). They are particularly useful when the standard concerns the number, distribution, and type of community contacts during a particular period of time.

Rating scales involve judgments of the relative level of behaviors, products, attitudes, or opinions that are either observed or reported. Rating scales are useful for addressing many "To what extent . . . ?" questions that cannot be answered objectively. Actually, rating scales will typically restate the general "extent" question to read "On a scale of 1–5, to what extent do observers or respondents perceive . . . ?" Rating scales for program monitoring purposes are typically completed by parents, program staff, program administrators, or program evaluators. Rating scales can be descriptions of behaviors, attitudes, or products. For example, to describe the extent to which IFSPs conform to some of the guidelines proposed by McGonigel (McGonigel, in press; McGonigel, Kaufman, & Johnson, 1991) a program administrator could develop a short instrument that lists five of McGonigel's criteria with which he or she is most concerned. The administrator could then ask each case coordinator to rate the extent to which the IFSPs for which he or she is responsible conform to each of the criteria (1 = very few of the IFSPs meet this criteria, 3 = some of the IFSPs meet this criteria, 5 = all of the IFSPs meet this criteria). If the administrator was interested in confirming staff ratings, he or she could evaluate the IFSPs for which the case coordinators, or a subset of them, were responsible, using the same rating instrument.

There are some existing rating scales that may be useful for internal monitoring. For example, The Family-Focused Rating Scale (Mahoney, O'Sullivan, & Dennebaum, 1990) is a rating scale that assesses the degree to which mothers perceive that intervention programs provide various service components. The Early Childhood Rating Scale (Harms & Clifford, 1980) is one of a number of scales that rate classroom environments. Other rating scales appropriate for internal monitoring are discussed elsewhere in this volume.

Checklists are lists of behaviors or product components that can be observed or reported. Checklists can be used to document the presence/absence, frequency, sequence, or duration of such behaviors or components; they are useful in addressing those "To what extent . . . " monitoring questions that can be broken down into specific behaviors or parts. Checklists can be completed by parents, staff, administrators, or evaluators.

Surveys and interviews may include checklists and/or rating scales, but also allow for more detailed feedback through narrative descriptions and opinions about program implementation from families, staff, or administrators. While interviews and surveys may be somewhat more difficult to compile and analyze, they can provide clarification and anecdotal information that is often useful to audiences.

Naturalistic descriptions typically involve an external evaluator spending time in a program observing various aspects of program functions; interviewing parents, staff, and administrators; and examining existing records before writing a description of how the program is actually operating. The external evaluator will have little prior knowledge of the intended policies, procedures, administrative or service delivery models, and so forth. The benefit of this approach is that decisionmakers receive feedback that is relatively free of bias. To the greatest extent possible, monitoring information should be acquired from multiple sources, using multiple methods, at multiple times, in order to ensure a representative description of the activity.

The two major models that are used for comparing a program standard to the program status are the criterion-based model and the judgment-based model. The criterion-based approach is used when the standard has been defined according to a minimally acceptable level of performance (e.g., 95% of IFSP meetings will be conducted within 3 weeks of the multidisciplinary assessment). By using data-collection procedures that provide information about the program component in the desired metric (e.g., examination of existing records or of a special log to document the total number of initial IFSP meetings conducted during the past year and the number of such meetings conducted within 3 weeks of the assessment), the evaluator can determine whether or not the criterion was met. If the criterion was not met, the evaluator may wish to examine the information gathered to ascertain whether there was any systemic reason for the failure (e.g., performance of a specific staff member, a large percentage of postponed IFSP meetings around holiday periods). Such detective work, essential in most evaluation activities, will help the decisionmaker determine how problematic the discrepancy is, and what the possible responses are.

More often, standards will not be framed in terms of absolute criteria (although the benefits of such criteria should not be overlooked). Rather, many standards are framed in a way that would make operationalization and the establishment of criterion levels difficult (e.g., "staff will fulfill their responsibilities through the prescribed transdisciplinary model"). The evaluator may use a variety of methods to gather information about performance of the standard (e.g., to describe whether staff were being transdisciplinary, the evaluator might use naturalistic observation, interviews, rating scales, observations during staffings, and/or existing IFSP and service delivery records). The evaluator and/or decisionmaker must judge whether the information shows that the standard is being met. Most standards that concern the quality of activities or products will require judgment-based discrepancy evaluation.

Goal attainment scaling (Kiresuk & Lund, 1976) is a valuable tool in monitoring the status, relative to standards, of administrative or service activities. Basically, goal attainment scaling involves operationally defining criteria that indicate that a goal or objective is being met adequately, criteria that would indicate that a goal was exceeded, and criteria that would indicate that a goal was not adequately achieved. A number is used (i.e., on a scale of −2 to +2) to reflect the level of attainment of each objective at any given time. This approach allows for the documentation and tracking of progress toward goal attainment across time. Procedures are available for standardizing goal-attainment scores so as to allow for comparisons across programs, objectives, children, personnel, and so forth.

A Program-Monitoring Case Example   The infant and toddler program proposed as a result of the needs assessment has been funded. The program keeps complete and ongoing records of information needed by the state's lead agency to comply with Part H. As the administrator receives the reporting forms, information is efficiently compiled and transferred to the forms. To document the delivery of a replicable model (a condition of the grant award) the administrator: 1) keeps daily logs of all services provided, by type, location, participants, duration, and cost; 2) surveys parents and service providers to assess congruence between the services provided and the services proposed by the model; and 3) periodically attends parent groups and classroom sessions to complete an observational measure of the congruence between observed and intended model-delivery characteristics. The administrator applies goal attainment scaling (GAS) on a biweekly basis as a method for judging the status of the program components relative to model criteria. GAS scores are compared across models and across time to assess the conformity of the program to the model ideal. Once a month the administrator meets with the staff to provide feedback about areas of the program that do and do not match the model ideal and to solicit discussion about the reasons for discrepancies. The administrator also periodically either modifies the model or suggests ways that staff can address unresolved discrepancies. Another area that the administrator periodically evaluates is the quality and appropriateness of IFSP objectives. The administrator has asked that staff ensure that all IFSP objectives conform to three standards—functionality, generality, and measurability (Notari & Bricker, 1990). Using guidelines and examples provided by Notari and Bricker (1990), the administrator judges objectives of randomly selected IFSPs. The administrator also collects information on other aspects of service delivery (e.g., staff job performance, interagency coordination) and administration (e.g., timeline of grant activities, budget expenditures, due-process concerns) which he or she typically compares to the grant agreement, policy and procedure manuals, and state regulations for services to infants and toddlers with disabilities. As discrepancies arise, they are documented and addressed with staff and the local Arc advisory board.

Impact Evaluation

Rossi and Freeman (1989) suggest five major motivations for conducting impact evaluation: 1) to determine whether a pilot demonstration has an impact sufficient to establish that a proposed program or policy is likely to have its intended effect; 2) to test the relative effectiveness of different variations in program elements; 3) to evaluate whether a program warrants expansion to other sites; 4) to demonstrate, when competing for limited resources or audiences, whether a particular program should be supported in preference to other programs; and 5) to determine whether modifications made in a program have achieved their intended effects. Unfortunately, these summative purposes of impact evaluation present actual or perceived threats to the status or funding of early intervention programs. In response to these threats, substantial pressure has been placed on early intervention programs to demonstrate, rather than evaluate, program success. A "skilled" evaluator is always able to find some evidence that a program is successful (or unsuccessful). A skilled grant writer can typically identify a set of outcome measures that, whether educationally relevant or not, will show improvement across time in a minimally competent program. Too often, success is measured by gains in norm-referenced measures that are not sensitive to program-related gains or curricular or individual objectives, using designs that can't prove that any gains are attributable to the program. While this section will provide information relevant to summative evaluation, greater attention will be given to the value of periodic impact evaluation for ongoing service improvement.

The perspective that impact evaluation is predominantly a summative endeavor (end-of-the-program renewal or termination of the program) has detracted from the formative importance (ongoing, diagnostic-remedial) of impact evaluation. While administrators, service providers, and other decisionmakers in programs serving infants and toddlers with disabilities will be called upon by funding agencies and other consumers to demonstrate effectiveness, there is latitude in outcomes that are appropriate indices of impact, and there is great value in formative applications of impact evaluation as a data-based tool for improving programs.

Questions and Decisions for Impact Evaluation   Impact evaluation of programs for infants with disabilities and their families involves three interrelated responsibilities: 1) assessing intended and unintended outcomes of a program; 2) establishing that such outcomes are, in part, the result of service or administrative components of the program; and, when possible, 3) isolating factors that contribute to inconsistencies in results (between subgroups or between expected and actual outcomes, for example). For example, an evaluator who establishes that infants and toddlers receiving services made, on the average, a 1-year gain in developmental age on a standardized test during a 12-month period must be able to establish that such a rate of gain is unlikely to have occurred in the absence of the program. If the evaluator is able to establish that program participants made greater gains than a similar group of infants and toddlers who received no treatment or an alternate treatment or that the rate of development for participants during intervention was substantially more accelerated than the rate before intervention, then the evaluator would be in a better position to argue that the program was at least in part responsible for the observed improvements. If the evaluator has reason to expect that the impact of the program may not be uniform for all participants, he or she may wish to examine how improvement varies as a function of potentially mediating factors (e.g., rate of attendance at the center-based program, parent participation in support and training activities, severity of impairment, participation in home-based vs. center-based services). Information that identifies potentially mediating factors can be used for modifying service provision, identifying staff-development needs, suggesting problems with the assessment measure being used, and informing service providers of specific issues to be sensitive to in their transactions with parents, children, and other consumers.

Programs can be expected to have direct or indirect impacts on infants and toddlers, parent–child relationships, social support, families, and communities. Ideally, program evaluation will assess outcomes across two or more of these consumers. Information on these outcomes is useful for providing feedback to program staff, program participants, funding sources, and other stakeholders. However, simply documenting basic outcomes of a program will do little to meet the goals of improving or remediating program functions. In order for impact evaluation to serve the needs of decisionmakers, evaluators must:

1. Clarify outcomes
2. Implement and document the intervention
3. Evaluate outcomes in a way that establishes that the program, at least in part, contributed to success
4. Investigate factors that mediate outcomes.

First, the relevant outcomes must be clarified. Success can be operationalized in many different ways for infants and toddlers, parents, and communities. If a program has clearly specified and operationally defined outcome objectives, this task is simplified. However, if a program has vague goals, such as "the program will facilitate development" or "parent–child interactions will improve as a result of intervention," then the targeted outcomes (development and parent–child interactions) will be too ambiguous to be useful. Any outcome being studied must be well-defined, in order to ensure that the measurement procedure used adequately reflects the intended concept (e.g., validity), and to ensure that any communication or application of the results of the gathered information is limited to the specific definition applied. For example, parent satisfaction can be defined as: 1) parent responses to general questions ("Please describe your general reaction to the quality of services that you and your son are receiving from the program") on a survey or interview, 2) parental ratings of their level of satisfaction with specific aspects of a program ("on a scale of 1–4 please rate your level of satisfaction with the process for developing the IFSP, service coordination services, feedback on your child's progress, etc."), or 3) unsolicited feedback to staff, parent advisory groups, or administration or funding agencies concerning parent satisfaction with services. Members of the evaluation team must clarify what is meant by these terms before procedures and methods for assessment can be determined.

Second, the intervention must be sufficiently well implemented and documented. This is essential for two reasons: it is impossible to claim that an intervention model had its intended effects if there is no evidence that the intended model was implemented, and to the extent that the mediating influences of program factors can be documented, the evaluation team will have a valuable aid to clarify decisionmaking. Program monitoring is therefore an essential component of impact evaluation. Furthermore, because programs are dynamic rather than static, there is a need to periodically monitor program operations in order to document any changes.

Third, the outcomes must be measured adequately and studied in a way that indicates that the program was at least partially responsible for the observed results. "Impact" implies the effect of one thing on another. The effect can be actual or perceived. Impact evaluations of infant/toddler programs involve, at least in part, comparisons over time. For example:

Have IFSP objectives been achieved *during the past 6 months*? Have there been any changes in children's developmental functioning *during the past year*?

Is there evidence that the social-competence gains seen in program participants *are maintained across time*?

Do parents perceive substantial changes in children's communication skills *since the time that the program was initiated*?

Are children achieving curricular goals *at a greater rate this year than last year*?

Have the families that received home visitation shown greater reductions in perceived stress *during the year* than families participating in the center-based program?

Documenting change over time for individuals involved in programs is necessary, but not, in itself, sufficient to establish that the program was responsible for any part of the change. Fundamentally, the evaluator must be able to compare an observed outcome to a reasonable estimate of what the outcome would have been if the consumer was not involved in the program or if the program was not effective. The "Sources and Methods" section below will address the use of metrics and methods to make such comparisons.

Fourth, administrators committed to ensuring quality outcomes must know not only the results of their program, but also the factors that account for any differences in these results. For example, administrators need to know not only what percentage of IFSP objectives are being met within a 6-month period, but also whether there are specific types of IFSP outcomes that the program is not serving adequately. This information will allow the administrator to plan staff development and IFSP reviews to facilitate monitoring of these under-achieved objectives and services aimed at them. Fundamentally, the distinction being made here is that decisionmakers have a need to not only describe outcomes, but also to investigate them. Rather than asking, "Is my program successful (in whatever ways the program defines success)?", the questions should be "In what ways is my program most successful? In what ways is my program least successful? What factors mediate the success, and how can I use this information to improve my program?"

The following is a representative sample of the formative questions that lend themselves to assisting with decisionmaking. Illustrative measurement techniques are provided for each general question.

Child Outcomes

1. To what extent does the program promote gains in important behavioral processes (e.g., engagement, levels of play)? (The outcome is often measured by observational scales or parent/ teacher judgmental reports of performance in naturalistic contexts.)

2. To what extent does the program prepare participants to function adequately in the social context? (This outcome is typically assessed using observational scales or parent/staff judgmental ratings/reports.)

3. To what extent does the program prepare participants for the next probable educational context they will experience? (This outcome is typically assessed using curriculum-referenced measures, staff judgment, progress toward IFSP objectives, and surveys of teachers of program graduates.)

4. To what extent and at what rate are IFSP objectives achieved? (This outcome is assessed using periodic reviews of measurable IFSP objectives and reviews of existing IFSPs, and by applying goal attainment scaling procedures where appropriate.)

5. To what extent and at what rate do participants make progress along a prespecified curricular continuum? (This goal is assessed using instruments that are referenced to the specific curriculum being used in the program.)

6. To what extent does the program promote gains in global developmental domains (e.g., cognition, receptive and expressive language, social, gross motor)? (This goal is assessed using standardized measures of elicited behaviors indicative of one or more developmental domains, or parental/staff judgments of child competence in developmental areas.)

Parent and Family Outcomes

7. To what extent and at what rate does the program achieve IFSP objectives? (This outcome is assessed using procedures described in #4 above.)
8. To what extent is parent–child interaction facilitated as a result of the program? (This outcome is assessed using observations of parent–child interaction and ratings/reports of parents and/or staff.)
9. To what extent is family functioning enhanced as a result of the program? (This outcome is typically assessed by rating scales completed by parents, interviews with family members, or sociometric techniques.)
10. What are the reactions to program processes and outcomes (satisfaction, acceptance, cooperation, etc.) expressed by family members? (These outcomes are typically assessed through rating scales, surveys, or interviews completed by parents. Minutes from parent-advisory meetings or other existing parent communications can also be used.)

Program and Community Outcomes

11. To what extent have specified program-level goals (e.g., number of children served, external funds accrued, expansion of services) been achieved? (Such outcomes are assessed through periodic comparisons of existing records on budget, service delivery, program characteristics, etc. to the targeted standards.)
12. What are the reactions (satisfaction, cooperation, commitment, assistance, support, etc.) of non-family stakeholders, such as staff, administrators, advisory boards, community agencies, and others, to the program? (These outcomes are assessed using procedures for nonfamily stakeholders discussed in #10, above.)

Three additional questions round out the challenges for impact evaluators seeking sufficient information to make specific data-based improvements within their programs:

1. What factors account for differences in these outcomes within a program? (To address this question, the evaluator must determine which factors might mediate outcomes, gather information on these mediating variables, as well as the outcomes of all individuals, and then assess the relationship of the factors to the outcomes.)

2. What factors account for differences in the extent to which gains in these outcomes are maintained across time and transitions? (To address this question, the evaluator must use repeated assessments of outcomes across time, gather information on factors that might mediate gains [e.g., degree of parental involvement, severity of the disability, nature of the outcome under consideration], and determine characteristics that differentiate those participants who do maintain gains from those who do not.)

3. What factors account for differences in the extent to which outcomes can be generalized to other contexts? (To address this question, the evaluator applies the methods in number 2 above using repeated measures across contexts, rather than across time.)

These questions are only illustrative. Decisionmakers, program administrators, program staff, and other stakeholders should contribute to identifying other meaningful outcomes of importance to formative or summative decisions within a program. No program evaluation could, or should, attempt to address all of these questions simultaneously. Evaluators should pursue only those evaluation questions that are within the resources of the program and can be expected to produce benefits that outweigh the anticipated costs of an evaluation. A shotgun approach to program evaluation, in which a wide spectrum of impacts are addressed simultaneously, is likely to be too costly or too cursory to provide information sufficient to accurately inform evaluation decisions. If resources and decisionmaking interests permit, programs should be encouraged to gather evaluation data during multiple measurement periods, from multiple sources, using multiple methods to measure child, interactional, family, and program outcomes.

Sources and Methods for Impact Evaluation   The sources of impact evaluation have been briefly introduced for each of the major outcome areas discussed above. For some of the outcome areas (behavioral processes, developmental domains, curricular progress, family functioning, parent–child interaction) a number of measures are already available for use. There are no instruments in any of these areas that are clearly superior for all purposes. Therefore, rather than listing a wide range of measures in these areas, we refer the readers to sources that will be useful in such selections. Sources of information on child assessment include: Bailey and Wolery (1989), Bracken (1991), McLean and McCormick (chap. 3, this volume), Snyder and Sheehan (in press), and Wachs and Sheehan (1988). Sources of information for family assessment include: Bailey and Simeonsson (1988), Dunst,

Trivette, and Deal (1989), Neisworth and Fewell (1990), and McLean and McCormick (chap. 3, this volume).

At times, due to the lack or costs of available measures, programs may wish to develop their own checklists, rating scales, interview protocols, or surveys to gather information. This is especially true when evaluating the beliefs and attitudes of parents and other stakeholders about a program and its outcomes. Since locally constructed measures are developed to gather answers to program-specific questions, there is a good likelihood that the information gathered will serve the needs of the program. However, the development of informal local measures is not a simple process. Surveys, for example, must consider the reading level and clarity of questions, the clarity of response formats, the ways that the responses can be summarized, means of gathering information about factors that might mediate responses (demographics, the type of services in which the child and parents participated, etc.), the adequacy of directions, the appropriateness of any rating scale used, and whether and where to place items that might be sensitive or threatening to the respondent. The reader who is interested in developing his or her own informal measures is referred to sources offering more advice on survey development, such as Neilsen and Buchanan (1991) or Sudman and Bradburn (1982). Harrison (1989) provides several examples of parental reaction surveys.

The outcomes resulting from the questions above can be documented using a variety of procedures, such as observations, open-ended surveys and interviews, curriculum-based measures, norm-referenced measures, rating scales and checklists, and the examination of existing records. The results of such outcome measures can be summarized by: 1) individual items (e.g., responses to a specific item on a rating scale, the highest item passed on an ordinal scale of infant development, the presence or absence of a targeted behavior type during a play assessment, the goal attainment score of an individual IFSP objective, or an anecdotal description of a single naturalistic observation), or by 2) the aggregate of a set of items (e.g., the total number or percent of IFSP objectives met, the total score on a rating scale of parent satisfaction, the total number of behaviors observed on a checklist, a developmental status score based on the number of items passed on a norm-referenced developmental measure, or a naturalistic description of IFSP staff meetings during a 1-month period).

The impact evaluator will typically be concerned about the amount or rates of changes in results across time (e.g., Does the typical rating for item 5 increase from the first measure to the second? What percentage of IFSP objectives were achieved during the first 6 months of services?). Documenting change across time for individuals or groups involved in programs is necessary, but not in itself sufficient to establish that the program was responsible for any part of the change. Fundamentally, the evaluator must be able to compare an observed outcome to a reasonable estimate of what the outcome would have been if the consumer was not involved in the program or if the program was not effective.

There are three major approaches for making such comparisons. First, the evaluator can focus on outcome measures that can be logically tied to the intervention and are not likely to be influenced by natural maturational processes. Examples of such outcomes include IFSP objectives, curriculum-based assessments, parental reactions, and program and community outcomes. The evaluator is able to make the reasonable assumption that gains in such outcomes are attributable to participation in the program. Simeonsson, Huntington, and Short (1982) illustrate the value of this approach in their application of GAS to IEP objectives.

Changes on standardized tests present a dilemma to impact evaluators. Several formulae have been proposed for calculating the rate of developmental change during a program (e.g., Bagnato & Neisworth, 1980; Simeonsson & Wiegerink, 1975; and Wolery, 1983) for one group of children. The use of these indices with infant and toddler programs has been criticized, due to the mismatch of the linearity of the indices with the nonlinearity of infant development (Fewell & Sandall, 1986; Rosenberg, Robinson, Finkler, & Rose, 1987). In addition, such measures do not necessarily reflect the rate of gain *due to* intervention, they simply record progress made *during* intervention. Evaluators are cautioned about the potential hazards of applying such ratio metrics in single-group comparisons.

A second approach involves the use of a control or comparison group. In this approach, two similar groups of children are identified and assigned to different conditions. One condition is the intervention program being tested and the other is typically an alternative treatment or no treatment. It is usually inconvenient or impossible to randomly assign children and staff to these conditions as a means of ensuring their equivalence before the intervention. More often, children will be assigned in such a way as to match the two groups on important characteristics (e.g., disability, developmental level, length of time in program, gender, age). Participants in both groups are administered the outcome measure before the intervention begins and at least one more time thereafter (e.g., annually). Basically, the results are analyzed to determine whether participants in the program made greater gains than their counterparts who did not participate in the program. This type of comparison can be used with most outcomes. When evaluators are convinced of the equivalence of the groups and that the differences in gains between the groups are large, the evaluator may not need statistical support for the results to assist in decisionmaking. A range of statistical procedures are also available for this type of method. In addition, this general method can be modified in a number of ways (having multiple outcomes, repeated measures across time, multiple factors aside from condition, statistically controlling pretest differences between groups, etc.). McConnell (1990) cautions that problems associated with group equivalence and the logistics and ethics of assembling and maintaining comparison groups must be considered before applying these methods.

The final approach involves collecting outcome information prior to (baseline), and periodically (on a set schedule) during, an intervention. By gathering data prior to initiating or modifying a program, the participants are able to serve as their own control/comparison group. The general design can be modified to include such strategies as alternating treatments after baseline, repeating baseline and treatment phases, using multiple outcome measures, collecting data in different contexts, or staggering the initiation or duration of treatments for different groups. As this method involves frequent data collection, it is most appropriate for outcomes that can be measured often without great cost to the program, interfering with the delivery of services, or sensitizing the child/parent to the instrument (practice effect). Behavioral measures of developmental processes (e.g., engagement), curricular outcomes, IFSP objectives, or functional skills are examples of appropriate outcomes. Results can be reported for groups or individuals at each measurement interval. While statistical procedures are available for analyzing such time-series data, the strength of the method for local evaluators is the ability to visually document trends. By graphing performance with time on the horizontal axis and degree of the outcome measure on the vertical axis, the evaluator is able to determine whether the intervention worked as expected and how much variability individuals or groups displayed. If group data indicates that, in general, the expected trends were present for a group, but greater variability in performance was evident in the group during intervention that before, the evaluator can examine graphs of data on individuals to determine if the intervention is differentially effective for identifiable groups of children.

Because of variations in children, families, and environments, and in the experiences that children in a program have, programs are not likely to produce uniform effects for all participants. The more an evaluator is able to uncover about factors that account for differences in program impact, the more information decisionmakers have for improving their services. There are two primary approaches to examining the relationships of mediating factors to outcomes. The first method involves the evaluation team identifying factors that might account for differences in outcomes, gathering data on mediating factors and outcomes, and then determining whether these differences do, in fact, exist. Potential mediating factors can be identified through research findings, recommended-practice standards, theory, or subjective experience. Often, the evaluator is able to use simple descriptive and graphic procedures to compare impacts for different groups. For example, bar charts can help decisionmakers visually compare how outcomes vary from one group to another. Likewise, scatterplots can illustrate the relationships that outcomes have to continuous variables. If more rigorous procedures are required, the relationship of the hypothesized mediating factors to outcomes can be determined through approaches such as experimental designs, single-subject designs, or hierarchical multiple-regression analysis. These planned tests are especially useful when evaluating outcomes and mediating factors that are easily, validly, and reliably quantified.

A second method for documenting mediating relationships is through discovery. That is, the evaluator attempts to understand the dynamics of a situation without any predisposing biases or expectations. Information is collected on outcomes and on the processes that appear to account for variations in such outcomes primarily through observation, interviews, and the examination of existing records. Types of discovery methods include naturalistic inquiry, critical-incidence studies, sociometry, and case-study procedures. Such qualitative approaches are especially useful when evaluating unintended outcomes and when gathering data that may be validly gathered through surveys or interviews or for which a meaningful standard of comparison cannot be determined. Odom and Shuster (1986) have applied this type of evaluation with positive results. Readers interested in more information on qualitative evaluation are referred to Patton (1990).

Impact Evaluation Case Example Based on discussions between the director of The Arc and the advisory board for the infant and toddler program, outcome evaluation efforts at the child, parent, and community level were planned. The major child outcome selected was progress toward IFSP objectives. Goal attainment scaling (GAS) was used by each intervenor for each IFSP objective. GAS involved operationally defining, for each IFSP objective: 1) the least favorable outcome (child's level of functioning prior to intervention), 2) the expected level of success on each objective, 3) the highest level of success that could be anticipated, 4) a less-than-expected level of success [between level 1 and level 2, above], and 5) a greater-than-expected level of success [between level 2 and level 3, above]. Similar to the approach advocated by Simeonsson et al. (1982), each IFSP objective was assigned a weight between 1 and 3 (assigned conjointly by parents and case manager) indicating its relative importance. Every 6 months, the attainment of each objective was scored between −2 and +2 (the least favorable outcome being −2 and the most favorable outcome +2). By multiplying these scores by the weight of the objective, a weighted goal-attainment score was determined for each objective. By summing the weighted GAS scores across all objectives, an index of relative efficacy was formulated. Index scores of 0 or greater indicate overall success for the child; index scores of less than 0 indicate that overall gains were less than expected. The average GAS index for participating children across a 12-month period was .25, indicating a slightly better-than-expected level of success on objectives for children in the program. The program administrator examined the GAS results for each case manager and by different levels of disability/risk to determine whether the results varied correspondingly with these factors. During the first 6-month period, a lower index was found for a single case coordinator. Following staff-development efforts and mentoring by a more experienced intervenor, no substantial difference in the GAS index between intervenors was found for the second 6 months.

Two important family-level outcomes of concern to the program were the reduction of stress and satisfaction with services. To evaluate changes in stress, parents completed the Parenting Stress Index (Abidin, 1983) prior to the beginning of intervention and again at the end of the first year. Results indicated a reduction in average stress scores during intervention. While no method (e.g., control-group design) was employed to substantiate that the reduction in stress was a result of service delivery, interviews with parents and informal logs of discussions during parent support/cluster groups indicated that parents attributed stress reduction, in part, to the availability of the program and the enabling efforts of the staff.

Parental satisfaction with the program and service delivery efforts were assessed twice each year using a survey developed by the staff, the administrator, and the advisory panel. The survey, which was completed anonymously (and included a pre-addressed stamped return envelope) was similar to the sample provided by Hanson and Lynch (1989).

The advisory board wanted to be certain that during the first year of operations the program was highly visible within the local community. Visibility was assessed by recording the number of requests for information about the program from parents, professionals, and community agencies during the first year and through a telephone survey of 100 community residents, administrators of five community service and educational agencies, and ten physicians (family physicians, obstetricians/gynecologists, and pediatricians) randomly sampled from the community and surveyed as to whether they were aware of the availability of the program.

Impact Evaluation Challenges   Evaluations of programs for infants with disabilities and their families are methodologically and conceptually difficult, due to a number of factors relating to the population. The following six concerns illustrate these difficulties. First, there is considerable heterogeneity in eligibility criteria. The population being served by any one program is likely to be determined by chronological age, level of developmental delay (between 20% delay and 75% delay, for example), and the presence of and one of a group of quite heterogeneous disabling conditions. This heterogeneity creates obstacles in impact evaluation.

Second, there is little agreement about the type of program outcomes that should be emphasized, and this leads to substantial ambiguity and uncertainty. This is complicated by the limited number of instruments with adequate psychometrics to measure broad or specific outcomes for infants and parents.

Third, infants and toddlers with disabilities or at risk for developmental problems typically have a restricted response repertoire. This may limit their ability to respond to the efforts of examiners to elicit behaviors on standardized tests. It also places greater demands on observers (parents, evaluators, staff) to be sensitive to behavioral performance, due to the muted, inconsistent, or atypical expressions of behavioral competencies.

Fourth, because many infants identified as being eligible for early intervention are likely to have substantial disabilities or delays, their abilities fall at the lower ends of most scales. Due to floor effects and regression to the mean, repeated assessment of groups of such children are likely, based on probability alone, to show gains. This effect further confounds interpretation of single-group, pretest–posttest designs.

Fifth, evaluators must be cautious of not becoming over-reliant on statistical significance. Evidence of statistical significance only indicates that differences or patterns are greater than would be expected by chance alone. It does not determine that the effect is meaningful from an intervention perspective. The determination of educational significance must be based on other criteria (see, for example, Tallmadge, 1977).

Finally, while there are many powerful designs that can be applied in evaluating the impacts of programs, logistical difficulties, ethical dilemmas, and the dynamic nature of program functioning may preclude their useful application in most early intervention programs.

Cost Evaluations

Fiscal resources for infant and toddler programs are scarce, and competition for available funds is high. Not all members of communities support the use of tax-based revenues to provide servicers to a limited portion of the population. For better or worse, programs providing services for infants and toddlers with disabilities exist in a context that demands not only evidence of the efficacy of services, but that such efficacy justifies program costs.

There are three basic types of cost evaluation: 1) cost analysis, 2) cost-effectiveness, and 3) cost–benefit analysis. All three types of cost evaluation begin with the determination of the approximate cost of services per child over a specific time period (day, week, month). Service costs include all tangible and intangible costs associated with personnel (e.g., salaries, benefits), travel, per diem costs, families (e.g., time lost in actual or potential work due to parental participation and transportation time), and resources (e.g., materials and supplies, equipment, space, insurance, and maintenance of facilities). These aggregate costs are then either: 1) divided by the number of children served during that period of time to establish average per capita expenditures (cost analysis), 2) examined in relation to a criterion (e.g., one month gain in mental age, noninstitutionalization as an adult) to establish the estimated per capita expenditure needed to reach the criterion (cost-effectiveness analysis [Levin, 1983]), or 3) compared to the aggregate value of actual program outcomes (cost–benefit analysis).

Gathering of such data and calculating such indices provides decisionmakers with information helpful for making cost-wise decisions about allocating resources and modifying programs. Cost analysis addresses the question "How expensive is my program, per recipient, for a given period of time?" Cost analysis may yield misleading results when comparing programs, because such analysis does not address the relative benefits of programs. For example, program A may be offered at a total cost of $1.00 per family per week while program B costs $2.00 per family per week. However, if program B reduces the likelihood that participants will require preschool services, but program A does not, the apparent value of program A is substantially reduced. Cost–benefit analysis improves on this approach by computing the monetary benefits associated with each approach (e.g., dollar savings per family from reduced intervention costs in preschool programs) by either subtracting costs from benefits (e.g., per capita profit) or dividing monetary benefits by the per family costs (per capita benefit-to-cost ratio), and comparing the metric between programs. The larger the benefit-to-cost ratio, the more efficient the program. Cost-effectiveness involves identifying a criterion outcome (e.g., placement in a regular kindergarten class) and then estimating the financial costs required to enable each child served by the infant/toddler program to meet this criterion. Cost-effectiveness analysis is a desirable approach when benefits cannot be calibrated in monetary units, but a salient criterion can be identified. Different programs or program variations with similar goals can be compared by cost-effectiveness. Cost evaluations require technical skills in identifying all relevant sources of costs and benefits (including the costs of opportunities that parents forgo because of their participation in the program), assigning monetary values to all outcomes and benefits (sometimes using complex econometric procedures), and then generating a meaningful metric. Therefore, most thorough cost evaluations will require the use of a technical consultant. The methods of cost evaluation are far too complex to adequately represent in a brief case study; the reader interested in a case example of cost evaluation with a preschool population is referred to Eiserman, McCoun, and Escobar (1990).

Ecological Evaluations

Programs for infants both influence and are influenced by the complex content within which they operate. Ecological evaluation documents the manner in which the program is incorporated into a community context and the extent to which it functions productively within the community ecology. Such evaluations examine community awareness and utilization of a program, collaboration between a program and related-service agencies, and the level of satisfaction that community representatives and service providers from other agencies express about a program. Essentially, ecological evaluation revisits needs assessment by examining the effectiveness of a program in light of its role in meeting community needs.

This discussion has only touched on the broad spectrum of measurement and design options; the complexities and options of evaluation methodology exceed the scope of this chapter. But greater complexity should not necessarily be equated with more utility. We argue that all evaluations of local programs should apply the simplest methodology and analysis appropriate for answering the evaluation questions. The simplicity will typically better serve practical decisionmaking; will more likely facilitate the decisionmaker's understanding of, and commitment to, an answer; and will more likely encourage the decisionmaker to pursue other program evaluation efforts in the future.

MANAGING PROGRAM
EVALUATIONS AND REPORTING RESULTS

Any effort to plan a program evaluation must attend to not only the congruence between question and method, but also to strategies for coordinating the components of the evaluation—activities, personnel, resources, and budget. Such a management plan defines the relationship between: 1) each of the major tasks required to answer an evaluation question, 2) timelines (beginning and end dates) estimated for completing each task, 3) the personnel used to complete each task (and the individual responsible for ensuring its completion), 4) the resources needed to complete each task (including staff time) and their costs, and 5) potential disruptions in services that may result. The management plan must provide reasonable assurances that the essential evaluation tasks can be achieved within an acceptable timeframe, with personnel and resources that are either available or affordable, and with minimal disruptions to the service delivery and administrative functions of the program. Supplemental detail should be provided on specific data collection procedures and dates, data entry and storage plans, and individuals responsible for ensuring the timelines and quality of each task. Harrison (1989) encourages administrators and evaluators to ensure that program staff have the opportunity to contribute to, or review, the management plan. The reader interested in examples of management structures is referred to Worthen and Sanders (1987). The reader interested in an example of a management plan appropriate for early intervention is referred to Suarez (1980). Every management plan must incorporate procedures to ensure that the evaluation is conducted, reported, and applied in a manner that is ethical and legal, with due regard for the rights and welfare of participants and audiences.

Results of an evaluation should be reported to the decisionmaker and other audiences in a manner that is clear, fair, understandable, and facilitative of decisionmaking. The report should describe the purposes of the evaluation, reasons for the evaluation, evaluation questions addressed, evaluation method used, findings relevant to the question and any additional findings of interest to the audiences, and recommendations (when requested). Conclusions and recommendations must be clearly justified and explained. All feedback resulting from an evaluation should be provided in a timely manner, in order to facilitate decisionmaking. Findings in a report should not be distorted by the evaluator's biases.

CONCLUDING COMMENTS

Some strides have been made since 1983, when Sheehan and Gallagher reviewed the literature on evaluating programs for infants with disabilities: the perspective on programs and their outcomes has become more holistic; the field is examining the appropriateness of alternatives to norm-referenced developmental measures for impact evaluation; and scholars are considering ways of better integrating program evaluation into the assessment and intervention aspects of programs (e.g., Bricker & Gumerlock, 1988). There is reason to be optimistic. Several recommendations may serve to further advance the methodologies and applications of program evaluation in early intervention during the 1990s. First, there is a need to make program evaluation an integral component of service delivery for local programs. This goal can be promoted by paying greater attention to program evaluation as a component of preservice and inservice training (the reader is referred to Bailey, Palsha, & Huntington [1990] for evidence of the recognized importance of evaluation, and to Stayton & Johnson [1990] for evidence of the minimal attention it receives in our training programs), and by promoting collaboration between universities and local programs to develop and initiate evaluation systems that can be integrated into the "real world" of infant and toddler programs. Second, the field can provide credible models of evaluation for programs by publishing and disseminating exemplary local program-evaluation reports or summaries that include discussions of how evaluation results were used for decisionmaking and program improvement. Finally, greater attention should be given to the importance of documenting stable and dynamic program characteristics, program objectives, and participant characteristics, due to the importance of such information for internal monitoring and impact evaluation. Clearly, gains are needed in methods and rigors of efficacy research as well. We argue that while program evaluation can learn much from efficacy research, it also needs to be able to grow up a bit on its own during the 1990s.

REFERENCES

Abidin, R.R. (1983). *Parenting stress index*. Charlottesville, VA: Pediatric Psychology Press.

Bagnato, S.J., & Neisworth, J.T. (1980). The intervention efficiency index: An approach to preschool program accountability. *Exceptional Children, 46*, 264–269.

Bailey, D.B., Palsha, S.A., & Huntington, G.S. (1990). Preservice preparation of special educators to serve infants with handicaps and their families: Current status and training needs. *Journal of Early Intervention, 14*(1), 43–54.

Bailey, D.B., & Simeonsson, R.J. (1988). *Family assessment in early intervention.* Columbus, OH: Charles E. Merrill.

Bailey, D.B., & Wolery, M. (1989). *Assessing infants and preschoolers with handicaps.* Columbus, OH: Charles E. Merrill.

Bracken, B.A. (1991). *The psychoeducational assessment of preschool children.* Newton, MA: Allyn & Bacon.

Bricker, D., & Gumerlock, S. (1988). Application of a three-level evaluation plan for monitoring child progress and program effects. *The Journal of Special Education, 22*(1), 66–81.

Bailey, D.B., & McWilliam, R.A. (1990). Normalizing early intervention. *Topics in Early Childhood Special Education, 10*(2), 33–47.

Carta, J.J., Schwartz, I.S., Atwater, J.B., & McConnell, S.R. (1991). Developmentally appropriate practice: Appraising its usefulness for young children with disabilities. *Topics in Early Childhood Special Education, 11*(1), 1–20.

Dunst, C.J., Trivette, C.M., & Deal, A.G. (1989). *Enabling and empowering families: Principles and guidelines for practice.* Cambridge, MA: Brookline Books.

Eiserman, W.D., McCoun, M., & Escobar, C.M. (1990). Cost-effectiveness analysis of two alternative program models for serving speech-disordered preschoolers. *Journal of Early Intervention, 14*(4), 297–313.

Fewell, R.R., & Sandall, S.R. (1986). Developmental testing of handicapped infants: A measurement dilemma. *Topics in Early Childhood Special Education, 6*(3), 86–99.

Hanson, M.J., & Lynch, E.W. (1989). *Early intervention: Implementing child and family services for infants and toddlers who are at-risk or disabled.* Austin, TX: PRO-ED.

Harms, T., & Clifford, R.M. (1980). *Early childhood environmental rating scale.* New York: Teachers' College Press.

Harrison, P.J. (1989). Evaluating programs. In M. Hanson & E. Lynch (Eds.), *Early intervention: Implementing child and family services for infants and toddlers who are at-risk or disabled* (pp. 360–397). Austin, TX: PRO-ED.

Johnson, B.H., McGonigel, M.J., & Kaufman, R.K. (1989). *Guidelines and recommended practices for the individualized family service plan.* Washington, DC: Association for the Care of Children's Health.

Johnson, B.H., McGonigel, M.J., & Kaufman, R.K. (1991). *Guidelines and recommended practices for the individualized family service plan* (2nd ed.). Washington, DC: Association for the Care for Children's Health.

Kiresuk, T., & Lund, S. (1976). Process and measurement using goal attainment scaling. In G. Glass (Ed.), *Evaluation studies review manual* (Vol. 1, pp. 383-399). Beverly Hills: Sage Publications.

Levin, H.M. (1983). *Cost-effectiveness: A primer.* Beverly Hills: Sage Publications.

Mahoney, G., O'Sullivan, P., & Dennebaum, J. (1990). Maternal perceptions of early intervention: A scale for assessing family-focused intervention. *Topics in Early Childhood Special Education, 10*(1), 1–15.

McConnell, S.R. (1990). Best practices in evaluating educational programs. In A. Thomas & G. Grimes (Eds.), *Best practices in school psychology—II* (pp. 357–370). Washington, DC: National Association of School Psychologists.

McGonigel, M.J. (1991). Philosophy and conceptual framework. In B. Johnson, M. McGonigel & R. Kaufman (Eds.), *Guidelines and recommended practices for the individualized family service plan* (2nd ed.). Washington, DC: Association for the Care of Children's Health.

McGonigel, M.J., Kaufman, R.K., & Johnson, B.H. (1991). A family-centered process for the individualized family service plan. *Journal of Early Intervention, 15*(1), 46–56.

McKillip, J. (1987). *Need analysis: Tools for the human services and education.* Beverly Hills: Sage Publications.

Neilsen, M.E., & Buchanan, N.K. (1991). Evaluating gifted programs with locally constructed instruments. In N.K. Buchanan & J.F. Feldhusen (Eds.), *Conducting research and evaluation in gifted education: A handbook of methods and applications* (pp. 275–310). New York: Teacher's College Press.

Neisworth, J.T., & Fewell, R.R. (Eds.). (1990). *Judgment-based assessment* [Special issue]. *Topics in Early Childhood Special Education, 10*(3).

Notari, A.R., & Bricker, D.D. (1990). The utility of a curriculum-based assessment instrument in the development of individualized education plans for infants and young children. *Journal of Early Intervention, 14,* 117–132.

Odom, S.L., & Shuster, S.K. (1986). Naturalistic inquiry and the assessment of young handicapped children and their families. *Topics in Early Childhood Special Education, 10,* 53–64.

Patton, M.Q. (1990). *Qualitative evaluation and research methods* (2nd ed.). Beverly Hills: Sage Publications.

Provus, M.M. (1971). *Discrepancy evaluation.* Berkeley, CA: McCutchan.

Rosenberg, S.A., Robinson, C.C., Finkler, D., & Rose, J.S. (1987). An empirical comparison of formulas evaluating early intervention program impact on development. *Exceptional Children, 54,* 213–219.

Rossi, P.H., & Freeman, H.E. (1989). *Evaluation: A systematic approach.* Beverly Hills: Sage Publications.

Sheehan, R., & Gallagher, R.J. (1983). Conducting evaluations of infant intervention programs. In S.G. Garwood & R.R. Fewell (Eds.), *Educating handicapped infants: Issues in development and intervention* (495–524). Rockville, MD: Aspen Publishers, Inc.

Simeonsson, R.J., Huntington, G.S., & Short, R.J. (1982). Individual differences and goals: An approach to the evaluation of child progress. *Topics in Early Childhood Special Education, 1*(4), 71–80.

Simeonsson, R.J., & Wiegerink, R. (1975). Accountability: A dilemma in infant intervention. *Exceptional Children, 45,* 474–481.

Snyder, S.W., & Sheehan, R.J. (in press). Assessment of cognitive functioning: An ecological perspective. In J. Siders & M. Huch (Eds.), *An ecological framework for team assessment of young children with handicaps.* Austin, TX: PRO-ED.

Stayton, V.D., & Johnson, L.J. (1990). Personnel preparation in early childhood special education: Assessment as a content area. *Journal of Early Intervention, 14*(4), 352–359.

Stufflebeam, D.L. (1983). The CIPP model for program evaluation. In G. Madaus, M. Scriven & D. Stufflebeam (Eds.), *Evaluation models: Viewpoints of educational and human services evaluation* (pp. 117–141). Boston: Kluwer-Nijhoff.

Suarez, T.M. (1980). *A planning guide for the evaluation of educational programs for young children and families*. Chapel Hill: University of North Carolina, TADS.

Sudman, S., & Bradburn, N.M. (1982). *Asking questions*. San Francisco: Jossey-Bass.

Tallmadge, G.K. (1977). *The Joint Dissemination Review Panel Ideabook*. Mountain View, CA: RMC Research Corporation. (ERIC Document Reproduction Service No. ED 148329).

Wachs, T.D., & Sheehan, R. (Eds.). (1988). *Assessment of young developmentally disabled children*. New York: Plenum.

Wolery, M. (1983). Proportional change index: An alternative for comparing child change data. *Exceptional Children, 50*, 167–170.

Worthen, B.R., & Sanders, J.R. (1987). *Educational evaluation: Alternative approaches and practical guidelines*. New York: Longman.

Some Perspectives on the Continuing Challenges in Early Intervention

S. Kenneth Thurman

Clearly, with the passage of PL 99-457, and subsequently PL 102-119, along with legislation in many individual states, early intervention has come of age and is now a very significant reality throughout much of the United States. Early intervention will not go away; nor should it. Each of the chapters in this volume provides the reader with current information on key components and issues pertinent to the implementation and maintenance of early intervention programs. However, as with any established service or policy, early intervention will continue to evolve with the passage of time. Early intervention has reached its adolescence, but there are issues and challenges that must be confronted before it can emerge into adulthood. Building on those chapters that have already been presented, this chapter attempts to provide perspective on some of the issues and challenges that will continue to face early intervention as it comes of age.

DEFINITIONS AND ELIGIBILITY

As Brown and Brown point out in Chapter 2, criteria for defining, identifying, and declaring infants and their families eligible for services vary widely from state to state and from locale to locale. Eligibility is a major issue because economic and human resources are limited, which leads to the conclusion that only certain children and their families can receive services. It is this frame of reference that leads Meisels and Wasik (1990) to stress the need for "identifying the 'right' children—those in greatest need of remediation" (p. 627). While there is no doubt that some infants and toddlers in our society are at greater risk for poorer developmental outcomes than are others, it is also true that all infants and toddlers require loving, nurturant environments if they are to develop to their greatest potential. Risk is a dynamic construct, and the degree of risk to which an individual child is exposed changes over time. For example, an infant who has two working parents may be at lower risk of living in poverty than he or she would be if one parent became disabled and was unable to work. As the degree of risk to an infant increases, the intensity of the intervention typically increases. It is important to realize that, as shown in the example above, it is not only infants who are at risk, but also their families. Early intervention has as one of its primary purposes the reduction of risk to individual children and their families. If early intervention is indeed committed to a family-centered approach, then it is necessary to establish criteria for the eligibility, not only of individual children, but also of families, for services. Thus, in determining eligibility, it may be just as necessary to screen families for certain risk factors (e.g., reduced economic resources, low levels of social support) as it is to screen individual infants. The point is simply that eligibility should be based on family parameters, which, of course, should include features of an individual child or children.

It is a basic right of all children to live in a compassionate, supportive, loving environment, which, to the greatest extent possible, limits the degree of risk to which he or she is exposed. The challenge to society is to provide programs that create these conditions. In the future, it will be important to consider intervention models that are flexible enough to provide whatever intervention is necessary, whether short-, medium-, or long-term, to minimize risks to infants and their families. Eligibility should be viewed as a continuum that has as its basis the degree of risk to which an infant and/or his or her family is exposed at any point in time. Thus, eligibility, like risk, is a dynamic rather than static phenomenon.

PREVENTION

Other authors (Brown & Brown, chap. 2, this volume; Upshur, 1990) have suggested that early intervention is a preventive activity. Certainly, the preceding discussion of eligibility and risk supports this notion. However, the challenge that remains is to discover means of prevention prior to birth. Clearly, to be most effective, in terms of both outcome and cost, it is important to prevent families from being at significant risk, even prior to the birth of a child. To accomplish this, an extension of services that are family centered and that help and support families is needed. Such efforts might include childrearing and birthing classes and programs to increase prenatal care and to provide jobs and economic security. Early intervention would, in a sense, become earlier intervention, or preventive intervention, in that families and single individuals who were of childbearing age would be eligible for services that were designed to reduce the risk to themselves and to their future children.

Essentially, the most effective preventive intervention programs focus on services that are required by all individuals in society. Thus, a preventive intervention program might be one that teaches high school students about childrearing, child development, and parenting. Another preventive intervention might provide in-home services or educational activities in child development and childrearing to any first-time parents. Other preventive programs include genetic counseling and family planning, as well as programs aimed at the enhancement of the health of childbearing women before and during pregnancy.

The nature of these preventive interventions should be universal. That is, they should be open to all citizens, and eligibility requirements should be as broad as possible. Parenting programs, for example, should be made available to all first-time parents, and these parents should not have to seek them out. All adolescents can benefit from learning about child development and childrearing, not just a select few. And all parents with infants in neonatal intensive care should be eligible for family support, not just those deemed problematic or under undue stress (see Thurman, Cornwell, & Korteland [1989] for an example of such a program).

Providing universal programs classified as preventive interventions does not discount the fact that some families and infants will require more intensive levels of services than others. Rather, the point is that certain basic needs are common to all families, and that if infants, regardless of their degree of risk, are to be nurtured by their family, then those basic needs must be attended to. While risk factors are more predominant in some sectors of society than in others, the fact remains, for example, that a pregnant woman who smokes cigarettes puts her infant at risk, whether she has an annual income of $5,000 or $5 million. Thus, a universal preventive program directed at smoking cessation in all pregnant women is probably justified. The particular approach used may vary, depending on the socioeconomic status or level of education of a particular mother, but the need to reduce smoking in pregnant women is no less important for one group of women than for another.

FAMILY CENTEREDNESS

The concept of family centeredness is featured throughout the chapters in this volume. For programs to be truly family centered, professionals must view their roles from a much different vantage point than they traditionally have. "Family centered" means more than involving parents in programs. It means more than simply providing parents with information and training, more than helping them to become substitute therapists and teachers for their children, and more than having a parent present at an IFSP meeting to sign forms. Being truly family centered means:

1. Accepting the family, and not just the child, as the focus of services
2. Recognizing and being responsive to the needs and desires of the family by letting *them* define what is in their own best interest
3. Forming a partnership with each family that is supportive of their needs, desires, and expectations
4. Accepting the unique social, moral, and cultural values of each family
5. Accepting that the degree of adaptive fit in the family affects each of its members, including the infant or toddler who is disabled or at risk
6. Accepting that the development of adaptive fit within the family is paramount to the ultimate development and adjustment of all family members (Thurman, 1985; Thurman & Widerstrom, 1990)
7. Recognizing that families define for themselves what is adaptive and that their definitions may vary from those that professionals have typically accepted
8. Working to reform and refine both the existing services and the existing delivery system in response to the expressed needs of families

Such a family-centered approach varies significantly from the more traditional child-centered approach, inasmuch as the family is seen as the client, and play an active role in the management of their own lives. Professionals in such a model do not dictate and direct, but rather educate, facilitate, empower, and cooperate with families in the provision of services. The following quotation from Thurman and Widerstrom (1990) is helpful in summarizing this point of view:

> Each family must be responded to on an individual basis, and early intervention providers, who are more and more committed to family empowerment, must realize that families, like children, differ. In summary, families should be given control over their lives, but it should also be remembered that some families will be more willing and able to take that control. Other families may feel empowered by making the decision to put control in the hands of the professional. [What is important here is that the family makes the decision and that the professional does not have the a priori expectation that she or he will be the one in control.] In essence, good early intervention service delivery depends on a philosophy that gives decision making power to families. . . . Professionals, of course, have the obligation to be responsive to the individual differences among families. (p. 273)

A family-centered approach requires that families and professionals be collaborators in the implementation of services and that families are given full authority to make the decisions that affect themselves and their child. The one exception to this rule is when a family's decisions place a child in clear and present danger through abuse or neglect. Unfortunately, the line between what is accepted by some cultures and what those from the dominant culture would define as abuse and neglect is sometimes fuzzy. In the opinion of this author, professionals must, in such cases, act to protect the best interest of the child, even if it becomes necessary to violate the tenets of family centeredness.

TRANSITION AND CONTINUITY

Rice and O'Brien (1990) have defined transitions as "points of change in services and personnel who coordinate and provide services" (p. 2). Their definition views transitions only in terms of service provision. In point of fact, however, families with infants and toddlers who are at risk or disabled undergo transitions that include not only the notion put forth by Rice and O'Brien, but can also include events that are not directly linked to the provision of services (e.g., loss of employment, death of a parent). The birth of an infant, especially for first-time parents, is itself a transition that can be affected by such factors as whether the parents are married, the number of years that they have been together, and their ages, attitudes toward childrearing, level of readiness to be a parent, and employment status (Michaels & Goldberg, 1988). When prematurity is a factor, the transition to parenthood may be even more difficult (Sammons & Lewis, 1985). Thus, on a broader level, transitions are events that have the potential to create stress in families, and that may require readjustment on the part of a family in order to maintain homeostasis.

From the perspective of family-centered services, coping with stressful events (i.e., transitions) is a family matter, but also calls upon professionals who have formed partnerships with families to be aware of these events and their potential for inducing stress. Professional partners must be facilitative and supportive during these times so that the effects of stress on the family can be reduced.

Furthermore, from a family-centered perspective, the issue is one of facilitating and maintaining continuity through the provision of social support. When sufficient and appropriate social support, as defined by the family, is available, it is more likely that continuity will be maintained and that the stress associated with life events will be minimized.

The notion of universal services and their link to prevention, discussed above, is also relevant in the present context. Every family needs a safety net that can help provide continuity in their lives and that can begin to function on-call. As suggested above, successfully accomplishing this depends on the establishment of family–professional partnerships that facilitate family independence and control.

Oftentimes, the nature of the established service delivery system is such that different agencies and/or service providers are responsible for different services. For example, in most states the lead agency for Part H (see Safer & Hamilton, chap. 1, this volume) is different from the agency designated to provide preschool services to children with disabilities. Collaboration, as discussed in Chapter 5, is necessary if a service system is to be responsive to families in a manner that facilitates continuity while minimizing stress. As Safer and Hamilton point out in Chapter 1: "for most states, the immediate challenge [in implementing Part H] was to transform existing fragmented services into a coordinated, comprehensive system of services throughout the state." Establishing and maintaining these service systems remains a major challenge (Gallagher, Harbin, Thomas, Clifford, & Wenger, 1988). The negative effects of transitions, or any stressful event that affects families, will only be prevented and minimized through the establishment of seamless service systems that are constructed to form partnerships between families and professionals so as to maintain continuity. Emphasizing the maintenance of continuity represents a proactive position that is preventive in nature and does not subscribe to the more common past practice of responding after an event has occurred.

Various models of planning for, and issues surrounding, prede-termined service transitions have been described in the literature (e.g., Bruder & Walker, 1990; Fowler, Hains, & Rosenkoetter, 1990; Hanline & Deppe, 1990; Hanline & Knowlton, 1988). While such ap-proaches can be useful, their basic rationale is one that fails to fully recognize the necessity of maintaining family continuity in response to stressful events in general, rather than developing plans and re-sponses to specific events. What is being suggested here is a more broad-based approach that is family centered and that creates the necessary safety net for families as they grow and develop along with their infants and toddlers.

ASSESSMENT IN CONTEXT

The family-centered approach being advocated raises additional chal-lenges for the field of early intervention in the area of assessment. The first is determining the role of the family in the assessment of infants and toddlers, an issue discussed by McLean and McCormick in Chapter 3 of this volume. Another issue that McLean and McCor-mick address is the "assessment" of families. They suggest that "from a family-centered perspective . . . the process of assessment of con-cerns, priorities, and resources becomes family-directed" and that the process should be a self-assessment by the family, rather than a deter-mination by the staff of the early intervention program. Another as-pect is the assessment of ecological fit, which goes beyond both the assessment of individual infants and toddlers and the determination of family needs and priorities, also examining the fit or mutual accep-tance between the child and the physical and social systems, examin-ing the mutual effects of one on the other and assuming that one role of intervention is to improve the functioning of interactive systems, as well as the function of the individual infant or toddler. The rationale and components of such an approach have been thoroughly eluci-dated by Thurman and Widerstrom (1990), and the interested reader is referred to that source.

Using the approach suggested by Thurman and Widerstrom (1990) also links the processes of assessment and intervention more closely. The importance of linking assessment information to inter-vention is hardly a new concept (cf. Bagnato, Neisworth, & Munson, 1989); however, used effectively, assessment based on the model pro-posed by Thurman and Widerstrom more closely links the assess-ment of a child's functional abilities with the actual ecological settings that are deemed important by the family. The challenge inherent in this approach is, again, to allow families themselves to determine what is important and to define their own degree of fit. Implementation of this approach will lead to a functional individualized assessment linked to outcomes that are defined by the system and that correspond to the competencies that are necessary in the ecological units of which a particular child is a member.

The challenge in implementing such an approach arises from the changes in the assumptions that underlie early intervention. From an ecological viewpoint, the assumption is that the child and system are interactive and that changes in one will affect (either positively or negatively) the other. These transactions play a major role in determining the ultimate developmental outcome for a child (Sameroff & Chandler, 1975; Sameroff & Fiese, 1990). As suggested above in the discussion of transition, the goal becomes not only to increase the developmental and behavioral functioning of the infant or toddler but also to maintain continuity within the family. Perhaps the most important means of maintaining continuity is understanding and facilitating high levels of fit within the family and other ecological settings. In addition, the functional nature of this approach more closely ties the targets of intervention to the real world of the child and family as they themselves see and define it.

To be useful, assessment must be ongoing and integrated with intervention. This practice is not only important within the context of program evaluation, as suggested by Snyder and Sheehan in Chapter 10 of this volume, but is fundamentally necessary in order to determine whether the desired changes are occurring in the child and ecological unit. Too often, assessment is seen as a separate and periodic function, rather than as a continuous function that should be integrated with intervention. This integration leads to what might be referred to as the intervention cycle, which is illustrated in Figure 1.

The intervention cycle ties together initial assessment, program planning, and intervention with ongoing assessment designed to provide program personnel with the data necessary to make informed decisions. Use of the intervention cycle creates a symbiotic relationship between intervention and assessment, rather than one in which assessment drives intervention while still remaining separate from it. A continuing challenge for early intervention is the implementation of programs that recognize that intervention and assessment are parts of the same process. Toward this end, Part H has differentiated assessment and evaluation; now the field itself needs to respond to these developments.

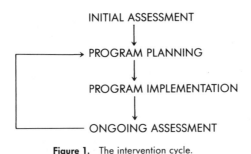

Figure 1.   The intervention cycle.

LEAST RESTRICTIVE ENVIRONMENTS AND NATURAL SETTINGS

Since the passage of PL 94-142 in 1975, the concept of least restrictive environment (LRE) (now referred to as "most inclusive environment") has become a guiding principle in the provision of services to children with special needs. PL 102-119, or IDEA, extends the principle of LRE to infant and toddler early intervention by calling for services to be delivered in "natural settings." The challenge for early intervention is to define what is meant by a natural setting. For example, what is the most inclusive setting for a 6-month-old infant with Down syndrome, or a 12-month-old who is ventilator dependent because of Bronchopulmonary dysplasia? If natural setting is defined as that which is most typical for infants of these ages, then these children would most likely be found living at home with their family, and perhaps attending some child care program during the day. Thus, one would argue that any early intervention services that were required would be offered in one of these settings. To accept this premise would essentially mean that center-based early intervention programs would cease to exist in their traditional form.

From the perspective of family-centered service delivery, however, the definition of "natural setting" could be left to the family. Thus, to be responsive to families, the provision of early intervention services must be made available in a wide variety of settings, from which families can choose the ones that are most "natural" in their own particular perception. A family with an infant with Down syndrome who chooses child care for their baby is entitled to early intervention services just as much as the family who chooses to have one parent quit working and stay home with their infant with Down syndrome. Each of these families has defined the "natural setting" for their baby differently. The challenge that confronts the field of early intervention is to develop a service delivery structure that can accommodate each of these families and their individual preferences regarding the placement of their baby. To accomplish this, early intervention systems will have to provide a wide range of flexible options in a truly family-centered manner and move away from many of their traditional service delivery practices.

PERSONNEL PREPARATION

In Chapter 9 of this volume, Brown and Rule discussed a number of issues related to the preparation of qualified personnel to serve in early intervention programs. The purpose here is not to reiterate the issues that they discuss, but to provide the reader with further perspective.

With the continued development of early intervention services, increasingly more personnel are going to be needed in the foreseeable future. There are several challenges associated with the development and maintenance of a cadre of well-prepared and effective personnel.

Many colleges and universities are developing preservice preparation programs for early intervention professionals. As Thurman et al. (1990) have pointed out:

> While many present college faculty members have had extensive experience in preparing special education and related services personnel generally, they have not had experience in the preparation of personnel for the birth–5 population. Further, present facilities may lack the necessary expertise for preparing such personnel. (p. 100)

To respond to this situation, the author and his colleagues have suggested several alternatives, including:

1. The development of post-doctoral experiences at institutions that already have established programs for preparing early intervention personnel
2. The development of faculty-exchange programs with early intervention service providers that would allow faculty to work as a team with staff from the provider agency in offering needed courses
3. The creation of faculty-development seminars that could be offered during the summer or semester breaks, with content focusing on relevant areas of early intervention
4. The development of a university mentoring system, in which faculty from universities with established early intervention personnel preparation programs would provide technical assistance and mentoring to faculty in other universities to develop the necessary expertise in early intervention (Thurman et al., 1990, p. 100)

It is interesting to note that the U.S. Department of Education, through the Office of Special Education Programs, Division of Educational Services, has identified as a funding priority the establishment of multistate consortia to provide inservice training to college and university faculty in the area of early intervention. Such programs will continue to be necessary in the near future if colleges and universities are going to be responsive to both the preservice and inservice personnel-preparation needs of the early intervention field.

Another challenge to the development of effective preservice personnel-preparation programs centers on the relationship between institutions of higher education (IHEs) and early intervention service providers. An effective collaborative relationship between IHEs and service providers is necessary to ensure that personnel preparation programs are able to provide their students with meaningful field experiences and internships, which Klein and Campbell (1990) have suggested are important components of preservice programs. The IHE–service provider relationship is also important in allowing university faculty to gain a better understanding of the competencies that are necessary in order to be an effective early intervention professional. These competencies can then be reflected in preservice personnel-preparation programs. Furthermore, such collaboration can facilitate the translation of theory and research into practice, which, in turn, should improve service provision.

For any field that is changing as quickly as is early intervention, ongoing staff development and inservice training will continue to present challenges. Models of inservice training that are responsive to developing trends and practices and that address the needs identified by program staff and administrators are needed. It is important that inservice programs are easily accessible and cost effective. Furthermore, inservice training efforts must be sensitive to the adult learner and must use training strategies that take individual learning characteristics into account. Klein and Campbell (1990) have suggested that inservice training may be a short-term solution to help alleviate current early intervention personnel shortages. They suggest that:

> to meet the ECSE [early childhood special education] training needs of professionals from the several disciplines currently employed in early intervention programs, in-service training models that combine didactic and practical experiences are a mechanism immediately available to prepare qualified personnel. (pp. 692–693)

They further suggest that "the development of innovative in-service training models, including the use of computerized modules and interactive videodiscs, holds promise for alleviating current personnel shortage" (p. 693).

Inservice training should not be seen only as a means to decrease personnel shortages, but also as a means to develop and maintain program quality. Many state and local agencies, as well as professional organizations, include ongoing inservice training as a requirement for maintenance of licensure, certification, and accreditation. An important outcome of effective preservice preparation should be to instill within program graduates an awareness of the need for continued professional development through lifelong learning, which further supports the need for effective and relevant inservice training programs.

EARLY INTERVENTION AND ADVOCACY

There can be little argument that the need for early intervention has been recognized through the passage of both state and federal legislation. Given these developments, it becomes easier to become complacent and assume that all families who require services, both preventive and remediative, will be served. However, the Part H program only solicits the participation of states. As Safer and Hamilton point out in Chapter 1 of this volume, it is not yet clear how many states will ultimately mandate early intervention services for infants and toddlers. The challenge of advocating the necessary levels of funding to ensure that the necessary services are provided also continues. In addition, early intervention personnel must advocate state-of-the-art services that adhere to recommended practice guidelines. As Safer and Hamilton discuss, the third purpose of Part H is the maintenance of quality; availability without quality will do little to respond to the needs of families and children. Many of the approaches discussed by Snyder and Sheehan in Chapter 10 of this volume can be helpful in determining and validating the quality of best practices. Their emphasis on formative evaluation is particularly important, because it is primarily through formative evaluation that program improvements are made. This does not discount the importance of cost effectiveness and cost–benefit analysis, which are important to legislators and public officials committed to conserving tax dollars or to using available dollars in the most effective way. Summative evaluation is also necessary, because to be an effective advocate, it is important to advocate what works. It is always easy to *believe* that what one is doing is best, but it is only through thorough, systematic evaluation that one's effectiveness can be validated. In addition, it is often easy to advocate the position that the source of any problem, and especially the lack of services, lies in inadequate funding. Beginning from this premise, it would be quite logical to always advocate for more money, although more money does not necessarily mean more or better programs. It is important to remember that early intervention, like all publicly funded programs, is competing for a piece of a finite pie. The challenge to the field is to develop cost-effective programs that meet the needs of the families in natural settings. Early intervention personnel must advocate for families and, through their partnership with families, teach them to advocate for themselves. Such advocacy is the basis of effective collaboration and service coordination, which, as discussed in Chapter 5 of this volume, is becoming the backbone of effective family-centered early intervention.

CONCLUDING COMMENTS

Edward Zigler, a long-time advocate of programs to promote the development of children and families, recently wrote (Zigler, 1990) that:

> Early intervention is now embraced by all elements of the political spectrum. Further, it is viewed as being of value not only for poor children but for other high-risk groups, including developmentally disabled and abused children. . . . The wide acceptance of the value of early intervention should not lead to hubris on the part of workers in the field . . . [because] many questions remain. (pp. ix–x)

The ultimate challenge for early intervention, then, is to continue to examine and answer those questions that remain outstanding. Only through such efforts will the field of early intervention move from adolescence to adulthood.

REFERENCES

Bagnato, S.J., Neisworth, J.T., & Munson, S.M. (1989). *Linking developmental assessment and early intervention: Curriculum-based prescriptions* (2nd ed.). Rockville, MD: Aspen Publishers, Inc.

Bruder, M.B., & Walker, L. (1990). Discharge planning: Hospital to home transitions for infants. *Topics in Early Childhood Special Education, 9*(4), 26–42.

Education for All Handicapped Children Act of 1975, PL 94-142. (August 23, 1977). Title 20, U.S.C. 1401 et seq: *U.S. Statutes at Large, 89,* 773–796.

Education of the Handicapped Act Amendments of 1986, PL 99-457. (October 8, 1986). Title 20, U.S.C. 1400 et seq: *U.S. Statutes at Large, 100,* 1145–1177.

Fowler, S.A., Hains, A.H., & Rosenkoetter, S.E. (1990). The transition between early intervention services and preschool services: Administrative and policy issues. *Topics in Early Childhood Special Education, 9*(40), 55–65.

Gallagher, J.J., Harbin, G., Thomas, D., Clifford, R., & Wenger, M. (1988). *Major policy issues in implementing Part H—P.L. 99-457 (infants and toddlers).* Chapel Hill, NC: Carolina Policy Studies Program, Frank Porter Graham Child Development Center, University of North Carolina.

Hanline, M.F., & Deppe, J. (1990). Discharging the premature infant: Family issues and implications for intervention. *Topics in Early Childhood Special Education, 9*(4), 15–25.

Hanline, M.F., & Knowlton, A. (1988). A collaborative model for providing support to parents during their child's transition from infant intervention to preschool special education public school programs. *Journal of the Division of Early Childhood, 12,* 116–125.

Individuals with Disabilities Education Act Amendments of 1991, PL 102-119. (October 7, 1991). Title 20, U.S.C. 1400 et seq: *U.S. Statutes at Large, 105,* 587–608.

Klein, N.K., & Campbell, P. (1990). Preparing personnel to serve at risk and disabled infants, toddlers, and preschoolers. In S.J. Meisels & J.P. Schonkoff (Eds.), *Handbook of early intervention* (pp. 679–699). Cambridge, England: Cambridge University Press.

Meisels, S.J., & Wasik, B.A. (1990). Who should be served? Identifying children in need of early intervention. In S.J. Meisels and J.P. Schonkoff (Eds.), *Handbook of early intervention* (pp. 605–632). Cambridge, England: Cambridge University Press.

Michaels, G.Y., & Goldberg, W.A. (Eds.). (1988). *The transition to parenthood: Current theory and research.* Cambridge, England: Cambridge University Press.

Rice, M.L., & O'Brien, M. (1990). Transitions: Times of change and accommodation. *Topics in Early Childhood Special Education, 9*(4), 1–14.

Sameroff, A.J., & Chandler, M.J. (1975). Reproductive risk and the continuum of caretaking casualty. In F.D. Horowitz, M. Hertehrington, S. Scarr-Salapatek, & G. Siegel (Eds.), *Review of child development research* (Vol. 4, pp. 187–244). Chicago: University of Chicago Press.

Sameroff, A.J., & Fiese, B.H. (1990). Transactional regulation and early intervention. In S.J. Meisels & J.P. Schonkoff (Eds.), *Handbook of early intervention* (pp. 119–149). Cambridge, England: Cambridge University Press.

Sammons, W.A.H., & Lewis, J.M. (1985). *Premature babies: A different beginning.* St. Louis: C.V. Mosby.

Thurman, S.K. (1985). Ecological congruence in the study of families with handicapped parents. In S.K. Thurman (Ed.), *Children of handicapped parents: Research and clinical perspectives* (pp. 35–46). Orlando: Academic Press.

Thurman, S.K., Brown, C., Bryan, M., Henderson, A., Klein, M.D., Sainato, D.M., & Wiley, T. (1990). Some perspectives on preparing personnel to work with at risk children birth to five. In L.M. Bullock & R.L. Simpson (Eds.), *Monograph on critical issues in special education: Implications for personnel preparation* (pp. 97–101). Denton, TX: University of North Texas, Programs in Special Education.

Thurman, S.K., Cornwell, J.R., & Korteland, C. (1989). The Liaison Infant Family Team (LIFT) project: An example of case study evaluation. *Infants and Young Children, 2*(2), 74–82.

Thurman, S.K., & Widerstrom, A.H. (1990). *Infants and young children with special needs: A developmental and ecological approach* (2nd ed.). Baltimore: Paul H. Brookes Publishing Co.

Upshur, C.C. (1990). Early intervention as prevention. In S.J. Meisels & J.P. Schonkoff (Eds.), *Handbook of early intervention* (pp. 633–651). Cambridge, England: Cambridge University Press.

Zigler, E.F. (1990). Foreword. In S.J. Meisels & J.P. Schonkoff (Eds.), *Handbook of early intervention* (pp. ix–xiv). Cambridge, England: Cambridge University Press.

Glossary

David Smith

Adaptive behavior   The ability to adjust to and meet the standards of personal independence expected for an individual's age and cultural group.

Affective   Pertaining to emotion, feeling, or attitude.

Amniocentesis   Method of testing for spina bifida and many biochemical or chromosomal disorders in which a needle is inserted through the mother's abdomen, a small amount of amniotic fluid is withdrawn, and chromosomes from the cells in the fluid are examined and tested.

Anoxia   Lack of oxygen, which can result in brain injury if prolonged.

Apgar score   Numerical expression of the condition of a newborn infant, generally rated at 1 minute, and again at 5 minutes, after birth, with scores in five areas—heart rate, respiration, muscle tone, reflex response, and color (0–2 points per area).

Apnea   Temporary perinatal suspension of breathing.

Arena assessment   Simultaneous assessment of a child by professionals of various disciplines to determine their eligibility for special services.

At-risk   Pertaining to children who are exposed to certain adverse genetic, prenatal, perinatal, postnatal, or environmental conditions that are known to cause, or are strongly correlated with the eventual appearance of, disabilities.

Audiologist   Professional who is trained to determine the nature and extent of hearing losses.

Auditory discrimination   Ability to distinguish one sound from another.

Bradycardia   Slowing of the heart rate to less than 60 beats per minute. This condition can be life threatening if left untreated.

Brain stem auditory evoked response (BAER)   Test to evaluate the processing of sound by the brain stem.

Case manager   *See* **Service coordinator.**

Central nervous system   The brain and spinal cord. It is this portion of the nervous system that is primarily involved in voluntary movement and thought processes.

Cerebral palsy   Major nonprogressive neuromuscular disorder caused by central nervous system injury that occurs during the developmental period. Any of the several forms of cerebral palsy can result in physical or communicative disorders.

Child find   Process of identifying children with disabilities.

Chorionic villus sampling (CVS)   Method for testing the chromosomes of an embryo at 9–11 weeks of pregnancy. A small number of placental cells are removed from the chorion through a catheter inserted through the cervix into the uterus, and chromosomes from the cells are examined under a microscope for abnormalities.

Cognitive   Pertaining to the act or process of perceiving or knowing.

Collaboration   Members of various disciplines working closely with one another, especially in communicating about the needs of children and their families.

Communicative disorder   Disorder of hearing, speech, voice, rhythm, or language that, singly or in combination with others, prevents an individual from adequately receiving communication from another person, communicating messages to another person, or both.

Community program or service   Localized educational, vocational, housing, or other service that is integrated into the community, rather than provided in an institutional setting.

Conductive hearing loss   Hearing loss caused by a blockage or other problem of the outer or middle ear that prevents sound from being transmitted (conducted) into the inner ear.

Congenital   Present at the time of birth.

Contracture   Shrinking or shortening of a muscle, tendon, or other tissue, which may result in distortion or disfiguration of the area of the body involved. If not treated with physical therapy, surgery, or other means, it becomes increasingly more severe and, eventually, irreversible.

Criterion-referenced tests   Tests or observations that compare a child's performance on a particular task to an established standard for that specific task.

Curriculum   All of the specific features of an intervention plan that have been chosen for use by a professional. Curricula may vary widely from setting to setting, but each curriculum reflects the skills, tasks, and behaviors that personnel have decided are important for children to acquire.

Cytomegalovirus (CMV)   Viral disease that may be asymptomatic or may mimic mononucleosis and can also lead to severe fetal malformations similar to those caused by congenital rubella.

Developmental approach   Concept that holds that individuals learn in the same way and in the same general sequences, but that they vary in their rate of learning. The developmental approach emphasizes Piagetian, cognitive, and sensorimotor stages of intelligence and a rigid sequence of steps in the acquisition of language skills.

Developmental assessment   Test that identifies the current level of an individual's maturation.

Developmental curriculum checklist   Checklist of behaviors often formulated by choosing items from standardized tests or scales and arranging them in a developmental sequence. These checklists are used as a guide in designing curricula and for recording individual children's progress through the curriculum.

Developmental milestone   Developmental goal that serves as a measure of developmental progress over time.

Developmentally appropriate practice (DAP)   Instructional guidelines that encompass both age-appropriate and individual-appropriate design to enhance children's development across the motor, language, social, and cognitive domains by encouraging child-initiated/directed active exploration and learning activities.

Diagnosis Process of determining the nature of a disorder on the basis of assessment and evaluation.

Diagnostic services Those services necessary to identify the presence of a disability, its cause, and complications associated with it, and to determine the extent to which the disability is likely to limit the individual's daily living and work activities.

Differential diagnosis Determination of which disorder or disorders may be present through systematic comparison and contrasting of all of the symptoms of the disorders.

Early and Periodic Screening, Diagnosis, and Treatment (EPSDT) Federally funded program to provide children of families receiving Medicaid with medical, dental, vision, and developmental screening, diagnosis, and treatment.

Empowerment Knowledge and behavior that allows an individual to acquire control in managing his or her life affairs.

Epidemiology The study of factors determining the frequency and distribution of disease.

Evaluation Appraisal of certain specific characteristics, such as intelligence, personality, physical development, or vocational ability of an individual. Under PL 99-457/102-119, *evaluation* refers to the process of determining developmental level in order to determine if a child is eligible for intervention services, and, if so, what specific types of services he or she needs. The evaluation consists of a series of tests covering all areas of development.

Facilitation Teaching technique that involves assisting an infant or child to perform a task or activity.

Family-focused approach Strategy that focuses intervention within the context of the family.

Family systems approach Philosophy that emphasizes the roles of different family members, the role of the family in larger social networks, and the impact of family and social networks on intervention efforts.

Fetal alcohol syndrome (FAS) Pattern of abnormality in infants due to maternal alcohol consumption. The major characteristics of this pattern are pre- and postnatal growth deficiency, facial and other physical anomalies, behavioral disorders, mental retardation, and some internal organ malformations or disorders. Less extensive evidence of this pattern is referred to as fetal alcohol effects.

Fine motor Precise, skilled movements that require the coordination of groups of small muscles; fine motor activities include fine eye–hand coordination tasks, speech, and tasks requiring oculomotor control, such as visual attending and tracking.

Generalization The successful transfer of skills and behaviors that are learned in a training environment to other environments.

Genetic counseling Service offered to prospective parents before conception, with a qualified counselor determining the likelihood that genetic defects will occur in offspring.

Gestation   Time period in which a developing baby is carried in the uterus; the period of pregnancy.

Gross motor   Movements that require the use of large muscle groups; gross motor activities include those involving body control, such as walking and running.

Habilitation   Teaching adaptive skills to children with disabilities.

Hyaline membrane disease   Condition that affects the lungs of newborn, especially premature infants, caused by the formation of a membrane between the lung capillaries and the tiny air sacs (alveoli) in the lung, which interferes with the passage of oxygen into the blood and of carbon dioxide out of the body after it returns to the lungs as waste. The condition can be life threatening.

Hydrocephalus   Pressure on the cortex caused by an excess of cerebrospinal fluid within the skull.

Hypertonia   High muscle tone. *See* **Muscle tone.**

Hypotonia   Low muscle tone. *See* **Muscle tone.**

Hypoxia   Reduction of oxygen content in body tissues.

Individualized family service plan (IFSP)   A planning process involving families and service providers for identifying a family's desired outcome and preferences for services for the child.

Interagency Coordinating Council (ICC)   A federally mandated, state-level committee appointed by the governor and comprising families, service providers, legislators, persons in personnel preparation, and agency representatives. The council's primary responsibility is to identify financial services and other support services.

Interdisciplinary team   Team composed of parents as well as professionals from several disciplines. Representatives of various professional disciplines separately assess children and families, but the team comes together at some point to discuss the results of their individual assessments and to develop plans for intervention. Interdisciplinary teams are characterized by formal channels of communication that encourage team members to share their information and discuss individual results.

Intraventricular hemorrhage (IVH)   Bleeding occurring in or around the ventricles of the brain.

Jaundice   Condition characterized by yellowness of the skin, whites of the eyes, mucous membranes, and body fluids due to a buildup of bile pigment resulting from excess destruction of red blood cells, or from a disturbance in the functioning of liver cells. The condition is often the result of liver disease or Rh incompatibility.

Karyotyping   Photographing the human chromosomes to examine them for the proper structure and amount of genetic material.

Large for gestational age (LGA)   A newborn whose weight falls above the 90th percentile for his or her gestational age.

Medicaid   Joint state and federal program that offers medical assistance to individuals with limited incomes.

Motor planning   Ability of the brain to conceive of, organize, and carry out a sequence of unfamiliar actions.

Motor skill   Combination of movements that has been practiced, such that specific coordination and control of muscle groups needed to execute a task have been learned.

Multidisciplinary team   Team on which professionals from several disciplines work independently of each other. The child being assessed is evaluated by each team member only in his or her own area of specialization. Upon completion of the assessments, the team members develop the part of the service plan related to their own disciplines, and then each member separately implements the planned intervention activities.

Muscle tone   Degree of elasticity or tension of muscles when at rest. Can be too low (hypotonia) or too high (hypertonia); abnormal tone causes developmental problems, particularly in motor areas, and can reflect brain injury. It also often impairs the child's ability to perceive tactile and proprioceptive input and to react to sensory input. Muscle tone must be high enough to keep the body upright against gravity but low enough to allow movement.

Neonatal   Pertaining to the first month after birth.

Neonatal intensive care unit (NICU)   Hospital facility that provides life support to newborns with complex medical needs.

Neonatologist   Specialist in pediatrics specifically trained to care for newborns.

Nervous system   The brain, spinal cord, nerves, and other parts of the system that carry "messages" (nerve impulses) to and from the brain, organs, and muscles of the body.

Neural tube defect   Any one of a group of birth defects in which the spine or cranium is abnormally open. Detected in utero through alpha-fetoprotein (AFP) screening, ultrasonography, or amniocentesis.

Neurodevelopmental treatment (NDT)   Approach to therapy that emphasizes inhibiting abnormal patterns of posture and movement and facilitates the greatest possible variety of innate normal basic motor patterns; used by physical, occupational, and speech-language therapists.

Neurologist   Doctor who specializes in the central nervous system (CNS).

Norms   Standardized performance levels derived from testing and categorizing the performance of a population.

Nurse   Professional who diagnoses and treats actual and potential medical and developmental problems.

Occupational therapist (OT)   Therapist who specializes in improving the development of fine motor and adaptive skills.

Ophthalmologist   Doctor of medicine (M.D.) licensed to practice medicine and surgery who specializes in the diagnosis and treatment of diseases and defects of the eye.

Optometrist   Doctor of optometry (O.D.); a licensed non-medical practitioner who measures refractive errors and eye muscle disturbances and prescribes glasses, low vision aids, and exercises.

Ordinal scales Evaluation instrument based on a hierarchical relationship among achievements at different levels; higher level achievements rely on skills obtained on preceding levels and encompass these lower-level abilities.

Orthosis Orthopedic appliance used to support, align, or improve the functioning of movable parts of the body, or to prevent or correct deformities.

Otolaryngologist Doctor who specializes in treating problems of the ears, nose, and throat.

Pediatric cardiologist Doctor who specializes in diagnosing and treating heart conditions in children.

Pediatric geneticist Doctor who studies genetics and the effects of genetic conditions on children.

Pediatrician Doctor who specializes in the development, growth, and diseases of childhood.

Perception Process of organizing and interpreting sensations received from internal and external stimuli.

Perceptual-motor Pertaining to the process of sensory input, integration, motor output, and feedback in perceptual-motor activities.

Perinatologist Specialist in obstetrics and gynecology trained to care for high-risk maternal and fetal patients.

Peripheral nervous system Parts of the nervous system other than the brain and spinal cord.

Phenylketonuria (PKU) Inability to metabolize the protein phenylalanine, which results in progressive brain injury and multiple disabilities, including mental retardation, hyperactivity, and seizures; can be diagnosed in newborns and treated through a phenylalanine-restricted diet.

Phototherapy One method of treatment for neonatal hyperbilirubinemia. The infant's skin is exposed to sunlight or to blue fluorescent bulbs, which destroys bilirubin through photo-sensitized oxidation.

Physiatrist Doctor who specializes in physical medicine and rehabilitation.

Physical therapist (P.T.) Therapist who works with an individual to help him or her overcome physical problems such as low muscle tone or weak muscles.

Positioning Placing a child in one of five basic postures—supine, prone, sidelying, sitting, or standing.

Post-term Born after 42 weeks gestation.

Posture Position of body that is assumed in order to execute a movement or to maintain steadiness of the body.

Premature baby Born at or before 36 weeks gestation, with weight at birth below 5.5 pounds.

Prenatal Period prior to birth.

Preterm Born at or before 36 weeks gestation.

Process-oriented assessment Method to evaluate a child's ability to perform tasks and how the child achieves tasks in natural settings.

Prone Lying face down.

Protective services System of social, legal, and other appropriate services that assist individuals who are unable to manage their own resources or to protect themselves from neglect, exploitation, or hazardous situations without assistance from others, and which helps them to exercise their rights as citizens.

Receptive language   Ability to understand spoken and written communication, as well as gestures.

Receptive language disorder   Difficulty in understanding language that is heard or read. A deficiency in processing, assimilating, and organizing incoming language.

Related services   Transportation, and such developmental, corrective, and other supportive services (including speech-language pathology and audiology, psychological services, physical and occupational therapy, recreation, and medical and counseling services—except that such medical services shall be for diagnostic and evaluation purposes only) as may be required to assist a child with a disability to benefit from early intervention; includes the early identification and assessment of disabling conditions in children.

Respite care   Program of temporary alternative care for persons with disabilities that permits families to take vacations, cope with emergencies, or obtain relief from the demands of constant special care.

Retinopathy of prematurity (ROP)   Damage to the retina that occurs in newborns exposed to high oxygen levels. (Formerly known as retrolental fibroplasia.)

Risk factor   An endogenous or exogenous variable strongly correlated with the evolution of developmental disabilities.

Screening   A series of health or educational tests given to large groups of children for the purpose of identifying those with, or at risk for, disabilities requiring further evaluation.

Self-care   Ability to care for one's self, including eating, dressing, bathing, and cleaning skills. Begins early with awareness, responsiveness, and participation in self-care activities.

Sensorimotor   Function that is both sensory and motor and implies that motor responses are affected by sensory stimuli; in sensorimotor activities more emphasis is placed on the types of sensory stimuli presented as part of the activity than on encouraging the child to attend to the activity.

Sensory ability   Ability to process sensations, such as touch, sound, light, smell, and movement.

Service coordinator   An individual who assists families and children in gaining access to and integrating necessary social, medical, educational, and other services.

Small for gestational age (SGA)   Any infant whose birth weight is in the lowest tenth percentile.

Spastic   Hypertonic, such that muscles are stiff and movements awkward.

Speech-language therapist   Therapist trained to assist people in improving their oral motor skills and in learning both receptive and expressive language.

Spina bifida   Disabling condition caused by the failure of the spine to close properly during fetal development.

Stimulation   The use of sounds, words, and other verbalizing to a child to encourage him or her to imitate or otherwise verbalize; to provide sensory information to bring about movement or some other behavioral response.

Supine   Lying on the back.

Supplemental security income (SSI)   Federal public assistance program for qualifying persons with disabilities.

Syndrome   A complex of symptoms that jointly characterize a disease or disability.

TORCH   Acronym for a group of congenital infections including Toxoplasmosis, Other infections, Rubella, Cytomegalovirus, and Herpes simplex.

Toxemia   Blood poisoning caused by a specific metabolic secretion chemically related to proteins.

Toxoplasmosis   Infectious disease caused by a microorganism; may be asymptomatic in adults but can lead to severe fetal malformations.

Transdisciplinary team   Team composed of professionals who cross disciplinary boundaries and thereby maximize communication, interaction, and cooperation among team members. Families are part of the team and are involved in setting goals and making programmatic decisions for themselves and their children. All decisions regarding assessment and program planning, implementation, and evaluation are made through team consensus. Although all team members share responsibility for the development of the service plan, it is carried out by the family and one other team member who is designated as the primary service provider.

Transition   Movement from one service-delivery setting to another.

Ventilator   Mechanical device that supplies oxygen and air under pressure to inflate the lungs; often called a *respirator*.

Ventricular septal defect   Abnormal opening between the right and left ventricle. Ventricular septal defects vary in size and may occur in either the membranes or muscular portion of the ventricular septum.

Visual acuity   Ability to see objects and their details; clarity of vision.

Vision specialist   Professional who assesses and evaluates visual functioning and coordinates services for children with visual impairments.

Index